Computational Social Science
Discovery and Prediction

Quantitative research in social science research is changing rapidly. Researchers have vast and complex arrays of data with which to work; we have incredible tools to sift through the data and recognize patterns in that data. There are now many sophisticated models that we can use to make sense of those patterns, and we have extremely powerful computational systems that help us accomplish these tasks quickly. This book focuses on some of the extraordinary work being conducted in computational social science – in academia, government, and the private sector – while highlighting current trends, challenges, and new directions. *Computational Social Science* showcases the innovative methodological tools being developed and applied by leading researchers in this new field, and shows how academics and the private sector are using many of these tools to solve problems in social science and public policy.

R. Michael Alvarez is a professor of political science at the California Institute of Technology. He is a fellow of the Society for Political Methodology. He is the coeditor of *Political Analysis* and of the Cambridge University Press series *Analytical Methods for Social Science*. He recently coauthored with Lonna Rae Atkeson and Thad E. Hall *Evaluating Elections: A Handbook of Methods and Standards*. He is also codirector of the Caltech/MIT Voting Technology Project.

Analytical Methods for Social Research

Analytical Methods for Social Research presents texts on empirical and formal methods for the social sciences. Volumes in the series address both the theoretical underpinnings of analytical techniques as well as their application in social research. Some series volumes are broad in scope, cutting across a number of disciplines. Others focus mainly on methodological applications within specific fields such as political science, sociology, demography, and public health. The series serves a mix of students and researchers in the social sciences and statistics.

Series Editors:

R. Michael Alvarez, California Institute of Technology
Nathaniel L. Beck, New York University
Stephen L. Morgan, Johns Hopkins University
Lawrence L. Wu, New York University

Other Titles in the Series:

Spatial Analysis for the Social Sciences, by David Darmofal
Time Series Analysis for the Social Sciences, by Janet M. Box-Steffensmeier,
    John R. Freeman, Matthew P. Hitt and Jon C. W. Pevehouse
Counterfactuals and Causal Inference, Second Edition, by Stephen L. Morgan and
    Christopher Winship
Statistical Modeling and Inference for Social Science, by Sean Gailmard
Formal Models of Domestic Politics, by Scott Gehlbach
*Counterfactuals and Causal Inference: Methods and Principles for Social
    Research*, by Stephen L. Morgan and Christopher Winship
Data Analysis Using Regression and Multilevel/Hierarchical Models,
    by Andrew Gelman and Jennifer Hill
Political Game Theory: An Introduction, by Nolan McCarty and
    Adam Meirowitz
Essential Mathematics for Political and Social Research, by Jeff Gill
Spatial Models of Parliamentary Voting, by Keith T. Poole
Ecological Inference: New Methodological Strategies, edited by Gary King,
    Ori Rosen, and Martin A. Tanner
Event History Modeling: A Guide for Social Scientists, by Janet M.
    Box-Steffensmeier and Bradford S. Jones

Computational Social Science

Discovery and Prediction

R. MICHAEL ALVAREZ

California Institute of Technology

CAMBRIDGE
UNIVERSITY PRESS

CAMBRIDGE
UNIVERSITY PRESS

University Printing House, Cambridge CB2 8BS, United Kingdom

One Liberty Plaza, 20th Floor, New York, NY 10006, USA

477 Williamstown Road, Port Melbourne, VIC 3207, Australia

4843/24, 2nd Floor, Ansari Road, Daryaganj, Delhi - 110002, India

79 Anson Road, #06-04/06, Singapore 079906

Cambridge University Press is part of the University of Cambridge.

It furthers the University's mission by disseminating knowledge in the pursuit of education, learning and research at the highest international levels of excellence.

www.cambridge.org
Information on this title: www.cambridge.org/9781107518414

© Cambridge University Press 2016

First published 2016

A catalogue record for this publication is available from the British Library

Library of Congress Cataloging in Publication data
Names: Alvarez, R. Michael, editor.
Title: Computational social science : discovery and prediction / R. Michael Alvarez.
Other titles: Computational social science (Cambridge University Press)
Description: New York, NY : Cambridge University Press, [2015] | Series: Analytical methods for social research | Includes bibliographical references and index.
Identifiers: LCCN 2015039154 | ISBN 9781107107885 (hardback : alk. paper) | ISBN 9781107518414 (pbk. : alk. paper)
Subjects: LCSH: Social sciences – Data processing. | Social sciences –Mathematical models. | Social sciences – Methodology.
Classification: LCC H61.3 .C6447 2015 | DDC 300.285 – dc23 LC record available at http://lccn.loc.gov/2015039154

ISBN 978-1-107-10788-5 Hardback
ISBN 978-1-107-51841-4 Paperback

Contents

Preface

Big Data Is Not About The Data!

Gary King

Institute for Quantitative Social Science, Harvard University

A few years ago, explaining what you did for a living to Dad, Aunt Rose, or your friend from high school was pretty complicated. Answering that you develop statistical estimators, work on numerical optimization, or, even better, are working on a great new Markov chain Monte Carlo implementation of a Bayesian model with heteroskedastic errors for automated text analysis is pretty much the definition of conversation stopper.

Then the media noticed the revolution that we're all a part of, and they glued a label to it. Now "Big Data" is what you and I do. As trivial as this change sounds, we should be grateful for it, as the name seems to resonate with the public and so it helps convey the importance of our field to others better than we had managed to do ourselves. Yet, now that we have everyone's attention, we need to start clarifying for others – and ourselves – what the revolution means. This is much of what this book is about.

Throughout, we need to remember that for the most part, Big Data is not about the data. Data is often easy to obtain and cheap, and more so every day. The analytics that turn piles of numbers into actionable insights are complex and become more sophisticated every day. The advances in making data cheap have been extremely valuable but mostly automatic results of other events in society; in contrast, the advances in the statistical algorithms to process the data have been spectacular and hard fought. Keeping the two straight is crucial for understanding the Big Data revolution and for continuing the progress we can make as a result of it.

Let us start with the data, the big data, and nothing but the data. For one, the massive increase in data production we see all across the economy is mostly

Albert J. Weatherhead III University Professor and Director, Institute for Quantitative Social Science, Harvard University (IQSS, 1737 Cambridge Street, Cambridge, MA 02138); GaryKing.org; king@harvard.edu; 617-500-7570.

a free byproduct of other developments underway for other purposes. If the HR team in your company or university installed new software this year, they will likely discover a little spigot that spews out data that, it will turn out, can be used for other purposes. Same for your payroll, IT infrastructure, heating and cooling, transportation, logistics, and most other systems. Even if you put no effort into increasing the data your institution produces, you will likely have a lot more a year from now than you do today. In many areas where you need to purchase data, you will find its prices dropping as it becomes commoditized and ever more automatically produced. And if you add to these trends a bit of effort or a bit of money, you will see vast increases in the billions of bits of data spewing forth.

Although the increase in the quantity and diversity of data is breathtaking, data alone does not a Big Data revolution make. The progress over the last few decades in analytics that make data actionable is also essential.

So Big Data is not mostly about the data. But it is also not about the "big" since the vast majority of data analyses involve relatively small data sets or small subsamples of larger data sets. And even many truly immense data sets do not require large-scale data analyses: if you wanted to know the average age in the U.S. population, and you had a census of 300 million ages, a random sample of a few thousand would yield accurate answers with far less effort.

Of course, the goal for most purposes is rarely creating the data set itself. Creating larger and larger quantities of data that is not used can even be downright harmful – more expensive, more time consuming, and more distracting – without any concomitant increase in insight into the problem at hand. Take the following data sources, each with massive increases in data pouring in, even more massive increases in the analytics challenge posed, and little progress possible without new developments in analytics.

Consider social media. The world now produces 650 million publicly available social media posts every day, the largest increase in the expressive capacity of humanity in the history of the world. Any one person can now write a post that has at least the potential to be read by billions of others. But yet no one person, without assistance from methods of automated text analysis, has the ability to understand what billions of others are saying. That is, when we think of social media data as data, it is nearly useless without some type of analytic capacity.

Or consider research into exercise. Until recently, the best data collection method was to ask survey questions, such as "did you exercise yesterday?" Suppose your survey respondent has an answer, is willing to tell it to you, intends to give a genuine response, and that response happens to be accurate. (Not likely, but at least possible.) Today, instead, we can collect nearly continuous time measurements on hundreds of thousands of people carrying cell phones with accelerometers and GPS or Fitbit-style wearables. In principle, the new data is tremendously more informative, but in practice what do you do with hundreds of millions of such unusual measurements? How do you use these data to distinguish an all-out sprint on a stationary bike from an all-in sit by a couch potato? How do you map accelerometer readings into heart beat or fitness measures? What is the right way to process huge numbers of traces on a map from GPS monitoring, all at different speeds and in different physical locations and conditions? Without analytics, and likely innovative analytics tuned to the task at hand, we're stuck paying to store a very nice pile of numbers without any insights in return.

Or consider measuring friendship networks. At one time, researchers would ask a small random sample of survey respondents to list for us their best friends, perhaps asking for their first names to reduce measurement error. Now, with appropriate permissions, we have the ability to collect from many more people a continuously updated list of phone calls, emails, text messages, social media connections, address books, or Bluetooth connections. But how do you combine, match, disambiguate, remove duplicates, and extract insights from these large and diverse sources of information?

Or consider measurements of economic development or public health in developing countries. Much academic work still assumes the veracity of officially reported governmental statistics, which are of dubious value in large parts of the world and just plain made up in others. Today, we can skip governments and mine satellite images of human-generated light at night, road networks, and other physical infrastructure. Internet penetration and use provide other sources of information. But how are you supposed to squeeze satellite images into a standard regression analysis expecting a rectangular data set? These data too require innovative analytics, which fortunately is improving fast.

Moore's Law is the historically accurate prediction that the speed and power of computers will double every 18 months, and the result of this repeated doubling has benefited most parts of society. However, compared to advances in analytics, Moore's Law is awfully slow. I've lost track of how many times a graduate student working with me has sped up an algorithm by a factor of 100 or 1,000 by working on a problem for more like 18 hours than 18 months.

Not long ago, a colleague came to the institute I direct and asked for help from our computing staff. The statistical program he was running every month started crashing because the volume of his data had increased and had overwhelmed his computer's capacity. He asked them to spec out what a new computer would cost so he could figure out how big a grant he would need to seek. The answer: $2 million. A graduate student noticed the answer, and she and I worked for an afternoon to improve his algorithm – which now runs on his off-the-shelf laptop in about 20 minutes. This is the magic of modern data analytics. As terrific as the developments summarized by Moore's Law, they don't come close to modern data science.

Whether you call what we all do by one of the long-standing names – such as statisticians, political methodologists, econometricians, sociological methodologists, machine-learning specialists, cliometricians, etc. – or some of the emerging names, such as big data analysts, data scientists, or computational social scientists, the current and likely future impact of these areas on the world is undeniable. From an institutional perspective, we see considerable power coming from the unprecedented and increasing connections and collaborations and even, to some extent, tentative unification across all these fields.

Throughout the history of each of these areas, the biggest impact has increasingly emerged from the tripartite combination of innovative statistical methods, novel computer science, and original theories in a field of substantive application. I hope this book will clarify for us all the distinctive perspectives and high impact that researchers in these areas have had. The benefits for the rest of academia, commerce, industry, government, and many other areas depend on it.

Introduction

R. Michael Alvarez

California Institute of Technology

This volume has its origins in the rapid and staggering changes occurring in computational social research. As one of the editors of *Political Analysis* (an academic journal that publishes research articles in political methodology) and *Analytical Methods for Social Research* (a book series), I know I am witnessing a major shift in social science research methodology. Researchers have vast (and complex) arrays of data to work with; we have incredible tools to sift through the data and recognize patterns in that data; there are now many sophisticated models that we can use to make sense of those patterns; and we have extremely powerful computational systems that help us accomplish these tasks quickly.

When I was in graduate school in the late 1980s and early 1990s, those of us who worked with survey and public opinion polling data were considered "big-N" researchers in the social sciences. When I teach introductory research methods in my graduate seminars at Caltech, I will often have students read the 1978 *American Political Science Review* paper by Steven J. Rosenstone and Raymond E. Wolfinger, "The Effect of Registration Laws on Voter Turnout." Today this paper seems straightforward to students: Rosenstone and Wolfinger simply collected information on state-by-state voter registration and administrative practices, and merged that with the November 1972 U.S. Census Bureau's Current Population voting supplement, which the authors report as having more than 93,000 respondents.[1] They then tested, using a relatively simple binary probit model, for the effects of various registration and election administration procedures on whether the survey respondent reported having voted in the 1972 federal general elections.

Most students of statistics, methodology, or econometrics today are familiar with the binary probit model and its near-cousin, binary logit. These are techniques that model the probability that an outcome is met (here, did a voter turn out in an election) based on the covariates or regressors on the right-hand side of the model. The parameters of the probit and logit model are typically fit via

1

maximum-likelihood optimization. Today a student could use an off-the-shelf statistics software package and replicate the original Rosenstone-Wolfinger analysis, literally in the blink of an eye, on his or her laptop computer.

Because students are accustomed to having such powerful tools as probit and logit, they often do not understand just how far applied social scientific research has advanced in the past few decades. For example, most of my students never even notice a critical sentence in the Rosenstone-Wolfinger paper: "Because of the tremendous cost of estimating a series of equations using all respondents in our sample, we took a subsample for the probit analysis" (page 28). Sometimes students see that statement and, scratching their heads, ask "What cost"?

If students are really interested, they may then read footnote 31 of the Rosenstone-Wolfinger article for further detail, which usually confuses them more: "Using the entire sample would have required about 50 *minutes* of computer time for each probit equation estimated" (page 28). Few students today realize that back when Rosenstone and Wolfinger were estimating the models for their paper, when probit models would take 50 minutes to run, they were likely using a mainframe computer. Accessing computer time usually required payment in the form of university research funds. These computational barriers seriously limited social science research.

I entered graduate school at a time when applied social science research computing was transitioning from mainframe computing to the personal computer. Some of my early applied research used what then would have been considered "big-N" American National Election Study (ANES) data sets, and employed maximum-likelihood techniques like probit and logit on mainframe computers at Duke University. A research project then required considerable thought and planning: if the university did not have the tapes containing the particular ANES data set that I wanted, we had to order the tapes from the ICPSR. Once the tapes were on campus and ready to be accessed, I had to write and submit jobs that would use IBM Job Control Language (JCL) to access the data set and to initiate some analytics routine using SAS language that followed the JCL. If I submitted a simple job in the afternoon, on the way to my office the next morning I could usually stop by the computing center for my printout. I could always tell, when entering the computer center, which jobs I had executed correctly: if there were boxes of green-and-white computer printouts with my name on them, that was a bad sign and usually implied thousands of pages of error messages; if there was a single sheet that usually meant that my JCL was a problem. A printout of a few dozen pages was usually a welcome sight.

Thus, technology limited what you could do as an applied researcher. Interactive and exploratory data analysis was impractical and in most cases impossible. Conducting extensive specification searches was time consuming. Running robustness tests, testing for the validity of important assumptions, and running other forms of model validation were seldom done. Integration, merging, or appending new data was difficult and time consuming, and typically not of interest. Estimation results were largely limited to the coefficient estimates and standard errors produced from the job's output file; producing interesting counterfactual estimates or fancy and colorful graphics was generally impossible and seldom done.

By the time my professional career began, it was possible to use computationally intensive iterative techniques like simple maximum-likelihood routines; yet much of the applied social science toolkit was based on tools that worked well in a computational environment of limited physical storage and limited memory. Tools like analysis of variance and simple ordinary least squares regression were the predominant methodological approaches in social science research, not because they were the best tools, but because they could be used in the computational facilities we had access to.

My point is that, because we could not combine interesting data sets easily, test the robustness of our assumptions readily, or produce informative secondary analyses to explain our results, the development of computational social science was hindered considerably. The computational resources available to researchers even shaped researchers' approaches, while limitations of physical storage and computer memory inhibited the use of large data sets and memory-intensive methods.

CHANGE IS GOOD

However, in the years since my graduate training, things have changed dramatically. Applied social science research has been greatly shaped by technological and computational innovations, and those changes are rapidly altering how we train our students, how we do research, and the types of problems we can study. Although there are many factors driving these changes, among the most important ones are the following:

- Easy and fast access, via the Internet, to data resources and databases. Whether through databases like the ICPSR, the Roper Center, or the Pew Research Center or from individual researchers themselves, today we have access to vast quantities of data that, through a speedy Internet connection, can be downloaded nearly instantly.
- Inexpensive computational power, including large amounts of inexpensive memory and physical storage. Cloud-based file storage means that large data arrays can be stored and accessed without straining local computer systems, and with parallel processing and cloud-based computation, very large-scale estimation problems can be made easily tractable.
- New forms of data (especially text) that can be easily obtained from many sources. The social media revolution – blogs, Facebook, Twitter, Tumblr, Instagram, and so on – is producing huge amounts of readily available data each minute.
- Open-source software and a culture of code-sharing. Most data scientists today use open-source platforms for data manipulation and modeling; for

example, R, Python, and Perl; code-sharing through platforms like GitHub makes such code easily accessible for researchers. It has also become "cool" to know how to write code, and with more researchers and practitioners writing sophisticated code using powerful analytical software languages, we will continue to be able to tackle ever more complex data sets and problems.

• More emphasis on and acceptance of multidisciplinary research. It is increasingly common for social scientists to work on data science teams with computer scientists, engineers, and those with other academic and professional backgrounds; research is more readily transported across traditional academic boundaries than in the past, facilitated by the increasing number of publication outlets and online communication of research products.

Of course, other transformations are occurring, but the aforementioned are some of the most significant forces. We see the results in articles in the leading journals of social sciences. For example, the first issue of 2015 for *Political Analysis* has three papers utilizing estimation methods that are computationally intensive: either via Bayesian methods (Traunmuller et al. 2015; Si et al. 2015) or using copula functions to model multiple political processes simultaneously (Chiba et al. 2015). Two papers focus on large-scale data generated from online activities, either Twitter status updates (Barbera 2015) or experiments conducted online (Guess 2015). And two papers undertake innovative causal modeling, one to model the incumbency advantage in Brazil (De Magalhaes 2015) and the other using voter registration data that has been merged with property sales records (Keele and Titiunik 2015). These studies would have been impractical or impossible to implement when I started my career: the data was not available, the files would have been difficult to store and manipulate, and the estimation approaches would have been computationally difficult or infeasible.

Some may grumble that all of this is just hoopla, that there is little going on other than researchers using increasingly sophisticated tools and data sets to answer the same old questions. Papers from the most recent issue of *Political Analysis* suggest that this is far from the case – the new data sets and analytical opportunities allow researchers to examine questions that could not be easily studied before and to conduct interesting and important research in cost-effective ways. And as readers will see in each of the chapters in this book, new data and new tools are allowing researchers to look at new questions and to examine the social world in ways that were impossible just a decade ago.

WHAT THIS BOOK IS ABOUT

The chapters in this book focus on some of the extraordinary work being conducted in *computational social science* – in academia, government, and the private sector – while highlighting current trends, challenges, and new directions. But it is important to tell readers what this book is about and the intentions behind putting this book together. This book is not about "big data." As Gary King notes in the Preface, the methodological and analytical changes focused on in this volume are really not about *the data*. Instead, the focus is on the methodological innovations driven by the availability of new types of data or by data of a different scale than has been previously possible. In other words, the chapters in this book all hinge on innovative computational tools used to answer lasting and important questions in social science and public policy, and thus I've titled the book *Computational Social Science*. Again, it's not the data, itself nor the "size" of the data that is critical to the innovations in this volume; the emphasis rather is on the cross-disciplinary applications of statistical, computational, and machine learning tools to the new types of data, at a larger scale, to learn more about politics and policy.

These innovations are difficult to compartmentalize and categorize; it is not easy to determine where computational social science is heading. In a recent symposium in *PS: Political Science & Politics*, a primary publication of the American Political Science Association, symposium editors William Roberts Clark and Matt Golder begin their introductory essay noting that the "big data revolution" is changing political science (Clark and Golder 2015). I suspect that one could easily find similar remarks from prominent economists, sociologists, epidemiologists, statisticians, and so on. In an effort to better understand developments in this field, I reached out to researchers developing new methodologies and innovative ways of looking at the new data that is proliferating at a rapid rate. Those contributions are included in the first part of this volume, which is titled "Computational Social Science Tools." The other set of contributions are from researchers using these new tools and methodologies to tackle important problems in social science and public policy. Those chapters are in the second part of the volume, "Computational Social Science Applications." The primary intention of the book is to showcase the new methodological tools being developed and applied by some of the leading researchers, and then to explain how academics and the private sector are using many of these tools to solve problems in social science and public policy.

The contributions are mainly focused on political science and public policy. I had originally cast a wide net, seeking contributions from economics, sociology, social and cognitive neuroscience, and psychology. Yet I realized that, by focusing on politics and policy, a sharper definition could emerge from the exciting new computational work in these areas. The focus on political science and policy also helps identify important new research opportunities (I'll return to those later in this Introduction), which are also touched on in many of the chapters and in the book's conclusion.

The first chapter is by Christopher Warshaw: "The Application of Big Data in Surveys to the Study of Elections, Public Opinion, and Representation." Warshaw is a leading scholar in the development of methods to link multiple public opinion polls or surveys, having already published a series of innovative and important papers in this emerging area of computational social science

(Caughey and Warshaw 2015; Tausanovitch and Warshaw 2013; Warshaw and Rodden 2012). Much of Warshaw's research agenda has focused on linking multiple polls or surveys, usually polling data collected by commercial survey research firms, and then using the linked data sets to study historical trends in public opinion after making statistical adjustments to ensure that the data analyses provide reasonable and valid inferences. Other components of Warshaw's work, including the research he presents in Chapter 1, use large-scale and big-N surveys and innovative statistical techniques to study political representation. As he argues, by using these new techniques, researchers can answer questions about representation and public opinion that they could not answer before. He points to a number of ways that this new approach to the study of public opinion and political representation can be improved, especially through the use of new causal inference methods in the large-scale public opinion polling framework.

The second chapter, by Margaret Roberts, Brandon Stewart, and Dustin Tingley, "Navigating the Local Modes of Big Data: The Case of Topic Models," focuses on text data. Their chapter looks closely at important analytic methods for studying text data, a topic these authors have a great deal of experience with.[2] The analysis of large-scale databases of text has become a growth area in recent years, in particular because so much textual information is readily available in electronic form, either through databases such as Lexis-Nexis, where data is produced by scraping text from websites, or from social media tools like Twitter or Facebook. Many methodologies have been developed to search through these large databases of text; one recent tool is the Latent Dirichlet Allocation (LDA) model, which is a type of "topic model" (Blei, Ng, and Jordan 2013; Blei 2012, 2014). Topic models are popular techniques because they search for underlying or "latent" commonalities across textual data based on word patterns reappearing in that data. Another way to think about topic models is that they are really data reduction techniques for very large arrays of textual data; by looking for repeating patterns of text they can identify patterns or themes that help classify or categorize textual data.

In Chapter 2, the authors examine a particular issue that can plague topic models like the structural topic model (STM, a type of LDA model that these authors have written about elsewhere; Roberts et al. 2014). The issue is multimodality and how it presents a problem for the estimation of topic models and the analysis of textual data. The problem of multimodality is a general one in optimization. Say that the underlying data-generating process in the real world really comprises two different phenomena. Consider Hillary Clinton. Assume that we had set up a Twitter tool some time in 2010 to track tweets associated with Clinton, and that tool has been collecting data since that time. We would have coverage that spans her time as secretary of state and then the early stages of her potential presidential candidacy (I'm writing this Introduction in the summer of 2015). It is likely that analyses of this data (for example, a topic model or some type of sentiment analysis) would encounter the problem of multimodality; the way in which people tweeted about Clinton while she was the chief diplomat for the United States is quite likely very different from the way people tweet about Clinton now. Roberts and her colleagues discuss these problems in textual data and how topic models like the STM deal with them.

The third chapter is by John Beieler, Patrick Brandt, Andrew Halterman, Philip Schrodt, and Erin Simpson, "Generating Political Event Data in Near Real Time: Opportunities and Challenges." This team focuses on methods to collect "event data," information that records an occurrence at a particular point in time. These event data are popular in the study of international relations, where for example scholars wish to collect data about international events, such as conflict or cooperation among nations, and then analyze these data from different perspectives – exploiting the dynamic nature of such data or the ways in which data like these can yield important patterns about networks or network effects. In the recent past, event data was typically collected and "coded" (translated into information that is machine readable) by human researchers; although human coding can often allow complex nuances or contexts to be deduced from the original source information (for example, a newspaper), such coding can be inaccurate, time consuming, and costly.

Machine coding of events data is a project that one of the authors, Philip Schrodt, has been engaged in for a considerable time. In particular, his work on the Kansas Event Data System (KEDS) is an early example of the utility of machine coding of large quantities of textual information into event data (Schrodt 1998). In Chapter 3, Schrodt and his colleagues discuss how the changing mass media environment, where media sources themselves are now fluid and dynamic, is altering how scholars approach the machine coding of event data; in particular they discuss how their Open Event Data Alliance (OEDA) approach provides a model for the development of large event data sets. The OEDA model, based on the principles of open data, open source code, and standardization of approaches for machine coding of event data, is an interesting one that might serve as the foundation for similar machine-driven data collections initiatives that will undoubtedly appear in the near future. Scholars and practitioners considering the merits of open data, open source code, and standardization of coding approaches in other areas where large arrays of textual data are collected and coded – for example, the study of social media – will find this chapter particularly interesting.

Next, in Chapter 4 Betsy Sinclair discusses modeling networks, a rapidly growing question in a number of academic fields, in the private sector, and in many different areas of public policy. Sinclair's recent book on political networks provides examples of the importance of studying networks and also demonstrates how difficult studying networks can be (Sinclair 2013). Much of the existing theoretical literature in political science and most of our methodological tools focus on individuals, organizations, candidates for office, politicians, nations, and so on; they are considered independent entities. For example, most of our theories and models of individual voting behavior assume that voters are making their decisions independently of the decisions of their family, colleagues, or friends. A typical empirical model of presidential voting behavior will include such factors as issues, partisanship, ideology, and demographic controls as explanatory variables, but will not typically include variables that might account for how voting decisions might depend on information from voters' friends, neighbors, family, or coworkers.

Sinclair's chapter, "Network Structure and Social Outcomes: Network Analysis for Social Science," provides an excellent overview of why studying networks is important for social science and gives some important background for how social scientists approach network analysis. As she points out, whether the networks are small or large, they are all computationally complex, which is no doubt why the study of networks was neglected in social science until we got to a point where we had sufficient computing power. Sinclair notes that if there are N individuals under study, they might be connected to 2^N other individuals in a network. In a small population of ten individuals, that's 1,024 possible connections. As Sinclair discusses, there are two primary approaches to studying these large and complex patterns of interconnections: spatial statistical approaches that assume that connections are more likely the closer that individuals are in an unobserved space, and exponential random graph models.[3] Sinclair's chapter is a fantastic primer for readers interested in learning more about network modeling.

In Chapter 5, Peter Foley writes about the estimation of political ideology in "Ideological Salience in Multiple Dimensions." Measuring political ideology has a long history in political science, because it is a central concept in the theoretical literature, in the study of elections and voting behavior, and in research on legislators and political representation.[4] The study of political ideology continues today, with scholars producing new and innovative ways to estimate the concept for voters and representatives (see, for example, Bonica 2014 or Barbera 2015).

Foley builds on these various literatures, starting with the foundation of formal political theory. He uses the formal conception of political ideology, which represents ideology spatially, and generalizes to allow for two spatial issue dimensions and a weighting of each dimension to reflect the importance of the issue dimension to the decision maker. The model that Foley develops allows for the simultaneous estimation of ideological placement and issue dimension weights; unsurprisingly this turns out to be computationally complex. This approach to the simultaneous estimation of placements and dimensional weights has great promise in both academia and other applied settings; for example, political campaigns and estimating simultaneously how a candidate or campaign's message might influence both the importance of an issue to a voter and the voter's preference on the issue.

In the sixth chapter, Daniel Conn and Christina Ramirez discuss the application of machine learning techniques to another important area of public and policy interest: biomedical research. Their chapter, titled "Random Forests and Fuzzy Forests in Biomedical Research," provides an excellent introduction to random forests for the interested reader. The random forest approach is best understood through the intuition behind classification and regression trees (CARTs). These "tree" methods proceed by breaking a high dimensional covariate space into smaller spaces and then producing something that can be depicted as a "tree." As Conn and Ramirez discuss in their chapter, a random forest model is then really a method that can estimate many trees (the "forest"). These models are very helpful in situations where the analyst has a data set with many covariates and where there are many potential interactions between the covariates that are not necessarily well known a priori by the researcher. Random forest models have seen some use in social science settings (see, for example, Grimmer and Stewart 2013), and as Conn and Ramirez argue, they will be increasingly used in the future.

The second part of the book, "Computational Social Science Applications," highlights ways in which today's computational social science is being applied to important problems.

It begins with a chapter that looks at mass political participation and political representation in a novel way. The team from NYU's Social Media and Political Participation Laboratory (Joshua Tucker, Jonathan Nagler, Megan Mac-Duffie Metzger, Pablo Barbera, Duncan Penfold-Brown, John Jost, and Richard Bonneau) uses a large trove of Twitter data to study recent mass protests in Turkey and Ukraine. As Tucker et al. argue in their chapter, social media tools like Twitter have become part of the political protest landscape, and some have argued that social media now plays an important role in the dissemination of information during political protests. Others, probably most famously Malcolm Gladwell (2010), have been skeptical about whether social media has altered the course of recent protest movements. Thus the question of whether social media tools help resolve collective action problems (e.g., Olson 1971) and help protest organizers better mobilize potential supporters is an important and open one.

Tucker and colleagues posit five necessary conditions that, if met, would support the hypothesis that social media plays an important role in facilitating political protest. They then utilized a python tool to collect all tweets that use keywords or hashtags relating to protest in the two nations under study; this tool yielded more than 40 million tweets! The authors then used the data to document support for their necessary conditions and to argue that social media tools play an important role in the development of political protest – and thus in potentially changing the nature of political representation in each nation. This is powerful stuff; these researchers provide evidence that supports the hypothesis that social media tools might be changing the basic calculus of collective action. In their conclusion they present a research agenda for further analysis to document and examine how these changes may be reshaping political participation throughout the world.

"Measuring Representational Style in the House: The Tea Party, Obama, and Legislators' Changing Expressed Priorities" (Chapter 8) comes from Justin Grimmer, one of the leading scholars using textual data sets – and developing tools to analyze those data sets – to study political representation. His recent book uses textual data in a number of interesting ways to build on the seminal work of Fenno (1978), providing an important new way to study the question of how political representatives communicate with their constituents (Grimmer 2013). In his chapter, Grimmer employs a large database of press releases from members of the U.S. House of Representatives, which he analyzes using a topic model like the one that Roberts and colleagues discussed in Chapter 2. Grimmer's focus in his use of topic models, however, is on estimating the nesting of topics, developed from topic modeling approaches discussed by Li and McCallum (2006). The method Grimmer presents in his chapter partitions a set of narrower topics within broader, more general topics. Methodologically, this approach helps advance the literature on topic models. But this contribution also has interesting substantive implications, because Grimmer is able to demonstrate both the general and specific ways that representatives communicate with their constituents.

Chapter 9 is written by a team of authors from the Fors Marsh Group: Brian Griepentrog, Sean Marsh, Sidney Carl Turner, and Sarah Evans. In "Using Social Marketing and Data Science to Make Government Smarter" they note that governments today are looking to use their resources more effectively and to engage in the development of data-driven policy. Simultaneously, increasing amounts of useful data are now available to governments, typically in two forms. Grienpentrog et al. distinguish between "tall" data (with a very large number of rows or observations) and "fat" data (with a very large number of covariates or predictors).

The authors discuss two government-sponsored research projects that illustrate how "tall" and "fat" data are being used by U.S. agencies to improve their decision making. The "tall" analytics example comes from a project for the U.S. Department of Agriculture, where they used data collected from agricultural inspections of travelers entering the United States, augmented by other data. The analysis helped the department improve outreach and marketing efforts, so as to prevent further risks to U.S. agriculture from diseases and pests originating abroad. The second example in their chapter looks at "fat" data through how their team has worked with the U.S. Department of Defense to estimate the population of American citizens abroad. This study involved the collection of a large (i.e., "fat") array of data arranged by country-years, and a model-based attempt to estimate, country-by-country, the number of American citizens residing, working, or studying in each country outside the United States. These estimates are being used by the Department of Defense in marketing and outreach efforts to help improve voter enfranchisement of American citizens abroad.

Chapter 10 provides another application of contemporary computational social science to an important contemporary problem – election fraud. In this chapter, Ines Levin, Julia Pomares, and I present new methodologies that can be used for the detection of potential election fraud in democratic elections. Fraud, or the manipulation of elections, has been a concern for as long as democratic elections have existed. In recent years there has been a great deal of research on the topic of detecting and mitigating electoral fraud (often called "election forensics," sort of a "CSI of election fraud").[5] Much of that research has used relatively simple statistical distribution tests (looking for multimodal distributions of election outcome data) or simple "digit tests." The increasing concern among scholars of elections, as we note in our chapter, is that these tests are now well known and thus could be easily foiled by a strategic adversary wanting to defraud an election.

In "Using Machine Learning Algorithms to Detect Election Fraud," Levin and colleagues present a variety of supervised and unsupervised machine learning algorithms and discuss their relative merits as election fraud detection tools. These techniques are applied to data taken from recent elections in Argentina, a country where there has historically been evidence of attempts at electoral manipulation (Cantu and Saiegh 2011). Contemporary Argentina is also an interesting case because of its recent push for electoral reform and various experiments with new forms of electronic voting technologies (Alvarez, Katz, and Pomares 2011; Alvarez et al. 2013; Pomares et al. 2014). The machine learning techniques used in this setting detected some significant anomalies. We argue that techniques like these should be further studied and developed because they seem ideally suited for the detection and mitigation of electoral fraud. These techniques also can be applied to a variety of other settings in which large data sets can be used forensically to detect anomalies and potential fraud, rooting out corruption and fraud in government expenditures through finding anomalies in financial and tax reporting.

Chapter 11, by Phillip Price and Andrew Gelman, is titled "Centralized Analysis of Local Data, with Dollars and Lives on the Line: Lessons from the Home Radon Experience." In this chapter, Price and Gelman tell an interesting story about their work studying residential radon gas risks across the United States. One of the interesting components of their chapter details the process by which they tried to piece together various types of data for their risk estimation model; their chapter provides cautionary advice that more data is not always good and that much effort needs to go into determining which data sets actually should be used in an applied predictive model like the one they were developing for estimating radon gas risks. More work needs to be done to provide clearer guidance for data scientists about how to assess the utility of different data sets in projects like this one; most of the attention in the literature has been on variable and model selection procedures.[6]

Price and Gelman's chapter tells a further cautionary tale, which is that sometimes government policy does not necessarily follow the guidance of computational social science research. Price and Gelman developed a model that showed the geographic distribution of radon gas risks, which implies that government policy should be heterogeneous; that is, the federal government should implement a flexible policy that would take into consideration how radon gas concentrations were measured in a home, when the measurements were taken, household size and makeup, and particulars of the home itself. Despite this proposal, the authors note that "the people we spoke with at the EPA resisted our efforts to create a calibrated decision analysis with different recommendations for different counties and house types; they wanted to stick with a uniform recommendation." There has been some apparent movement by state and local governments to adopt more flexible standards recently, along the recommendations made by Price and Gelman.

The volume concludes with a chapter by Hanna Wallach, "Computational Social Science: Toward a Collaborative Future." Wallach's own research is at the intersection of computer science and social science. In her chapter she summarizes how work in this new interdisciplinary area is distinct from the more traditional research that characterizes the two fields. Importantly, Wallach concludes the book with a forward-looking discussion about the future of the field. Her prescriptions for the continued development of computational social science, especially improving how future generations of students are trained and how we need to develop a strong professional infrastructure (of funding and publishing opportunities) to sustain their success, need to be read by all who are interested in the continued growth of this new interdisciplinary field.

Finally, I've created a Dataverse for the authors in this book to use to give readers access to their data and code. The Dataverse is located at https://dataverse.harvard.edu/dataverse/CSS, and I encourage readers who are interested in using the data or code from the chapters in this book to visit that site.

WHAT THIS BOOK DOES NOT COVER

Just as it is important to discuss what this book covers, it is important to discuss what this book does not consider. First, theory. There has been some concern that research generally in the area of data science is not theoretically driven. It's easy to see where these criticisms originate, because it is often the case that data used in many studies has particular problems that necessitate the use of tools to render the data tractable for analysis. For example, data sets may have a lot of missing data, requiring the use of multiple imputation. Or they may have hundreds of columns of potential covariates, which might call for the use of techniques to reduce the dimensionality of the data set. Although the tools used to alleviate these problems might look to some like simple "data mining," they can also be used within the context of the typical approach that social scientists take to research – using some sort of a priori theory to help specify estimation models and to generate hypotheses to test. That is, the new tools of data science are not themselves leading to a less theoretical social science; rather they can and should be used in conjunction with social science theory (Monroe et al. 2015). Although this is an important and timely discussion, it is not one that the chapters in this book engage.

Relatedly, there has long been a tradition in the social sciences of using computers to examine complex problems that often do not have simple analytical solutions. There are canonical examples in political science; for example, the simulation analysis of the 1960 and 1964 presidential elections by Ithiel de Sola Pool, Robert Abelson, and Samuel Popkin (1965) or Robert Axelrod's paper on the evolution of cooperation (1981). There is also now a rich literature on agent-based modeling, recently reviewed by de Marchi and Page (2014). The contributions in this book are not focused on this area of computational social science, and readers interested in those topics should consult the large literature that de Marchi and Page (2014) discuss.

Another important emerging set of questions regard privacy, data security, and confidentiality. These are critical questions, and although some of the challenges presented by these questions are described later in this Introduction, a comprehensive discussion of the current state of debate would take a book of its own. Researchers generally understand the ethical principles regarding research and human subjects, as have been articulated in the "Belmont Report."[7] For example, most public-release individual-level data is made available only after the personally identifiable information (PII) has been removed; this has long been the case for public-release survey data from entities like the U.S. Census Bureau, the American National Election Studies, or the General Social Surveys. However, at the same time, researchers would like to integrate other information with these public-release data sets; for example, contextual data that might be linked to the geographies in which each individual in the particular survey files resides. It is, of course, possible that the linkage of survey responses, contextual data, and other information enable secondary users of these data sets to identify otherwise anonymous survey respondents, a possibility that has led some of the providers of these public-release data sets to release the data only at higher levels of geographic information (and in some cases not at all).[8]

Concerns about anonymity and confidentiality are not new. For example, Latanya Sweeney wrote about a number of examples (focused on medical data) of how data that has been de-identified (all obvious identifying information removed) can be combined with other data sets and how one can then re-identify the data; she proposed a number of methods in that paper to mitigate these problems (Sweeney 1997). These concerns, of course, have not disappeared; rather they have intensified in recent years as cyber attacks against major banks, corporations, and government agencies have proliferated. Recently the White House issued an important study of data privacy issues in response to these concerns, and there is no doubt that policy makers will pay more attention to how to mitigate these problems in the future.[9] Research into mechanisms underlying potential solutions like differential privacy needs to continue (e.g., Heffetz and Ligett 2014).

Of course, the examination of linked data sets can yield important information that policy makers can use to make effective and efficient policy. One example is a project that I worked on with three data scientists, in collaboration with election administrators in Washington and Oregon (Alvarez et al. 2009). We linked the voter registration data sets for the two states and looked for duplicate records. This project helped election officials in both states cull duplicates (using a procedure we developed in which the individuals on the matched list were contacted and asked if they wanted the older registration records canceled). This analysis identified a small number of potential instances of double voting that were investigated by election officials in both states. Thus, this analysis helped election officials in both states produce better voter registration lists, which potentially saves them money because they won't be sending voting information or ballots to individuals who are no longer residents of their state. Clearly, researchers can work with policy makers to help them find ways to use their data to make government more effective and efficient, but researchers also need clear guidelines about how to undertake these studies in ways that will ensure the appropriate confidentiality and anonymity of information in these data sets.

Relatedly, there are important questions being debated about how the research community should best share data and code, in particular material that forms the basis for published research results. Journals like *Political Analysis* have adopted rigorous replication policies, and other social science journals are slowly moving in that direction. In computational social science we must continue to develop new mechanisms for researchers to share access to data and code and even to computational facilities. Although these are important issues for the continued evolution of research in this area, they are not highlighted in this book (though I do return to them later in this Introduction).

Finally, the authors who have contributed to this volume generally come from backgrounds in political science or public policy. Their chapters largely focus on examples and applications from those substantive areas, as I've summarized earlier. This substantive focus is intentional; as editor, I sought out excellent research from political science or public policy to highlight which methods and approaches of computational social science are being used in these areas. There, of course, are important and interesting contributions to this emerging field that primarily interest computer scientists and also those involved in other fields of social science (sociology, economics, cognitive and social neurosciences, for some examples). Numerous collections of essays could be published about those fields, and I hope to see more research in those areas, published in venues where their joint contributions can be easily seen. (Indeed, increasingly we are looking for books for the Cambridge Analytic Methods for Social Research series that present advances in computational methodologies in these related areas of social science.)

NEW THEMES

Among the most difficult aspects of editing a volume like this – aside from repeated readings of the chapters and reflecting on their contribution to the field – is providing guidance to students, scholars, and practitioners. I've read a lot of material while developing this volume, talked with students and colleagues, and seen work presented online and in conferences. I've come to find that there are four big challenges confronting research in this emerging field.

First, we need to do a better job of data visualization. Data and methods are becoming more complicated, yet computational sophistication enables us to find patterns in data and reveal those patterns heretofore unavailable. Visionaries in the field like Edward Tufte have been pushing us toward better visualization for decades. We need to start taking Tufte's advice more seriously.[10] Each year I spend a week talking with my advanced graduate students about advanced data visualization, and I walk them through some of my favorite examples. One of those is the "MoneyBombs" visualization from David Lazer's research group; the visualization shows the geographic distribution of political contributions made throughout the 2012 election, associated with the presidential campaign in the Boston area.[11] This visualization allows the viewer to watch the distribution of financial support for each candidate, over time and space. This is a wonderful example of visualization of data for analysis of important public policy questions.

But the problem is that, although there are great examples of cool and useful ways to visually present data to make patterns and results pop for readers or viewers, we haven't been able to translate those examples into our published work very well. For example, *Political Analysis* will only publish color graphics in the journal itself if the author pays a fee; the journal will publish color graphics for free in the electronic version of a published paper. Yet even if we publish color figures they are still two-dimensional depictions of data or results. Until journals offer truly interactive data visualization tools, authors will continue to use very limited data visualizations in their formal, peer-reviewed, research – and that will continue to stymie the development of great examples of data visualization in published research.[12] Journals, publishers, editors, and professional societies will need to come together to develop means by which sophisticated data visualizations can become part of academic publishing.

We also need to incorporate visualization into our teaching and training of students, methodologists, and data scientists. Although I know that some of us spend a session or two on visualization in some of our methods classes, and that there are courses on data visualization at many colleges and universities, visualization needs to be built into each and every data science and methods class we teach. Although there are good reasons to have stand-alone visualization courses, we must teach the coming generations of data scientists how to develop usable and sophisticated yet intuitive visualization tools for all stages of a data analytics project.

A second big challenge is posed by audio, images, and video. As a number of the chapters in this book demonstrate, researchers have made an enormous amount of progress analyzing text data. Even a decade ago most text information was processed or coded manually, which was labor intensive, time consuming, and potentially unreliable (because coders sometimes interpret text differently). However, similar progress has not been made analyzing audio, images, and video, despite the enormous amount of audio and video content available. For example, at the time of this writing, YouTube reports that each minute 300 hours of video are uploaded.[13] Although many of these videos are of family pets doing silly (and irrelevant) things, it is also the case that YouTube (and Facebook, Tumblr, Twitter, Pinterest, Vine, and many other similar sites) has important content that the computational social scientist should be interested in using for analysis.

A great example concerns political candidates. On April 12, 2015, Hillary Clinton announced her formal entrance into the 2016 campaign via a video recording (now available on YouTube).[14] There's a lot of important information in this video announcement: the different voters who are portrayed in the video, their physical context and movement, what they say and how they say it, and, of course, the statements by Hillary Clinton at the end. All of this is important information that could be coded manually, but we need to develop the tools to automate this process.

Undoubtedly this is just one of what will be hundreds of videos that will be produced by the Clinton campaign alone. There will be hundreds, perhaps thousands, of campaign videos produced by the candidates' campaigns and by independent expenditure groups in the 2016 presidential race alone. Add to that other federal campaigns in 2016, other state candidate races, and, of course, ballot measures; an incredible quantity of important information is going to be disseminated to the electorate in the 2016 election cycle, and computational social science must begin to tackle how to automate the collection and coding of this information if we want to understand the strategies and dynamics of the modern political campaign.

And not just political scientists will want to analyze this audio and visual data; so will sociologists, psychologists, economists, anthropologists, and other social sciences. So much of modern life is now recorded and disseminated via audio and video, and computational social scientists will need to develop the tools to obtain, store, process, and analyze these data – or we won't be able to properly understand contemporary politics, social interactions, marketing and business strategy, and many other phenomena.

A third big challenge is to develop even better approaches for the statistical analysis of networks. The formal and quantitative study of social, political, and economic networks has advanced in amazing ways in recent years; interested readers can consult the reviews by Snijders (2011) or Jackson (2008). Research on many types of networks – for example, networks of voters, political contributors, interest groups, or lobbyists – has been hampered by data limitations.

Most of the traditional approaches used to collect data for the study of social behavior do not collect detailed information about the networks that the individual or entity might participate in (for example, the American National Election Studies and, for that matter, most of the important larger scale political, economic, and social surveys of behavior). Collecting this information vastly complicates the typical survey research project, but methodologists will need to figure out ways to collect it, either directly as part of the interview itself or through information from respondents' use of social media, for example.[15]

Even more important, though, will be the development of quantitative tools to study networks of networks, how networks interact with each other, and how they change over time and space. These are all very difficult statistical and computational problems; although scholars who study networks are well aware of these complicated aspects of networks they are also aware that the challenges ahead lie in collecting the information and developing the methodologies needed to study network interactions and changes over time.

A great example comes from the study of political fundraising; in recent election cycles it has become clear that networks of contributors are being developed to take advantage of network structure to collect larger and larger amounts of money for candidates and causes. However, how these fundraising networks interrelate, how they interact with each other, and most important how they change over time (especially given changes in campaign finance rules and regulations), have not been studied in sufficient depth or detail. The lack of a strong quantitative base of research on how these fundraising networks interact, or how they evolve in response to changes in campaign finance laws and regulations, leaves policy makers, advocates, and the public with insufficient knowledge of how elections are financed and by whom.

Clearly this is a pressing public policy problem; helping inform the policy debate in this area will require the collection of better data on contributors and contributions, as well as stronger methodologies for analyzing the networks, their interactions, and how they evolve over time.

The final challenge is a broader one and has to do with research ethics and transparency, topics mentioned earlier. Many colleagues working on the quantitative side of computational social science today are asking big and important questions, and the scientific community must continue supporting them. Incumbent in that ambition is considerable responsibility; we need to be careful that when we undertake radically new studies using new forms of data and analytic tools we pay attention to the ethics of how data is collected from individuals, how that data is stored, and what is reported in analyses of these data. All researchers are aware of the ethical principles enshrined in important statements like the 1979 Belmont Report, which lays out the basic principles of the ethical treatment of human subjects.[16] Researchers must take care when starting innovative and ambitious research projects and ensure that appropriate steps are taken to obtain informed consent (where possible) and to protect research subjects.

An example of the need for caution comes from the 2014 publication in the *Proceedings of the National Academy of Sciences* (PNAS) of a study by Kramer, Guillory, and Hancock, "Experimental Evidence of Massive-Scale Emotional Contagion through Social Networks." The authors used an innovative experiment with Facebook users; selected Facebook subjects saw information in their friends' posts on their News Feed that was manipulated by the researchers to either have more positive or more negative emotional content. The authors used the data from these experiments to study emotional contagion through Facebook networks. Almost immediately after publication of this paper by PNAS, however, controversy ensued regarding whether appropriate steps were taken to provide subjects in the study with informed consent, as well as the ability to not participate in the study if they did not want to be involved.

The editor-in-chief of PNAS wrote an "Editorial Expression of Concern" about the matter, concluding by saying, "It is nevertheless a matter of concern that the collection of the data by Facebook may have involved practices that were not fully consistent with the principles of obtaining informed consent and allowing participants to opt out."[17] This debate has continued, and the lessons are instructive – following the principles of the Belmont Report is critical. Scholars should consult with their Institutional Review Boards (IRBs) to understand if their research needs further review and possible alteration, so that where necessary, informed consent is obtained and the potential for harming human subjects is eliminated or minimized. Researchers who are not at institutions with IRBs should take steps to ensure that their work complies with these same human subjects provisions; private companies or nonprofits doing research with human subjects can develop IRB-like processes and procedures or get assistance from third-party groups and organizations.

The flip side of this discussion, though, is that IRBs at colleges and universities must develop procedures for educating and advising researchers and graduate students about ethical issues, as well as more flexible and expedient means for questions and feedback. All too often I hear stories from colleagues and others about lengthy waits just to get a question answered from their IRB or to get relatively minor changes in research protocols reviewed and approved. No doubt, the work of IRBs is difficult, especially in a dynamic and rapidly changing research environment like social science; yet an efficient and accurate question and review process is necessary.

A related issue is the transparency of research, in particular the code and data used to produce research results by computational social scientists. These are issues that have seen considerable discussion in recent years, and professional societies, journals, and other organizations associated with social scientific research have all undertaken important steps to improve research transparency. In the distant past, when a research paper might have relied on some simple analysis of a commonly used data set on a mainframe computer, research transparency was not such an issue; the data was commonly available (for example, an ANES study), and the code would be a few dozen lines of SPSS or

SAS commands. However, many papers published today do not use data that is easily available to other researchers; the code might be complex and lengthy, which creates complications for students or scholars who might wish to use code and data for teaching purposes, to see if they can reproduce a study's results, or to use as a foundation for an extension or related research.

Professional societies like the American Political Science Association (APSA) have come up with important initiatives (APSA's Data Access and Research Transparency [DART]). Many scholarly journals are beginning to require authors to provide all of the materials needed to reproduce the results in the paper, either as part of the paper's initial submission or on acceptance for publication (leaders in this area in political science are the *Quarterly Journal of Political Science* and *Political Analysis*). Initiatives like the Dataverse project at Harvard University are providing a user-friendly infrastructure that scholars and journals can use for permanent archiving of replication materials.[18] These are all steps in the right direction, and they are actions that all quantitative journals in social science should take in the future.

Last, and perhaps most important, computational social scientists teaching the next generation of researchers and scholars must work to ensure that students understand research transparency and research ethics. Materials on research transparency and research ethics should be added to methodological training courses in masters and doctoral programs; colleges and universities should consider creating courses around these topics, especially the complexities of human subjects research. Students should be taught to develop research plans before they begin big projects (like a master's thesis or doctoral research); as part of these plans they should develop and discuss how they will use human subjects in their work and how they plan to develop software, compute code, and databases that can eventually be shared with the larger research community.

CONCLUSION

Computational social science is developing at a dizzying pace. Most researchers have a laptop or desktop computer that has more memory, more processing capability, and more storage space than available just two decades ago. The accumulation of decades of polling and survey data, along with the widespread availability of other types of information that can be linked to polls and surveys, has led to impressive developments in a number of areas of behavioral analysis. The ability to accumulate vast arrays of textual data, whether from media databases or scraped from blogs or social media sites, has yielded advances in the collection, storage, and analysis of information that decades ago would have been coded by hand. All of these innovations in computational social science are themselves being used to produce new understandings of political representation, voter and legislative behavior, social mobilization, and health care and medical policy, to name a few of the examples discussed in the chapters that follow. It will be interesting to witness the next two decades and to participate in the evolution of this new field of computational social science. Judging from the contributions in this book, the future of computational social science looks bright.

ACKNOWLEDGMENTS

The chapters that follow are all interesting and important, and I hope they will point to new directions for the emerging field of computational social science. In addition to thanking the many authors of these chapters for their help, I want to thank Gary King and Hanna Wallach for writing the Preface and Conclusion, respectively. Robert Dreesen deserves a great deal of credit; his good-natured and helpful suggestions, comments, and prodding helped push this project from a vague idea into a completed book. Recent Caltech students, both undergraduate and graduate, have provided ideas and suggestions, and have listened to me talk about some of the themes of this book over the past two years, and I've learned a great deal from them: thanks to Nailen Matschke, Sean McKenna, Lucas Nunez, Allyson Pellissier, Jacob Shenker, Welmar Rosado, and Eugene Vinitsky. Ines Levin and Peter Foley have also contributed greatly to this book, both as graduate students and, more recently, as colleagues. Neal Beck provided an enormous amount of feedback throughout this project, from start to finish, and along the way influenced how I think about this field. I also want to thank my colleagues at the journal *Political Analysis*, especially my co-editor Jonathan Katz, and our many fantastic authors who continue to send manuscripts that keep me busy and informed about advances in political methodology. Sabrina De Jaegher provided invaluable assistance at a number of stages in this project.

Most important, I want to thank my family, Sarah Hamm-Alvarez and Sophia Alvarez, for their support and understanding while I worked on this book.

Notes

1. Rosenstone and Wolfinger's exuberance about their "big-N" data set is interesting to quote: writing in their paper about the data and why it is important for their study, they point out the "sheer size of the sample: 93,339 respondents were interviewed" (page 26).
2. For example, see Grimmer and Stewart 2013; Lucas et al. 2015; Roberts et al. 2014; and King et al. 2013.
3. See Franzese and Hayes 2007; Cranmer and Desmarais 2010.
4. Political ideology plays an important role in the spatial model of voting (Downs 1957; Black 1958). Discussions of political ideology featured prominently in some of the early foundational works of political behavior in the United States (Campbell et al. 1964; Lane 1962; Converse 1964; Stokes 1963). Finally, ideology features centrally in the literature on legislative behavior and representation (e.g., Poole 2005).

5. See the essays in Alvarez, Hall, and Hyde (2008) for a discussion of both historical concerns about electoral fraud and manipulation and the development of a series of approaches for statistical fraud detection.

6. For example, questions of variable and model selection are discussed in a number of chapters in this volume, including Chapters 10 (Levin et al.) and 6 (Conn and Ramirez). A good contemporary reference for these procedures is Hastie, Tibshirani, and Friedman (2011).

7. See http://www.hhs.gov/ohrp/humansubjects/guidance/belmont.html.

8. For example, the National Health Interview Survey data restricts the availability of low-level geographic identifiers in their public-release data, see http://www.cdc .gov/rdc/geocodes/geowt_nhis.htm.

9. See "Big Data: Seizing Opportunities, Preserving Values." May 2014, https://www .whitehouse.gov/sites/default/files/docs/big_data_privacy_report_5.1.14_final_print .pdf.

10. Tufte's books have been very influential, and I have used them in my graduate teaching and my own research (Tufte 2001). Another great reference for how we can do better with data visualization is Steele and Iliinsky (2010).

11. See http://www.vispolitics.com/index.html.

12. It is, of course, possible for journals today to publish multidimensional, colorful, and interactive graphics online in the form of something like supplementary materials. However, that's not an ideal solution because many readers will still engage with the publication in print form and may not be able to experience the graphic as intended.

13. https://www.youtube.com/yt/press/statistics.

14. https://youtu.be/0uY7gLZDmn4.

15. Collecting data about individual political and social networks also raises a slew of important questions about privacy and confidentiality, which are well beyond the scope of this book.

16. The Belmont Report is available from http://ohsr.od.nih.gov/guidelines/belmont .html.

17. The letter from the editor-in-chief is available from http://www.pnas.org/cgi/doi/ 10.1073/pnas.1412469111.

18. In fact, I've used the Harvard Dataverse to set up a data and code archive for the authors of this book, at https://dataverse.harvard.edu/dataverse/CSS.

References

Alvarez, R. Michael, Thad E. Hall, and Susan D. Hyde. 2008. *Election Fraud: Detecting and Deterring Electoral Manipulation*. Washington, DC: Brookings Institution Press.

Alvarez, R. Michael, Jeff Jonas, William E. Winkler and Rebecca N. Wright. 2009. "Interstate Voter Registration Database Matching: The Oregon-Washington 2008 Pilot Project." EVT/WOTE 2009, https://www.usenix.org/legacy/event/evtwote09/ tech/full_papers/alvarez.pdf.

Alvarez, R. Michael, Gabriel Katz, and Julia Pomares. 2011. "The Impact of New Technologies on Voter Confidence in Latin America: Evidence from e-voting Experiments in Argentina and Colombia." *Journal of Information Technology and Politics*, 8(2), 199–217.

Alvarez, R. Michael, Ines Levin, Julia Pomares, and Marcelo Leiras. 2013. "Voting Made Safe and Easy: The Impact of e-Voting on Citizen Perceptions." *Political Science Research and Methods*, 1(1), 117–137.

Axelrod, Robert. 1981. "The Emergence of Cooperation among Egoists." *American Political Science Review*, 75(2), 306–318.

Barbera, Pablo. 2015. "Birds of the Same Feather Tweet Together: Bayesian Ideal Point Estimation Using Twitter Data." *Political Analysis*, 23(1), 76–91.

Black, Duncan. 1958. *The Theory of Committees and Elections*. New York: Cambridge University Press.

Blei, David M. 2012. "Probabilistic Topic Models." *Communications of the ACM*, 55(4), 77–84.

Blei, David M. 2014. "Build, Compute, Critique, Repeat: Data Analysis with Latent Variable Models." *Annual Review of Statistics and Its Application*, 1, 203–232.

Blei, David M., Andrew Y. Ng, and Michael I. Jordan. 2003. "Latent Dirichlet Allocation." *Journal of Machine Learning Research*, 3, 993–1022.

Bonica, Adam. 2014. "Mapping the Ideological Marketplace." *American Journal of Political Science*, 58(2), 367–386.

Campbell, Angus, Philip E. Converse, Warren E. Miller and Donald E. Stokes. 1964. *The American Voter*, abridged edition. New York: John Wiley and Sons.

Cantu, Francisco and Sebastian M. Saiegh. 2011. "Fraudulent Democracy? An Analysis of Argentina's Infamous Decade Using Supervised Machine Learning." *Political Analysis*, 19(4), 409–433.

Caughey, Devin and Christopher Warshaw. 2015. "Dynamic Estimation of Latent Opinion Using a Hierarchical Group-Level IRT Model." *Political Analysis*, 23(2), 197–211.

Chiba, Daina, Lanny W. Martin, and Randolph T. Stevenson. 2015. "A Copula Approach to the Problem of Selection Bias in Models of Government Survival." *Political Analysis*, 23(1), 42–58.

Clark, William Roberts and Matt Golder. 2015. "Big Data, Causal Inference, and Formal Theory: Contradictory Trends in Political Science?: Introduction." *PS: Political Science & Politics*, 48(1), 65–70.

Converse, Philip E. 1964. "The Nature of Belief Systems in Mass Publics." In D. E. Apter, editor, *Ideology and Discontent*. New York: Free Press.

Cranmer, Skyler and Bruce A. Desmarais. 2010. "Inferential Network Analysis with Exponential Graph Models." *Political Analysis*, 19(1), 66–86.

De Magalhaes, Leandro. 2015. "Incumbency Effects in a Comparative Perspective: Evidence from Brazilian Mayoral Elections." *Political Analysis*, 23(1), 133–126.

de Marchi, Scott and Scott E. Page. 2014. "Agent-Based Models." *Annual Review of Political Science*, 17, 1–20.

Downs, Anthony. 1957. *An Economic Theory of Democracy*. New York: Harper and Row.

Fenno, F. Richard. Jr. 1978. *Home Style: House Members in Their Districts*. Boston: Little, Brown.

Franzese, Robert and Jude Hayes. 2007. "Spatial-Econometric Models of Cross-Sectional Interdependence in Political-Science Panel and Time-Series-Cross-Section Data." *Political Analysis*, 15(2), 140–164.

Gladwell, Malcolm. 2010. "Small Change: Why the Revolution Will Not Be Tweeted." *The New Yorker*, http://www.newyorker.com/magazine/2010/10/04/small-change-3.

Grimmer, Justin. 2013. *Representational Style: What Legislators Say and Why It Matters*. New York: Cambridge University Press.

Grimmer, Justin and Brandon M. Stewart. 2013. "Text as Data: The Promise and Pitfalls of Automatic Content Analysis Methods for Political Texts." *Political Analysis*, 21(3), 267–297.

Hastie, Trevor, Robert Tibshirani, and Jerome Friedman. 2011. *The Elements of Statistical Learning: Data Mining, Inference, and Prediction*, 2nd ed. New York: Springer.

Heffetz, Ori and Katrina Ligett. 2014. "Privacy and Data-Based Research." *Journal of Economic Perspectives*, 28(2), 75–98.

Jackson, Matthew O. 2008. *Social and Economic Networks*. Princeton: Princeton University Press.

Keele, Luke J. and Rocio Titiunik. 2015. "Geographic Boundaries as Regression Discontinuities." *Political Analysis*, 23(1), 127–155.

King, Gary, Jennifer Pan, and Margaret E. Roberts. 2013. "How Censorship in China Allows Government Criticism but Silences Collective Expression." *American Political Science Review*, 107(2), 326–343.

Kramer, Adam D., Jamie E. Guillory, and Jeffrey T. Hancock, 2014. Proceedings of the National Academy of Sciences, 111(24), 8788–8790.

Lane, Robert E. 1962. *Political Ideology: Why the American Common Man Believes What He Does*. New York: Free Press.

Li, Wei and Andrew McCallum. 2006. "Pachinko Allocation: DAG-Structured Mixture Models of Topic Correlations." *International Conference on Machine Learning (ICML)*, 577–584.

Lucas, Christopher, Richard A. Nielsen, Margaret E. Roberts, Brandon M. Stewart, Alex Storer, and Dustin Tingley. 2015. "Computer-Assisted Text Analysis for Comparative Politics", Political Analysis, 23(2), 254–277.

Monroe, Burt L., Jennifer Pan, Margaret E. Roberts, Maya Sen, and Betsy Sinclair. 2015. "No! Formal Theory, Causal Inference, and Big Data are Not Contradictory Trends in Political Science." *PS: Political Science and Politics*, 48(1), 71–74.

Olson, Mancur. 1971. *The Logic of Collective Action: Public Goods and the Theory of Groups*. 2nd ed. Cambridge, MA: Harvard University Press.

Pomares, Julia, Ines Levin, and R. Michael Alvarez. 2014. "Do Voters and Poll Workers Differ in their Attitudes toward e-voting? Evidence from the First e-election in Salta, Argentina." USENIX *Journal of Election Technology and Systems (JETS)*, 2(2), https://www.usenix.org/system/files/conference/evtwote14/jets_0202-pomares.pdf.

Pool, Ithiel de Sola, Robert P. Abelson, and Samuel Popkin. 1965. *Candidates, Issues & Strategies: A Computer Simulation of the 1960 and 1964 Presidential Elections*, revised edition. Cambridge, MA: MIT Press.

Poole, Keith T. 2005. *Spatial Models of Parliamentary Voting*. New York: Cambridge University Press.

Roberts, Margaret E., Brandon M. Stewart, Dustin Tingley, Christopher Lucas, Jetson Leder-Luis, Shana Kushner Gadarian, Bethany Albertson, and David G. Rand. 2014. "Structural Topic Models for Open-Ended Survey Responses." *American Journal of Political Science*, 58(4), 1064–1082.

Rosenstone, Steven J. and Raymond E. Wolfinger. 1978. "The Effect of Registration Laws on Voter Turnout." *American Political Science Review*, 72(1), 22–45.

Schrodt, Philip A. 1998. "Kansas Event Data System (K-E-D-S)." University of Kansas, http://eventdata.parusanalytics.com/keds.dir/kedsmanual.pdf.

Si, Yajuan, Jerome P. Reiter, and D. Sunshine Hillygus. 2015. "Semi-Parametric Selection Models for Potentially Non-Ignorable Attrition in Panel Studies with Refreshment Samples." *Political Analysis*, 23(1), 92–112.

Sinclair, Betsy. 2013. *The Social Citizen*. Chicago: University of Chicago Press.

Snijders, Tom A. B. 2011. "Statistical Models for Social Networks." *Annual Review of Sociology*, 37, 131–153.

Steele, Julie and Noah Iliinsky, 2010. *Beautiful Visualization: Looking at Data through the Eyes of Experts*. Sebastopol, CA: O'Reilly Media.

Stokes, Donald. 1963. "Spatial Models of Party Competition." *American Political Science Review*, 57, 368–377.

Sweeney, Latanya. 1997. "Weaving Technology and Policy Together to Maintain Confidentiality." *Journal of Law, Medicine and Ethics*, 25, 98–10.

Tausanovitch, Chris and Christopher Warshaw. 2013."Measuring Constituent Policy Preferences in Congress, State Legislatures and Cities."*Journal of Politics*, 75(2), 330–342.

Traunmuller, Richard, Andreas Murr, and Jeff Gill. 2015."Modeling Latent Information in Voting Data with Dirichlet Process Priors."*Political Analysis*, 23(1), 1–20.

Tufte, Edward. 2001. *The Visual Display of Quantitative Information*. Cheshire, CT: Graphics Press.

Warshaw, Christopher and Jonathan Rodden. 2012. "How Should We Measure District-Level Public Opinion on Individual Issues?" *Journal of Politics*, 74(1), 203–219.

PART 1

COMPUTATIONAL SOCIAL SCIENCE TOOLS

1

The Application of Big Data in Surveys to the Study of Elections, Public Opinion, and Representation*

Christopher Warshaw[†]

Department of Political Science, Massachusetts Institute of Technology

1 INTRODUCTION

Until recently, political scientists relied primarily on a small number of academic surveys that were extremely limited in size and scope. Their small sample sizes made them unsuitable for examining variation in public opinion across subpopulations, such as between Hispanics and Asian Americans. These surveys were also ill suited for examining public opinion at the subnational level. Recently, however, there has been a revolution in scholars' ability to access large data sets of public opinion data and in their ability to leverage the full array of survey data at their disposal.

Over the past decade, the amount of available public opinion has exploded due to the increasing availability of large archives of commercial polls that were collected over the past 75 years. In addition, advances in cooperative survey research have dramatically expanded the sample sizes in individual academic surveys (Ansolabehere and Rivers, 2013). At the same time, a broad array of statistical advances have improved scholars' ability to make substantive inferences from the full array of available survey data. Researchers have developed new model-based weights to compensate for the unrepresentativeness of survey data from earlier time periods (e.g., Berinsky, 2006; Berinsky et al., 2011). Moreover, they have developed new techniques to estimate the attitudes of small geographic areas and demographic groups (Gelman and Little, 1997; Park, Gelman, and Bafumi, 2004). These methodological advances have enabled scholars to measure the mass public's ideology and policy views at a variety of geographic scales, such as states, congressional districts, state

* I am grateful for feedback on this manuscript from Michael Alvarez, Devin Caughey, and Matto Mildenberger. All mistakes, however, are my own.
† Assistant Professor, Department of Political Science, Massachusetts Institute of Technology, cwarshaw@mit.edu.

legislative districts, and even large cities and towns. Moreover, scholars have developed new methods to leverage historical survey data to examine changes in public opinion over time (Stimson, 1991; Caughey and Warshaw, 2015; Enns and Koch, 2013).

These advances in the measurement of public opinion have enabled scholars to perform nuanced studies on political representation and accountability at the local (Tausanovitch and Warshaw, 2014), state (Lax and Phillips, 2009*a*; Pacheco, 2013), and federal levels (Ansolabehere and Jones, 2010; Bafumi and Herron, 2010; Clinton, 2006; Hill, 2014). Scholars have found that policy outcomes at each geographic level are responsive to public opinion. They have also examined whether particular political institutions, such as direct democracy or nonpartisan elections, enhance the relationship between public opinion and salient political outcomes (Canes-Wrone, Clark, and Kelly, 2014; Lax and Phillips, 2011). This work could eventually provide new insights into how institutional reforms might improve democratic governance. In addition, scholars have developed innovative approaches to pool together public opinion data to forecast election results (Linzer, 2013; Lock and Gelman, 2010). Future work on representation will examine the relationship between public opinion and political outcomes in increasingly diverse contexts. It will also combine survey data with information from political texts (Grimmer and Stewart, 2013), as well as campaign contributions (Bonica, 2014) and voter files (Ansolabehere and Hersh, 2012).

2 BIG DATA IN PUBLIC OPINION

Perhaps the most basic functions of surveys are to summarize public opinion and enable researchers to examine variation over time or space, as well as across geographic and demographic subgroups. However, traditional academic surveys, such as the American National Election Survey, had only limited utility for these purposes. These surveys gave scholars a snapshot of public opinion on a wide variety of topics. But they were only conducted every two or four years, which made them useful for examining long-term trends, but less suitable for studying more granular fluctuations in public opinion. Their small sample sizes also made them unsuitable for examining variation in public opinion across geographic and demographic subgroups (Ansolabehere and Rivers, 2013).

Over the past decade, however, the amount of survey data available to researchers has expanded dramatically. Much of this progress has occurred due to the efforts of the Roper Center for Public Opinion. The Roper Center has collected more than 20,000 polls from hundreds of survey firms, and data from many of these surveys are available at the individual level. For instance, the Roper Center has individual-level data available from more than 2,500 Gallup polls, as well as millions of survey responses from other commercial polls conducted by the *New York Times*, CBS News, ABC News, *USA Today*, the *Los Angeles Times*, and many other organizations.

These commercial polls have huge potential for research. The temporal coverage of these surveys goes back to the Great Depression. They include questions about respondents' views on thousands of different political issues, which enables researchers to examine changes in issue attitudes over time. In addition, they include a huge number of questions about elections at a variety of different levels. Finally, they include valuable information on the evolution of the mass public's partisanship (Enns and Koch, 2013; Wilkins, 2014).

Of course, these commercial surveys are not well suited for some research questions. For instance, they rarely include questions about media usage, which limits their utility for communications scholars. They also have only limited questions about citizens' views on members of Congress and elected officials at the subnational level. To address questions such as these, scholars have developed several novel large-scale surveys over the past 15 years. In 2000, and then again in 2004 and 2008, researchers at the University of Pennsylvania's Annenberg School of Communications surveyed more than fifty thousand people over the course of the presidential election campaign about their views on the campaign, as well as a number of other issues. Although the original motivation of these surveys was to study campaign effects, scholars have used them for a variety of other purposes. For instance, scholars have taken advantage of the National Annenberg Election Survey's (NAES) large sample size to estimate public opinion at the subnational level (e.g., Carsey and Harden, 2010; Tausanovitch and Warshaw, 2013). However, although the NAES was a huge advance over previous academic surveys, it also had a number of limitations. Most importantly, it focused primarily on the presidential election and only had a small number of survey questions about congressional or state elections.

In recent years, new innovations in survey research have emerged. The most prominent example is the Cooperative Congressional Election Study (CCES). The CCES was conceived in 2005 as a consortium that could produce large sample surveys out of numerous small sample surveys (Ansolabehere and Rivers, 2013). Over its first seven years, the CCES has produced more than 150 individual team surveys, as well as a master file of more than 200,000 aggregate survey responses to common questions on respondents' voting behavior, party identification, issue preferences, and so forth.

Although the NAES and CCES are well suited for many purposes, they go into the field too late to help predict campaign outcomes before they happen. As a result, a variety of pundits and scholars have built models to pool together data from many commercial polls (Linzer, 2013; Lock and Gelman, 2010). More recently, scholars have sought to use convenience samples to predict election outcomes. For instance, Wang et al. (2015) uses survey responses from hundreds of thousands of Xbox players to predict the 2012 presidential election results. These convenience samples often have the benefit of being available much faster than traditional surveys. They are also well suited for experimental research (e.g., Berinsky, Huber, and Lenz, 2012). However, it is challenging to build models that adjust for response bias to make them representative of the population.

3 SURVEY AND SAMPLING DESIGN

There are a number of sampling and design issues that researchers wishing to pool surveys need to surmount. Scholars often want to pool together data about a particular issue from a number of different surveys. However, the wording of questions can differ slightly across surveys. It is often difficult to decide whether the wordings of similar questions on different surveys are close enough to justify pooling the responses. Moreover, researchers need to be mindful of differences in the response categories for different items. For instance, Likert response categories are generally not comparable with dichotomous or other non-Likert response categories (Bishop et al., 1978). To mitigate these issues, researchers should only pool survey questions with similar wording and response categories.

An even more difficult problem is that different surveys employ a variety of different sampling methodologies. In the very early years of survey research, pollsters made little attempt to gather representative samples of the population.[1] In the mid-1930s, George Gallup and other pollsters introduced a technique called quota sampling (Berinsky, 2006). In quota-based samples, survey researchers sought to interview predetermined proportions of people from a number of different segments of the population. Although this approach yielded much better results than the earlier convenience samples, a problem was that interviewers were given wide discretion in selecting which people to interview within each population segment. Unfortunately, the people selected tended to be better educated and wealthier than the general population.[2] For many years, this response bias led academic scholars to eschew the usage of quota-based surveys. In recent years, however, researchers have developed model-based weighting techniques to mitigate selection bias from quota sampling (Berinsky, 2006). A research team is currently developing weights for all quota-based samples hosted by the Roper Center, which should soon be available for public use (Berinsky et al., 2011).

In the 1950s, many surveys switched to area-probability, or "cluster," sampling.[3] In this approach, researchers sample a set of "areas," such as cities or census tracts. Then, they randomly create a sample of a set of people in each community to interview. This approach was largely driven by the high cost of flying face-to-face interviewers to communities around the country. When properly weighted, these surveys are well suited for examining national-level trends in public opinion. However, area-probability samples are not necessarily representative at the subnational levels.[4] To address this problem, scholars could use model-based weights or pool area-probability surveys across time in order to ensure there is a more diverse set of areas in the samples (Brace et al., 2002; Stollwerk, 2012).

In the 1960s and 1970s, commercial survey firms switched from face-to-face interviews to phone interviews using random-digit dialing (RDD). This new approach yielded samples that were more representative of the population at a variety of geographic scales than quota or area-probability samples. However, nonresponse can be a significant problem for phone-based surveys. Over time, the rate of nonresponse to phone surveys has grown significantly (Kohut et al., 2012). As a result, researchers using phone samples should generally apply some sort of design or model-based weights to their analyses.[5]

The low response rates of RDD surveys and the desire to obtain larger sample sizes have led survey researchers to seek other sampling approaches in recent years. Most importantly, researchers have developed a number of innovative survey designs over the Internet, such as the Cooperative Congressional Election Study (CCES) discussed earlier (Ansolabehere and Rivers, 2013). The CCES uses a model-based sampling design, in which members of an online opt-in panel are matched to a synthetic frame of the population. This matched sample generally requires further weighting because the matching used for sample selection is imperfect. Of course, there is no guarantee that this approach yields samples that are representative of the population. However, the CCES appears to produce accurate predictions of recent elections (Ansolabehere and Rivers, 2013). More generally, Ansolabehere and Schaffner (2014) find that a carefully executed opt-in Internet panel produces estimates that are as accurate as a telephone survey.

4 SMALL AREA ESTIMATION

In many cases, researchers hope to use the broad array of survey data at their disposal to learn about public opinion at the subnational level. The most straightforward way to estimate citizens' attitudes at the subnational level is to use data from a simple random sample (SRS) that asks respondents for their preferences on individual issues. Lax and Phillips (2009b) calls this approach "disaggregation." The primary advantage of disaggregation is that scholars can estimate public opinion using only the respondent's survey response and place of residence (e.g., Erikson, Wright, and McIver, 1993; Brace et al., 2002). Thus, it is very straightforward for applied researchers to generate estimates of public opinion in each geographic unit. However, there are rarely enough respondents to generate precise estimates of the preferences of people in small geographic areas using simple disaggregation. Most surveys have only a handful of respondents in each state. Even large academic surveys generally only have a few dozen respondents in particular congressional districts or cities.[6]

Moreover, as we have seen, most surveys require the application of design or model-based weights to ensure that they are representative of the population. Unfortunately, the "prepackaged" weights included in survey data rarely ensure that the sample is representative at the subnational level. In addition, even if it were possible to construct a set of poststratification weights at the subnational level, the raw survey samples are typically too sparse to weight them to match the joint population distribution in small geographic areas (Caughey and Wang, 2014).

An alternative strategy introduced by Gelman and Little (1997) and Park, Gelman, and Bafumi (2004) is to estimate subnational public opinion using a technique called multilevel regression and poststratification (MRP).[7] The idea behind MRP is to model respondents' opinion hierarchically based on demographic and geographic predictors by partially pooling respondents in different geographic areas to an extent determined by the data. The smoothed estimates of opinion in each geographic-demographic cell (i.e., Hispanic women with a college education in Texas) are then weighted to match the cells' proportion in the population, yielding estimates of average opinion in each area. These weights are generally built using poststratification-based population targets.[8] But they sometimes include more complicated weighting designs (Ghitza and Gelman, 2013; Caughey and Warshaw, 2015). Several research teams have shown that MRP-based estimates of public opinion are almost always more accurate than estimates based on disaggregation of national surveys. Moreover, MRP models generate predictions of public opinion at the subnational level that are generally highly correlated with "actual" opinion even with survey samples of only a few thousand people (Park, Gelman, and Bafumi, 2004; Lax and Phillips, 2009*b*; Warshaw and Rodden, 2012). Moreover, Wang et al. (2015) show that MRP models may even be useful with convenience samples.

Scholars can build simple MRP models in R or Stata.[9] For more complicated models, they may wish to use fully Bayesian software such as Jags or Stan (see, e.g., Gelman and Hill, 2006). These fully Bayesian software packages also allow uncertainty in the posterior estimates of public opinion to be modeled more accurately.

As an example of how MRP models look in practice, I estimated the percentage of people who support gay marriage in each city with more than 50,000 people.[10] In this case, each individual's opinion on gay marriage is estimated as a function of his or her demographics, city, and state (for individual i, with indexes r, g, e, c, and s for race, gender, education category, city, and state, respectively). This information is incorporated using the following hierarchical model for responses:

$$\Pr(y_i = 1) = logit^{-1}\left(\gamma_0 + \alpha_{r[i]}^{race} + \alpha_{g[i]}^{gender} + \alpha_{e[i]}^{edu} + \alpha_{c[i]}^{city}\right)$$

where

$$\alpha_{r[i]}^{race} \text{ for } r = 1, \ldots, 4 \qquad (1)$$

$$\alpha_{g[i]}^{gender} \text{ for } r = 1, 2$$

$$\alpha_{e[i]}^{edu} \text{ for } e = 1, \ldots, 5$$

The city effect are then modeled as a function of the state into which the city falls, the city's average income, the percentage of the city's residents that are military veterans, and the percentage of couples in each city that are same-sex couples. The state effects, in turn, are modeled as a function of the region into which the state falls, the percentage of the state's residents that are union members, and the state's percentage of evangelical or Mormon residents. The second stage is poststratification. In this stage, I use the multilevel regression to make a prediction of public opinion in each demographic-geographic subtype. The estimates for each geographic-demographic group are then weighted by the percentages of each type in the actual city populations. Finally, these predictions are summed to produce an estimate of the proportion of people in each city that support same-sex marriage.[11]

Figure 1.1 shows public opinion on gay marriage in cities with more than 250,000 people. There is significant variation in public opinion on gay marriage across cities. Not surprisingly, Minneapolis, San Francisco, Washington, DC, and Seattle are four of the most liberal cities in the country on gay marriage. Memphis, Oklahoma City, and Jacksonville, are three of the most conservative cities.

An important question in the study of representation is whether policy outcomes at the local level are responsive to public opinion. Figure 1.2 shows that there is a strong correlation between the rights that municipalities grant to gay employees and public opinion on same-sex marriage.[12] Cities with greater support for same-sex marriage are much more likely to provide strong protections to gay employees. This suggests that city governments are responsive to the views of their citizens on gay rights (see also Palus, 2010; Tausanovitch and Warshaw, 2014).[13]

The use of MRP models to study questions of political representation and accountability has exploded in recent years. In recent years, scholars have begun examining factors that lead to variation in the performance of MRP models (Warshaw and Rodden, 2012; Buttice and Highton, 2013; Lax and Phillips, 2013). This work has led to several preliminary guidelines for researchers using MRP models in applied work. First, the price of MRP models' efficient estimates is a dependence on modeling assumptions, which is most acute in small survey samples. For instance, a survey sample with 1,500 respondents might have no respondents in the state of Wyoming. This means that the estimates of opinion in Wyoming would be entirely driven by the model (i.e., respondents in demographically similar states), rather than by respondents in Wyoming. This example illustrates that while MPR models enable inferences to be made with relatively small sample sizes, researchers should be cautious about making inferences about geographic units with few or no respondents. The combination, however, of MRP models with the larger survey data sets that are now available enables researchers to make accurate inferences about opinion in small states like Wyoming, as well as even smaller geographic units such as towns, school districts, neighborhoods, and city council districts.

Second, researchers should generally only use samples in MRP models where the survey respondents are a random sample of their geographic-demographic type. This condition is not met by convenience samples or area-probability

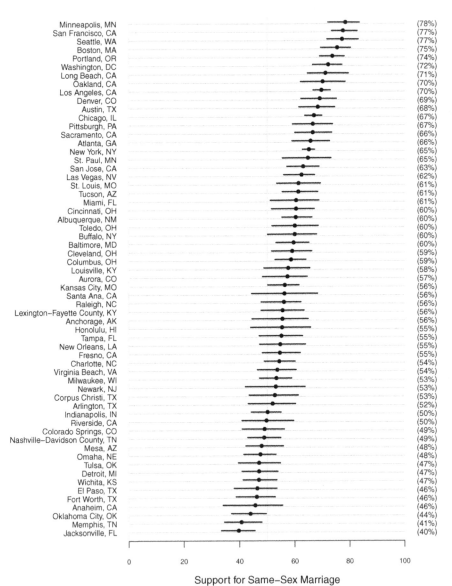

FIGURE 1.1. City responsiveness to public opinion on gay rights. This graph shows the association between public opinion on same-sex marriage in each city and an index of the rights that municipalities grant to gay employees.

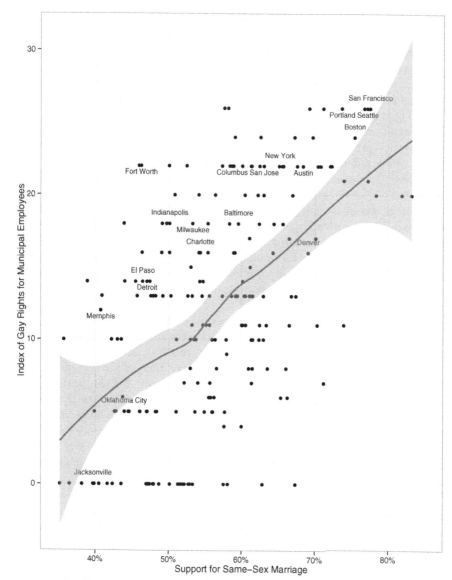

FIGURE 1.2. City responsiveness to public opinion on gay rights. This graph shows the association between public opinion on same-sex marriage in each city and an index of the rights that municipalities grant to gay employees.

samples such as the ANES or the GSS. However, a variety of scholars are currently building more complicated weighting models that allow analysts to account for the nonrepresentativeness of convenience (Wang et al., 2015) and area-probability samples (Stollwerk, 2012) at the local level.

In addition, scholars should generally use at least one predictor at each geographic level in the multilevel model (Lax and Phillips, 2013). Moreover, researchers should explain why they believe that the geographic covariates are strong proxies for the opinion being estimated (Buttice and Highton, 2013).[14] In general, stronger predictors in the multilevel model will lead to better estimates of public opinion (Warshaw and Rodden, 2012).[15] However, researchers should be mindful of endogeneity concerns. For instance, scholars should generally avoid including election results as covariates in an MRP model that is partially designed to predict other election results. They should also avoid using public opinion data in their model that is measured after the substantive outcome (e.g., policy outcome or roll-call vote) that public opinion is hypothesized to affect.[16]

Another lesson is that scholars usually do not need to use a complicated first-stage model with a large number of interactions between predictors when the substantive goal is to estimate public opinion at the state level (Lax and Phillips, 2013). However, more complicated first-stage models can be useful when the goal is to model the opinion of small demographic groups within states or other geographic units. For instance, Ghitza and Gelman (2013) built a nuanced model with a complicated set of interactions that enables them to model the voting behavior of different income and racial groups in each state.

Another issue is that researchers need to determine how to handle temporal dynamics in their analysis. For instance, scholars could choose to assume that public opinion does not change much over time, which would enable them to pool together data over many years (Erikson, Wright, and McIver, 1993; Lax and Phillips, 2009a). Alternatively, they could assume that public opinion is changing dramatically over time and then estimate every year separately. Between these two extremes, scholars could partially smooth temporal dynamics in their estimates (Pacheco, 2011; Caughey and Warshaw, 2015).[17] Regardless of which choice they make, scholars should theoretically justify the degree to which data is pooled together over time in their analysis.

Scholars should also be mindful that there is always uncertainty in public opinion estimates generated from survey data.[18] It is important to take this uncertainty into account in any substantive analysis (Lax and Phillips, 2013; Kastellec et al., forthcoming). Doing so is particularly important when the estimates of public opinion are used as a predictor in a regression model (see Gelman and Hill, 2006, 542).

Finally, scholars should always evaluate the quality of their MRP estimates. Ideally, they should conduct both convergent and construct validation (Adcock and Collier, 2001). To evaluate the convergent validity of a model, it is useful to either perform splitsample validation (Lax and Phillips, 2009b; Buttice and Highton, 2013; but see Wang and Gelman, 2014) or out-of-sample validation. One way to conduct out-of-sample validation is to compare MRP estimates of public opinion in a particular state with the results of state-level polls. It is also useful to evaluate a model's construct validity by comparing the estimates to theoretically related concepts. For instance, scholars could compare

MRP-based estimates of public opinion on same-sex marriage with the results of ballot initiatives to ban (or allow) gays to marry (Warshaw and Rodden, 2012). If the model's estimates are valid, they should be highly correlated with the initiative results, as well as other theoretically related concepts.

The next generation of work in small area estimation will likely focus on improving scholars' ability to estimate the preferences of small subconstituencies at the local level, such as Hispanic voters in Texas or people in Iowa without a high school education (Ghitza and Gelman, 2013). To do this, it may draw on richer sources of auxiliary geographic information (Selb and Munzert, 2011). The next generation of work will also likely focus on expanding scholars' ability to model changes in public opinion at the subnational level (e.g., Pacheco, 2011; Caughey and Warshaw, 2015). For instance, future work might examine how state-level public opinion on gay rights or climate change has changed over the past decade.

5 MEASURING IDEOLOGY AND OTHER LATENT VARIABLES

Although public opinion on individual issues is useful for many purposes, researchers often care more about estimating latent constructs that cannot be measured directly (Treier and Jackman, 2008). For instance, researchers might wish to measure the policy liberalism ("ideal points")[19] of survey respondents (Bafumi and Herron, 2010; Tausanovitch and Warshaw, 2013) or legislators (Clinton, Jackman, and Rivers, 2004), whereas election forecasters might wish to measure citizens' propensity to turn out to vote based on their responses on a survey. To estimate these latent constructs, scholars have developed a variety of measurement models.[20]

The most common class of measurement models in recent years comes out of item response theory (IRT). The conventional two-parameter IRT model introduced to political science by Clinton, Jackman, and Rivers (2004) characterizes each response $y_{ij} \in \{0, 1\}$ as a function of subject i's latent *ability* (θ_i), the *difficulty* (α_j) and *discrimination* (β_j) of item j, and an error term (e_{ij}), where

$$\Pr[y_{ij} = 1] = \Phi(\beta_j \theta_i - \alpha_j), \tag{2}$$

where Φ is the standard normal CDF (Jackman, 2009, 455; Fox, 2010, 10). β_j is referred to as the "discrimination" parameter because it captures the degree to which the latent trait affects the probability of a yes answer. If β_j is 0, then question j tells us nothing about the latent variable being measured. We would expect β_j to be close to 0 if we ask a completely irrelevant question, such as one about the respondent's favorite color. The "cut point" is the value of α_j / β_j at which the probabilities of answering yes or no to a question are 50–50. Scholars can run relatively simple IRT models using off-the-shelf software such as Simon Jackman's `ideal` function in the R package `pscl` (Jackman, 2012). For more complicated IRT models, they can use fully Bayesian software such as Jags or Stan.

Like other dimension-reduction methods, such as additive scales or factor analysis, IRT models benefit from the reduction in measurement error that comes from using multiple indicators of a single construct (Ansolabehere, Rodden, and Snyder, 2008). However, IRT models also offer a number of methodological advantages over alternative methods. In particular, they can be motivated by an explicit spatial utility model appropriate for dichotomous data (Clinton, Jackman, and Rivers, 2004, 356). Bayesian IRT models also allow easy characterization of the uncertainty around any parameter estimates (Jackman, 2000). Researchers should bear in mind that IRT models generally have less measurement error when more items (e.g., roll-call votes or survey questions) are available to measure the latent construct and these items discriminate well between individuals in different regions of the scale (Tausanovitch and Warshaw, 2011). In the case of policy preferences this may mean that the question is more closely related to left-right ideology, is easier for respondents to understand, or simply taps more clearly into the primary cleavage of politics rather than more idiosyncratic concerns.

More generally, an important challenge facing researchers who wish to deploy IRT models is that it is impossible to directly compare latent constructs if they are estimated using disjoint sets of people answering disjoint sets of choices (e.g., respondents to two different surveys with no overlapping items). To overcome this problem, researchers need to "bridge" respondents from different surveys into the same latent space using common actors or items (see, e.g., Bafumi and Herron, 2010; Bailey, 2007).[21] Regardless of the precise bridging method used, an important assumption of IRT models is that some set of item parameters are constant across groups (Lewis and Tausanovitch, 2013). For instance, the cut points for a given set of items (i.e., survey question) should be similar across groups both cross-sectionally and over time. Although this assumption may seem innocuous, the context of the questions may be different over time or across groups. For instance, the status quo may have changed on particular items over time. In the future, scholars should seek to explicitly verify the assumption of constant item parameters for any bridging items between groups. Scholars should also experiment with allowing the item parameters for individual survey questions to evolve over time in their IRT models (Caughey and Warshaw, 2015).

One of the frontiers of IRT modeling is to estimate the latent policy preferences of legislators and other political elites in the same ideological space as ordinary citizens (Jessee, 2009). This would enable researchers to directly compare the preferences of elites and voters. For instance, they could examine whether legislators are more extreme than voters in their constituency (Bafumi and Herron, 2010). Most commonly, scholars seek to jointly scale elites and the mass public using common questions in the manner described earlier. However, Lewis and Tausanovitch (2013) show that the constant item parameters assumption often fails in this case. They suggest that this could be because legislators take positions in a context that is fundamentally different from the context of public opinion polling. At the very least, these findings suggest that researchers need to be cautious about jointly scaling elites and the mass public. Moreover, they need to be attentive to differences in the contexts of elites and survey respondents.

Another emerging line of research is to combine IRT and MRP models to measure the public's latent policy liberalism at the subnational level. For instance, Tausanovitch and Warshaw (2013) combined IRT and MRP models to estimate the policy preferences of states, legislative districts, and cities over the past decade. Their approach, however, can only be applied under very specific conditions.[22]

A more general approach for estimating the average latent preferences of the mass public at the level of geographic units such as states or congressional districts is to use a Bayesian dynamic hierarchical IRT model that is estimated at the level of demographic groups rather than individuals (Lewis, 2001; McGann, 2014). This enables scholars to use data from surveys that only ask one or two questions about the latent construct of interest, which would be impossible with conventional IRT models at the individual level. For example, Caughey and Warshaw (2015) developed a model that estimates latent group opinion in each year as a function of demographic and geographic characteristics, smoothing the hierarchical parameters over time via a dynamic linear model. The group-level estimates from this model can be weighted to generate estimates for geographic units. This approach enables scholars to measure ideology and other latent variables across geographic space and over time in a unified framework. For instance, it could be used to estimate the mass public's policy liberalism in each state over the past fifty years. Indeed, Figure 1.3 shows how the mass public's policy liberalism has changed at the state level between 1965 and 2010 (Caughey and Warshaw, 2014). It indicates that only a few states' policy liberalism has shifted substantially over time (Erikson, Wright, and McIver, 2006). Southern states such as Mississippi and Alabama have become somewhat more conservative over time, whereas states in New England have become somewhat more liberal.

6 APPLICATIONS

In this section, I review recent work that combines large-scale survey data with recent advances in statistical techniques to tackle important substantive questions in political science.

6.1 Descriptive Analysis

The growing availability of thousands of surveys over the entire span of the last half-century has revolutionized scholars' ability to study variation in public opinion in earlier time periods. For instance, until recently, scholars had

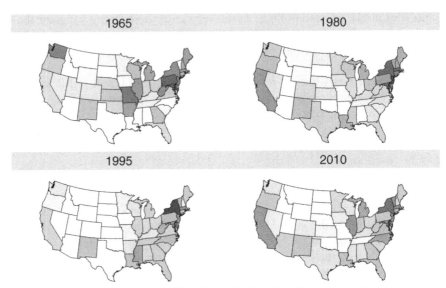

FIGURE 1.3. Average state policy liberalism, 1965–2010. The estimates have been recentered and standardized in each year to accentuate the color contrasts.

little knowledge of public opinion on the New Deal in the 1930s. However Berinsky et al. (2011) compiled more than 400 public opinion polls undertaken between 1936 and 1945. They also developed a series of weights to mitigate the problems introduced by the quota-sampling procedures employed at the time. They examine the evolution of public opinion during this period on a variety of different policy issues. For instance, they find that although most Americans expressed basic support for unions, support dropped by about 10 points between 1937 and 1941. Schickler and Caughey (2011) show that the decline in support for unions during this period was particularly large in the South.

The availability of thousands of historical surveys has also enabled scholars to examine long-term changes in the partisan composition of the electorate. Wilkins (2014) compiles hundreds of thousands of individual respondents from more than 600 Gallup polls between 1950 to 2011 to study the evolution of the electorate's ideological and partisan composition. He finds that there was an asymmetric shift of conservatives toward Republican identification during the 1980s, which led to a large increase in Republican party identification. Gillon, Ladd, and Meredith (2013) pool more than 1,800 Gallup polls between 1953 and 2012 to examine the gender gap in partisanship. They show that the modern partisan gender gap emerged in the late 1970s, gradually increased until the mid-1990s, and since has plateaued. None of these studies would have been possible without the availability of millions of survey respondents going back to the mid-20th century.

Other recent work has used the new statistical tools described earlier, as well as the growing availability of survey data, to measure the attitudes of geographic and demographic sub-constituencies with increasing precision. For instance, Lax and Phillips (2009*a*) use MRP to measure state-level public opinion on gay-rights issues in the 2000s. Using a similar approach Elmendorf and Spencer (2014) examine variation in racial stereotyping across states. They find that significant levels of anti-black racial stereotyping continue to be present in many southern states, as well as in several Great Plains and mountain states.

One of the frontiers in this line of research is to examine how the opinions of geographic and demographic subconstituencies have changed over time (e.g., Pacheco, 2011). A number of scholars have examined opinion change on individual issues (e.g., Pacheco, 2014; Shirley and Gelman, 2014). For instance, Pacheco (2014) examines changes in state-level opinion in recent years on education and welfare, abortion, the death penalty, and presidential approval. Other scholars have examined changes in the public's overall policy liberalism or mood at the state level (Enns and Koch, 2013; Caughey and Warshaw, 2014, 2015).

Another exciting line of research is working on building dynamic forecasts of election outcomes at the subnational level. Recently, scholars have developed innovative approaches to pool together public opinion data to forecast presidential election results at the state and national level (Linzer, 2013; Lock and Gelman, 2010). The next generation of forecasting models will likely be used to predict congressional and state legislative election results.

6.2 Representation & Elections

The foundation of representative democracy is the assumption that citizens' preferences should correspond with and inform elected officials' behavior. There is a large body of research on the dyadic relationship between legislators' roll-call behavior and public opinion in their district. These studies generally find that legislators' roll-call positions are correlated with the general ideological preferences of their districts (e.g., Clinton, 2006). However, there is little evidence that candidates' positions converge on the median voter (Ansolabehere, Snyder, and Stewart, 2001; Lee, Moretti, and Butler, 2004). Instead, legislators appear to be more ideologically extreme than voters (Bafumi and Herron, 2010). Moreover, Democrats and Republicans represent the same electorates very differently. One recent study finds that a Democratic and Republican legislator elected by the same district will disagree with one another on more than one out of three bills (Fowler and Hall, forthcoming).

If legislators' positions are not converging on the median voter, perhaps they are converging on the positions of other subconstituencies in each district, such as primary voters, donors, or activists. Of course, this question is impossible to examine without good estimates of public opinion at the subnational level. As a result, scholars made little progress on understanding the relationship between legislators' positions and the preferences of sub-constituencies in their districts until recently. Clinton (2006) kicked off the modern era of research in this area with an innovative study in which he pooled data on more than 100,000 survey respondents surveys from two different large-scale surveys in 1999–2000. He finds that the ideology of same-party constituents has a disproportionate influence on the roll-call behavior of members of the 106th House of Representatives (1999–2000). Similarly, Bafumi and Herron (2010) use a novel survey design in the Cooperative Congressional Election Study to show that "members of Congress, both Senators and Representatives, are more representative of state partisans than they are of state medians" in the 109th and 110th Congresses (2005–2008). More recent studies of the effect of subconstituencies on representation use MRP to model the preferences of Democrats and Republicans in each constituency. Kastellec et al. (forthcoming) find that senators more heavily weight their partisan base when casting roll-call votes on Supreme Court confirmation. Indeed, when their state median voter and party median voter disagree, senators strongly favor the latter. Hill (2014) studies the relationship between the ideology of partisan subconstituencies and a wider range of roll-call votes. In contrast to the results of Kastellec et al. (forthcoming), he finds that primary and general electorate preferences have roughly equal influence on voting in Congress.

Although scholars will continue to make progress on the study of representation at the federal level, the frontier of research on representation in American politics is to examine the links between public opinion and political outcomes at the state and local levels. Until recently, the lack of sufficient public opinion data has stymied research on representation at the state and local level. As Jessica Trounstine put it only a few years ago, "in order to explain how well and under what conditions [local] policy reflects constituent preferences, we need…some knowledge of different constituents' preferences…at the local level" (Trounstine, 2010, 413–414).

The availability of new data and statistical methods, however, has revolutionized scholars' ability to study representation at the subnational level. Moreover, scholars have made great progress on evaluating whether particular institutions enhance the link between public opinion and political outcomes. For instance, Lax and Phillips (2011) use MRP to estimate state-level public opinion on dozens of individual issues in the 2000s. Then, they look at whether public policy outcomes on these issues are responsive and congruent with public opinion. Overall, they find a strong link between public opinion and policy. They also examine whether institutions affect the link between public opinion and state policy outcomes. They find that legislative professionalism and term limits improve responsiveness, whereas direct democracy and elected courts have no affect on representation.

In another recent study, Tausanovitch and Warshaw (2014) examine representation at the municipal level by pooling together seven large-scale surveys and estimating each respondents' latent policy liberalism in a common space. Then, they use MRP models to estimate the mean policy liberalism of citizens in every city in the country with more than 20,000 people. They find that city policy outcomes are extremely responsive to citizens' policy preferences. However, no institution, such as term limits or direct democracy, consistently improves responsiveness. Berkman and Plutzer (2005) use a similar approach to examine representation in school districts. They pooled together a number of years from the General Social Survey (GSS) and employ a technique similar to MRP to estimate public opinion on school spending in each district. They find that school spending is responsive to public opinion. Moreover, they find that institutions affect the relationship of public opinion to school spending.

A limitation of virtually all of the existing studies on representation at the state and local level is that they use cross-sectional research designs. This makes it impossible to examine policy change, which is both theoretically limiting and problematic for strong causal inference since the temporal order of the variables cannot be established (Lowery, Gray, and Hager, 1989; Ringquist and Garand, 1999). Indeed, most existing studies cannot rule out reverse causation. For instance, more liberal policies could lead to more liberal public opinion (cf. Lenz, 2013). The next generation of studies in this area should examine whether *changes* in public opinion lead to *changes* in policy outcomes. This will require a new generation of modeling approaches that enable scholars to build dynamic estimates of public opinion that change over time.

7 CONCLUSION

In recent years, there has been a revolution in scholars' ability to access large data sets of public opinion data and to leverage the full array of survey data at their disposal. This has enabled scholars to estimate public opinion at a variety of geographic levels for increasingly small groups of people. Moreover, it has enabled researchers to address nuanced questions related to representation and accountability in American politics.

Future work in this area should tackle several linked methodological challenges. First, researchers need to continue to develop better tools to integrate representative samples and convenience samples (Wang et al., 2015). Second, scholars need to overcome challenges that have limited their ability to put the preferences of elites and the mass public into the same space (Lewis and Tausanovitch, 2013). This will enable them to study whether institutions such as direct democracy or term limits improve the level of ideological congruence between elected officials and the mass public. Third, they need to build better models to estimate changes in public opinion over time at the subnational level (Caughey and Warshaw, 2015). This will enable them to examine whether changes in public opinion lead to changes in policy outcomes. There also needs to be more work to integrate survey data with other types of political data. For instance, scholars of representation might be able to improve their estimates of the latent preferences of small geographic subconstituencies by linking public opinion data with information on political donations and social networks (see, e.g., Bonica, 2014).

There also needs to be more attention to integrating causal inference methods with large-scale observational survey data. Indeed, accurate measures of public opinion alone are insufficient to address key theoretical question if these new data are not paired with strong research designs. For instance, researchers could combine survey data and causal inference methods to examine whether the incumbency effect varies across partisan or ideological subgroups. They could also examine how changes in the partisan control of various levels of government influence public opinion.

Scholars are likely to leverage the expansion in the availability of large-scale public opinion data, as well as new techniques in small area estimation, to examine questions of representation and accountability at the state and local level. They will likely focus on whether the opinions of small demographic groups affect political outcomes. For instance, they might examine whether legislators are more responsive to wealthy or well-educated constituents (e.g., Erikson and Bhatti, 2011). They might also examine whether an increase in polarization among partisan elites and donors at the local level has contributed to polarization in Congress. Finally, there is likely to be a new generation of election forecasting models at the subnational level in the coming years. Forecasters are likely to use the increasingly large survey samples available to them to model the outcomes of gubernatorial, congressional, and state legislative elections.

Notes

1. For instance, Literary Digest conducted a mail-in survey during the 1936 presidential campaign that attracted a huge sample of more than two million responses (Wang et al., 2015). Despite this massive sample, the magazine incorrectly predicted a landslide victory for Republican candidate Alf Landon over Franklin Roosevelt. The problem was that the respondents to the magazine's poll were largely automobile and telephone owners as well as the magazine's own subscribers, which overrepresented Landon's core constituencies (Squire, 1988).
2. For instance, Berinsky (2006) reports that only about 10% of the population in 1940 had at least some college education, while nearly 30% of a 1940 Gallup poll sample had some college education.
3. The General Social Survey (GSS) and the National Election Survey (ANES) continue to use a variant of this approach.
4. For instance, imagine that Ann Arbor was the community selected for interviewers to visit in Michigan. The sample of households in this community would certainly not be representative of the population of Michigan.

5. Researchers should be aware, however, that the application of design or model-based weights does not necessarily yield unbiased estimates of public opinion if there is still a nonrandom probability of response even conditional on the covariates in the weighting model.

6. For instance, the 2010 Cooperative Congressional Election Study has about 50,000 respondents. This seems like a massive sample; yet there are barely a hundred respondents in any given congressional district and many fewer in individual state legislative districts, cities, or counties.

7. Other scholars have also developed a number of related approaches for small area estimation (see, e.g., Selb and Munzert, 2011). But MRP remains the most prominent.

8. See Caughey and Wang (2014) for a discussion of the complications that can emerge when constructing post-stratification-based weights in earlier time periods.

9. Kastellec, Lax, and Phillips (2010) provide a useful primer on building MRP models in R. Also, Warshaw and Rodden (2012) provide replication code in R to build an MRP model of public opinion in congressional and state legislative districts.

10. I used data from the 2010, 2011, 2012, and 2013 Cooperative Congressional Election Studies (CCES), and 10 Pew Foundation surveys conducted between 2010–2013. In all, the model includes data from more than 47,000 survey respondents in cities. For simplicity, I dropped "don't know" responses. In a more in-depth substantive analysis of this issue, however, "don't know" responses would be modeled rather than deleted.

11. The correlation between the MRP-based estimates and simple, disaggregated estimates of public opinion on same-sex marriage is .92. In addition, the correlation with Tausanovitch and Warshaw (2014)'s broader measure of the policy conservatism of the mass public in each city is .64. Finally, the estimates have strong face validity. Thus, there is substantial reason to believe that these estimates are accurately capturing public opinion on same-sex marriage.

12. The data on the rights that municipalities grant to gay employees is derived from the Human Rights Campaign's Municipal Equality Index (MEI), which scores how well approximately 300 cities support the LGBT people who live and work there.

13. Note that more work would have to be done to show a *causal* link between public opinion and gay rights policies, but at the very least, the correlational evidence in Figure 1.2 suggests a robust role for public opinion.

14. To develop a closer theoretical link between the covariates in the multilevel model and the opinion being modeled, some previous work suggests that scholars should customize the MRP model for their particular substantive application (Warshaw and Rodden, 2012). For instance, a researcher seeking subnational public opinion estimates on climate change might want to include covariates related to pollution or the impacts of global warming.

15. In the future, research should assess whether machine learning algorithms could be used to choose predictors in the MRP model (Caughey and Wang, 2014; Elmendorf and Spencer, 2014).

16. Given data limitations, scholars often choose to pool together public opinion data over many years for their MRP models. In this case, scholars should show that public opinion is relatively stable across the entire time frame, that and there is no reverse causation where policy changes lead to changes in public opinion.

17. One benefit of partially smoothing temporal dynamics over time is that it renders the model less sensitive to cross-sectional modeling assumptions. For instance, the estimates of public opinion in Georgia would be primarily a function of opinion in Georgia in the previous time period, rather than opinion in demographically similar states, as in a normal MRP model.

18. This is true whether the estimates are generated using disaggregation, MRP, or some other model-based approach.

19. Ideal points are a measure of individuals' latent liberalism or conservatism based on their stated policy preferences on surveys, roll-call votes, or judicial decisions.

20. See Jackman (2008) for more on measurement models.

21. This is most commonly done by using an overlapping set of choices and/or people to bridge individuals into a common space. In some cases, there may be enough common survey questions on different surveys to bridge together the latent construct across surveys without any additional work. In other cases, there may not be enough survey items to bridge together the respondents. In this case, one potential solution is to ask an original survey with questions that overlap with the ones on earlier surveys. For instance, Tausanovitch and Warshaw (2013) link together respondents from seven previous surveys using the module they placed on the 2010 Cooperative Congressional Election Survey. In this module, they asked 1,300 survey respondents a large number of questions with wording identical to questions asked on other, previous surveys. These common questions allow them to place the policy preferences of respondents from the previous surveys on a common scale.

22. First, it requires that each individual survey respondent be asked a large number of issue questions. This means that it would not be applicable to earlier eras when each survey tended to include only a handful of policy questions. Second, it requires substantial computational resources to estimate the latent ideology of hundreds of thousands of individuals.

References

Adcock, Robert and David Collier. 2001. "Measurement Validity: A Shared Standard for Qualitative and Quantitative Research." *American Political Science Review* 95(3):529–546.

Ansolabehere, Stephen and Eitan Hersh. 2012. "Validation: What Big Data Reveal about Survey Misreporting and the Real Electorate." *Political Analysis* 20(4):437–459.

Ansolabehere, Stephen and Philip Edward Jones. 2010. "Constituents' Responses to Congressional Roll-Call Voting." *American Journal of Political Science* 54(3):583–597.

Ansolabehere, Stephen and Douglas Rivers. 2013. "Cooperative Survey Research." *Annual Review of Political Science* 16:307–329.

Ansolabehere, Stephen, Jonathan Rodden, and James M. Snyder Jr. 2008. "The Strength of Issues: Using Multiple Measures to Gauge Preference Stability, Ideological Constraint, and Issue Voting." *American Political Science Review* 102(2):215–232.

Ansolabehere, Stephen and Brian F. Schaffner. 2014. "Does Survey Mode Still Matter? Findings from a 2010 Multi-Mode Comparison." *Political Analysis* 22(3):285–303.

Ansolabehere, Stephen, James M. Snyder Jr., and Charles Stewart III. 2001. "Candidate Positioning in U.S. House Elections." *American Journal of Political Science* 45(1):136–159.

Bafumi, Joseph and Michael C. Herron. 2010. "Leapfrog Representation and Extremism: A Study of American Voters and Their Members in Congress." *American Political Science Review* 104(3):519–542.

Bailey, Michael A. 2007. "Comparable Preference Estimates across Time and Institutions for the Court, Congress, and Presidency." *American Journal of Political Science* 51(3):433–448.

Berinsky, Adam J. 2006. "American Public Opinion in the 1930s and 1940s: The Analysis of Quota-Controlled Sample Survey Data." *Public Opinion Quarterly* 70(4):499–529.

Berinsky, Adam J., Gregory A. Huber, and Gabriel S. Lenz. 2012. "Evaluating Online Labor Markets for Experimental Research: Amazon.com's Mechanical Turk." *Political Analysis* 20(3):351–368.

Berinsky, Adam J., Eleanor Neff Powell, Eric Schickler, and Ian Brett Yohai. 2011. "Revisiting Public Opinion in the 1930s and 1940s." *PS: Political Science & Politics* 44(3):515–520.

Berkman, Michael B. and Eric Plutzer. 2005. *Ten Thousand Democracies: Politics and Public Opinion in America's School Districts.* Washington, DC: Georgetown University Press.

Bishop, George F., Robert W. Oldendick, Alfred J. Tuchfarber, and Stephen E. Bennett. 1978. "Changing Structure of Mass Belief Systems: Fact or Artifact?" *Journal of Politics* 40(3):781–787.

Bonica, Adam. 2014. "Mapping the Ideological Marketplace." *American Journal of Political Science* 58(2):367–386.

Brace, Paul, Kellie Sims-Butler, Kevin Arceneaux, and Martin Johnson. 2002. "Public Opinion in the American States: New Perspectives Using National Survey Data." *American Journal of Political Science* 46:173–189.

Buttice, Matthew K. and Benjamin Highton. 2013. "How Does Multilevel Regression and Poststratification Perform with Conventional National Surveys?" *Political Analysis* 21(4):449–467.

Canes-Wrone, Brandice, Tom S. Clark, and Jason P. Kelly. 2014. "Judicial Selection and Death Penalty Decisions." *American Political Science Review* 108(1):23–39.

Carsey, Thomas M. and Jeffrey J. Harden. 2010. "New Measures of Partisanship, Ideology, and Policy Mood in the American States." *State Politics & Policy Quarterly* 10(2):136–156.

Caughey, Devin and Mallory Wang. 2014. "Bayesian Population Interpolation and Lasso-Based Target Selection in Survey Weighting." Working Paper.

Caughey, Devin and Christopher Warshaw. 2015. "Dynamic Estimation of Latent Public Opinion Using a Hierarchical Group-Level IRT Model." *Political Analysis*, 23(2):197–211.

Caughey, Devin and Christopher Warshaw. 2014. "Dynamic Representation in the American States, 1960–2012." Working Paper.

Clinton, Joshua D. 2006. "Representation in Congress: Constituents and Roll Calls in the 106th House." *Journal of Politics* 68(2):397–409.

Clinton, Joshua, Simon Jackman, and Douglas Rivers. 2004. "The Statistical Analysis of Roll Call Data." *American Political Science Review* 98(2):355–370.

Elmendorf, Christopher S. and Douglas M. Spencer. 2014. "The Geography of Racial Stereotyping: Evidence and Implications for VRA Preclearance after Shelby County." *California Law Review* 102(5):1123–1180.

Enns, Peter K. and Julianna Koch. 2013. "Public Opinion in the U.S. States: 1956 to 2010." *State Politics and Policy Quarterly* 13(3):349–372.

Erikson, Robert S. and Yosef Bhatti. 2011. "How Poorly Are the Poor Represented in the US Senate?" In *Who Gets Represented*, ed. Peter Enns and Christopher Wlezien. New York: Russell Sage Foundation, pp. 223–246.

Erikson, Robert S., Gerald C. Wright, and John P. McIver. 1993. *Statehouse Democracy: Public Opinion and Policy in the American States*. New York: Cambridge University Press.

Erikson, Robert S., Gerald C. Wright, and John P. McIver. 2006. "Public Opinion in the States: A Quarter Century of Change and Stability." In *Public Opinion in State Politics*, ed. Jeffrey E. Cohen. Palo Alto, CA: Stanford University Press, pp. 229–253.

Fowler, Anthony and Andrew Hall. Forthcoming. "Long Term Consequences of Elections." British Journal of Political Science.

Fox, Jean-Paul. 2010. *Bayesian Item Response Modeling: Theory and Applications*. New York: Springer (PDF ebook).

Gelman, Andrew and Jennifer Hill. 2006. *Data Analysis Using Regression and Hierarchical/Multilevel Models*. New York: Cambridge University Press.

Gelman, Andrew and Thomas C. Little. 1997. "Poststratification into Many Categories Using Hierarchical Logistic Regression." *Survey Methodology* 23(2):127–135.

Ghitza, Yair and Andrew Gelman. 2013. "Deep Interactions with MRP: Election Turnout and Voting Patterns among Small Electoral Subgroups." *American Journal of Political Science* 57(3):762–776.

Gillon, Daniel Q., Jonathan M. Ladd, and Marc Meredith. 2013. "Education, Party Polarization and the Origins of the Partisan Gender Gap." Working Paper.

Grimmer, Justin and Brandon M. Stewart. 2013. "Text as Data: The Promise and Pitfalls of Automatic Content Analysis Methods for Political Texts." *Political Analysis* 21(3):267–297.

Hill, Seth. 2014. "Primary Electorates and Member Ideology in the U.S. House." Working Paper.

Jackman, Simon. 2000. "Estimation and Inference Are Missing Data Problems: Unifying Social Science Statistics via Bayesian Simulation." *Political Analysis* 8(4):307–332.

Jackman, Simon. 2008. "Measurement." In *The Oxford Handbook of Political Methodology*. Oxford Handbooks Online.

Jackman, Simon. 2009. *Bayesian Analysis for the Social Sciences*. Hoboken, NJ: Wiley.

Jackman, Simon. 2012. "pscl: Classes and Methods for R Developed in the Political Science Computational Laboratory, Stanford University." Department of Political Science, Stanford University. R package version 1.04.4. http://pscl.stanford.edu.

Jessee, Stephen A. 2009. "Spatial Voting in the 2004 Presidential Election." *American Political Science Review* 103(1):59–81.

Kastellec, Jonathan P., Jeffrey R. Lax, Michael Malecki, and Justin H. Phillips. Forthcoming. "Polarizing the Electoral Connection: Partisan Representation in Supreme Court Confrontation Politics." Journal of Politics.

Kastellec, Jonathan P., Jeffrey R. Lax, and Justin Phillips. 2010. "Estimating State Public Opinion with Multi-Level Regression and Poststratification Using R." Unpublished Manuscript.

Kohut, Andrew, Scott Keeter, Carroll Doherty, Michael Dimock, and Leah Christian. 2012. "Assessing the Representativeness of Public Opinion Surveys." Washington, DC: Pew Research Center.

Lax, Jeffrey R. and Justin H. Phillips. 2009*a*. "Gay Rights in the States: Public Opinion and Policy Responsiveness." *American Political Science Review* 103(3):367–386.

Lax, Jeffrey R. and Justin H. Phillips. 2009*b*. "How Should We Estimate Public Opinion in the States?" *American Journal of Political Science* 53(1):107–121.

Lax, Jeffrey R. and Justin H. Phillips. 2011. "The Democratic Deficit in the States." *American Journal of Political Science* 56(1):148–166.

Lax, Jeffrey R. and Justin H. Phillips. 2013. "How Should We Estimate Sub-National Opinion using MRP? Preliminary Findings and Recommendations." Working Paper.

Lee, David S., Enrico Moretti, and Matthew J. Butler. 2004. "Do Voters Affect or Elect Policies? Evidence from the U.S. House." *Quarterly Journal of Economics* 119(3):807–859.

Lenz, Gabriel S. 2013. *Follow the Leader? How Voters Respond to Politicians' Policies and Performance*. Chicago: University of Chicago Press.

Lewis, Jeffrey B. 2001. "Estimating Voter Preference Distributions from Individual-Level Voting Data." *Political Analysis* 9(3):275–297.

Lewis, Jeffrey and Chris Tausanovitch. 2013. "Has Joint Scaling Solved the Achen Objection to Miller and Stokes?" Working Paper.

Linzer, Drew A. 2013. "Dynamic Bayesian Forecasting of Presidential Elections in the States." *Journal of the American Statistical Association* 108(501):124–134.

Lock, Kari and Andrew Gelman. 2010. "Bayesian Combination of State Polls and Election Forecasts." *Political Analysis* 18(3):337–348.

Lowery, David, Virginia Gray, and Gregory Hager. 1989. "Public Opinion and Policy Change in the American States." *American Politics Research* 17(1):3–31.

McGann, Anthony J. 2014. "Estimating the Political Center from Aggregate Data: An Item Response Theory Alternative to the Stimson Dyad Ratios Algorithm." *Political Analysis* 22(1):115–129.

Pacheco, Julianna. 2011. "Using National Surveys to Measure Dynamic US State Public Opinion: A Guideline for Scholars and an Application." *State Politics & Policy Quarterly* 1(4):415–439.

Pacheco, Julianna. 2013. "The Thermostatic Model of Responsiveness in the American States." *State Politics & Policy Quarterly* 13(3):306–332.

Pacheco, Julianna. 2014. "Measuring and Evaluating Changes in State Opinion across Eight Issues." *American Politics Research* 42(6):986–1009.

Palus, Christine Kelleher. 2010. "Responsiveness in American Local Governments." *State and Local Government Review* 42(2):133–150.

Park, David K., Andrew Gelman, and Joseph Bafumi. 2004. "Bayesian Multilevel Estimation with Poststratification: State-Level Estimates from National Polls." *Political Analysis* 12(4):375–385.

Ringquist, Evan J. and James C. Garand. 1999. "Policy Change in the American States." In *American State and Local Politics: Directions for the 21st Century*, ed. Ronald E. Weber and Paul Brace. New York: Chatham House: Seven Bridges Press, pp. 268–299.

Schickler, Eric and Devin Caughey. 2011. "Public Opinion, Organized Labor, and the Limits of New Deal Liberalism, 1936–1945." *Studies in American Political Development* 25(02):162–189.

Selb, Peter and Simon Munzert. 2011. "Estimating Constituency Preferences from Sparse Survey Data Using Auxiliary Geographic Information." *Political Analysis* 19(4):455–470.

Shirley, Kenneth E. and Andrew Gelman. 2014. "Hierarchical Models for Estimating State and Demographic Trends in US Death Penalty Public Opinion." *Journal of the Royal Statistical Society: Series A (Statistics in Society)* 178(1):1–28.

Squire, Peverill. 1988. "Why the 1936 Literary Digest Poll Failed." *Public Opinion Quarterly* 52(1):125–133.

Stimson, James A. 1991. *Public Opinion in America: Moods, Cycles, and Swings.* Boulder, CO: Westview.

Stollwerk, Alissa. 2012. "Estimating Subnational Opinion with Cluster-Sampled Polls: Challenges and Suggestions." Paper presenting at the 2012 APSA Annual Meeting.

Tausanovitch, Chris and Christopher Warshaw. 2011. "How Should We Choose Survey Questions to Measure Citizens' Policy Preferences?" Working Paper.

Tausanovitch, Chris and Christopher Warshaw. 2013. "Measuring Constituent Policy Preferences in Congress, State Legislatures and Cities." *Journal of Politics* 75(2):330–342.

Tausanovitch, Chris and Christopher Warshaw. 2014. "Representation in Municipal Government." *American Political Science Review* 108(3):605–641.

Treier, Shawn and Simon Jackman. 2008. "Democracy as a Latent Variable." *American Journal of Political Science* 52(1):201–217.

Trounstine, Jessica. 2010. "Representation and Accountability in Cities." *Annual Review of Political Science* 13:407–423.

Wang, Wei and Andrew Gelman. 2014. "Difficulty of Selecting among Multilevel Models using Predictive Accuracy." *Statistics at its Interface* 7(1):1–88.

Wang, Wei, David Rothschild, Sharad, Goel, and Andrew Gelman. 2015. "Forecasting Elections with Non-Representative Polls." *International Journal of Forecasting* 31(3):980–991.

Warshaw, Christopher and Jonathan Rodden. 2012. "How Should We Measure District-Level Public Opinion on Individual Issues?" *Journal of Politics* 74(1):203–219.

Wilkins, Arjun S. 2014. "Ideological Sorting and the Transformation of American Politics." Working Paper.

2

Navigating the Local Modes of Big Data
*The Case of Topic Models**

Margaret E. Roberts
University of California, San Diego

Brandon M. Stewart
Princeton University

Dustin Tingley
Harvard University

1 INTRODUCTION

Each day humans generate massive volumes of data in a variety of different forms (Lazer et al., 2009). For example, digitized texts provide a rich source of political content through standard media sources such as newspapers, as well as newer forms of political discourse such as tweets and blog posts. In this chapter we analyze a corpus of 13,246 posts that were written for six political blogs during the course of the 2008 U.S. presidential election. But this is just one small example. An aggregator of nearly every document produced by the U.S. federal government, voxgov.com, has collected more than eight million documents from 2010–2014, including over a million tweets from members of Congress. These data open new possibilities for studies of all aspect of political life from public opinion (Hopkins and King, 2010) to political control (King, Pan, and Roberts, 2013) to political representation (Grimmer, 2013).

The explosion of new sources of political data has been met by the rapid development of new statistical tools for meeting the challenges of analyzing "big data." (National Research Council, 2013; Grimmer and Stewart, 2013; Fan, Han, and Liu, 2014). A prominent example in the field of text analysis is latent Dirichlet allocation (LDA) (Blei, Ng, and Jordan, 2003; Blei, 2012),

* The research assistance of Antonio Coppola, under the support of the Harvard BLISS program, was extremely valuable for this chapter. Our thanks to participants in the Harris School Political Economy workshop and Princeton University Political Methodology workshop for reinforcing the need to write this chapter, and to Scott de Marchi, Jetson Leder-Luis, Jimmy Foulds, Padhraic Smyth, and Hanna Wallach for their comments. An R package for estimating the structural topic model is freely available at www.structuraltopicmodel.com.

a topic model that uses patterns of word co-occurrences to discover latent themes across documents. Topic models can help us deal with the reality that large data sets of text are also typically unstructured. In this chapter we focus on a particular variant of LDA, the structural topic model (STM) (Roberts et al., 2014), which provides a framework to relate the corpus structure we do have (in the form of document-level metadata) with the inferred topical structure of the model.

Techniques for automated text analysis have been thoroughly reviewed elsewhere (Grimmer and Stewart, 2013). We instead focus on a less often discussed feature of topic models and of latent variable models more broadly: multimodality. That is, the models discussed here give rise to optimization problems that are nonconvex. Thus, unlike workhorse tools such as linear regression, the solution we find can be sensitive to our starting values (in technical parlance, the function we are optimizing has multiple modes). We engage directly with this issue of multimodality, helping the reader understand why it arises and what can be done about it. We provide concrete ways to think about multimodality in topic models, as well as tools for dealing and engaging with it. For example, we enable researchers to ask these questions. How substantively different are the results of different model solutions? Is a "topic," which heuristically can be thought of as a collection of commonly co-occurring words, likely to appear across many solutions of the model? Furthermore, is our key finding between a variable (such as partisan affiliation) and the prevalence of topic usage stable over multiple solutions to the model?

We also discuss initialization strategies for choosing the starting values in a model with multiple modes. Although seldom discussed, these initialization strategies become increasingly important as the size of the data grows and the computational cost of running the model even a single time rises. Starting the algorithm at better starting values not only leads to improved solutions but can also result in dramatically faster convergence.

The outline of this chapter is as follows. In Section 2 we introduce the problem of multimodality and provide several examples of models with multiple modes. In Section 3 we focus on the particular case of topic models and highlight some of the practical problems that can arise in applied research. In Section 4 we introduce a set of tools that allow users to explore the consequences of multimodality in topic models by assessing the stability of findings across multiple runs of the model. In Sections 5 and 6 we discuss procedures for carefully initializing models that may produce better solutions. Finally Section 7 concludes by returning to the constraints and opportunities afforded by big data in light of the statistical tools we have to analyze it.

2 INTRODUCTION TO MULTIMODALITY

Multimodality occurs when the function we are trying to optimize is not globally concave.[1] Thus, when we converge to a solution, we are unsure whether we have converged to a point that is the global maximum or simply a local maximum. In statistical models, the function we are typically trying to maximize is the likelihood function, and when this function is not concave the solution we arrive at can be dependent on our starting values. This issue occurs in many classes of statistical models, but is particularly relevant in those where (1) the data-generating process of the data comes from a mixture of distributions or contains latent variables, which the likelihood then reflects; (2) ridges (essentially flat regions) in the likelihood function appear due to constraints applied to the statistical model; or (3) some parameters are unidentified and therefore multiple solutions exist for the same model. The ability to diagnose and navigate multimodality decreases with the dimension of the parameter space, as visualizing and estimating the likelihood become more difficult in higher dimensions and more complicated models.

Multimodality is particularly prevalent in the context of big data because the same latent variable models that are useful for analyzing largely unstructured data also lead to challenging optimization problems. The models we employ in this setting often involve mixtures of distributions, complicated constraints, and likelihoods that are difficult to visualize because the models contain hundreds, sometimes thousands of parameters. Although simple models from the exponential family with concave likelihoods like regression or lasso (Tibshirani, 1996) still play an important role in big-data applications (Mullainathan, 2014; Belloni, Chernozhukov, and Hansen, 2014), there is an increasing interest in the use of more complex models for discovering latent patterns and structure (National Research Council, 2013). While the latent variable models can bring new insights, they also introduce a complex optimization problem with many modes.

In this section we build up for the reader intuitions about what can lead to multimodality. We first discuss a convex, univariate Gaussian maximum likelihood model that is easily optimized to provide contrast for the nonconvex models we describe later in the section. Then, we extend the univariate Gaussian to a simple mixture of Gaussians and provide an intuition for why mixture models can be multimodal. Last, we connect the simple mixture of Gaussians to topic models and describe how these models, and generally models for big data, contain *latent variables* (variables in the data-generating process that are not observed), which will mean they are more likely to be multimodal.

2.1 Convex Models

To start, we present an example of a convex model in which multimodality is not a problem. A strictly concave function only has (at most) one maximum and has no local maxima. This is convenient for optimization because when the optimization procedure[2] has found a maximum of a concave likelihood function, it has clearly reached the global maximum if only one exists. The natural parameter space for regression models with a stochastic component in the exponential family are convex and therefore are easily optimized (Efron et al., 1978).

We begin with a simple Gaussian (normal) model with mean μ and variance σ.[2,3] In the next section we show how we can generalize this basic setup to a more flexible Gaussian mixture model.

$$Y \sim N(\mu, \sigma^2)$$

The normal distribution is from the exponential family, and therefore the likelihood is concave. This is easy to see by deriving the log-likelihood:

$$L(\mu|y) \propto N(y|\mu, \sigma^2)$$

$$= (2\pi\sigma^2)^{-1/2} \exp\left(\frac{-(y_i - \mu)^2}{2\sigma^2}\right)$$

$$\ln L(\mu|y) = -\frac{n}{2}\ln(2\pi\sigma^2) - \frac{\sum_{i=1}^{n} y_i^2}{2\sigma^2} + \frac{\sum_{i=1}^{n} y_i^2}{\sigma^2} + \left(\frac{-n}{2\sigma^2}\right)\mu^2$$

If we take the second derivative of the log-likelihood, we get $\frac{-n}{\sigma^2}$. Since n and σ^2 are always positive, the second derivative is always negative.[4] For a fixed σ^2, in a function with only one parameter such as this one, a negative second derivative is sufficient for the likelihood to be convex.[5] As a result, this model is not multimodal. When estimated, the same parameter estimates will be returned regardless of the starting values.[6]

2.2 Mixture Models

Now consider a model where the stochastic component is a combination of Gaussians, instead of one Gaussian with a mean and standard deviation. Imagine a case where the dependent variable could be drawn from one of two different normal distributions. In this data-generating process the Gaussian distribution that the observation is drawn from is first chosen with a particular probability. Then, the value of the dependent variable is drawn from the chosen Gaussian with a particular mean and variance.

For example, say you were trying to model the height of people within a population. Further, you only observed the heights of the people in the population, not any other information about them. You might assume a model where first you draw with 0.5 probability whether the person is male or female. Based on their gender, you would draw the height either from a distribution with a "taller" mean (if the person were male) or from a normal distribution with a "shorter" mean (if the person were female). This is a simple mixture model, because as the data (the heights) would be drawn from a mixture of distributions.

Formally, the data-generating process for this model, a simple Gaussian mixture model, is as follows:

1. Randomly select a distribution d_i with probability $P(d_i) = w_i$, where $\sum w_i = 1$.

2. From the selected distribution, draw $y \sim N(\mu_i, \sigma_i^2)$.

The log-likelihood for this model becomes

$$\ln L(y | \mu_1, \mu2, \sigma_1^2, \sigma_2^2) = \sum_{n=1}^{N} \ln \left(\sum_{k=1}^{K} w_k N(y_n | \mu_k, \sigma_k^2) \right)$$

This model has more parameters to maximize than the normal regression model described in the previous section because (1) the probability of each distribution must be estimated *and* (2) the mean and variance of each distribution must be estimated. Further, the model is considered a *latent variable model* because the latent distribution variables d_i are not observed, but are rather generated as an intermediate step within the data-generating process. Because it is unknown from which distribution each data point comes (the data do not tell us which data points are men and which are women), we cannot solve this problem using the familiar tools of regression. In practice, the maximum likelihood estimate is typically solved using heuristics such as the expectation maximization algorithm (Dempster, Laird, and Rubin, 1977), which alternates between estimating the latent membership variable d_i (the unknown gender in our case) and the parameters of the distribution (the expected height and variance for each gender).[7]

It is easy to see that the estimates of each distribution's parameters will depend on the data points assigned to it and that the estimates of the latent variables will depend on distribution parameters. Because we need one to easily estimate the other, we choose a starting value to initialize our estimator. Unfortunately, different starting values can lead to different final solutions when the optimization method gets stuck in a local maximum. Despite the problems with multimodality, mixture models are often more accurate descriptions for data-generating processes than more traditional regression models, particularly for data that may have quite complicated underlying data-generating processes (e.g., Deb and Trivedi, 2002; DuMouchel, 1999; Fan, Han, and Liu, 2014; Grimmer and Stewart, 2013).

2.3 Latent Dirichlet Allocation

Later in the core sections of this chapter, we address approaches to dealing with multimodality in models of text data. In anticipation of this discussion, we now introduce the latent Dirichlet allocation (LDA) (Blei, Ng, and Jordan, 2003), one of the most popular statistical models of text. We use the intuition from the simple mixture model described in the previous section to provide an intuition for why LDA and similar models are multimodal.

LDA is a mixed membership topic model, meaning that each document is assumed to be a "mixture" of topics. Topics are mathematically described as a probability vector over all V words within a corpus. For example, a topic about summer might place higher probabilities on the words "sun," "vacation," and "summer," and lower probabilities on words such as "cold" or "snow." Each topical vector has a probability assigned to each word within the corpus and therefore is a vector of length V. Topics are typically described by the most probable words for that corpus. The "topic matrix" β contains K (the number of topics estimated from the data) rows of topical vectors, each of length V.

For each document, the data-generating process first decides the number of words within the document N. Then, it draws how much of the document will be in each topic (out of K topics), assigning a probability to each of K topics in the vector θ ($\sum_K \theta = 1$). It then assigns each word within the document to a topic, with probabilities θ. Last, it draws each word for the document from each of the topic probability distributions in β.

More formally, the data-generating process for each document in LDA is as follows:

1. First, the length of the document is chosen from a Poisson, with prior η: $N \sim \text{Poisson}(\eta)$.
2. Next, the proportion of the document in each topic is drawn, with prior α: $\theta \sim \text{Dir}(\alpha)$
3. Last, for each of the N words,
   - A topic for the word is chosen: $z_n \sim \text{Multinomial}(\theta)$.
   - The word is chosen from the topic matrix β, selecting the topic that was chosen z_n: $w_n \sim \text{Multinomial}(\beta^{z_n})$.

The reader should already be able to note that LDA is a more complicated version of the mixture of Gaussians described previously in this section. First, we draw from a distribution that determines the proportion of a document within each topic and the topic assignment for each word. Then, given the topic assignment for each word, we draw the words that we observed within the documents. Although the process is much more complicated, it closely follows the previous section where first we drew a "latent" variable (the distribution (male or female) of the height) and then drew the data (height itself).

Similar to the mixture of Gaussians, optimization of LDA is difficult because of the "latent" parameters that must be drawn before the data is finally drawn. In LDA, these parameters are the proportion of a document in each topic (θ) and the topic assignment for each word (z_n) and are not observed. Similar to the mixture model case, we can optimize the model using a variant of the EM algorithm called variational EM.[8] In the expectation step, we first make a best guess as to the θ and z_n for each individual document, and in the maximization step, we optimize the remaining parameters (in this case β) assuming θ and z_n. We iterate between the expectation and maximization steps until convergence is reached.[9]

This approach maximizes the marginal likelihood (the probability of the data given β and α), which we can use as the objective function for maximizing the model. To get an intuition for the marginal likelihood, first we find the joint distribution of parameters and data:

$$p(\theta, z, w | \alpha, \beta) = p(\theta | \alpha) \prod_{n=1}^{N} p(z_n | \theta) p(w_n | z_n, \beta)$$

To find the probability of the words marginalized over the latent parameters, we integrate over z_n and θ:

$$p(w | \alpha, \beta) = \int p(\theta | \alpha) \prod_{n=1}^{N} \sum_{z_n} p(z_n | \theta) p(w_n | z_n, \beta) d\theta$$

The marginal likelihood itself is intractable in the case of LDA because of the coupling of β and θ, which leads to a an intractable integration problem. The variational EM approach uses Jensen's inequality to create a lower bound on the marginal likelihood, which we can maximize via coordinate ascent. That is, the algorithm is alternating between updating the content of the topics (β) and the topical makeup of a document (θ). It is this alternating maximization strategy that leads to multiple local optima. If we we could jointly optimize β and θ, we would likely have fewer issues of local modes, but the coupling in the marginal likelihood makes this unfeasible.

3 THE CASE OF TOPIC MODELS

Multimodality occurs in a huge number of statistical models.[10] In the rest of this chapter we focus on unsupervised latent variable models. In practice we use latent variable models to discover low-dimensional latent structure that can explain high-dimensional data. These models have been broadly applied throughout the social sciences to analyze large bodies of texts (Grimmer and Stewart, 2013), discover categories of diseases (Doshi-Velez, Ge, and Kohane, 2014; Ruiz et al., 2014), study human cognition (Tenenbaum et al., 2011), develop ontologies of political events (O'Connor, Stewart and Smith, 2013), build recommendation systems (Lim and Teh, 2007) and reveal the structure of biological and social networks (Airoldi et al., 2009; Hoff, Raftery, and Handcock, 2002). As we have suggested, the flexibility of latent variable models often leads to difficult statistical inference problems, and standard approaches often suffer from highly multimodal solutions.

Statistical topic models are rapidly growing in prominence within political science (Grimmer, 2010a; Quinn et al., 2010; Lauderdale and Clark, 2014; Roberts et al., 2014) as well as in other fields (Goldstone et al., 2014; Reich et al., 2015). Here we focus on latent Dirichlet allocation (LDA), which, as discussed in the previous section, models each document as a mixture over topics (Blei, Ng, and Jordan, 2003; Blei, 2012). The *mixed* membership form provides a more flexible representation than the single membership mixture model, but at the cost of an optimization problem with many more local optima.[11]

The posterior of the LDA model cannot be computed in closed form. Two popular approximate inference algorithms are collapsed Gibbs sampling (Griffiths and Steyvers, 2004) and variational inference (Blei, Ng, and Jordan, 2003). In this context, both methods can be seen as a form of alternating maximization; in Gibbs sampling we randomly draw from a single parameter conditional on the others, and in variational inference we update a single parameter averaging over the other parameters with respect to the approximating distribution (Grimmer, 2010b). This process of alternating conditional updates, necessitated by the inability to directly integrate over the posterior, leads to a sensitivity to the starting values of the parameters. The myriad solutions that can result from different starting points are well known among computer scientists, but are infrequently discussed.[12]

In fact, we can be more precise about the difficulty of the LDA inference problem by introducing some terminology from theoretical computer science. Nondeterministic polynomial-time-hard (NP-hard) problems are a class of problems that it is strongly suspected cannot be solved in polynomial time.[13] A more complete definition is beyond the scope of this chapter, but the classification conveys a sense of the difficulty of a problem. Maximum likelihood estimation can be shown to be NP-hard even for LDA models with only two topics (Sontag and Roy, 2011; Arora, Ge, and Moitra, 2012). These hardness results suggest not only why local optima are a characteristic of the LDA problem but also why they cannot be easily addressed by changes in the inference algorithm. That is, we can reasonably conjecture from these results that, without additional assumptions to make the problem tractable, it would be impossible to develop a computationally practical, globally optimal inference algorithm for LDA.[14]

How then do we address the practical problem of multimodality in topic models? In this section, we advocate selecting a solution using a broader set of criteria than just the value of the objective function. In the next section we make the argument for looking beyond the objective function when evaluating local modes. We then discuss some specific methods for choosing a single model for analysis. Finally we consider how to assess the stability of the chosen result across many different runs. Throughout we use LDA as a running example, but the arguments are more broadly applicable. In particular we see how they play out in an applied example using the related STM in subsequent sections.

3.1 Evaluating Local Modes

There is a disconnect between the way we evaluate topic models and the way we use them (Blei, 2012). The likelihood function and common evaluation metrics reward models that are predictive of unseen words, but our interest is rarely in predicting the words in a document; instead we want a model that provides a semantically coherent, substantively interesting summary of the documents (Grimmer and Stewart, 2013). This disconnect is not easily remedied; our models and evaluation metrics focus on prediction because it is the most tractable approximation to a human judgment of utility that ultimately must be made on a case-by-case basis. This perspective informs an approach to dealing with multimodality that emphasizes selecting a particular run not solely on the basis of which model yields the highest value of the objective function, but also includes other external assessments of model quality.

If our sole criterion of success were the ability to maximize the objective function, our path would be clear. We would simply generate a large number of candidate solutions by running the model repeatedly with different starting values and then select the one with the highest value. In variational approximations this metric is neatly defined in a single value: the lower bound on the marginal likelihood. We could simply calculate the bound for each model and choose the largest value.

In a general sense, this procedure is both intuitive and well supported theoretically. Not only is the lower bound the objective function we are optimizing but also, as a lower bound on the marginal evidence, it is precisely the quantity commonly used in approaches to Bayesian model selection (Kass and Raftery, 1995; Bishop et al., 2006; Grimmer, 2010*b*). These methods will pick the best model, given the assumptions of the data-generating process, but that may not be the one that is most interesting (Grimmer and Stewart, 2013). While for the purposes of estimating the model we need to rely on our assumptions about the data-generating process, we need not maintain these commitments when making our final selection. This allows us to access a richer set of tools for evaluating model quality.

The implication of this argument is that if we found the global optimum we might not choose to use it. This seems counterintuitive at first, but various forms of the argument have a long tradition in statistics. Consider the argument that we should choose a model on the basis of cross-validation or other forms of held-out prediction. This is the most commonly used evaluation metric for topic models (Wallach et al., 2009; Foulds and Smyth, 2014) and also has a strong tradition in political science (Beck, King, and Zeng, 2000; De Marchi, Gelpi, and Grynaviski, 2004; Ward, Greenhill, and Bakke, 2010). Selecting a model that maximizes a held-out predictive measure implies that we may not choose the model that maximizes the *in-sample* objective function. In settings where forecasting is the primary goal, the ability to predict a held-out sample is the clear gold standard; however, in the case of topic models, prediction is not the only relevant standard.

Implicit in this argument is the claim that the objective function need not directly correspond with human judgment. In human evaluations of topic coherence, selecting model parameters to maximize predictive log-likelihood can actually lead to a mild decrease in assessment of human interpretability (Chang et al., 2009; Lau, Newman, and Baldwin, 2014). Domain expert assessment (Mimno et al., 2011) and alignment to reference concepts

(Chuang et al., 2013) have consistently shown that selecting on the objective function alone does not necessarily yield the same model as human selection.

This is not to say that the objective function is completely useless; we have after all chosen to optimize it. Rather our claim is that among *locally optimal solutions*, model fit statistics provide a weak signal of model quality as judged by human analysts. Due to the nature of the optimization problem we find ourselves having fit a number of candidate models and given that we already have them, it would be wasteful to evaluate them only on the basis of the objective function.

One reaction to this situation would be to improve the objective of the model until it matched a human perception of quality. Unfortunately, this is theoretically impossible across all possible tasks (Grimmer and King, 2011; Wolpert and Macready, 1997). Moreover, the inference problem is already particularly complex, and modifications tend to result in even more intractable models (Mimno et al., 2011).

At the end of the day we trust the objective function enough to optimize it when fitting the model, but not enough to let it be the surrogate for the selection process. Instead, we want to explore the model and its implications, a process that is closely related to the literature on posterior predictive checks (Mimno and Blei, 2011; Blei, 2014; Gelman et al., 2013). In the next section we treat the question of how to choose a particular model for analysis, which we call the reference model. In Section 3.3 we explain how to assess the stability of results across multiple models.

3.2 Finding a Reference Model

Choosing a single reference model for analysis is challenging. The ideal selection criterion is the utility of the model for the analyst, which is an inherently subjective and application-specific assessment (Grimmer and King, 2011; Grimmer and Stewart, 2013). There is an inherent tradeoff in selection criteria between how time intensive the criterion is for the analyst and how closely it approximates the theoretical ideal. In this section we outline methods that span the range of high quality to highly automated.

Manual Review

The most thorough and time-intensive process is a manual review and validation of the model. This entails reading several example documents for each topic and carefully examine the topic-word distributions to verify that the topics are capturing a single well-defined concept. Depending on the number of topics and the length of the documents, this may be a daunting task in itself.

We may also want to consider information beyond the content of the documents themselves. In the social sciences we often have a rich source of additional information in document metadata. Mapping the relations between topics and a document's author (Grimmer, 2010*a*) or date (Quinn et al., 2010) is an important part of understanding if the model is functioning. When an existing typology of the documents is available, we can evaluate how well it corresponds to the inferred topics (Chuang et al., 2013). Ideally we hope that the model will convey some things we already know, allowing us to validate it, while also providing us with some novel insights. The different types of validation criteria have been well developed in the literature for measurement models and content analysis (Quinn et al. 2010; Grimmer and Stewart 2013; Krippendorff 2012).[15]

Manual evaluations of this sort are essentially custom procedures designed specifically for a particular analysis, and they require a large amount of an analyst's time. They are an important and necessary tool for validation of the final model, but are too expensive for evaluation of each candidate model.

Semi-Automated Analysis

A less labor-intensive approach is the human analysis of automated model summaries. The idea is to develop some generic tools for quickly evaluating a model, even if some human intervention is required to make a decision. For topic models we can summarize a topic by looking at the most probable or distinctive words. These word lists can be supplemented by focused reading of documents highly associated with a particular topic. These types of summaries arise naturally from the parameters of the model in the case of LDA, and most latent variable models have some approximate equivalents.

Recent work in information visualization has moved toward the development of automatically generated topic model browsers (Chuang, Manning, and Heer, 2012; Gardner et al., 2010; Chaney and Blei, 2012). Similar approaches have been used to provide browsers that focus on the exploration of covariate effects on word use (O'Connor, 2014). The best of these approaches embody the information visualization mantra of "overview first, zoom and filter, details on demand" (Shneiderman, 1996), which encapsulates the goal of a system that can seamlessly move from high-level model summaries such as word lists all the way down to the document reading experience. Some systems can even incorporate user feedback to allow for an interactive topic modeling experience (Hu et al., 2014). Visualization of topic models is an active area of research that promises to vastly improve the analyst's interaction with the model.

Complete Automated Approaches

The fastest evaluation metrics are those that are completely automated. The most natural metric is the objective function, which is generally either a bound or an approximation to the marginal likelihood (Grimmer, 2010*b*). The default standard within the computer science literature is held-out likelihood, which provides a measure of how predictive the model is for unseen documents

(Wallach et al., 2009; Foulds and Smyth, 2014). Evaluating how well the model predicts new data is appealing in its simplicity, but a predictive model need not be the most semantically interpretable.

Automated metrics can also be useful for narrowing the selection of candidate models that are then evaluated using more labor-intensive approaches. In Roberts et al. (2014) we consider two summary measures: semantic coherence (Mimno et al., 2011), which captures the tendency of a topic's high-probability words to co-occur in the same document, and exclusivity, which captures whether those high-probability words are specific to a single topic. We use these summaries as a coarse filter to focus our attention on a subset of promising candidate models.

Choosing a Balance

This provides only a coarse overview of some of the strategies for choosing a model. Necessarily, model choice is dictated by the particular problem at hand. Once a model is chosen there is always a subjective process of assigning a label to the topic, which implicitly involves arguing that the model representation (a distribution over words) is a good proxy for some theoretical concept represented by the label. Regardless of how the model is chosen, careful validation of the topic to ensure it fits with the theoretical concept is key (Grimmer and Stewart, 2013).

3.3 Assessing Stability

Once we have committed to a particular model and unpacked the publishable findings, we may want to know how stable the finding is across different initializations (i.e., starting values of the optimization algorithm). This serves two distinct purposes: first, we get a sense of how improbable it is that we found the particular local mode we are analyzing, and second, we learn how sensitive the finding is to other arrangements of the parameters.

The first purpose is the most straightforward. We want to build confidence in our readers and in ourselves that we did not stumble across the result completely by chance. The instability across individual runs of LDA has been criticized as unsettling by applied users across fields (Koltcov, Koltsova, and Nikolenko, 2014; Lancichinetti et al., 2014). Understanding how topics map on to the results across runs builds trust in the results (Chuang et al., 2013).

We can also use stability to assess how sensitive our finding is to other configurations of the topics. If a researcher identifies a topic as about "economics," is there some other version of that topic that looks substantially similar but yields contradictory results? These situations can arise when a particular topic or group of topics is of interest, but the model is sensitive to the way the remainder of the topics are allocated. Careful examination of the topic may confirm that it is about "economics," but that it fails to reveal similar content outside the topic that might reasonably be included. Examining the "economics" topic across a large set of models provides a sense of the different representations of the topic supported by the data.

4 SIMILARITY BETWEEN TOPICS ACROSS MODES

In this section we develop tools for assessing the stability of findings of interest across local modes. We start by setting up a running example that uses STM to analyze a corpus of political blogs. We then illustrate several approaches to assessing how similar a pair of topics is to each other. We then show how these metrics can be aggregated to the topic level, to the model level, or across covariates.

The methods we present here serve two related purposes. First, we provide some intuition for the variety of solutions that arise from local modes. Especially for those primarily familiar with globally convex models, this provides a sense of what to expect when using or reading about latent variable models. The methods themselves can also be useful as diagnostics for practictioners. Indeed we show through examples how examination of stability can lead to useful insights about the data and model.

4.1 Political Blogs

To make our discussion concrete we turn to a specific data set: a collection of 13,246 blog posts from American political blogs written during the 2008 presidential election (Eisenstein and Xing, 2010).[16] Six blogs – American Thinker, Digby, Hot Air, Michelle Malkin, Think Progress, and Talking Points Memo – were used to construct the corpus. Each blog is given a rating: liberal or conservative. For each blog post the day of the post is recorded. After stemming and removing a standard list of stopwords and words that appeared in fewer than 1% of the documents, there is left a vocabulary of 2,653 words.

To analyze these texts we use STM (Roberts et al., 2014). STM is a mixed membership topic model in the style of LDA that allows for the inclusion of document-level covariates, in this case rating (liberal/conservative) and time (day of the post). We use the stm package in R that uses a fast variational EM algorithm. We specify topic prevalence as a function of the partisan rating and a smooth function of time. We estimated the model 685 times, initializing with a short run of LDA (we return to this in Section 5).[17] We note that this set of runs holds a number of things constant, including choices in preprocessing (e.g., stopword removal, stemming) and specification of the model (e.g., the STM prevalence formula, number of topics) that could also lead to differences in model fit.

We briefly define a minimal amount of notation for use in later sections. Let $K = 100$ be the user-selected number of topics, $V = 2,653$ be the size of the vocabulary, and $D = 13,246$ be the number of documents. Mixed membership topic models, including LDA and STM, can be summarized by two matrices

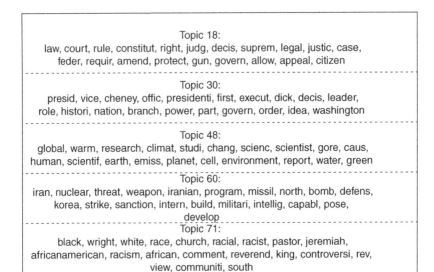

FIGURE 2.1. Five example topics from the reference model. These are given the labels Supreme Court, Cheney, global warming, Iran/N.K. nukes, and Wright, respectively.

of parameters. β is a row-normalized K-by-V matrix of topic-word distributions. The entry $\beta_{k,v}$ can be interpreted as the probability of observing the v-th word in topic k. θ is a row-normalized D-by-K matrix of the document-topic distributions. The entry $\theta_{d,k}$ can be interpreted as the proportion of words in document d that arise from topic k. Both LDA and STM can be framed as a factorization of the row-normalized D-by-V empirical word count matrix W, such that $W \approx \theta\beta$. We use the θ and β matrices to compare the models.

To simplify the resulting discussion, we choose as our reference model the sample maximum of the variational bound. We do not recommend using the sample maximum in general as the selection criteria (for reasons discussed in previous section), but it allows us to proceed more quickly to the comparison of results.

The hundred topics estimated in the model cover a huge range of issues spanning the political dimensions of the 2008 presidential election. We select five topics that illustrate different properties of stability to use as running examples.

Figure 2.1 shows the top 20 most probable words for each of the example topics: Supreme Court rulings, Vice President Cheney, global warming research, nuclear weapons issues in Iran and North Korea, and the controversy surrounding Barack Obama's former pastor, Jeremiah Wright.

4.2 Comparing Topics

Our first step is to ask whether there are any differences between the different runs of the model at all. If each run is equivalent up to numerical precision, the question of multimodality would be moot. To answer this question we need a way to measure whether two topics generated across different runs are in fact comparable.

We can compare the similarity of two models by comparing the topic-word distribution β or the document-topic distribution θ. Using β implies that two topics are considered similar if they generate similar observed words. Using θ assesses two topics as similar if they load in the same patterns across the corpus. Although both approaches are useful, β will tend to contract on the true posterior faster than θ, resulting in a less noisy measure. This is because the number of documents will tend to grow faster than the number of unique words in the vocabulary. Before proceeding to pairwise similarity metrics, we need to align topics across runs.

Alignment

Consider a simple case where we have two runs of the model. We first need to establish which two topics from each run to compare. The topic numbers are arbitrary across each run, which on its own is unproblematic, but means that we need to do something additional in order to compare topics to each other across runs. We call the process of deciding which topics to compare the "process of alignment." The alignment itself is determined by some metric of similarity typically on the topic-word distribution. Here we use the inner product between the rows of β.

Given the similarity metric there are at least two reasonable approaches to aligning topics, both of which will yield the same result when the topics are in fact identical up to permutation of the topic numbers. First, we can let each topic in one run of the model choose its favorite in another run of the model, even if that involves a topic being chosen multiple times. We call this process "local alignment" because each topic in the reference model is making a local choice that is independent of the choices of all other topics. A second approach is to choose a one-to-one matching that maximizes the sum of similarities across all the topic pairs. We call this the "global alignment" because each topic's match is contingent on the selection of all other topics. Although this formulation results in a combinatorial optimization problem, it can be solved efficiently using the Hungarian algorithm (Kuhn, 1955).[18] We use global alignment here. The local alignment produced essentially the same relative trends.

Pairwise Similarity

Once we have a candidate alignment we can calculate distance metrics between two topics across model runs. An intuitive measure of distance is the L_1 norm, which is the sum of the absolute value of the difference. It is defined as

$$L_1 = \sum_v \left| \beta_{k,v}^{\text{ref}} - \beta_{k,v}^{\text{cand}} \right|$$

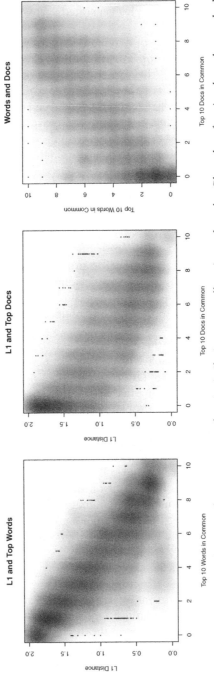

FIGURE 2.2. Relation between three measures of topic similarity across all topics and modes. Plotted surface is a kernel smoothed density estimate.

and has a range: [0,2]. We discuss alternate metrics, but we use L_1 because the result is easy to conceptualize. We discuss the implications of alternative distance metrics in Section 4.5.

We need not constrain ourselves to distance metrics on the parameter space. As an alternative, we compare the number of the top 10 most probable words shared by the reference topic and its match. The result ranges from $\{0, \ldots, 10\}$, indicating the number of words matched.

We can establish the comparable metric for documents. Ranking documents by their use of a particular topic, we can count the overlap in the number of the 10 documents most strongly associated with a topic. This metric ranges from $\{0, \ldots, 10\}$ with 10 indicating complete agreement in the two sets.

Figure 2.2 plots the relations between each of these three metrics across the aligned topics. Each pair of metrics is strongly correlated in the theoretically anticipated direction. Also as expected, the measure based on the documents is somewhat noisier than the corresponding measure based on the words.

This figure also provides us with some insight on the similarities across solutions. Topics range from nearly perfectly aligned to having almost no correspondence. This suggests that there are substantial semantic differences across local modes that could lead to significant differences in interpretation.

4.3 Aggregations

The pairwise similarities shown in Figure 2.2 are useful for contextualizing the full range of topic pairs; however, to make these metrics more interpretable it is helpful to aggregate up to either the model level or the topic level. Aggregation at the model level gives us a sense of how well the local modes approximate the reference model by taking the average over each topic. Aggregation to the topic level gives us information about how stable a given topic in the reference model is across runs.

Model-Level Aggregations

We start with aggregations to the model level. In this case we have a natural summary metric of the complete model: the approximation to the bound on the marginal likelihood.

In Figure 2.3 we plot each of the three similarity metrics on the Y-axis against the approximate bound on the X-axis. The outlier (upper right corner of the first two plots, and lower right of the third) is the reference model, which is, by definition, an exact match for itself. The dashed line marks a natural reference point (5 of 10 words or documents in the left two plots, and an L_1 distance in the middle of the range for the third). The solid line shows the simple linear trend.

The trend between the lower bound and the other three similarity metrics suggests that the objective function can be useful as a coarse measure of

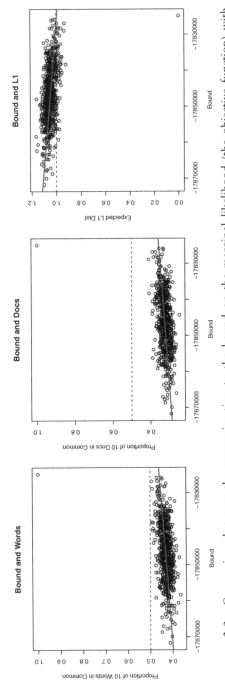

FIGURE 2.3. Comparison between the approximation to the bound on the marginal likelihood (the objective function) with similarity metrics aggregated to the model level.

similarity. That is, as the bound of each of the runs approaches the reference model, all three metrics reveal similarity increasing on average. However, it is only a coarse metric because of the large variance relative to the size of the trend. The high variance around the trend reinforces the observation that, among candidate models with comparable levels of model fit (as measured by the objective function), there is considerable semantic variety in the discovered topics.

Topic-Level Aggregations

Aggregation to the topic level provides us with a measure of how stable a topic within the reference model is across different runs. This helps address the applied situation where a researcher has identified a topic of interest, but wants some understanding of how frequently it occurs across multiple runs of the model.

The distribution over topics is plotted in Figure 2.4 where each topic is represented by the average value of the statistic over the different model runs. The five example topics are each denoted by the dashed lines and a label. In each plot the distribution varies over essentially the full range of the metric, indicating that some topics are extremely stable across all of the runs whereas others are essentially unique to the reference model.

The example topics help explain where some of this variance is coming from. The climate change topic is one of the most stable across all three of the metrics. This reflects the rather specialized language in these blog posts. In a political context, words such as "climate" are very exclusive to a particular topic. These specialized words help pin down the topic, resulting in fewer distinct locally optimal solutions.

One of the least stable topics across runs is the Cheney topic. In the reference model the topic is primarily about Vice President Cheney, whereas other models include broader coverage of the Bush presidency. As an example we chose the local model that is farthest away from the reference model in L_1 distance. In Table 2.1 we compare the two versions of the topic by comparing the topic-specific probabilities of observing 18 terms. These terms define the set of words that have probability of at least 0.01 in one of the two models. We can see that, although both topics discuss Cheney, the local model discusses President Bush using words such as Bush, Bush's, and George, which have negligible probability under the reference model version of the topic.

Topic-level stability analysis focuses the analyst's attention on the semantic content covered by a topic. As an analyst, our responsibility is to choose a label for a topic that clearly communicates to the reader what semantic content is included in a topic. We emphasize that an unstable topic is not inferior or less substantively interesting. Depending on the question, a topic that combines discussion of Cheney and the Bush presidency may be more interesting than a topic that just covers the vice president. However, the instability in the topic alerts us that the topic in the reference model is specific to Cheney, with discussion of the Bush presidency being included in a separate topic.

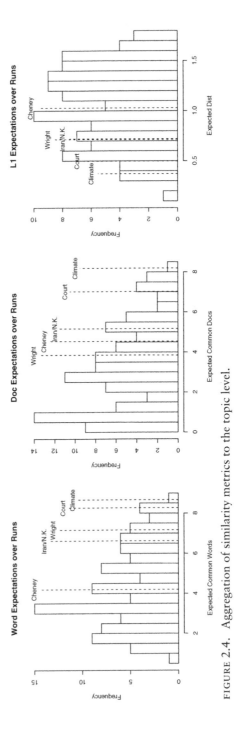

FIGURE 2.4. Aggregation of similarity metrics to the topic level.

TABLE 2.1. *Topic-Specific Probabilities of Observing 18 Words in the Cheney Topic in Both the Reference Model and a Local Solution Far Away from It*

Term	Ref. Model	Local Model
administr	<.0005	0.104
bush	<.0005	0.275
bush'	<.0005	0.0191
cheney	0.0464	0.0279
decis	0.0178	0.0060
dick	0.0195	0.0109
execut	0.0226	0.0022
first	0.0253	0.0001
georg	<.0005	0.0480
histori	0.0104	0.0099
leader	0.0134	<.0005
nation	0.0102	<.0005
offic	0.0414	0.0209
presid	0.5302	0.2868
presidenti	0.0254	0.0003
role	0.0129	0.0001
term	0.0025	0.0130
vice	0.0512	0.0251

Note: Included words have a probability of at least 0.01 under one of the two versions of the topics. The reference model topic is focused primarily on Vice President Cheney, whereas the local mode includes broader coverage of the Bush presidency.

4.4 Covariate Effect Stability

In applied use of STM, we are often interested in the role played by covariates in driving topical prevalence. Indeed this is a principal advantage of the STM framework: it allows for the inclusion of covariate information in the estimation process and facilitates the estimation of covariate effects on the resulting model. In the Poliblog corpus, we can examine the role of partisanship in topical coverage. We start by unpacking the partisanship effects for our example topics in the reference model. We then show how to assess the stability of these findings across other local modes.

Unpacking Covariate Effects

Figure 2.5 plots the expected proportion of topic use in conservative blogs minus the expected proportion of topic use in liberal blogs under the reference model. Thus topics more associated with the conservative blogs appear to the right of zero.

We briefly contextualize the partisan effects in this set of topics. Conservative attention to the Supreme Court topic is primarily driven by the June 2008

Partisan Rating Effects by Topic

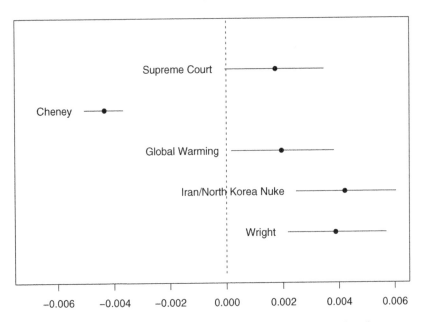

Expected Difference in Topic Proportion (Conservative minus Liberal)

FIGURE 2.5. Differences in topical coverage by rating (controlling for time). Effects to the right of 0 indicate a topic more heavily used by conservatives. Lines indicate 95% confidence intervals using the "global" approximation to measurement uncertainty (Roberts et al., 2014).

Heller v. District of Columbia case that Struck down parts of the *Firearms Control Regulations Act of 1975* on Second Amendment grounds. As discussed in the previous section the Cheney topic is primarily about Dick Cheney's legacy on the vice presidency. The coverage is mainly from liberal blogs and is predominantly critical in tone.

The greater conservative attention to global warming is initially surprising given that it is typically a more liberal issue, but it should be remembered that these blogs were posted in 2008, which was before the more recent trend (at time of writing) in liberal assertiveness. We explore this further by examining the posts most associated with this topic. Figure 2.6 shows the first 300 characters of the three posts most associated with the topic. The first and third posts are critical of global warming, whereas the second post describes a report warning against climate change. The first and third are as expected from a conservative blog, and the second is from a Liberal blog.

The Iran and North Korea nuclear weapons topic shows a conservative effect consistent with increased attention to security topics and consistent

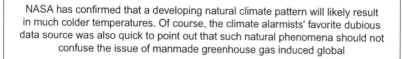

NASA has confirmed that a developing natural climate pattern will likely result in much colder temperatures. Of course, the climate alarmists' favorite dubious data source was also quick to point out that such natural phenomena should not confuse the issue of manmade greenhouse gas induced global

- -

Climate change report forecasts global sea levels to rise up to 4 feet by 2100. According to a new report led by the U.S. Geological Survey, the U.S. faces the possibility of much more rapid climate change by the end of the century than previous studies have suggested. The report,

- -

Deathly news for the religion of Global Warming. Looks like at least one prominent scientific group has changed its mind about the irrefutability of evidence regarding man made climate change. The American Physical Society representing nearly 50,000 physicists "has reversed its stance on climate

FIGURE 2.6. The first 300 characters of the three posts most associated with the global warming topic. Posts 1 and 3 come from *American Thinker* and post 2 comes from *Think Progress*.

with conventional views that issue ownership of security is much greater for Republicans. Finally the scandal involving Reverend Jeremeiah Wright, which is critical of then Democratic primary candidate Barack Obama, is more prevalent on conservative blogs.

Stability across Models

How stable are these effects are across other plausible local modes? A simple way to evaluate this stability is to align the topics to the reference model and then calculate the effect for each topic.[19] Although this process produces a distribution over effect sizes, it is important to emphasize the conceptual challenges in interpreting the results. Each model is estimating the effect of the partisan rating, but on a slightly different version of the topic. Thus differences arise for two reasons: the document-topic assignments may be different, but also the topics themselves capture different concepts. The alignment ensures that this concept is the most similar to our reference model (given the alignment method and the similarity metric), but they are not necessarily conceptually identical.

Figure 2.7 plots the distribution of effect sizes. Beginning with the first plot on the top left, we see that the partisan effect for the Supreme Court topic in the reference model has one of the largest observed values across all of the local modes. Not only is the reference model effect out in the tail but also the distribution over effect sizes includes negative as well as positive values. What accounts for this difference? Comparing the most probable words in the

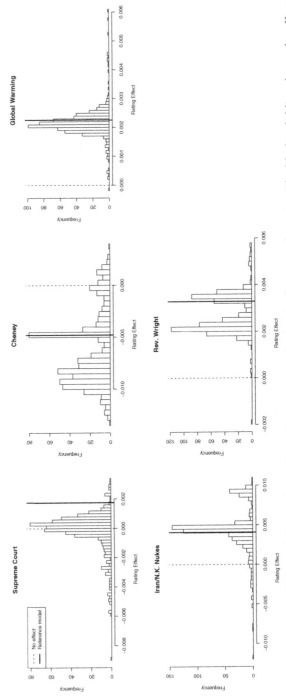

FIGURE 2.7. Distribution of the partisan rating effect across modes for the five example topics. The black solid line shows the effect at the reference mode, and the black dashed line marks an effect size of 0.

reference model with those in an aligned topic for one of the models with a strong liberal effect provides an indication of the differences:

> Reference Model: law, court, rule, constitut, right, judg, decis, suprem, legal, justic, case, feder, requir, amend, protect, gun, govern, allow, appeal, citizen
>
> Local Mode: court, tortur, law, justic, legal, rule, judg, suprem, case, interrog, detaine, lawyer, cia, constitut, guantanamo, decis, prison, violat, prosecut, administr

The local mode includes significant discussion of the legal issues surrounding the use of torture and the operation of Guantanamo Bay. By contrast, our reference has a completely separate topic that captures this discussion (top words: tortur, prison, cia, interrog, detaine, use, guantanamo). Thus the fact that the effect size we found is considerably out in the tail of the histogram does not mean that the finding is not valid, but it does suggest that it is very sensitive to the content of the legal cases and the way in which relevant information about legal issues is spread across the other topics.

The second plot in Figure 2.7 shows the Cheney topic. Here we see a distribution with three modes where the reference model sits directly on top of the most typical point. Following the discussion in the previous section, this reflects the difference between having the topic focus exclusively on Vice President Cheney as opposed to including the broader Bush presidency.

The global warming case (third plot) is the most clear-cut, with most of the solutions producing extremely similar effect sizes. This reflects the relatively specialized vocabulary in discussing climate change, which allows the allocation of topics to be less ambiguous across solutions.

The Iran and North Korea topic is a case where, like the Supreme Court topic there is substantial spread across the models. However, in contrast to the Supreme Court topic, the reference model is quite close to the majority of the solutions. Here the largest source of variation is primarily in whether both Iran and North Korea are grouped within the same topic.

Finally, the topic on Reverend Wright shows another case where the reference model is largely consistent with the local modes. There is some distinction between topics that contain coverage of the scandal and those that also contain elements of the positive liberal coverage that followed Barack Obama's speech on the matter ("A More Perfect Union").

These examples highlight the value of local modes for contextualizing the finding in our reference model. By seeing alternative models, such as a Supreme Court topic that focuses on either gun control or the use of torture, we become more attuned to exactly what concepts are included within the model. This in turn allows us to choose labels that more precisely represent the topic's semantic content.

Differences from Alignment

While most of these analyses are insensitive to the method of aligning topics, we do observe significant differences in the covariate effects. Global alignments tend to result in more cases where there are several clusters of effect sizes. Consider for example, the Cheney topic (top-center of Figure 2.7). In the example discussed in Section 4.3 we saw that the matching topic in another model included both discussion of the Bush presidency and Cheney. If the global alignment had assigned that topic to the Bush reference model topic, that would leave it unavailable for the Cheney reference model topic. This tends to manifest in the covariate effect distributions as clusters of certain covariate effect sizes. We still find the global alignment the most useful, however, because it ensures that we are not omitting any topics from the comparison models.

4.5 Additional Comparisons and Related Work

The examples provided here focused on a particular data set with a specific number of topics. Here we briefly discuss findings from additional settings and related work in the literature.

Different Number of Topics

We ran the set of experiments discussed earlier under the same data set with $K = 50$ topics and observed essentially the same patterns and trends reported. Smaller experiments at $K = 20$ revealed higher levels of instability across runs with increased instances of topics that are very poorly aligned. We conjecture that this is primarily a matter of how well the number of topics fit the specific data set, rather than a statement about small numbers of topics in general.[20] If instability was solely a function of the number of topics, we would expect substantially poorer performance in this extreme case. That the instability would be connected to selecting too few topics for a given data set certainly makes intuitive sense, but additional investigation would be necessary to make conclusive statements.

Alternative Distance Measures

In the results discussed earlier, we used two basic measures of distance between the topic-word distributions. We aligned the topics using a dot product measure, and we presented calculations based on L_1 distance. We also performed experiments using a cosine similarity metric (essentially the dot product rescaled by the L_2 norm of the vectors).

The results, depicted in Figure 2.8, show slightly less clear correlations between the similarity metric and the top words and top documents measure. Specifically there are many cases where high cosine similarity topic appears with a comparatively low number of top words or documents in common. Manual examination of topics in these settings demonstrated that this was primarily

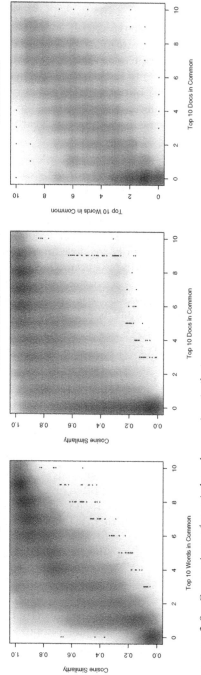

FIGURE 2.8. Comparison of metric based on cosine similarity.

connected with topics where the majority of the probability mass loaded onto fewer than 10 words.[21]

Koltcov, Koltsova, and Nikolenko (2014), in a similar investigation of stability in LDA, guard against the possibility of L_1-style calculations being dominated by the long tail of infrequently occurring words. To guard against this we tested a version where we only calculated the distance over the minimal set of words accounting for 75% of a topic's probability mass within the reference model. The results are substantially the same, but with slightly less noise. We opted to maintain the versions we presented earlier to allow for simpler interpretation.

Alternative Approaches

The similarity metrics described here are automated approximations to semantic similarity. All of the metrics equally penalize deviations from the reference model, regardless of whether they are in the direction of a semantically related word or not. One solution would be to embed words within a vector space such that semantically related words are close together and then calculate differences relative to this space (Mikolov et al., 2013). This has the advantage of more sharply penalizing differences between topics that involve words that are semantically unrelated. However, to perform the word embeddings, we need an extremely large text corpus, which limits the applicability to smaller document settings.[22]

Finally, our focus here has primarily been on estimating similarity across a large number of models. Chuang et al. (2013) focus on comparing two topic models and introduce a rich typology of correspondence between them, including topics that are fused, repeated, junk (unmatched), or resolved (well matched) relative to the reference model. These comparisons require a bit more technical machinery, but can elegantly handle comparisons between a reference and candidate model with different numbers of topics.

This section has presented several approaches to comparing topics across different runs of a model. These methods provide not only a measure of the reference model's stability but also can often give the analyst useful diagnostic information about the contents of the topics. The discussion, however, leaves open the important question of whether there are ways to increase the quality of model runs at the estimation stage. In the next section we discuss approaches to initialization that maximize the quality of the initial runs.

5 INITIALIZATION

When the function we are optimizing is well behaved and globally concave, any starting point will result in the same global solution. Thus initialization of the parameters becomes a trivial detail, possibly chosen to save on computational costs.[23] In the multimodal setting, our initialization influences our final solution. When the computational cost of inference in the model is extremely low, we can simply randomly initialize the parameters and repeat until we have identified the same maximum several times. However, in latent variable models not only may we never encounter a repeat solution but also each solution to the model may be very computationally expensive, a problem that is exacerbated in big-data settings. If fitting a topic model on a million documents takes a week of computational time, rerunning it a thousand different times is not a reasonable strategy. A well-known but little-discussed aspect of statistical optimization is that careful initialization can be an incredibly powerful tool (McLachlan and Peel, 2004; Murphy, 2012).

Before returning to the case of topic models, we consider the simpler case of k-means, a central algorithm in the clustering literature closely related to the normal mixture model discussed in Section 2.2. The k-means example helps provide some intuition about the role of "smart" initialization. In Section 5.2, we return to the case of topic models and discuss how simpler models such as LDA can be used to initialize more complex models such as STM. In Section 5.3, we provide a simulation study that shows that the LDA-based initialization yields higher values of the approximate evidence lower bound than random initialization.

The initialization approaches we consider in this section are stochastic, and so each time the procedure is repeated we may obtain a different solution. Thus our goal is to initialize such that we produce better solutions in expectation. In special cases such as k-means, we may even be able to obtain provable guarantees on the number of trials necessary to come within a certain tolerance of the global solution.

An alternative approach is to explore deterministic approaches to initialization. In Section 6 we outline very recent research that yields deterministic initializations with excellent performance.

5.1 k-Means

The k-Means algorithm is arguably the central algorithm of the clustering literature. Not only is it important in its own right as a problem in clustering and computational geometry but it is also a common component of larger systems. Because algorithms for k-means are extremely fast and easily parallelized, it has widespread applications in big-data settings (Bishop et al., 2006).[24]

k-Means algorithms use an alternating optimization strategy to find a partition of units into k distinct clusters such that Euclidean distance between the units and their nearest center is minimized. Finding the optimal partition of units under the k-means objective function is a combinatorial optimization problem that is known to be NP-hard (Mahajan, Nimbhorkar, and Varadarajan, 2009). This manifests itself in a tendency of k-means algorithms to get stuck in local optima. Nevertheless, it is the most widely used clustering algorithm in practice.

Under the most popular heuristic, cluster centers are chosen randomly from the data points (Lloyd, 1982). Estimation then proceeds by iterating between assigning data points to their closest center and recomputing the location of the cluster center given those points. The result is an incredibly fast procedure, but one that can produce arbitrarily bad partitions relative to the global optimum (Arthur and Vassilvitskii, 2007).

A substantial advance in the literature on the problem came with the development of the k-means++ algorithm (Arthur and Vassilvitskii, 2007). The idea is extremely simple: by using a careful seeding of the initial centers we can make probabilistic guarantees on recovery relative to the optimal solution. The seeding strategy is based on selecting the first center uniformly at random from the data points and then choosing subsequent centers at random, but reweighting to prioritize data points that are not near a previously chosen center.

The k-means++ algorithm highlights an important general point: carefully considering the initialization procedure can be an important tool for dealing with multimodality in practice. This is an important difference from problems that are globally convex, where starting values are important only for increasing speed or avoiding numerical instability. It is interesting to note that, despite being both simple conceptually and incredibly effective in practice, the k-means++ heuristic was not discovered until 25 years after Lloyd's algorithm. Heuristics for solving this problem continue to be an active area of research (Bahmani et al., 2012; Nielsen and Nock, 2014).

5.2 What Makes a Good Initialization?

A good initialization strategy needs to balance the cost of solving for the initial state with the expected improvement in the objective. If the cost of finding the initial values of the parameters is high relative to the model-fitting process, then you might as well use that computational time to randomly restart the original algorithm. Thus the art to initializing a model is finding a procedure that places the model in the right region of the parameter space with as few calculations as possible. The k-means++ algorithm is an excellent example of an incredibly low-cost initialization.

In cases where the the model itself is straightforward and the cost of inference rises rapidly with the number of units, a simple but powerful strategy is to run the model on a small subsample of the data. This is generally a good default, particularly in the big-data regime where the computation is costly solely due to scale.

Another steadfast default approach is to initialize a complicated model with a simpler model or algorithm for which inference is easy. The simpler algorithm can often put you into a good region of the parameter space without expending the higher costs of the more complex method. Indeed, this is why the k-means algorithm is often used to initialize more complex mixture models (McLachlan and Peel, 2004; Bishop et al., 2006).

In the case of STM, there is a natural simpler model, LDA. Due to the Dirichlet-multinomial conjugacy in LDA we can perform inference using a fast collapsed Gibbs sampler (Griffiths and Steyvers, 2004). They key here is

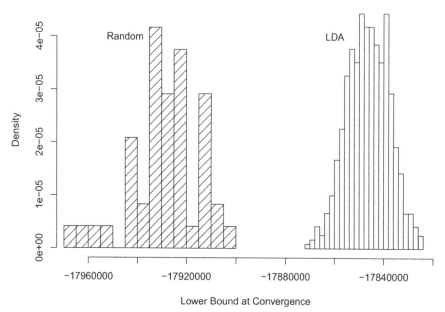

FIGURE 2.9. A comparison of initialization strategies for the $K = 100$ STM models.

that the conjugacy of the model allows for all parameters except the token-level topic latent variables to be integrated out. The result is a very fast sampler that has been heavily optimized (Yao, Mimno, and McCallum, 2009). The cost of inference is linear in the number of individual words (tokens) in the text.[25]

Because LDA is itself multimodal, the result is an initialization that is different each time. Thus like the k-means++ algorithm, this approach places STM in a good region of the parameter space, but still allows for variation across runs. The initialization for the LDA algorithm itself is just a random assignment of the tokens, so we do not have a problem of infinite regress.

5.3 The Effects of Initialization

Unlike the case of the k-means++ algorithm, we cannot make theoretical guarantees on the quality of LDA as a method for initializing STM.[26] This naturally leads us to ask about how it performs as an initialization in practice. To investigate this issue we compared the objective function values in the 685 model runs initialized with LDA to a set of 50 runs initialized from random starting values.[27] Figure 2.9 plots the resulting distributions over the final level of the objective function.

These substantial gains come at a very low computational cost courtesy of the efficient Gibbs sampler in the lda package (Chang, 2012). The initialization process takes only a few seconds to complete 50 iterations of the 2.6 million tokens in the Poliblog data. Indeed this is why initializing with LDA is the current default method in the stm package in R. Furthermore, not only do the LDA initialized models performed uniformly better but they also converged significantly more quickly. Most of the LDA models took between 60 to 120 iterations to converge, whereas the randomly initialized versions took close to 200 iterations. Interestingly, we were not able to increase the average quality by running the sampler longer, suggesting that without considerable further effort this may be close to the optimal strategy for this type of initialization.

6 GLOBAL SOLUTIONS

In the previous sections we discussed how nonconvex models can lead to inference algorithms that exhibit multimodality. For the important case of topic models we provided a series of tools both for exploring a set of local modes and for improving the average quality of our solutions through careful initialization. These approaches work well in settings where it is feasible to run the model many times. However, in the truly big-data setting, every single optimization of the model may be so costly that we want to strictly limit the number of times we run the model.

In this section we introduce recent innovations in theoretical computer science that allow for global optimization of nonconvex models using *spectral learning*. As we show, these algorithms introduce additional assumptions into the model to achieve tractable inference with provable guarantees of recovering the globally optimal parameters. Following the logic of Section 5, we use an algorithm for LDA as an initialization to the STM. Our results suggest that this hybrid strategy can be a useful technique for tackling big-data problems.

We remind the reader that these techniques are very much "on the frontier," and so the substantive implications for applied projects have not been charted out, something that is beyond the scope of this chapter. Furthermore, we emphasize that these initialization strategies do not "solve" the multimodality problem. These techniques do not yield a correct answer, and even though they do very well at maximizing the approximate evidence lower bound, this does not mean that the solution is optimal with respect to other criteria (as discussed earlier). The types of robustness exercises discussed earlier should continue to be an important part of the research process. Nevertheless, we find that these deterministic initialization procedures are a promising contribution to the topic modeling toolkit.

6.1 Introduction to Spectral Learning

When we define an inference procedure we would like to be able to prove that the algorithm will converge to the global optimum. For the types of problems that we discuss here, we generally settle for heuristics, such as expectation-maximization, which has provable convergence to a local optimum (Dempster, Laird, and Rubin, 1977), or MCMC algorithms, which have no finite sample guarantees but will asymptotically recover the posterior (Robert and Casella, 2004). In practice both approaches get stuck in local optima.

Here we describe a class of spectral learning algorithms for estimating the parameters of latent variable models while retaining guarantees of globally optimal convergence.[28] The key insight is that by using matrix (or array) decomposition techniques we can recover the parameters from low-order moments of the data. This approach relies on a method of moments inferential framework, as opposed to the likelihood-based framework we have adopted thus far (Pearson, 1894; King, 1989; Anandkumar, Ge, Hsu, Kakade and Telgarsky, 2014). In models with certain structures this can lead to procedures with provable theoretical guarantees of recovering the true parameters, as well as algorithms that are naturally scalable.

Spectral algorithms have been applied to a wide array of models: Gaussian mixture models (Hsu and Kakade, 2013), hidden Markov models (Anandkumar, Hsu, and Kakade, 2012), latent tree models (Song, Xing, and Parikh, 2011), community detection on a graph (Anandkumar, Ge, Hsu and Kakade, 2014), dictionary learning (Arora, Ge, and Moitra, 2014), and many others (Anandkumar, Ge, Hsu, Kakade and Telgarsky, 2014). Of particular interest for our purposes is the development of spectral approaches to estimating topic models (Arora, Ge, and Moitra, 2012; Anandkumar, Liu, Hsu, Foster, and Kakade, 2012). There are two basic approaches to spectral learning in LDA that differ in their assumptions and methods. For clarity we focus on a simple and scalable algorithm developed in Arora, Ge, Halpern, et al. (2013).

The discussion of these methods is unavoidably more technical than the previous material. However, the common theme is straightforward: we are making stronger assumptions about the model in order to obtain an algorithm that does not suffer from problems of local modes. Importantly for our case we use the spectral algorithm as an initialization, rather than as a procedure to fit the model. In doing so we weaken our reliance on the assumptions in the spectral algorithm while still achieving its desirable properties. In this sense the spectral learning algorithms are complementary to the likelihood-based approach we have considered here (Anandkumar, Ge, Hsu, Kakade and Telgarsky, 2014).

6.2 An Algorithm for LDA

Here we briefly describe the intuition behind the inference algorithm of Arora, Ge, Halpern, et al. (2013) that uses a non-negative matrix factorization (NMF)[29] to recover the model parameters from the word co-occurrence matrix, as we show later, to separate the β parameter (the topic distributions) from the data. The main input to the algorithm is a matrix of word-word co-occurrences that is of size V-by-V where V is the number of the words in the vocabulary. Normalizing this matrix so all entries sum to 1, we get the matrix Q. If we assume that Q is constructed from an infinite number of documents, then it is the second-order moment matrix, and the element $Q_{i,j}$ has the interpretation as the probability of observing word i and word j in the same document. We can write the Q matrix in terms of the model parameters as

$$Q = \mathbb{E}\left[\beta^T \theta^T \theta \beta\right] \tag{1}$$

$$= \beta^T \mathbb{E}\left[\theta^T \theta\right] \beta, \tag{2}$$

where the second line follows by treating the parameters as fixed but unknown. Arora, Ge, Halpern, et al. (2013) show that we can recover β^T from the rest of the parameters using a non-negative matrix factorization.

The NMF problem is also NP-hard in general (Vavasis, 2009) and suffers from the same local mode problems as LDA in practice (Gillis, 2014). However recent work by Arora, Ge, Kannan, and Moitra (2012) showed that we can provably compute the NMF for the class of matrices that satisfy the *separability* condition (Donoho and Stodden, 2003). In this context, separability assumes that for each topic there is at least one word, called an anchor word, that is assigned only to that topic. The anchor word for topic k does not need to be in every document about topic k, but if a document contains the anchor word, we know that it is at least partially about topic k. Separability implies that all non-anchor word rows of the Q matrix can be recovered as a convex combination of the anchor rows (Arora, Ge, Halpern, et al., 2013). Thus if we can identify the anchors, we can solve for β using convex optimization methods.

Thus the algorithm of Arora, Ge, Halpern, et al. (2013) proceeds in two parts. First we identify the anchors, and then given the anchors we uncover the model parameters β. Crucially these steps do not need to be iterated and are not sensitive to the starting values of the algorithm. There are many different approaches to these two steps that differ in computational complexity and robustness to noise (Kumar, Sindhwani, and Kambadur, 2012; Recht et al., 2012; Gillis and Luce, 2014; Ding, Rohban, Ishwar, and Saligrama, 2013).[30]

Advantages

The main advantage of the Arora, Ge, Halpern, et al. (2013) algorithm is that we can give theoretical guarantees that it will recover the optimal parameters (given the model and separability assumption). In practice this means that we completely sidestep the multimodality concerns described in this chapter. The second crucial advantage is that the method is extremely scalable. Note that Q is V-by-V, and thus the algorithm does not increase in complexity with the number of documents. This means that, for a fixed vocabulary size, the cost of doing inference on a million documents is essentially the same as inference for a hundred. This is an incredibly useful property for the big-data setting. Many of the algorithms cited earlier for other models are similarly scalable.[31]

Disadvantages

Naturally there are practical drawbacks to spectral algorithms. Because we are substituting the observed sample moments for the population moments, spectral methods require a lot of data to perform well. In experiments on synthetic data reported in Arora, Ge, Halpern, et al. (2013), spectral methods only approach the accuracy of Gibbs sampling at around 40,000 documents. This is particularly troubling because as the power-law distribution of natural language ensures that we will need an incredibly large number of documents to estimate co-occurrences of highly infrequent words. In practice this is addressed by filtering out low-frequency words before performing anchor selection.

The second major concern is that spectral methods lean more heavily on the model assumptions, which can lead to somewhat less interpretable models in real data (Nguyen, Hu, and Boyd-Graber, 2014). Finally, as a practical matter the spectral method only recovers the topic word distributions β so additional methods are still required to infer the document-topic proportions. These can be obtained by a single pass of Gibbs sampling or variational inference (Roberts et al., 2014).

6.3 Spectral Learning as Initialization

Here we apply the Arora, Ge, Halpern, et al. (2013) algorithm as an initialization for the structural topic model. Using the spectral method as an initialization weakens our reliance on the assumptions of the methods. For example, our initialization will have anchor words, but once we begin variational inference of STM, those anchor words are free to move some of their probability mass onto other topics. Thus we simply use the spectral algorithm to place us into an optimal region of the space. Because the spectral method is deterministic, we also only need to run the model once.

We apply the algorithm as an initialization for the same 100-topic model of the Poliblog corpus used previously. Note that the approximately 13,000-document corpus is smaller than previous findings would suggest are necessary to match the quality of Gibbs sampling.

Figure 2.10 shows the results of the model with the spectral initialization. Not only is the result dramatically better with respect to the lower bound than the random and LDA initializations but also the model converged considerably faster as well.[32] Because our focus here is on introducing this class of algorithms, we do not go through the process of reinterpreting the 100-topic model.

6.4 Future Directions

Spectral algorithms are a very active area of current research. Here we focused on a particular algorithm that leverages non-negative matrix factorization under a separability assumption. There have been several algorithmic

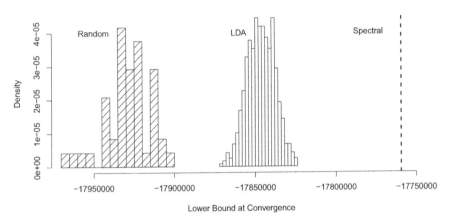

FIGURE 2.10. A comparison of the spectral initialization strategy to random and LDA for the $K = 100$ STM models. The dashed line denotes the result of the spectral initialized solution.

improvements since Arora, Ge, Kannan, and Moitra (2012) introduced the anchor-based method (Recht et al., 2012; Kumar, Sindhwani, and Kambadur, 2012; Ding, Rohban, Ishwar, and Saligrama, 2013; Gillis and Luce, 2014; Gillis, 2014; Zhou, Bilmes, and Guestrin, 2014). There has also been substantial work applying the approach to other problem domains (Arora, Ge, Moitra, and Sachdeva, 2012; Arora, Ge, and Moitra, 2014; Arora, Bhaskara, Ge, and Ma, 2014; Zhou, Bilmes, and Guestrin, 2014).

A separate line of work uses higher order moments of the data along with tools for array (tensor) decomposition (Anandkumar, Ge, Hsu, Kakade and Telgarsky, 2014). These methods have also resulted in algorithms for an incredibly rich set of applications and models. Importantly we can also use this framework to develop algorithms for LDA with provable global convergence guarantees (Anandkumar, Liu, Hsu, Foster, and Kakade, 2012; Anandkumar, Hsu, Javanmard, and Kakade, 2013).[33] This work differs in both the assumptions and methods used. Crucially the tensor method of moments approach uses the third moments of the data, which may require an even higher sample size to accurately estimate.[34]

7 CONCLUSION

Alongside rapid increases in data and processing power have come the development and deployment of a range of new data analysis tools. All of these tools enable new insights and new ways of looking at data that even a decade ago would have been difficult. In this chapter, we focus on the problem of multimodality that affects many of these tools, with specific attention to topic models for textual data. The purpose of this chapter has been to convey an understanding of where this multimodality comes from and then engage in a sustained discussion about what to do about multimodality from an applied perspective when analyzing text data.

Any modeling approach requires transparency about both process and guiding principles. The topic models we focus on in this chapter are no different in this respect from more traditional statistical tools. Even in traditional general linear models, there is always the choice of model specification in both variables and functional form. Although multimodality brings new issues to the table, the responsibility of the researcher to carefully validate the chosen model is fundamentally the same. This is true regardless of whether the choice between competing models arises due to a nonconvex latent variable model or due to the selection of an important model-tuning parameter in a globally convex problem. Thus even if multimodality is an unfamiliar problem, social scientists can draw on the same set of best practices that they employ throughout their research.

An important practical contribution of this chapter is that it extends the set of tools available to scholars using topic models in applied research. While we have focused on STM, many of the procedures we use are helpful for a broader class of latent variable models. For instance, the approaches to aligning topics and calculating stability across runs can all be applied directly to the broader class of statistical topic models and with minor modifications to most latent variable models.

We see great potential for the analysis of "big" data in the social sciences, but rather than focus on the data we have taken a more methodological focus. We think this has important implications not only for methodological development but also could structure the types of questions we ask and the types of data sets we seek to build. Methodologically, we think that there will be important advances in areas such as optimal initialization strategies, which will be especially important as our data sets grow in size. From an applied perspective, users will be unlikely to want to wait for extended periods of time to get even a single set of results. Advances in computational power need to be matched with smart ways to leverage that power. From a research design perspective, we think more focus should be put on bringing greater structure to so-called unstructured data. In the STM we focus on the inclusion of metadata for modeling and hypothesis testing, but this is only one possible use. Can more direct supervision help us with issues of multimodality? Of course, in the end, big data will be at its best when there is active dialogue between those who pose the big question and those who might provide the big answers.

Notes

1. In this chapter, we refer to convex optimization problems and convex models as those where the likelihood is globally concave and therefore has one maximum, instead of a globally convex likelihood with one minimum. Our main interest, however, is in the number of modes the likelihood has.

2. There exist a large number of optimization procedures for finding optima of a particular function; see Boyd and Vandenberghe (2009) for a review.

3. This model is equivalent to a normal linear regression that only models the intercept; that is, without regressors.

4. See King (1989) for a more in-depth discussion of this example.

5. For multidimensional likelihoods, if the Hessian is positive definite, the model will be strictly convex (only has one optimum); if it is positive semi-definite, it will be convex (two points may share a optimum on the same plane.)

6. Other normal linear regression models that are sometimes used in big data applications include lasso (Tibshirani, 1996).

7. Although see additional strategies for the lower dimensional case in Kalai, Moitra, and Valiant (2012).

8. Variational inference provides an approximation to the posterior distribution that falls within a tractable parametric family, unlike EM, which provides a point estimate of the model parameters. Here we simplify some of the differences between these approaches by referring to variational inference as optimizing the "model parameters" rather than the parameters of the approximating posterior. For more information, see Jordan et al. (1998); Grimmer (2010*b*); and Bishop et al. (2006).

9. The posterior distribution of LDA can also be estimated using Gibbs sampling; see Griffiths and Steyvers (2004) for more information.

10. For example, neural network models (Cochocki and Unbehauen, 1993), which allow for layered combinations of the model matrix, are extremely useful for modeling more complex data-generating processes (Beck, King, and Zeng, 2000). However, they too often suffer from extremely multimodal likelihoods, and rarely is the global maximum found (Bishop et al., 2006; De Marchi, Gelpi, and Grynaviski, 2004). Additional examples include Bayesian nonparametric processes (Teh et al., 2006; Griffiths and Tenenbaum, 2004), hidden Markov models (Rabiner and Juang, 1986; Park, 2012), switching time series models (Hamilton, 1989), and seemingly unrelated regression models (Srivastava and Giles, 1987; Drton and Richardson, 2004), to name a few. The item response (IRT) model (Hambleton, 1991), popular in political science (Poole and Rosenthal, 1997), is unidentified because solutions that are rotations of each other can exist for the same set of data (Poole and Rosenthal, 1997; Rivers, 2003). To estimate the model, a few parameters must first be pinned down before the rest of the parameters can be known. In essence, there are multiple and sometimes equally likely solutions to the same problem. While different from multimodality in the previous examples, "multiple solutions" of an unidentified likelihood can also be classified under models with likelihoods that have multiple modes.

11. LDA, and mixture models more generally, have $K!$ substantively identical modes arising from posterior invariance to label switching (i.e., permutation of the order of the topics). This type of multimodality is only a nuisance because each of the modes will yield the same inferences in an applied setting.

12. For example, Blei (2012) provides an excellent overview of LDA and related models, but does not mention the issue of local optima at all. The original paper introducing LDA mentions local optima only in passing to warn against degenerate initializations (Blei, Ng, and Jordan, 2003). Notable exceptions to this trend are Koltcov, Koltsova, and Nikolenko (2014) and Lancichinetti et al. (2014), which investigate the stability more directly, as do our the efforts in this chapter.

13. That is, if $P \neq NP$ then this is the case. However, there is no formal proof that $P \neq NP$.

14. The exact connection between NP-hard complexity and local modes is difficult to concisely state. Not all convex problems can be provably solved in polynomial time (de Klerk and Pasechnik, 2002). However it is sufficient for the argument here to establish that the hardness results imply that there is something inherently difficult about the nature of the problem, which makes it unlikely that a computationally practical algorithm with global convergence properties exists without adding assumptions.

15. Quinn et al. (2010) present five types of validity for topic models: external, semantic, discriminant, predictive, and hypothesis.

16. The CMU Poliblog corpus is available at http://sailing.cs.cmu.edu/socialmedia/blog2008.html, and documentation on the blogs is available at http://www.sailing.cs.cmu.edu/socialmedia/blog2008.pdf. A sample of 5,000 posts is also available in the stm package.

17. Each model is run to convergence (a relative change of less than 10^{-5} in the objective).

18. The Hungarian algorithm is a polynomial time algorithm for solving the linear sum assignment problem. Given a K by K matrix, where entry i, j gives the cost of matching row i to columns j, the Hungarian algorithm finds the optimal assignment of rows to columns such that the cost is minimized. The Hungarian algorithm guarantees that this can be solved in $O(K^3)$ time (Papadimitriou and Steiglitz, 1998). We use the implementation in the clue package in R (Hornik, 2005).

19. This is similar to the permutation test methodology developed in Roberts et al. (2014). In Roberts et al. (2014) we are interested in testing whether our finding on the effect of the binary treatment indicator is driven by including it as a topic prevalence covariate (that is, are we at risk of baking in our conclusion?). We randomly permute the treatment indicator across documents and rerun the model. In each case we calculate the *largest* treatment effect observed within the data across *all topics* and compare this distribution to the observed level. If we were baking in the conclusion, the model would discover large treatment effects even though the treatment indicator had been randomly assigned. In practice the observed effect is substantially larger than the randomly permuted data sets, suggesting that the model is working as expected. Here we are *aligning the topics* first and then comparing effect sizes across model runs.

20. In Roberts et al. (2014) we examined a small open-ended survey response data set with $K = 3$ and found results to be extremely stable even under a more demanding permutation test.

21. Chuang et al. (2013) presented a number of different distance metrics (e.g., testing KL divergence, cosine metric, and Spearman rank coefficient) against human judgments of similarity. They find that the cosine metric most directly matches human judgment and that it could even be further improved using a rescaled dot product measure that they introduced. The strong findings for the cosine metric provide an interesting contrast to Figure 2.8 and suggest that it may perform better in other circumstances.

22. An alternate strategy is to cast the notion of distance between topics entirely in the realm of human judgments. This is essentially the approach of Grimmer and

King (2011), which offers experimental protocols for evaluating similarity between topics.

23. We mean well behaved because in practice even globally convex problems can be sensitive to starting values due to practical issues in numerical optimization.

24. By easily parallelized, we mean that it can be easily fit into the Map-Reduce paradigm (Dean and Ghemawat, 2008). The algorithm is still serial in the iterations, but the expensive calculations within each iteration can be performed in parallel.

25. Also crucially the collapsed sampler mixes dramatically faster than an uncollapsed version (Carpenter, 2010; Asuncion Jr., 2011). By integrating out the topic-word distribution β we are implicitly updating the global parameters every time we take a new sample at the document level. As a result we only need a few passes through the data to reach a good region of the parameter space.

26. Such a theoretical analysis is likely possible under a certain set of assumptions, but would lead to a lengthy and technical digression here.

27. Specifically we initialize topic-word distributions with random draws from a Dirichlet distribution and set the document-topic proportion prior mean to zero. This is the commonly used initialization procedure in many variational algorithms for LDA.

28. Spectral methods derive their name from the use of tools from linear algebra that are connected to the spectral theorem. Here we use an inclusive definition of spectral learning that includes methods using a variety of matrix and array decomposition techniques beyond the canonical singular value decomposition.

29. NMF is similar to a singular value decomposition except that all elements of the decomposition are constrained to be non-negative.

30. Anchor selection methods use either a sparse regression framework (Recht et al., 2012) or appeal to geometric properties of the anchors (Kumar, Sindhwani, and Kambadur, 2012). See Gillis (2014) for a summary of these approaches. For our experiments here, we focus the approach defined in Arora, Ge, Halpern, et al. (2013), which falls into the geometric properties camp. They use a combinatorial search based on a modified Gram Schmidt orthogonalization process for the anchor selection. Parameter recovery then uses an exponentiated gradient descent algorithm (Kivinen and Warmuth, 1997) with an L_2 norm loss.

31. A good example is the mixed membership stochastic blockmodel, which is, loosely speaking, LDA for community detection on a network (Airoldi et al., 2009). Huang et al. (Forthcoming) give a spectral algorithm that learns hundreds of communities in a network of millions of nodes in under 10 minutes.

32. It took 25 iterations to converge after the spectral initialization, compared to 60 iterations for LDA initialization and close to 200 iterations for random initialization.

33. Technically the work in Anandkumar, Liu, Hsu, Foster, and Kakade (2012) uses an approach called excess correlation analysis, which involves two singular value decompositions on the second and third moments of the data. The approach based on the tensor method of moments strategy is described in Anandkumar, Ge, Hsu, Kakade and Telgarsky (2014) and applies to a wider class of models. We group them together here because they emerged from the same research group and use similar techniques.

34. An excellent discussion of differing assumptions of spectral methods is given in Ding, Ishwar, Rohban, and Saligrama (2013).

References

Airoldi, Edoardo M., David M. Blei, Stephen E. Fienberg, and Eric P. Xing. 2009. "Mixed membership stochastic blockmodels." In *Advances in Neural Information Processing Systems*. pp. 33–40.

Anandkumar, Animashree, Rong Ge, Daniel Hsu, and Sham M. Kakade. 2014. "A tensor approach to learning mixed membership community models." *Journal of Machine Learning Research* 15:2239–2312. http://jmlr.org/papers/v15/anandkumar14a.html.

Anandkumar, Animashree, Rong Ge, Daniel Hsu, Sham M. Kakade, and Matus Telgarsky. 2014. "Tensor decompositions for learning latent variable models." *Journal of Machine Learning Research* 15:2773–2832. http://jmlr.org/papers/v15/anandkumar14b.html.

Anandkumar, Animashree, Yi-kai Liu, Daniel J. Hsu, Dean P. Foster, and Sham M. Kakade. 2012. "A spectral algorithm for latent Dirichlet allocation." In *Advances in neural information processing systems*. pp. 917–925.

Anandkumar, Animashree, Daniel Hsu, Adel Javanmard, and Sham Kakade. 2013. "Learning linear bayesian networks with latent variables." In *Proceedings of the 30th International Conference on Machine Learning*. pp. 249–257.

Anandkumar, Animashree, Daniel Hsu, and Sham M. Kakade. 2012. "A method of moments for mixture models and hidden Markov models." *arXiv preprint arXiv:1203.0683*.

Arora, Sanjeev, Rong Ge, Yonatan Halpern, David Mimno, Ankur Moitra, David Sontag, Yichen Wu, and Michael Zhu. 2013. "A practical algorithm for topic modeling with provable guarantees." In *Proceedings of the 30th International Conference on Machine Learning*. pp. 280–288.

Arora, Sanjeev, Rong Ge, Ravindran Kannan, and Ankur Moitra. 2012. "Computing a nonnegative matrix factorization–provably." In *Proceedings of the Forty-Fourth Annual ACM Symposium on Theory of Computing*. ACM. pp. 145–162.

Arora, Sanjeev, Aditya Bhaskara, Rong Ge, and Tengyu Ma. 2014. "Provable bounds for learning some deep representations." In *Proceedings of the 31st International Conference on Machine Learning*. 32. pp. 584–592.

Arora, Sanjeev, Rong Ge, and Ankur Moitra. 2012. "Learning topic models – going beyond SVD." In *Foundations of Computer Science (FOCS), 2012 IEEE. 53rd Annual Symposium on*. IEEE. pp. 1–10.

Arora, Sanjeev, Rong Ge, and Ankur Moitra. 2014. "New algorithms for learning incoherent and overcomplete dictionaries." In *Proceedings of The 27th Conference on Learning Theory*. 35. pp. 779–806.

Arora, Sanjeev, Rong Ge, Ankur Moitra, and Sushant Sachdeva. 2012. "Provable ICA with unknown Gaussian noise, with implications for Gaussian mixtures and autoencoders." In *Advances in Neural Information Processing Systems*. pp. 2375–2383.

Arthur, David and Sergei Vassilvitskii. 2007. "k-means++: The advantages of careful seeding." In *Proceedings of the Eighteenth Annual ACM-SIAM Symposium on Discrete Algorithms*. Society for Industrial and Applied Mathematics. pp. 1027–1035.

Asuncion Jr., Arthur Uy. 2011. "Distributed and accelerated inference algorithms for probabilistic graphical models." Technical report. California State University at Long Beach.

Bahmani, Bahman, Benjamin Moseley, Andrea Vattani, Ravi Kumar, and Sergei Vassilvitskii. 2012. "Scalable k-means++." *Proceedings of the VLDB Endowment* 5(7):622–633.

Beck, Nathaniel, Gary King, and Langche Zeng. 2000. "Improving quantitative studies of international conflict: A conjecture." *American Political Science Review* 94:21–36.

Belloni, Alexandre, Victor Chernozhukov, and Christian Hansen. 2014. "High-dimensional methods and inference on structural and treatment effects." *Journal of Economic Perspectives* 28(2):29–50.

Bishop, Christopher M., et al. 2006. *Pattern recognition and machine learning*. Vol. 1. Springer: New York.

Blei, David M. 2012. "Probabilistic topic models." *Communications of the ACM* 55(4):77–84.

Blei, David M. 2014. "Build, compute, critique, repeat: Data analysis with latent variable models." *Annual Review of Statistics and Its Application* 1:203–232.

Blei, David M, Andrew Y. Ng, and Michael I. Jordan. 2003. "Latent Dirichlet allocation." *Journal of Machine Learning Research* 3:993–1022.

Boyd, Stephen and Lieven Vandenberghe. 2009. *Convex optimization*. Cambridge University Press.

Carpenter, Bob. 2010. "Integrating out multinomial parameters in latent Dirichlet allocation and naive Bayes for collapsed Gibbs sampling." Technical report. LingPipe.

Chaney, Allison June-Barlow and David M. Blei. 2012. "Visualizing topic models." In *International Conference on Web and Social Media*.

Chang, Jonathan. 2012. *lda: Collapsed Gibbs sampling methods for topic models*. R package version 1.3.2. http://CRAN.R-project.org/package=lda.

Chang, Jonathan, Sean Gerrish, Chong Wang, Jordan L. Boyd-Graber, and David M. Blei. 2009. "Reading tea leaves: How humans interpret topic models." In *Advances in Neural Information Processing Systems*. pp. 288–296.

Chuang, Jason, Christopher D. Manning, and Jeffrey Heer. 2012. "Termite: Visualization techniques for assessing textual topic models." In *Proceedings of the International Working Conference on Advanced Visual Interfaces*. ACM. pp. 74–77.

Chuang, Jason, Sonal Gupta, Christopher Manning, and Jeffrey Heer. 2013. "Topic model diagnostics: Assessing domain relevance via topical alignment." In *Proceedings of the 30th International Conference on Machine Learning (ICML-13)*. pp. 612–620.

Cochocki, A. and Rolf Unbehauen. 1993. *Neural networks for optimization and signal processing*. John Wiley & Sons.

Dean, Jeffrey and Sanjay Ghemawat. 2008. "MapReduce: Simplified data processing on large clusters." *Communications of the ACM* 51(1):107–113.

Deb, Partha and Pravin K. Trivedi. 2002. "The structure of demand for health care: Latent class versus two-part models." *Journal of Health Economics* 21(4):601–625.

de Klerk, Etienne and Dmitrii V. Pasechnik. 2002. "Approximation of the stability number of a graph via copositive programming." *SIAM Journal on Optimization* 12(4):875–892.

De Marchi, Scott, Christopher Gelpi, and Jeffrey D. Grynaviski. 2004. "Untangling neural nets." *American Political Science Review* 98(2):371–378.

Dempster, Arthur P., Nan M. Laird, and Donald B. Rubin. 1977. "Maximum likelihood from incomplete data via the EM algorithm." *Journal of the Royal Statistical Society. Series B (Methodological)*. pp. 1–38.

Ding, Weicong, Prakash Ishwar, Mohammad H. Rohban, and Venkatesh Saligrama. 2013. "Necessary and sufficient conditions for novel word detection in separable topic models." *arXiv preprint arXiv:1310.7994*.

Ding, Weicong, Mohammad H. Rohban, Prakash Ishwar, and Venkatesh Saligrama. 2013. "Topic discovery through data dependent and random projections." *arXiv preprint arXiv:1303.3664*.

Donoho, David and Victoria Stodden. 2003. "When does non-negative matrix factorization give a correct decomposition into parts?" In *Advances in Neural Information Processing Systems*. pp. 1141–1148.

Doshi-Velez, Finale, Yaorong Ge, and Isaac Kohane. 2014. "Comorbidity clusters in autism spectrum disorders: An electronic health record time-series analysis." *Pediatrics* 133(1):e54–e63.

Drton, Mathias and Thomas S. Richardson. 2004. "Multimodality of the likelihood in the bivariate seemingly unrelated regressions model." *Biometrika* 91(2): 383–392.

DuMouchel, William. 1999. "Bayesian data mining in large frequency tables, with an application to the FDA spontaneous reporting system." *American Statistician* 53(3):177–190.

Efron, Bradley et al. 1978. "The geometry of exponential families." *Annals of Statistics* 6(2):362–376.

Eisenstein, Jacob and Eric Xing. 2010. "The CMU 2008 Political Blog Corpus."

Fan, Jianqing, Fang Han, and Han Liu. 2014. "Challenges of Big Data analysis." *National Science Review* 1:293–324.

Foulds, J. R. and P. Smyth. 2014. "Annealing paths for the evaluation of topic models." In *Proceedings of the Thirtieth Conference Conference on Uncertainty in Artificial Intelligence*.

Gardner, Matthew J., Joshua Lutes, Jeff Lund, Josh Hansen, Dan Walker, Eric Ringger, and Kevin Seppi. 2010. "The topic browser: An interactive tool for browsing topic models." In *NIPS Workshop on Challenges of Data Visualization*.

Gelman, Andrew, John B. Carlin, Hal S. Stern, David B. Dunson, Aki Vehtari, and Donald B. Rubin. 2013. *Bayesian data analysis*. CRC press.

Gillis, Nicolas. 2014. "The why and how of nonnegative matrix factorization." In *Regularization, Optimization, Kernels, and Support Vector Machines*. J.A.K. Suykens, M. Signoretto and A. Argyriou (eds), Chapman & Hall/CRC, Machine Learning and Pattern Recognition Series. pp. 257–291.

Gillis, Nicolas, and Robert, Luce. 2014. "Robust near-separable nonnegative matrix factorization using linear optimization." *Journal of Machine Learning Research* 15 (Apr). pp. 1249–1280.

Goldstone, Andrew and Ted Underwood, et al. 2014. "The Quiet Transformations of Literary Studies: What Thirteen Thousand Scholars Could Tell Us." New Literary History 45, no. 3:359–384.

Griffiths, D.M.B.T.L. and M.I.J.J.B. Tenenbaum. 2004. "Hierarchical topic models and the nested Chinese restaurant process." *Advances in Neural Information Processing Systems* 16:17.

Griffiths, Thomas L. and Mark Steyvers. 2004. "Finding scientific topics." *Proceedings of the National Academy of Sciences* 101(Suppl 1):5228–5235.

Grimmer, Justin. 2010a. "A Bayesian hierarchical topic model for political texts: Measuring expressed agendas in Senate press releases." *Political Analysis* 18(1):1–35.

Grimmer, Justin. 2010b. "An introduction to Bayesian inference via variational approximations." *Political Analysis* 19(1):32–47.

Grimmer, Justin. 2013. *Representational style in Congress: What legislators say and why it matters*. Cambridge University Press.

Grimmer, Justin and Gary King. 2011. "General purpose computer-assisted clustering and conceptualization." *Proceedings of the National Academy of Sciences* 108(7):2643–2650.

Grimmer, Justin and Brandon M. Stewart. 2013. "Text as data: The promise and pitfalls of automatic content analysis methods for political texts." *Political Analysis* 21(3): 267–297.

Hambleton, Ronald K. 1991. *Fundamentals of item response theory*. Vol. 2. Sage publications.

Hamilton, James D. 1989. "A new approach to the economic analysis of nonstationary time series and the business cycle." *Econometrica: Journal of the Econometric Society* 57(2): 357–384.

Hoff, Peter D., Adrian E. Raftery, and Mark S. Handcock. 2002. "Latent space approaches to social network analysis." *Journal of the American Statistical Association* 97(460):1090–1098.

Hopkins, Daniel J. and Gary King. 2010. "A method of automated nonparametric content analysis for social science." *American Journal of Political Science* 54(1):229–247.

Hornik, Kurt. 2005. "A clue for cluster ensembles." *Journal of Statistical Software* 14(12).

Hsu, Daniel and Sham M. Kakade. 2013. "Learning mixtures of spherical Gaussians: Moment methods and spectral decompositions. In *Proceedings of the 4th Conference on Innovations in Theoretical Computer Science*. ACM. pp. 11–20.

Hu, Yuening, Jordan Boyd-Graber, Brianna Satinoff, and Alison Smith. 2014. "Interactive topic modeling." *Machine Learning* 95(3):423–469.

Huang, Furong, U.N. Niranjan, M. Hakeem, and Animashree Anandkumar. Forthcoming. "Online tensor methods for learning latent variable models." *Journal of Machine Learning Research*. arXiv:1309.0787.

Jordan, Michael I., Zoubin Ghahramani, Tommi S. Jaakkola, and Lawrence K. Saul. 1998. *An introduction to variational methods for graphical models*. Springer.

Kalai, Adam Tauman, Ankur Moitra, and Gregory Valiant. 2012. "Disentangling Gaussians." *Communications of the ACM* 55(2):113–120.

Kass, Robert E. and Adrian E. Raftery. 1995. "Bayes factors." *Journal of the American Statistical Association* 90(430):773–795.

King, Gary. 1989. *Unifying political methodology*. Cambridge University Press.

King, Gary, Jennifer Pan, and Margaret E. Roberts. 2013. "How censorship in China allows government criticism but silences collective expression." *American Political Science Review* 107(02):326–343.

Kivinen, Jyrki and Manfred K. Warmuth. 1997. "Exponentiated gradient versus gradient descent for linear predictors." *Information and Computation* 132(1):1–63.

Koltcov, Sergei, Olessia Koltsova, and Sergey Nikolenko. 2014. "Latent Dirichlet allocation: Stability and applications to studies of user-generated content." In *Proceedings of the 2014 ACM Conference on Web Science*. ACM. pp. 161–165.

Krippendorff, Klaus. 2012. *Content analysis: An introduction to its methodology*. Sage.

Kuhn, Harold W. 1955. "The Hungarian method for the assignment problem." *Naval Research Logistics Quarterly* 2(1–2):83–97.

Kumar, Abhishek, Vikas Sindhwani, and Prabhanjan Kambadur. 2012. "Fast conical hull algorithms for near-separable non-negative matrix factorization." *arXiv preprint arXiv:1210.1190*.

Lancichinetti, Andrea, M. Irmak Sirer, Jane X. Wang, Daniel Acuna, Konrad Körding, and Luís A. Nunes Amaral. 2014. "A high-reproducibility and high-accuracy method for automated topic classification." *arXiv preprint arXiv:1402.0422.*

Lau, Jey Han, David Newman, and Timothy Baldwin. 2014. "Machine reading tea leaves: Automatically evaluating topic coherence and topic model quality." In *Proceedings of the European Chapter of the Association for Computational Linguistics.*

Lauderdale, Benjamin E. and Tom S. Clark. 2014. "Scaling politically meaningful dimensions using texts and votes." *American Journal of Political Science* 58(3):754–771.

Lazer, David, Alex Sandy Pentland, Lada Adamic, Sinan Aral, Albert Laszlo Barabasi, Devon Brewer, Nicholas Christakis, Noshir Contractor, James Fowler, Myron Gutmann, et al. 2009. "Life in the network: The coming age of computational social science." *Science* 323(5915):721.

Lim, Yew Jin and Yee Whye Teh. 2007. "Variational Bayesian approach to movie rating prediction." In *Proceedings of KDD Cup and Workshop.* Vol. 7. Citeseer. pp. 15–21.

Lloyd, Stuart. 1982. "Least squares quantization in PCM." *IEEE Transactions on Information Theory* 28(2):129–137.

Mahajan, Meena, Prajakta Nimbhorkar, and Kasturi Varadarajan. 2009. "The planar k-means problem is NP-hard." In *WALCOM: Algorithms and Computation.* Springer. pp. 274–285.

McLachlan, Geoffrey and David Peel. 2004. *Finite mixture models.* John Wiley & Sons.

Mikolov, Tomas, Ilya Sutskever, Kai Chen, Greg S. Corrado, and Jeff Dean. 2013. "Distributed representations of words and phrases and their compositionality." In *Advances in Neural Information Processing Systems.* pp. 3111–3119.

Mimno, David and David Blei. 2011. "Bayesian checking for topic models." In *Proceedings of the Conference on Empirical Methods in Natural Language Processing.* Association for Computational Linguistics. pp. 227–237.

Mimno, David, Hanna M. Wallach, Edmund Talley, Miriam Leenders, and Andrew McCallum. 2011. "Optimizing semantic coherence in topic models." In *Proceedings of the Conference on Empirical Methods in Natural Language Processing.* Association for Computational Linguistics. pp. 262–272.

Mullainathan, Sendhil. 2014. "What big data means for social science." Behavioral and Experimental Seminar.

Murphy, Kevin P. 2012. *Machine learning: A probabilistic perspective.* MIT press.

National Research. Council. 2013. *Frontiers in massive data analysis.* National Academies Press.

Nguyen, Thang, Yuening Hu, and Jordan, Boyd-Graber. 2014. "Anchors regularized: Adding robustness and extensibility to scalable topic-modeling algorithms." In *Proceedings of the 52nd Annual Meeting of the Association for Computational Linguistics (Volume 1: Long Papers).* Baltimore, Maryland: Association for Computational Linguistics. pp. 359–369. http://www.aclweb.org/anthology/P14-1034.

Nielsen, Frank and Richard Nock. 2014. "Further heuristics for *k*-means: The merge-and-split heuristic and the (k, l)-means." *arXiv preprint arXiv:1406.6314.*

O'Connor, Brendan. 2014. "MiTextExplorer: Linked brushing and mutual information for exploratory text data analysis." In *Proceedings of the Workshop on Interactive Language Learning, Visualization, and Interfaces.* Association for Computational Linguistics. pp. 1–13.

O'Connor, Brendan, Brandon M. Stewart, and Noah A. Smith. 2013. "Learning to extract international relations from political context." In *Proceedings of the 51st Annual Meeting of the Association for Computational Linguistics (Volume 1: Long Papers)*. Sofia, Bulgaria: Association for Computational Linguistics. pp. 1094–1104. http://www.aclweb.org/anthology/P13-1108.

Papadimitriou, Christos H. and Kenneth Steiglitz. 1998. *Combinatorial optimization: Algorithms and complexity*. Courier Dover Publications.

Park, Jong Hee. 2012. "A unified method for dynamic and cross-sectional heterogeneity: Introducing hidden Markov panel models." *American Journal of Political Science* 56(4):1040–1054.

Pearson, Karl. 1894. "Contributions to the mathematical theory of evolution." *Philosophical Transactions of the Royal Society of London. A*. pp. 71–110.

Poole, Keith T. and Howard Rosenthal. 1997. *Congress: A political-economic history of roll call voting*. Oxford University Press.

Quinn, Kevin M., Burt L. Monroe, Michael Colaresi, Michael H. Crespin, and Dragomir R. Radev. 2010. "How to analyze political attention with minimal assumptions and costs." *American Journal of Political Science* 54(1):209–228.

Rabiner, Lawrence and Biing-Hwang Juang. 1986. "An introduction to hidden Markov models." *ASSP Magazine, IEEE* 3(1):4–16.

Recht, Ben, Christopher Re, Joel Tropp, and Victor Bittorf. 2012. "Factoring nonnegative matrices with linear programs." In *Advances in Neural Information Processing Systems*. pp. 1214–1222.

Reich, Justin, Dustin Tingley, Jetson Leder-Luis, Margaret E. Roberts, and Brandon M. Stewart. 2015. Computer Assisted Reading and Discovery for Student Generated Text in Massive Open Online Courses. *Journal of Learning Analytics*. 2(1):156–184.

Rivers, Douglas. 2003. "Identification of multidimensional spatial voting models." Typescript. Stanford University.

Robert, Christian P. and George Casella. 2004. *Monte Carlo statistical methods*. Vol. 319. Springer: New York.

Roberts, Margaret E., Brandon M. Stewart, Dustin Tingley, Christopher Lucas, Jetson Leder-Luis, Shana Kushner Gadarian, Bethany Albertson, and David G. Rand. 2014. "Structural topic models for open-ended survey responses." *American Journal of Political Science*. 58(4):1064–1082.

Ruiz, Francisco J. R., Isabel Valera, Carlos Blanco, and Fernando Perez-Cruz. 2014. "Bayesian nonparametric comorbidity analysis of psychiatric disorders." *Journal of Machine Learning Research* 15:1215–1247. http://jmlr.org/papers/v15/ruiz14a.html.

Shneiderman, Ben. 1996. "The eyes have it: A task by data type taxonomy for information visualizations." In *Proceedings of the IEEE Symposium on Visual Languages*. pp. 336–343.

Song, Le, Eric P. Xing, and Ankur P. Parikh. 2011. "A spectral algorithm for latent tree graphical models." In *Proceedings of the 28th International Conference on Machine Learning (ICML-11)*. pp. 1065–1072.

Sontag, David and Dan Roy. 2011. "Complexity of inference in latent Dirichlet allocation." In *Advances in Neural Information Processing Systems*. pp. 1008–1016.

Srivastava, Virendera K. and David E. A. Giles. 1987. *Seemingly unrelated regression equations models: Estimation and inference*. Vol. 80. CRC Press.

Teh, Yee Whye, Michael I. Jordan, Matthew J. Beal, and David M. Blei. 2006. "Hierarchical Dirichlet processes." *Journal of the American Statistical Association* 101(476).

Tenenbaum, Joshua B., Charles Kemp, Thomas L. Griffiths, and Noah D. Goodman. 2011. "How to grow a mind: Statistics, structure, and abstraction." *Science* 331(6022):1279–1285.

Tibshirani, Robert. 1996. "Regression shrinkage and selection via the lasso." *Journal of the Royal Statistical Society. Series B (Methodological)*, pp. 267–288.

Vavasis, Stephen A. 2009. "On the complexity of nonnegative matrix factorization." *SIAM Journal on Optimization* 20(3):1364–1377.

Wallach, Hanna M., Iain Murray, Ruslan Salakhutdinov, and David Mimno. 2009. "Evaluation methods for topic models." In *Proceedings of the 26th Annual International Conference on Machine Learning.* ACM. pp. 1105–1112.

Ward, Michael D., Brian D., Greenhill, and Kristin M. Bakke. 2010. "The perils of policy by p-value: Predicting civil conflicts." *Journal of Peace Research* 47(4):363–375.

Wolpert, David H. and William G. Macready. 1997. "No free lunch theorems for optimization." *IEEE Transactions on Evolutionary Computation* 1(1):67–82.

Yao, Limin, David Mimno, and Andrew McCallum. 2009. "Efficient methods for topic model inference on streaming document collections." In *Proceedings of the 15th ACM SIGKDD International Conference on Knowledge Discovery and Data Mining.* ACM. pp. 937–946.

Zhou, Tianyi, Jeff Bilmes, and Carlos Guestrin. 2014. "Divide-and-conquer learning by anchoring a conical hull." *arXiv preprint arXiv:1406.5752.*

3

Generating Political Event Data in Near Real Time

Opportunities and Challenges

John Beieler
Pennsylvania State University, john.b30@gmail.com

Patrick T. Brandt
University of Texas, Dallas, pbrandt@utdallas.edu

Andrew Halterman
Caerus Associates, ahalterman0@gmail.com

Philip A. Schrodt
Parus Analytical Systems, schrodt735@gmail.com

Erin M. Simpson
Caerus Associates, emsimpson@gmail.com

1 INTRODUCTION

Political event data are records of interactions among political actors using common codes for actors and actions, allowing for the aggregate analysis of political behaviors. These data include both material interactions between political entities and verbal statements. Such data are common in international relations, recording the spoken or direct actions between nation-states and other political entities. Event data can be generated through either human-coded or machine-based methods. Human-coded event data efforts continue to dominate research on global protests and social movements, although data sets in international relations have led the movement toward automated coding.[1] While humans are better able to extract the meaning in sentences using background knowledge and innate abilities for dealing with complex grammatical constructions, human coding is dramatically more labor and time intensive than machine-coding approaches for anything but small or one-off data sets. Machine-coded methods can attain 70–80% accuracy when compared to a human-coded "gold standard," which is comparable to, and in some cases exceeds, the inter-coder reliability of human coding (King and Lowe, 2004). This makes the

98

machine-coded methods quite scalable in terms of costs and time and thus attractive to academic, government, and private sector researchers.[2]

King (2011) notes that the ability to code and process political texts to generate records like event data will be *de rigueur* in the later part of the 21st century. Machine-readable text about politics, including news reports, speeches, press conferences, and intelligence reports, are already the basis of many political analyses. The ever-increasing availability of such texts presents both opportunities and challenges because they are a form of "big data." Even processing just the lead sentences of Reuters and Agence France-Presse (AFP) news reports for the Levant from 1979–2011 generates more than 140,000 distinct time-series records (http://eventdata.parusanalytics.com/data.dir/levant.html), and these sentences could also be processed as a much larger set of network relationships. One recent effort to expand event data collection outside of this geographical region – albeit without the event de-duplication found in most event data sets – has generated nearly a quarter of a billion records. Extrapolating from our coding experience with the Levant and our initial experiments with the EL:DIABLO coding system described later, we estimate that a data collection with duplication controls like that for the Levant data set will generate around *4,000 to 8,000 distinct records per day* for the entire globe.

The growth in machine-readable texts is well documented. It is driven by increased online publishing of traditional sources such as AFP and Reuters, the expansion of more localized outlets that provide regular reporting in English and publish these reports on the Web, and the emergence of new international sources such as BBC World Monitoring, al-Jazeera, Xinhua, and the All-Africa aggregation service. This growth allows for unprecedented "remote sensing" of political entities that might have once been disregarded or only caught as international reporters made their regional rounds. Although these shifts in the media landscape and global internet connectivity present distinct opportunities for new applications, they also create a number of technical challenges. The underlying data-generating process for event data is not static; rather, it is highly dynamic, requiring researchers to engage in frequent (if not constant) validation efforts.

Our discussion begins with the upsides of these big-data opportunities before moving to the darker side of the challenges. We then move on to discuss a new alternative network of scholars, researchers, nonprofit organizations, and for-profit entities that we are organizing to work on these issues – the Open Event Data Alliance (OEDA) – which is based on other data collaborations, such as the Linguistics Data Consortium (http://www.ldc.upenn.edu/), Health Data Consortium http://www.healthdataconsortium.org/), and Open Geospatial Consortium (http://www.opengeospatial.org). This network should help identify key challenges and coordinate efforts to resolve them in a transparent manner. In particular, a network of dedicated scholars, analysts, and practitioners is necessary to create event data systems that consistently meet two criteria:

1. persistence and reliability: the system is stable, even in the event of a funding or contract interruption;
2. replicability: the system is sufficiently transparent and well documented that new teams or analysts can readily pick up where others have left.

To meet these standards, successful event data systems must pass the following critical tests:

- archival depth: data available at least to 2001 and preferably to 1989 (i.e., post–Cold War);
- validity and reliability: the events, actors, and locations are accurately coded;
- consistency: the data are coded into common, open standards and updates are versioned;
- transparency to the user: analysts can interface with and drill down to a citation or, when possible without violating intellectual property restrictions, the source text;
- flexibility and sharing: analyst teams across departments, universities, and agencies can analyze the same source data and the source code is easily read, forked, and modified.

Many existing approaches fail to meet these standards. Some emphasize "big" data over "good" data, resulting in very large but incredibly noisy volumes of political events. For others, the choice to commoditize the data (via analytical services) creates rigid and expensive data sets that are difficult or impossible to customize, share, or extend.

2 OPPORTUNITIES

The upsides of machine-coded event data are manifestly clear. As a viable alternative to human coders to create a data set, machine-coding has significantly lower costs that come in several forms. First a mature system has nearly zero marginal costs (literally zero if, as with event data, the texts are also acquired automatically). Furthermore, it is much easier and cheaper to adapt an existing machine-coding system (e.g., the cluster of programs and dictionaries described here) than it is to train coders in an existing protocol. Put another way, most of the costs of a human-coding system – largely training – are lost when the coders leave (the development of training materials being the exception); in contrast, most of the costs of machine-coding system are cumulative and reuseable (the exception being material that can no longer to be used because of changes in formats). As open source resources become more widely available, even these upfront costs are dropping.

Second, machine-based systems can do near-real-time coding, if that is of interest: no human system has ever managed this. They also scale very easily, whereas human systems probably have increasing marginal costs due to the need to keep coders consistent. However, these advantages are only relevant if you are scaling and want to do near-real-time coding, which is increasingly of interest for forecasting models such as those described in Brandt et al. (2011) and O'Brien (2010).

Third, machine-coding systems are completely transparent, consistent, and replicable, which given the increasing concern about replicability, is a major benefit. These features are also important when one anticipates the continuing need to code a data set over a long period of time. For example, the KEDS Levant data have now been maintained for close to a quarter-century: it is nearly impossible (or at best is extremely costly) to maintain consistency in human systems across that span of time. Or one may not want to maintain that consistency, given changes in theoretical issues or in coding ontologies, and with machine coding (assuming one has retained the source texts), recoding can be done inexpensively.

Contemporary automated methods can achieve 70+% accuracy against a human-coded "gold standard" (Best et al., 2013; King and Lowe, 2004), which is comparable to the accuracy of human coding in a single well-managed project and probably substantially better than the intercoder reliability of data sets that are coded over long periods of time and at multiple institutions. To a certain extent, comparisons with human coding are irrelevant since the contemporary volume of reports is such that human coding is simply not an option for near-real-time data. But if one is going to use software to carry out these tasks, it must have the same level of openness and reporting as the codebooks used in traditional human coding: the rules or algorithms used for the coding of events need to to be open source and public, as one sees, for example, in the human-coded data sets archived at the Inter-University Consortium for Social and Political Research (http://www.icpsr.umich.edu/) or like those developed for the older open source TABARI system (http://eventdata.parusanalytics.com/software.dir/tabari.html) originally developed at the University of Kansas. As with these earlier standards, openness allows for (1) transparency and replication and (2) improvement, modification, and future refinements. Both are necessary for scholarly inquiry, as well as nonacademic applications.

New features that we focus on here are ease of use, the ability to recode the data according to new ontologies, and the ability to inexpensively provide near-real-time updating. But realizing these opportunities forces researchers to address a related set of issues: (1) price and demand, (2) dictionary and ontology development, (3) new languages, and (4) new and lower cost uses to process, visualize, and model the event data.

2.1 Marginal Cost

The impact of the Internet on event data generation and analysis cannot be overstated. In the pre-1990s era, to have a copy of either source materials or coded text, one needed to send away to a data depository for a 5-kg nine-track magnetic tape reel, a compact disk, reels of microfilm, or whatever other media were prevalent at the time and, then analyze it with costly proprietary software. But in the contemporary environment, news reports on the Web and open-source software capable of coding and analyzing this near-real-time data are now available at small to zero marginal cost. For example, the EL:DIABLO system we describe later can be installed on any Linux system or virtualized, functioning as a "coding engine in a box." Using this or some other open-source system, along with other open-source tools such as R and Python, researchers can build custom actor and verb dictionaries, feed these into a common coding engine to create customized event data sets for specific projects, and then analyze these with tools shared across the research community.

2.2 Automated Dictionary Updates

Access to new computational tools and to the enormous amount of news text on the Internet opens up new possibilities for refining and improving event data. Given the density of source texts, it may be possible to automate portions of the development of new actor or verb dictionaries. This spares future generations of undergraduates the tedious task of entering Nigerian warlords' names into text files one at a time or reading dozens of news reports to locate a new verb phrase that is not in the existing dictionaries but usefully could be (we discuss additional related challenges later).

Automated identification of new actors can provide a powerful early warning of emerging terrorist or insurgent groups or of new factions in old ones. The international news media often refer to new groups or actors in surprisingly consistent ways. For months in 1996 Reuters and AFP highlighted the actions of a "radical new student group" in Afghanistan; only later did the international media consistently call this group the "Taliban." Similar patterns hold for groups such as Boko Haram and shape-shifting splinter groups like Jabhat al-Nusra and the Islamic State in Iraq and the Levant (ISIL). Systematic review of noun phrases left uncoded by event data parsers can easily reveal shifts in the playing field of key international actors.[3] Though less common in political science circles, actor frequencies and interactions found in event data are also amenable to certain kinds of network analysis, including measures of centrality and betweenness.

Under funding from the U.S. National Science Foundation's Political Science program, the TABARI system has developed very extensive open-source dictionaries for the identification of political actors. Central to these is the 32,000-line `CountryInfo.txt`, a general-purpose file intended to facilitate natural language processing of news reports and political texts. This covers about 240 countries and administrative units (e.g. American Samoa, Christmas Island, Hong Kong, Greenland); fields include adjectival forms and synonyms of the country name, the capital city and cities with populations over one-million, regions and geographical features (WordNet meronyms), leaders from http://rulers.org, and members of government from the *CIA World Leaders* open database. This has been supplemented by names obtained from lists of major corporations, NGOs and IGOs, and some militarized groups such as al-Qaeda.

The CountryInfo.txt and the ancillary dictionaries do not, however, catch all names. For example, they do not include opposition leaders unless they have been in government or the names of new militarized groups, nor do they provide all equivalent forms of a name (e.g., "President Obama," "President Barack Obama," "United States President Barack Hussein Obama" and so forth). To some extent, this process of identifying equivalent forms can be automated, and there are some very sophisticated named entity recognition (NER) methods available in open-source software – for example, using conditional random fields and hidden Markov models – though the NER issue is relatively simple for political actors found in news reports, who usually have regularized names and titles.

With fully parsed text – for example the Treebank parse format that can be produced by a number of open-source parsers – NER is fairly straightforward – actors are always noun phrases – and can be done with modest enhancements of the existing systems. However, at the time of this writing no open source system exists for doing this. More generally, there is a very large literature on NER that has not been fully incorporated into the event coding analytical repertoire. Most of the work, in fact, is not actually the identification of new actors – once an existing actor list has been established, most politically significant actors persist for years and often decades – but disambiguating actors via the phrases that correspond to them. New actors are generally introduced in context, so it is relatively easy to figure out the appropriate codes. Network-based approaches such as the combination of Bayesian, network, and rule-based approaches instantiated in the entity resolution system of Getoor and Machanavajjhala (2013) are very promising in this regard.[4]

That said, it is easy to exaggerate the level of effort required here: as shown in Tables 3.1 and 3.2 references to political actors are highly asymmetrically distributed with an extremely long tail – essentially a classical rank-size distribution – and a small amount of effort devoted to those that are frequently mentioned will be sufficient to get almost all of the useful information. Although practical automated methods should be encouraged, there is little reason to invest substantial resources in developing specialized software (which may in the end fail anyway) for a task that could be more effectively done by a small number of trusted and trained coders working a few tens of hours per week at $20/hour.

While machine-augmented development of event-phrase dictionaries is more difficult than dealing with actor dictionaries, with fully parsed texts it is fairly straightforward: one simply looks for sentences containing actors as subjects and objects that are not coding with the existing verb phrases,

Computational Social Science

TABLE 3.1. *Actor Distribution: High-Frequency Cases*

Phrase	Proportion of Events
China	11.86%
United States	11.56%
Russian Federation	8.43%
Japan	7.99%
North Korea	5.33%
India	5.24%
South Korea	3.45%
Chinese	3.44%
UN	3.14%
Taiwan	3.13%
Pakistan	3.10%
Thailand	2.88%
Australia	2.48%
Iraq	2.23%
United Kingdom	2.08%
Indonesia	1.96%

Source texts are from the research phase of the DARPA ICEWS project (O'Brien, 2010) and consequently emphasize Asian actors.

TABLE 3.2. *Actor Distribution: Sample of the Tail*

Phrase	Proportion of Events
Hamid Karzai	0.01%
President (Angola)	0.01%
Yang Hyong Sop	0.01%
Kashmir State	0.01%
Ehud Olmert	0.01%
Police (Sri Lanka)	0.01%
Vojislav Kostunica	0.01%
Commerce Minist (India)	0.01%
Parliament (Iran)	0.01%
President (Yemen)	0.01%
Foreign Minist (Netherlands)	0.01%
Director General (IAEA)	0.01%
Liu Qi	0.01%
Yang Jiechi	0.01%
Business (Hong Kong)	0.01%
President (Namibia)	0.01%
Police (China)	0.01%
Business (France)	0.01%

From the research phase of the DARPA ICEWS O'Brien (2010) project.

cluster these sentences based on word counts with synonym sets, and then identify the distinguishing phrases. That said, there are actually four related issues here:

- incorporating an entirely new class of events into an existing ontology, essentially an orthogonality issue;
- filling in the details of an existing class that has been properly classified at the cue category level (e.g., protests);
- dealing with misclassification of events that should be coded;
- dealing with false positives that should not be coded at all, which is largely a standard text classification task for which mature technologies exist.

We also believe more effort should be made to establish an open and replicable framework for event dictionary development. Such a framework would facilitate the continued diffusion of event data into other specialized domains and should leverage existing automated dictionary development algorithms and techniques (e.g., Riloff, 1996) for event pattern extraction. These algorithms take as inputs collections of relevant (in-domain) and irrelevant (out-of-domain) texts, event phrases, and event characteristics for learning and can be modified to extend existing event dictionaries or develop new specialized ones.[5]

2.3 New Languages

There are now opportunities to move past English-language source material and code event data in local languages based on automated dictionary development. The Stanford CoreNLP system, an invaluable open-source resource powering next-generation event coders, provides support for natural language processing in Mandarin, Arabic, German, and French. Custom efforts have been used to create data sets of more than nine million events from 2000–2010 to study Mexican drug violence (Osorio, 2013).[6] While some language skills will be required to test the validity of this newly generated data, the high-volume processing will be fully automated and not require language skills.

An open issue, and one likely to remain open for some time, is whether it will be more effective to use machine translation to convert files to English and then code them with the existing English-language dictionaries that have had decades of development, or whether language-specific coding programs need to be developed. In all likelihood, a combination of the two approaches will be used: languages where there is a large amount of codable text available (and English-language news coverage is poor), probably initially Spanish, Arabic and Mandarin, could have language-specific coders, whereas less common languages such as Farsi and German would use machine translations. This will be particularly useful for languages such as French, German, and Russian where there has been a substantial commercial investment in machine translation. Machine translations of the English language event-phrase dictionaries may also provide a starting point for coders in additional languages, but the prevalence of idiomatic expressions in political texts will present challenges.

2.4 New Uses

Contemporary analytical and visualization tools make it much easier to perform more elaborate analysis with event data than was possible in even the past 5 to 10 years. These tools are particularly valuable for nontechnical end users who are interested in gaining insights generated by event data, but are unlikely to develop their own algorithms or forecasting models. At the same time, for more technical users, near-real-time data enable time series and network models to analyze the interactions of conflict and cooperation dynamics over both space and time with high observational granularity in both dimensions.

The promise of low-cost near-real-time data availability allows researchers to monitor conflicts around the world, without the costs and complications of war-zone field research, provided there are reasonably accurate reports on these conflict somewhere on the Web. This ability to create baseline models of conflict dynamics in far-flung places is particularly valuable to those interested in a disparate set of potential wars and other crises. Because the marginal costs of data collection are so low, it is possible to effectively monitor hot spots from the Straits of Hormuz to the South China Sea, and burgeoning protest movements from Brazil to Burma.

This baseline data can also be fed into increasingly sophisticated forecasting models. For example, Bagozzi (2011), Brandt and Freeman (2006), Brandt et al. (2008), Brandt et al. (2011), and Yonamine (2013) all offer different applications of forecasting inter- and intrastate conflict based on event data. These studies primarily use large, regional collections of event data to predict conflict among a small set of endogenous actors. The forecasts typically are about the general trend in the different number of event types. A recent paper by Chadefaux (2014) uses machine-coded mentions of "tensions" in global news reports among nations to construct a weekly index over more than the last century to predict inter- and intrastate wars. The index does a very good job:

> Using only information available at the time, the onset of a war within the next few months could be predicted with up to 85% confidence and predictions significantly improved upon existing methods both in terms of binary predictions (as measured by the area under the curve) and calibration (measured by the Brier score). Predictions also extend well before the onset of war – more than one year prior to interstate wars, and six months prior to civil wars – giving policymakers significant additional warning time. (Chadefaux, 2014, 5)

Thus, big event data can serve as both objects of prediction and critical predictors in many forecasting methods in international politics.

As breakthough big-data applications, event data have already started to make contributions. O'Brien (2010) documents the Integrated Crisis Early Warning System competition. In that federal grant competition, three competing teams were using the same structural data to predict political and civil conflict across the globe. Only Lockheed-Martin, which was using event data coded using the open-source TABARI coder, was able to pass the required benchmarks to win the research award. Zeitzoff (2011) uses social media data from Twitter accounts of Hamas and the Israeli Defense Forces (IDF) to look at the evolution of the Israeli-Palestinian conflict during the 2008-2009 Gaza conflict. One key finding is that there is a time-shift in the IDF Twitter postings that matches to European and American news cycles.

These are but two recent high-profile contributions. Clearly there is additional room to extend earlier, large event data studies such as those by Goldstein et al. (2001) on systemic dynamics of Middle East conflict and U.S. influence, Gerner and Schrodt (1998) on the effects of media coverage and early warning models in the Middle East, and Schrodt and Gerner (1996) on cluster-based warning indicators for Middle East conflict.

3 CHALLENGES

Until very recently political event data analysis was a very small and specialized domain, and the individuals working within that domain were, for the most part, PhD-level political scientists with quantitative training, who had specific theoretical questions in mind. As a consequence, they were familiar with the limitations of data in general and with the specific problems of data based on the international news media. During the early development, multiple conferences resulted in book-length discussions of the nuances of the approach (e.g., Azar et al., 1972; Burgess and Lawton, 1972; Azar and Ben-Dak, 1975; Merritt et al., 1993). This continued through the 1990s and 2000s as the community gradually shifted from human-coded to machine-coded data, which introduced new complications. Throughout these discussions, the community recognized several core limitations throughout the data-generation process. These form the basis of the challenges to big event data.

3.1 Input Challenges and Coverage Issues

Event data are subject to the reporting biases of the news media, which, for the most part, "follow the money": they are more likely to report from wealthy areas or areas where wealthy people have interests. While the availability of local sources has changed this bias somewhat, it generally just shifts the biases downward rather than eliminating them (reports from a less developed country will still be biased toward the major cities). Reports are also subject to "media fatigue" and "if it bleeds, it leads": novel events are reported more frequently than routine events, and violent events are reported more commonly than nonviolent ones. In some cases, such as models that forecast political instability, these biases are not a problem: the volume of news coverage itself can sometimes be a useful leading indicator. In other cases – for example, those attempting to assess the frequency and efficacy of nonviolent protest – changes in coverage levels can be very problematic. The effects of these biases on statistical inference have been discussed in Davenport and Ball (2002) and Reeves et al. (2006).

Almost all uses of event data depend on access to historical event data going back at least several years. Collecting and securing the rights to back material are two of the greatest challenges for event data projects. Access to major national newspapers and newswire archives can be very expensive, whereas the archives of smaller papers and non-U.S. sources may be impossible to locate. Without sufficient news coverage, forecasting models will lack enough training data, and researchers studying particular time periods and locations may not be able to answer the questions they pose to the data.

3.2 Production Challenges

In addition to addressing the inherent limitations of media coverage patterns and the difficulties associated with collecting a suitable archive of news text, event data projects face issues associated with the technical process of extracting and coding event data from text.

3.2.1 Limits of the Ontologies

Event data ontologies were developed to address specific problems, typically dealing with forecasting violent political conflict and, before the 1990s, interstate conflict in the context of the Cold War. The data sets only code the behaviors that were seen as interesting given the interests of the individuals who paid for and developed them. They do not code "everything."

The original event data sets were focused on nation-states. There are a very limited number of such actors, and they change only rarely and usually as well-anticipated events. Contemporary event data analysis, in contrast, is usually focusing at the substate level, where important actors, both state (e.g., heads of state and cabinet members) and nonstate (particularly militarized groups) can be transient. Balancing the need to get data on all actors – which provides more detail than can be analyzed – while still tracking persistent actors (for example, al-Qaeda, Boko Haram, and the Taliban as militarized nonstate actors) is a major issue.

At present, CAMEO (Schrodt, 2012b; Schrodt et al., 2009) and IDEA (Bond et al., 2003) are the only two event coding ontologies in wide use for event data, though a variety of actor-level coding systems exist in various conflict data sets (Bernauer and Gleditsch, 2012; Schrodt, 2012a). CAMEO has four advantages: it modified the Cold War era coding systems to be more appropriate for automated coding; it is thoroughly documented; it has been implemented in open-source dictionaries that have been used in multiple projects; and it contains a very extensive ontology for coding actors. The disadvantage is that it was developed specifically to code international mediation and has not been extended to deal with events outside of the traditional political interactions. The two advantages of IDEA are that it contains a number of extensions and has integrated the half-dozen or so different ontologies available in the early 2000s. Its disadvantages are that it retains a number of legacy codings from the pre-automated coding era, its documentation is not very extensive, it has no actor ontology comparable to that found in CAMEO, and there is only a single proprietary implementation.

Schrodt and Bagozzi (2013) have demonstrated that the existing event ontologies are probably picking up only about half of the events that are arguably "political," with the single biggest missing category being routine democratic processes (elections and parliamentary debate). More generally, the core extensions should include natural disasters, disease, criminal activity, financial activity, refugees and related humanitarian issues, human rights violations, and electoral and parliamentary activity. The growing widespread interest in event data beyond the study of conflict highlights the need for more specialized coding schemes. Indeed, the development and maintenance of specialized ontologies are primary objectives of the Open Event Data Alliance described later.

While both CAMEO and IDEA have been used as comprehensive schemes – and IDEA was explicitly designed with this in mind – we are not entirely convinced this use is practical as the event data world expands for both pragmatic and theoretical reasons: different projects will require more or less detail on various types of events, and maintenance of a single scheme that entails all possible distinctions that might be relevant to political analysis could quickly become impractical and, being impractical, will not be used. The alternative is to encourage the development of multiple coding frameworks that are compatible at some level – perhaps the two- and three-digit event codes – but not all levels. Similar efforts could be devoted to actor coding: there are about 10 coding systems in wide use for national-state actors – including multiple ISO systems, multiple COW systems, multiple FIPS systems – but analysis of substate actors is far less standardized. Efforts are underway to address this and standardization should be increased, though any such efforts are labor intensive.

Finally, there are options of semi- and unsupervised detection of events and actors. New event detection (NED) is an established field, built in large part by DARPA's Topic Detection and Tracking (TDT) initiative from 1997 to 2004. Although research continues on NED, it proceeds with little overlap with the work on event data. NED seeks to differentiate genuinely new stories from reports about ongoing or past events in streaming text. The earliest approaches relied on term frequency-inverse document frequency (TF-IDF) as a metric to determine whether two stories were similar or not (Kumaran and Allan, 2004, 2005; Roberts and Harbagiu, 2011). TF-IDF measures the importance of words in a document by counting how often they occur in that document, compared to how often they occur in a larger corpus of text. Advances in NED have come largely as the result of better computing power and advancements in machine learning algorithms. For instance, Kumaran and Allan (2004) expanded the naïve TF-IDF framework to include pre-sorting of documents into different topics (using latent Dirichlet allocation), each with its own term frequency, thereby allowing for more sensible comparisons of term frequencies and improving the system's performance. Improvements were added by Roberts and Harbagiu (2011), who use sophisticated natural language processing and named-entity recognition (NER) to more accurately assess the actors, locations, and times involved in an event. This approach outperforms the standard TF-IDF metric and Kumaran and Allan's method. Future work will most likely incorporate improvements in NER, including with Stanford's CoreNLP. As the accuracy of NED improves, it should be incorporated into machine-generated event data. A NED system operating in parallel with event extraction and coding would dramatically improve the ability of consumers of the event data to flag new situations and emerging crises.

3.2.2 De-Duplication

As the number of sources used to generate event data increased – incredibly by contemporary standards, the early human-coded data sets typically used only a single source, usually the *New York Times* – the problem of duplicate event reports increased exponentially. Duplicates can occur both when a news source reports on a developing story – a bombing in a major city can easily generate a dozen stories even from a single source – and when multiple local sources retransmit stories (often with some editing) provided by wire services. "Near-duplicate detection" is an imperfect and computationally intensive process when done with the original text, and usually shortcuts such as "one-a-day" filtering – only allowing one instance of any given *source – event – target* triple per day – are used instead. In the absence of such filtering, however, event data sets will wildly exaggerate both the number of events and the importance of locations that are well connected to global English-language media.

3.2.3 Geolocation

Recent event data sets such as GDELT (http://gdeltproject.org/) and ACLED (http://www.acleddata.com/) offer the promise of geolocations of events that allow for spatiotemporal analyses of international relations events using the wide variety of new geospatial statistical and visualization tools that have become available in recent years. Given the importance of geography in international and intrastate relations, the location of events becomes even more critical. That said, even in a "small" data context, geolocation is a difficult challenge.

So long as one has actor-location references in the text and the event has an unambiguous known physical locations, such as the site of a demonstration or a military clash, geolocation is straightforward: for example, the major demonstrations in Tahrir Square in Cairo and Independence Square in Kiev could be unambiguously located. But a report "Demonstrations occurred in major cities across Egypt" provides little codeable information. The location may also be irrelevant or unknown; for example, in pronouncements made on the Web by militant groups.

Even known locations can present problems. Consider the following challenge:

The U.S. Secretary of State, speaking from Paris, denounced Russian president Vladimir Putin's support of Syria.

This describes a U.S. action toward Russia. But even when available software and dictionaries disambiguate the actors and parse the sentence, an ontological coding issue remains on the "location" of this event. Although "Paris" is the physical location of the announcement, it could easily be the *least* interesting location in the sentence, particularly if Kerry just happened to be in Paris at the time he made the announcement, which could as easily have been made in Berlin, London, or Cape Cod. Conversely, if Kerry were in Paris to discuss the Syrian situation with his French counterparts, the reference to "Paris" is important. While the political event data community has been working on the issue of event and actor ontologies for about 50 years, the issue of location ontologies is quite new, and the example here is only one of many unresolved issues.

Although the names of countries and major cities are usually unambiguous – the former Soviet state "Georgia" and the U.S. state "Georgia" being one of the few exceptions – disambiguation of smaller sites can present additional problems. For example, the widely used http://www.geonames.org/ site returns 101 matches for "Sidi Moussa" in Algeria and 137 for Morocco, and many countries, not just Ukraine, have an "Independence Square." Geonames.org generally provides excellent coverage, but there are still a few conflict areas where coverage in limited, notably the Democratic Republic of Congo.

In addition to the onotological challenges of geolocation, it poses specific technical challenges that have yet to be fully surmounted in event data sets. Generally, geolocation proceeds in three steps: (1) find all place names in a given text, (2) obtain geographic coordinates of said locations, and (3) determine which of these is the location of the event. Step one is a problem to which a fair amount of attention has been paid. Named-entity recognition systems, such as the one developed by Stanford,[7] do an acceptable job of pulling locations out of the text, though there is, of course, some slippage in terms of accuracy. The second step constitutes an area of active research as seen by projects developed at Pennsylvania State University[8] and by commercial entities such as Berico Technologies.[9] These systems attempt to make determinations about whether the Cairo mentioned in a text is Cairo, Egypt, or Cairo, Illinois. They do a mostly acceptable job, but are perhaps less accurate than ideal. This stage is certainly more difficult than identifying place names as outlined in step one. The final step is to determine the "aboutness" of a text. In other words, what one location best represents the actions or events described in the text? This is an extremely difficult problem, especially given that humans might not necessarily agree on the single location in a text. However, some projects have attempted to tackle this question, such as CLIFF[10] by the MIT Center for Civic Media.

As the preceding discussion has outlined, geolocation is not a single problem, but instead comprises of many individual steps that must be combined to create a successful geolocation system. When added to the more general issues with geolocating event data – does a given event actually need a location, what about events that need a location but the underlying text makes no mention of a location? – it becomes apparent that event data geolocation is an issue that is likely not conquerable by a single individual or by pasting together existing technologies that are not specifically designed for the task.

3.3 Analysis and Community Challenges

Once event data is produced from text, end users of the data and the research community more broadly face a number of challenges related to sustaining, validating, and updating event data sets and producing accurate inference and predictions using the data.

While our focus here is on improving the quality of the data-generation process, we and the Open Event Data Alliance are working to improve the final analytic uses of the data once it has been produced. Event data are noisy – this was true even in the era of human-coded data sets – and consequently are best used with methods that have explicit models for errors (most importantly, out-of-sample testing). The highly idiosyncratic patterns that people claim – always after the fact – to be specific "triggers" are just a psychological artifact of "hindsight bias," which Kahneman (2011) discusses in detail: they are not actually present in the data. Forecasts not made about the future or, at minimum, a hold-out sample should be discounted.

Transparency

In our opinion – and this is what motivated the formation of the Open Event Data Alliance (OEDA) – event data are impossible to evaluate unless they are fully transparent: this has been a problem with both GDELT and ICEWS. There are simply too many decisions that have to be made, and minor changes in protocols can make big differences in the coding. Black boxes will not work, nor will the "one data set to rule them all approach" that was common when event data were much more expensive than they are now.

Costs

"Big data" is a two-edged sword in the sense that too many funders are looking for easy solutions – typically involving unsupervised learning algorithms – to everything and are reluctant to fund sloggy human-coded efforts (for example in actor dictionary development and coding "gold standard" cases), even when these were vital to bringing analytical efforts to their current levels. These are crucial issues in developing these data.

High-quality or large-scope event data in near-real time bring a number of costs. Servers and programmer time are needed to produce data, and expert labor is required to update dictionaries and ontologies as needed. At present, dictionary updates employ a suite of tools that can handle both parsing of text and capturing information via NER on new actors to foster further dictionary development. This is an active research area and one in need of additional inputs and algorithms such as the topic modeling approach of O'Connor et al. (2013).

Compared to many methods of collecting social science data – for example, surveys and any human-coded data collection – the *marginal* costs of event data are very low; in fact they are very close to zero. However, improvements in coding bring both labor and infrastructure costs. Older pattern-based coders could run effectively on very limited hardware, even an aging laptop. As the systems have become more sophisticated and the volume of reports grows, computational costs become a limiting factor. For example, the pattern-based TABARI program could code about 1,000 to 2,000 sentences per second (depending on the hardware and dictionaries), whereas the Stanford CoreNLP parser works at about 5 sentences per second on typical hardware, so any high-volume coding project requires access to a computing cluster. While dictionaries do not need constant updating, they do require periodic updating or they will be biased toward persistent actors, and updating is a task that requires large amounts of semi-skilled labor. Over the longer term, formats and technologies change and the coding software must be adapted, bringing additional costs in software developer time.

Replication
Well-documented automated coding efforts that generate big data face the problem of replication: how does someone verify the source data, its coding, and subsequent analysis? In the next section, we describe some ways that the OEDA can supplement open data collection and offer replication standards that will be good for both industry and academia.

Sharing the code and coding standards for these data is more complex. Just providing a static data set and a series of codes that process the data does not work (i.e., we cannot put this data easily into the Dataverse because that system was not designed for data sets that were constantly updated). Using more dynamic versioning and shared collaboration environments, such as Github, can be fruitful, but presents issues for setting and benchmarking standards for data and analysis replication.

Customization and Versioning
All of these issues are be exacerbated by the proliferation of custom-tailored event data sets built with specialized dictionaries. OEDA can play a role in

comparing accuracy across data sets, recording how each data set was created, and potentially assisting with the maintenance of custom data sets after projects or publications are completed.

Producers and users of data sets should be comfortable versioning their data sets in the same way that software developers version their software releases. Rapid "hotfix" updates and bleeding-edge features can be incorporated in newer versions so that people who want the features can get quick access, but people using these data sets for forecasting or for comparison over time should have access to stable releases and be confident that these versions' availability will continue for years. Maintaining, hosting, and explaining those versions is another role an organization like OEDA should play.

Unfortunately, as event data became popularized in the early 2010s, first in the policy community and then in the popular press, these caveats were either ignored or the data sets were oversold in grandiose terms as providing a "God's-eye view" of world activity. At the same time, the data were criticized for being noisy and prone to error, although this criticism was typically based only on the examination of a few dozen cases out of data sets containing hundreds of thousands of cases. The fact that those errors would be completely irrelevant in a statistical analysis, and have been part of the event data enterprise since its beginnings more than 50 years ago, was not appreciated. The caveats extend to *any* automated coding of texts because of the need for validation and good understandings of the data-generation process (Grimmer and Stewart, 2013).

These issues will be present to some degree in all event data sets. The most effective mitigation of these issues is to make all aspects of the event-generation process as transparent as possible. Transparency in large-scale event data projects allows users of all stripes to understand all aspects of the data-generation process and thus these limitations. It also allows for community revisions and improvements, consistent with the OEDA approach. Our current answer to the issue of transparency is the creation of a standardized environment for the creation of event data, which we refer to as EL:DIABLO (Event/Location: Data set In A Box, Linux-Option).[11]

EL:DIABLO makes use of common technologies within the software development community, specifically a virtual machine created using Vagrant, to ease the setup of an event data coding environment.[12] The deployment of this environment within a virtual machine allows other researchers or analysts to deploy the exact code we use to generate event data. This helps with many of the issues described earlier. The entire processing pipeline is transparent and easily replicable; a single file describes all of the software used and the underlying dependencies for that software. This approach also allows easy customization and versioning of the processing pipeline. Customization of the pipeline is simply a matter of changing a few lines of code in either the setup script for EL:DIABLO or the underlying code. Versioning is simple as well: one needs to simply make changes to the setup script and release it under a new version tied to the generated data.

Validation

Finally, validation considerations for quality need to be built into the process. This is probably an area where the event data community has put in the least effort, in large part because it can only be done with very expensive coding by well-trained and coordinated coders. As event data methods are scaled or updated, there need to be gold standards against which to compare the code and algorithms. At present, we lack a common set of test cases or data against which to evaluate these decisions. One goal of OEDA is to present such a test suite of cases that have been human validated, so that there is a common standard against which improvements can be measured.

4 THE OPEN EVENT DATA ALLIANCE (OEDA)

The Open Event Data Alliance (OEDA) is a consortium, in the process of incorporation as a limited liability corporation, of for-profit organizations, not-for-profit organizations, and individuals committed to facilitating the development, adoption, and analysis of social and political event data through

- the provision of open access data sets;
- the development of open-source software and coding ontologies for these purposes; and
- the creation of standards for documenting the source data used for event data because texts cannot be typically directly shared due to licensing and intellectual property concerns.

The prime objective of OEDA is to provide reliable, open access, multi-sourced political event data sets that are updated on at least a daily to weekly basis, that are transparent and documented with respect to the origin of the source texts, and that use one or more of the open coding ontologies supported by the organization. We hope to be able to fulfill this objective solely as an aggregator rather than by generating such data; in particular, we expect to link to multiple data sets, either sharing a common format or being supported by software that will translate into that format. However, generating data will be kept open as an option if it is deemed necessary to ensure a reliable resource. When suitable sources are available, preference will be given to data that are also transparent with respect to the use of open-source coding engines and dictionaries, but OEDA will support data sets that have been produced in part or in total by using proprietary methods, provided the resulting data are open access, documented, and clear of intellectual property issues.

The objective of OEDA is not to provide "one data set to rule them all," and as such it takes no position on the relative appropriateness or validity of various event data sets – although it may support research on scientific comparisons of various data sets, including those provided by its members. Rather it seeks to provide a stable, credible, and recognized data source that can be used to support the research and development efforts of the community.

Following the model of the Linguistic Data Consortium, as opportunities arise, OEDA expects to negotiate and become the intellectual property license holder for news texts that can be used to produce open access event data sets. These licenses could include those that restrict the text (but not the derived data) to use within the organization, that provide access only to the membership, and that provide for open access.

OEDA will not seek to compete with its membership for the provision of research and analysis. It will undertake the development of open-source software and standards in circumstances where these needs have been identified as not being met in a timely fashion as determined by its board of directors and board of advisors. When opportunities arise, the organization will actively seek funding for workshops on common standards and for training.

As resources and voluntary efforts allow, OEDA expects to participate in the conferences and workshops of other professional organizations, both to disseminate results of its own work and to provide training. Although the organization may on occasion initiate independent conferences, these are not the primary purpose of OEDA. We do not anticipate the establishment of a journal, magazine, or any other periodic communication, but will maintain various forms of electronic communications. The organization will give no awards, particularly those involving the recruitment of committees.

In summary, we anticipate that OEDA will engage in the following activities:

- maintenance of a set of reliable – 24/7/365 availability – Internet-based open access, multisourced social and political event data sets that are updated on at least a daily or weekly basis. When practical, this will be done by aggregating existing data sets but if needed the organization will generate its own data using open-source resources. This data will be maintained in reliable, mirrored archives.
- licensing of texts of news sources that can be used for the production of open access data;
- development of specialized coding software, particularly for computationally intensive tasks such as parsing and machine translation;
- enhancement of dictionaries using open formats:

  - named-entity updates
  - expansion/refinement of actor, event, and thematic ontologies
  - maintaining dictionary development expertise

- maintenance of a blog, Listserv, and servers, as well as contributing in other electronic media as may arise through future social and technological developments. The servers will contain a versioned archive of various open-source resources;
- development of voluntary open standards for resources such as data formats (and software to translate between formats), coding ontologies, and dictionaries, as well as the development of "best practices" for coding protocols;

- legal defense of any challenges to open source materials or coordination of such efforts with other organizations such as the Electronic Frontier Foundation as resources permit;
- sponsorship of training and best-practice workshops at professional meetings as opportunities allow and, if there is sufficient demand, sponsorship of one or more independent conferences.

This model has been widely used in other software projects (e.g., consider parallels to open-source Linux distributions or the statistical software R), but it has not been an applied model in terms of developing software or data practices in political science. This model moves the development practice from outside of the pure academic environment and asks outside researchers, companies, and other users of these data (e.g., political risk analysts, finance professionals) to provide input both in terms of substantive contributions to the codebase and feedback on the resultant data. Further, it sponsors a research community around event data that can lead to new uses and developments.

5 CONCLUSIONS

Few domains of quantitative political science stand to benefit from the big-data explosion as much as automated event data. The ability to build large-scale, global event data sets from news reports in near-real time is what pushes this area of political science into the realm of big data. Its possibilities create a unique set of opportunities and challenges, both for the producers and consumers of such data. To realize these opportunities – and appropriately address the challenges – we believe it is necessary for researchers across the academic, policy, and private sectors to engage collaboratively to build a persistent, transparent, and replicable system for generating valid global events.

The issues faced by those developing and analyzing event data are far from unique; many other domains of the burgeoning field of data science are working through similar concerns as research teams work to develop new tools and techniques that are both rigorous and usable. The democratization of big data through the combination of open access to data sets on the Web and inexpensive access to tools through open-source software means that data analysis and visualization are now available to a wide community, not simply to a cloister of PhD-trained political scientists at research universities. While this opens new space for innovation and collaboration, it also requires researchers who generate data to do so in a thoughtful way. Our proposed criteria for working with event data need to be upheld by the community working with these data, thereby creating opportunities for the depth, validity, transparency, consistency, and community necessary to manage such a big-data project over the long term – and further extending to the consideration of gold standards, new ontologies, dictionaries, and so on.

As we have seen in other major scientific big-data projects such as those in linguistics, genomics, astronomy, demography, and geography, the challenges associated with global, near-real time event data cannot be solved (well) by any one researcher or even any single research team. Establishing effective norms in this domain will enable a coordinating function for the wider event data community to quickly resolve technical issues like de-duplication and machine translation, before moving on to the meatier questions of geolocation, foreign language dictionaries, and forecasting.

The OEDA initiative that we outline here serves as a way to address the big-data opportunities and challenges outlined in this chapter. Providing a common and open set of tools (EL:DIABLO, PETRARCH, etc.), standards, and community expectations will generate new data and more efforts focused on how it is generated and improved. We believe this is an important step for any project that aspires to be big data since it ensures that transparency and replication are at the fore. With time, we hope that OEDA will be a model for high-quality open collaboration and innovation across the public and private sectors and provide a foundation for a period of rapid innovation in tools and applications of event data comparable to that seen in other successful open-source projects.

Notes

1. They are also part of legislative studies where the spoken and vote-based actions of legislators generate events of interest.
2. There is a related literature in computer simulation on "event data." It works with audit trails to look at the traffic in a network. Although this work clearly shares some similarities with what we are discussing here, we do not address this variant.
3. http://petrarch.readthedocs.org/en/latest/.
4. See also http://www.youtube.com/watch?v=Vo-v3ptPmdQ.
5. See research by NLP Research Group at University of Utah: http://www.cs.utah .edu/~riloff/publications.html.
6. For a re-implementation of TABARI in Spanish see Javier Osorio's EventusID software, http://www.javierosorio.net/#!software/cqbi.
7. http://nlp.stanford.edu/software/CRF-NER.shtml.
8. http://geotxt.org/.
9. http://clavin.bericotechnologies.com/.
10. http://cliff.mediameter.org/.
11. More information on EL:DIABLO can be found at https://openeventdata.github .io/eldiablo/.
12. http://www.vagrantup.com/.

References

Azar, E. E. and J. Ben-Dak (1975). *Theory and Practice of Events Research*. New York: Gordon and Breach.

Azar, E. E., R. A. Brody, and C. A. McClelland (Eds.) (1972). *International Events Interaction Analysis: Some Research Considerations*. Beverly Hills: Sage Publications.

Bagozzi, B. E. (2011). Forecasting civil conflict with zero-inflated count models. Manuscript. Pennsylvania State University.

Bernauer, T. and N. P. Gleditsch (2012, August). Special issue: Event data. *International Interactions 38*(4).

Best, R. H., C. Carpino, and M. J. C. Crescenzi (2013). An analysis of the TABARI coding system. *Conflict Management and Peace Science 30*(4), 335–348.

Bond, D., J. Bond, C. Oh, J. C. Jenkins, and C. L. Taylor (2003). Integrated data for events analysis (IDEA): An event typology for automated events data development. *Journal of Peace Research 40*(6), 733–745.

Brandt, P. T., M. P. Colaresi, and J. R. Freeman (2008). The dynamics of reciprocity, accountability and credibility. *Journal of Conflict Resolution 52*(3), 343–374.

Brandt, P. T. and J. R. Freeman (2006). Advances in Bayesian time series modeling and the study of politics: Theory testing, forecasting, and policy analysis. *Political Analysis 14*(1), 1–36.

Brandt, P. T., J. R. Freeman, and P. A. Schrodt (2011). Real time, time series forecasting of political conflict. *Conflict Management and Peace Science 28*, 41–64.

Burgess, P. M. and R. W. Lawton (1972). *Indicators of International Behavior: An Assessment of Events Data Research*. Beverly Hills: Sage Publications.

Chadefaux, T. (2014). Early warning signals for war in the news. *Journal of Peace Research 51*(1), 5–18.

Davenport, C. and P. Ball (2002). Views to a kill: Exploring the implications of source selection in the case of Guatemalan state terror, 1977–1995. *Journal of Conflict Resolution 46*(3), 427–450.

Gerner, D. J. and P. A. Schrodt (1998). The effects of media coverage on crisis assessment and early warning in the Middle East. In S. Schmeidl and H. Adelman (Eds.), *Early Warning and Early Response*. Columbia University Press-Columbia International Affairs Online.

Getoor, L. and A. Machanavajjhala (2013). Entity resolution for big data. In *Proceedings of the 19th ACM SIGKDD International Conference on Knowledge Discovery and Data Mining*, KDD '13, New York, pp. 1527–1527.

Goldstein, J. S., J. C. Pevehouse, D. J. Gerner, and S. Telhami (2001). Dynamics of Middle East conflict and US influence. *Journal of Conflict Resolution 45*(5), 594–620.

Grimmer, J. and B. M. Stewart (2013). Text as data: The promise and pitfalls of automatic content analysis methods for political texts. *Political Analysis 21*, 267–297.

Kahneman, D. (2011). *Thinking Fast and Slow*. New York: Farrar, Straus and Giroux.

King, G. (2011). Ensuring the data-rich future of the social sciences. *Science (Washington) 331*(6018), 719–721.

King, G. and W. Lowe (2004). An automated information extraction tool for international conflict data with performance as good as human coders: A rare events evaluation design. *International Organization 57*(3), 617–642.

Kumaran, G. and J. Allan (2004). Text classification and named entities for new event detection. In *Proceedings of the 27th Annual International ACM SIGIR Conference on Research and Development in Information Retrieval*, SIGIR '04, pp. 297–304.

Kumaran, G. and J. Allan (2005). Using names and topics for new event detection. In *Proceedings of Human Language Technology Conference and Conference on Empirical Methods in Natural Language Processing (HLT/EMNLP)*, pp. 121–128.

Merritt, R. L., R. G. Muncaster, and D. A. Zinnes (Eds.) (1993). *International Event Data Developments: DDIR Phase II.* Ann Arbor: University of Michigan Press.

O'Brien, S. P. (2010). Crisis early warning and decision support: Contemporary approaches and thoughts on future research. *International Studies Review 12*(1), 87–104.

O'Connor, B., B. M. Stewart, and N. A. Smith (2013). Learning to extract international relations from political context. In *Proceedings of the Association of Computational Linguistics,* Sofia, Bulgaria, pp. 1094–1104.

Osorio, J. (2013). The contagion of drug violence: Spatio-temporal dynamics of the Mexican war on drugs. Unpublished manuscript.

Reeves, A., S. Shellman, and B. Stewart (2006). Fair & balanced or fit to print? The effects of media sources on statistical inferences. In *International Studies Association Conference,* pp. 22–25.

Riloff, E. (1996). An empirical study of automated dictionary construction for information extraction in three domains. *Artificial Intelligence 85*(1), 101–134.

Roberts, K. and S. Harbagiu (2011). Detecting new and emerging events in streaming news documents. *International Journal of Sematic Computing 5*(4).

Schrodt, P. A. (2012a, August). Precedents, progress and prospects in political event data. *International Interactions 38*(4), 546–569.

Schrodt, P. A. (2012b). *Conflict and Mediation Event Observations (CAMEO) Codebook.* http://eventdata.psu.edu/data.dir/cameo.html.

Schrodt, P. A. and B. Bagozzi (2013, April). Detecting the dimensions of news reports using latent Dirichlet allocation models. Annual Meeting of the International Studies Association, San Francisco.

Schrodt, P. A. and D. J. Gerner (1996). Cluster-based early warning indicators for political change in the Middle East, 1979–1996. Annual Meeting of the American Political Science Association, San Francisco.

Schrodt, P. A., D. J. Gerner, and Ö. Yilmaz (2009). Conflict and mediation event observations (CAMEO): An event data framework for a post-Cold War world. In J. Bercovitch and S. Gartner (Eds.), *International Conflict Mediation: New Approaches and Findings.* New York: Routledge, pp. 287–304.

Yonamine, J. (2013). *A Nuanced Study of Political Conflict Using the Global Data set of Events Location And Tone (GDELT) Data set.* PhD thesis, Pennsylvania State University.

Zeitzoff, T. (2011). Using social media to measure conflict dynamics: An application to the 2008–2009 Gaza conflict. *Journal of Conflict Resolution 55*(6), 938–969.

4

Network Structure and Social Outcomes

*Network Analysis for Social Science**

Betsy Sinclair[†]
Washington University in St Louis

1 WHY SHOULD SOCIAL SCIENTISTS STUDY NETWORKS?

Human behavior is characterized by connections to others. We define ourselves by these connections: our families, our friends, our neighbors, our co-workers all form a social geography. Social scientists who study networks serve as cartographers for these social plains, identifying actors who influence others. In their overview of the study of political networks, McClurg and Young (2011) state, "We would probably all agree that one primary tie among political scientists is our emphasis on power, and understanding how and why power is used. We are all inherently interested in the exercise of power between and among individuals and groups and the implications that this exercise holds for social outcomes. We contend that this unifying concept is, at its very core, relational." Social scientists have an interest in relational social science, with roles as either researchers directly focusing on relationships between actors or else as scholars accounting for interdependence among actors and institutions in their analyses.

Additionally, we have seen an explosion in the availability of networked data. With the rise of social media, the relationships between ordinary citizens and political elites, among ordinary citizens, and even among political elites is more easily quantified. When once scholars of Congress had to "soak and poke" to understand a legislator's relationship with her constituents (Fenno 1978), now it is possible to directly observe the connections that legislators establish with their constituents over Twitter, as well as the connections between the constituents themselves (Barbera 2015), the donations made to legislators and

* I thank participants from the University of Iowa and University of Southern California Master Class sessions on political networks for their comments and suggestions on this material.
† Department of Political Science, 1 Brookings Drive, St Louis, MO 63130; bsinclai@wustl.edu.

121

from one legislator to another (Bonica 2014), and the relationships between friends that lead one friend to influence another to cast a ballot (Bond et al. 2012). The availability of these new data resources demands new empirical techniques in part because of these resources' sheer magnitude and in part because the relational structure of the data allows different analyses than ever before. This chapter focuses not on the computational innovation but rather on the empirical strategies.

A range of scholars from political science to sociology to economics to even physics have innovated to develop empirical techniques to account for networked relationships.[1] Interestingly these methods are applied to a range of substantive questions. Existing scholarship has documented that any two Americans are connected by six intermediaries (Milgram 1967), for example, and that any two unrelated Web pages are separated by only 19 links (Albert, Jeong, and Barabasi 1999). For another example, all of the 19 hijackers responsible for the 9/11 disaster could be tied together using shared and available data (such as addresses, telephone numbers, and frequent-flier numbers) and a disproportionate number of network metrics converged on the leader Mohamad Atta (Krebs 2001). Across substantive questions it is consistently clear that citizens are connected to other citizens and that our political and economic institutions are connected to each other. The structure of those connections has the potential to yield meaningful insight into the kinds of outcomes that are possible or expected. The goal of this chapter is to introduce the reader to a range of tools of network analysis that provide insights into a variety of social science problems. First the chapter focuses on those tools best designed for exploratory data analyses – visualizing a network and producing simple summary statistics of the network's characteristics. It then turns to a range of effective strategies to draw causal inferences.

Visualization of networks can provide answers – and quick ones – to all kinds of questions. If you want to be a law school professor, where should you get your JD? By simply visualizing the network of "sending" and "receiving" schools – by drawing a network where two universities are linked if one hired a JD who graduated from another – it is pretty clear that the best bet is to have gone to Yale or Harvard. A quick comparison to a similar network for political science faculty demonstrates that this network is much more diverse.

Quantification of networks can similarly provide surprising answers. Why did the Medici rise to power in Renaissance Florence? They were neither the most powerful nor wealthiest family. By visualizing the Medici family's marriages with other powerful families, it is possible to see how they are central to the network of Florentine families. Quantifying the strength of the Medici position in the network and noting that this family dominates all standard network quantification metrics in terms of the marriage network suggest that it is not that surprising they were the most powerful family at the end of the Renaissance in Florence. Other quantification tools can also provide surprising insights (such as those related to community detection).

Neither of these tools (visualization and quantification), however, allows us to test hypotheses, although they are useful for exploratory data analyses. Randomized field experiments have made great forays into providing designs for explicitly testing the role of network ties in influencing outcomes of interest for social scientists. These experimental designs have been pushed into the field because of serious concerns about the endogeneity between the outcome of interest and the variables that generate a network tie. Much of the observational work in this area has suffered from this criticism (and in fact some current statistical work addresses this problem). Even these experimental designs, however, are subject to a set of assumptions about the data-generating process. Consequently, a separate line of researchers have suggested that the best tools that social scientists can offer to test networks are those that explicitly test models. The final section of this chapter explores the tension between testing specific models and designing randomized trials.

Social scientists are increasingly interested in relationships. Whether those relationships are between countries, between individuals, or between institutions, the field of social networks has offered a number of useful tools to gain insight into how the structure of these relationships influences outcomes of interest. This chapter aims to advance the appropriate use of these tools in the social sciences.

2 WHAT IS AND IS NOT A NETWORK?

Before proceeding with a discussion of the vast array of empirical tools available for social scientists, it is important to first define what is and is not a network. The field of network analysis has been quite generous, so a network is typically defined as a set of actors and their relationships where the range of potential actors and relationships is defined quite broadly. Nodes typically represent actors or institutions, whereas edges represent connections between such entities. Edges can be either directed, to represent connections that flow from one node to another, or undirected. They can simply signify the existence of a connection, taking on a discrete value of 0 or 1, or they can be weighted to reflect the strength of the connection between two nodes.

Key to this definition of a network is that relationships describe how the actors are connected. These networks can be cities connected by interstate highways, scholars connected by collaborations (Berardo 2009), or even bills introduced in the House of Representatives that are connected by their committee of reference (Gailmard and Patty 2013). It is the responsibility of the researcher to posit a network where the relationships are something meaningful. What is not a network? An instance of data that is not a network is one where the edges have no social or relational meaning – suppose, for example, you drew a network based on numbers from a phone book that had the same last four digits. While these actors (the phone numbers) do have something in common (the last four digits), the edges have no role in defining a relationship between them.[2] Yet edges (relationships) can represent a wide class of potential connections, including social ties, the flow of goods between firms of countries, or the linkages between various actors or institutions. The type of network under study is frequently defined by the relationships that connect the actors. For example, a *social network* is a social structure made up of a set of social actors (such as individuals or organizations) and of a complex set of the dyadic ties between these actors (Wasserman and Faust 1994), whereas a *political network* consists of the social network structure that focuses on politics, elections, or government (Sinclair 2012).

After a network is defined, it is then possible to conduct an analysis. This next section reviews several common tools used to quantify characteristics of a network. Although these are summary statistics and do not easily lend themselves to statistical tests, they do often provide clear insights into the association between the structure of a network and its outcomes, suggesting the possibility that it is through networked influence that these outcomes occur.

3 NETWORK ESTIMATION

What is important to focus on when considering the importance of networks? Each person or institution is connected to a myriad of potential other actors. The first step in network estimation is simply to properly define the network. The definition, paired with a visualization of the network's structure, can sometimes yield great insights (for example, defining the academic hiring market for law and political science as a network between institutions that grant terminal degrees and those that hire faculty). Yet not every network can be easily visualized to capture the key insight. Quantification of the network characteristics, then, can either support the insight gained by visualization or more frequently helps provide evidence that the structure corresponds with a pattern of influence posited by the researcher. This section reviews some of the most common quantification tools using a handful of canonical examples in the network literature . Additionally, there are a range of more sophisticated tools, such as those designed to detect communities, that can be employed when studying social networks. These tools look for the presence of key structures and can handle very large networks where visualizing the structure of the network is simply not feasible.

3.1 Visualizing Structure

The hiring of graduates from law schools and graduate schools for academic positions is a good example of how simply visualizing a network is can yield insights into the structure of an institution, in this case the academic hiring market. Here, the actors are the academic institutions that grant the degrees and the academic institutions that might hire the graduates for professorial positions. Edges represent a hire and are directed, with the sending institution granting the degree and the receiving institution hiring the graduate. It is possible to draw these networks for both law schools and for political science departments and then to compare whether these two different fields have very different hiring structures (Katz et al. 2011). Interestingly, they do. Law schools are primarily populated with individuals who received degrees from Yale or Harvard, whereas political science departments are populated with individuals who received their degrees from a much more diverse array of institutions. Merely by drawing the figure that characterizes this network we learn something about the hiring norms in these two respective fields. Networks have the power to yield insights when they are simply visualized.

During the 1400s, Florence, Italy, was ruled by an oligarchy of elite families. The Medici family rose to power in Florence, despite having less wealth and less political power than other ruling families in Florence at that point in time. A question that has long puzzled historians was how to understand the Medici rise to power. By simply visualizing the structure of the network it is easy to grasp the insight that Florentine family marriages allowed them to secure influence in the early 15th century (Padgett 1993). Indeed, Cosimo de Medici, "the godfather of the Renaissance," orchestrated strategic marriages to ensure a central position within the Florentine social network. This data is frequently used in the network community to illustrate the importance of network quantification tools.

To understand the Medici rise to power, it is possible to plot the marriage network and then capture the essence of how the strategic choice of marriages resulted in the Medici family becoming central figures in the Florentine social network. In this network, each node represents one of the elite families. Each link represents a marriage between members of two families. Figure 4.1 presents this network.[3] Again, by doing nothing other than plotting the network figure, it is possible to gain insight into the Florentine power structure.

In terms of the social-political structure of the Florentine families, the Strozzi had the most wealth at the start of the 15th century. Why did they not rise to power and instead the Medici did? Looking at this network it is clear that the Medici are better positioned. They look more central to the network. How much more central are they? The next section quantifies this characteristic.

3.2 Network Quantification

How can we quantify network position? What types of characteristics, for example, make the Medici more central to the network than the Strozzi? To illustrate the differences between the Strozzi and the Medici, for example, we can use two common network quantification tools. First, *degree centrality* counts the number of edges for each node. In this case, that means that we count the number of families to which a given family is linked through marriages. Second, *betweenness centrality* calculates the fraction of the total number of shortest paths between any two nodes on which a particular node

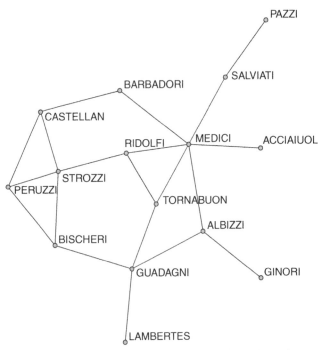

FIGURE 4.1. Florentine family marriages in the early 15th century.

lies. In this case, we consider paths to be marriages and then consider the fraction of the total number of shortest paths between any two families on which a particular family lies. Returning to the Florentine marriage network shown in Figure 4.1, it is easy to add up the number of ties to discover that the degree centrality of the Medici is 6, whereas the degree centrality of the Strozzi is 4. This is only one way in which the Medici are better positioned. If instead we were to calculate their respective betweenness centrality, the Medici have a betweenness centrality of .522, whereas the Strozzi have a betweenness centrality of .103. The intuition behind betweenness centrality is that if these edges were roads, and if you were committed to driving the shortest distance (where distance is calculated by the number of nodes you pass through) between any two nodes, you would want to know which actor was on the greatest fraction of shortest paths for any possible set of paths. For example, consider the shortest paths between the Barbadori and the Guadagni families. There are two such paths: Barbadori-Medici-Albizzi-Guadagni and Barbadori-Medici-Tornabuon-Guadagni. The Medici lie on both paths, and the Strozzi lie on neither.

Networks are frequently quantified using four types of values (1) degree centrality, which calculates how connected a node is to his neighbors; (2) closeness,

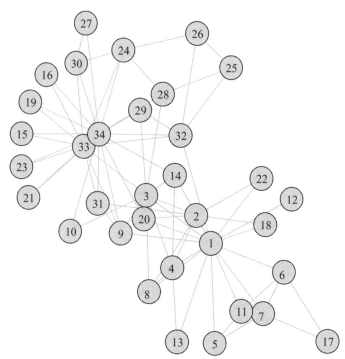

FIGURE 4.2. The karate club.

which calculates how easily a node can reach other nodes; (3) betweenness centrality, which calculates how important a node is in terms of connecting other nodes, and (4) eigenvector centrality, which estimates how important, central, or influential a node's neighbors are.

To illustrate all four of these tools, we turn to another canonical data set – the "karate club" data. A researcher documented observations from a karate club at a Midwestern university for three years, from 1970–1972 (Zachary 1977). The club's activities included both social activities (parties, dances, and banquets, for example) and regularly scheduled karate lessons. The club president and the part-time karate instructor disagreed over the price of karate lessons and more specifically under whose authority it fell to raise prices. Over time, the club became divided over this issue. After a series of confrontations, the supporters of the karate instructor resigned and formed a new organization. The structure of friendships within the club – that is, those individuals who consistently interacted outside of the karate lessons – provides a high degree of prediction into who would split into which group after the subsequent confrontation.[4]

To visualize this network, the nodes are the individual members, and the links are their social interactions. The network can then be seen in Figure 4.2.

TABLE 4.1. *Quantifying Network Position: The Karate Club*

Node	Degree	Closeness	Betweenness	Eigenvector
1	16	0.017	231.07	0.952
2	9	0.014	28.47	0.712
3	10	0.016	75.85	0.849
...	...	...	...	...
12	1	0.011	0.00	0.141

It is easily possible to calculate each of these four centrality quantifications for each node, which I do in Table 4.1. To illustrate their differences, focus on nodes 1 and 2 versus node 12. As is clear from the visualized Figure 4.2, nodes 1 and 2 are much more central to the karate network than node 12: they have a higher degree (16 and 9 versus 1), closeness (.017 and .014 versus .011), and eigenvector centrality (.952 and .712 versus .141). When focusing on their betweenness, however, it is clear that node 1 – which is quite critical in terms of connecting other parts of the network – has the most influence. Node 1's betweenness centrality is 231.07, whereas node 2's betweenness centrality is 28.47 (less even than node 3 with a betweenness centrality of 75.85). Node 12 has a betweenness centrality of 0.

Since the karate club network is small, it is easy to compare our intuitions with the quantified values in Table 4.1. These kinds of quantification tools are now frequently used across the social sciences to gain additional insight into how the structure of a network can relate to the influence of particular individual nodes. For example, in a pioneering study on legislative cosponsorship, Fowler (2006) focuses on the most and least connected legislators in the 108th U.S. House of Representatives, where legislators are nodes and are connected by their cosponsorship decisions. Looking at the 20 most central legislators, we see a preponderance of legislative leadership and other representatives reknowned for their legislative prowess. None of the 20 least central legislators are household names. We can sometimes explain changes in these centrality measures as well. In understanding which legislators are most central in the California State Assembly, for example, before and after the California blanket primary, it is clear that those legislators elected under a blanket primary system are more likely to be influential to both parties (Alvarez and Sinclair 2012). The quantification of social network measurements can then associate network characteristics with outcomes of interest.

3.3 Community Detection

Another example of the quantification of networks that can play a key role in linking the geography of a network to social science outcomes is that of community detection. In this case, we theorize that there exists a latent social structure of a network that is often not fully observable and thus needs to be constructed from the set of observed ties between nodes. We formally define a *network community* as a subset of a social network graph that is more internally connected than externally connected. Community detection allows us to uncover the structures that split a network into communities. Uncovering these kinds of structures allows us to address questions such as the following. Are there specific biases in a society, such as in hiring or publishing? Are there systematic ways to classify and categorize political ideologies or economic patterns of behavior?

One main advantage of using community detection algorithms is that they do not presuppose knowledge of the number and size of the underlying groups. That is, it is possible to apply a community detection algorithm to a network and to find a result that indeed there are no specific communities within that network. Alternatively, the algorithm could unearth many separate communities. One limitation of these algorithms is that they typically can only find non-overlapping communities.

These algorithms have been used in a number of different applications that appear sensible and where the communities that are detected correspond with our understanding of communities that are present within that particular data. For example, Newman (2004) uses a community detection algorithm to detect the pages on a website using the hyperlinks between them, and Porter et al. (2005) use a related algorithm to detect congressional committees using roll-call votes. Some of these analyses require enormous computational power, such as those that analyze the purchasing decisions by Amazon customers with respect to books on American politics, political blogs, or coauthor networks (Girvan and Newman 2002).

In Figure 4.3 using the canonical "karate club" data, I rely on modularity maximization, formalized by Girvan and Newman (2002). There are many possible alternatives, but this algorithm seems particularly robust when handling large networks of data. I first define modularity. Let e be a symmetric $n \times n$ matrix where each element e_{ij} represents the fraction of all edges that link community i to vertices in community j. Modularity is defined, then, as

$$Q = \sum_i \left(e_{ii} - a_i^2\right) = \mathrm{Tr}\, \mathbf{e} - \|\mathbf{e}^2\|,$$

where a_i is defined as the row sums, $a_i = \sum_j e_{ij}$. Tr e, the trace of e, gives the sum of edges connecting vertices in the same community, and $\|\mathbf{e}^2\|$ represents the sum of the elements of the matrix $\mathbf{e}^2$. We can think of $\|\mathbf{e}^2\|$ as measuring, holding the detected community structure fixed, the expected number of edges connecting communities if connections between vertices were random. Modularity, Q, can then take on values between 0 and 1. A value of 0 implies no more community edges than would be expected. To calculate modularity in this context, we first calculate betweenness (the number of shortest paths that run along

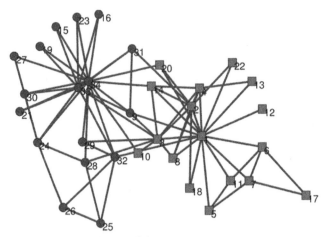

FIGURE 4.3. The karate club communities.

a given edge) for every edge. We then remove edge with the highest between-ness score because this edge is most likely to connect communities as opposed to lie within communities. We then estimate modularity, which measures the number of within-community edges relative to a null model of a random graph with the same degree distribution. After this phase, the betweenness scores are recalculated within the new graph and the process repeats, continuing to remove edges until modularity is maximized.

Here I apply modularity maximization to the karate club data, where edges represent shared social activities and nodes represent members. The algorithm detects two communities, which are shown in Figure 4.3.

Like the previous examples, these two communities that are discovered correspond to what we know about this data. Recall in the previous section we described how the karate club split into two separate factions after the disagreement over the price of karate lessons. This example illustrates that the topography for the split – that the people who interacted socially were divided into two membership groups – was already set before the disagreement took place.

Although in this case the community detection algorithm was successful, the field of network science has done little to develop serious hypotheses tests. We have no notion of a test statistic in the case of modularity maximization, but rather are simply drawing a comparison to a null model (a random net-work) without any formalized statistics. In the field of network analysis, there are many possible algorithms to detect communities within the observed net-works.[5] Much of the literature takes an "inter-occular test" approach, looking for whether the communities that are detected fit some kind of "common sense" for what is "known" about the network ex ante. Thus the difficulty for these methods is that they are primarily designed to provide tools for exploratory social science. They are interesting and allow us to develop hypotheses about social geography, but for networks to advance in the social sciences, we need to improve our ability to draw inferences about networks.

4 NETWORK INFERENCE

The key goals for a successful marriage between network science and social science are to generate two key empirical tools: first, a test statistic that allows a comparison to a null model to evaluate how likely we are to construct the network measurements at random, and second, a way to allow network traits to explain outcomes in a causal framework. Although little has been done to advance to the appropriate null model comparisons, because network measurements are frequently used as explanatory variables in regression-type model, then threats to inference come primarily from measurement error. This chapter focuses on causal inference.

Scholars have made key advances in terms of causal inference and networks. The question of causal inference is a fundamental one to all social science: we are interested in questions of cause and effect. In the field of network science, we frequently observe associations or correlations between network parameters (centrality, for example) and other outcomes, but these associations may not be causal. In particular the field has been plagued with criticisms regarding selection biases. Friends become friends because of shared interests or characteristics, for example, and these shared traits may lead to shared outcomes regardless of the friendship. In the following subsections, I discuss some of the strategies that can be employed to allow serious causal inference with networks.

4.1 Observational Approaches and Endogeneity

Several of the most well-known social science studies that involve networks are penned by Nicholas Christakis and James Fowler (2009). In these studies, they frequently test whether health outcomes spread through networks (obesity, smoking, loneliness, etc.). The key concern they have faced in their analyses is that people select their social networks (their families and friends) because of shared traits (proclivities toward particular health outcomes or geography, for example) that are causally associated with these health outcomes. This produces an omitted variable bias problem with the additional complication that the people in the network are not independent of each other.

For purpose of illustration I focus on the Christakis and Fowler study (2007) on the spread of obesity through a social network. Their data includes 12,067 people (5,125 "egos" and the remaining "alters") from the Framingham Heart Study. The data was collected from 1971 to 2003. Egos took part in physical exams that measured their weight in regular intervals over this 32-year time frame. Egos also identified social ties – they were asked to provide the names of individuals who could help locate them for repeat health evaluations. Because of the geographic nature of the study, many of the social ties who were named (the "alters") were also in the study, and thus this data provides both longitudinal network data and longitudinal health data.

The study then explains obesity (at time t + 1) as a function of obesity (at time t), the alter's obesity (at time t and t + 1), the geographic distance between the alter and the ego, and finally a set of ego attributes (age, sex, and education). Its principal finding is that the alter's obesity is a significant predictor of the ego's obesity. The study gives three possible explanations for its findings: homophily (that the egos associate with like alters), confounding (that the egos and alters share unobserved attributes or experiences), or social influence. By explicitly controlling for the alter's weight at time t, the study argues that homophily is not the most likely explanation. By explicitly controlling for geography, the study finds that decreasing geographic distance does not increase the probability of obesity, potentially ruling out confounding (moreover, because not every ego-alter pair names each other as friends, the effect is only observed in the direction of the named friendship). Thus, the study concludes, the most likely explanation is social influence.

Although this study has been criticized by a number of scholars, the most compelling critique has come from Shalizi and Thomas (2011). They argue that unfortunately the limitations in the statistical modeling of observational network data in general result in very limited capabilities to draw causal inferences without exceptionally strong assumptions. In particular they argue that additional explanations cannot be ruled out in the Christakis and Fowler approach. They motivate their work asking, "If your friend Joey jumped off a bridge, would you jump too?" and then go on to say that if the answer is "yes," it could be because (a) Joey inspires you (social influence), (b) your friendship is founded on a shared love of jumping off bridges (homophily), or (c) your friendship is founded on a common risk-seeking propensity (confounding). Unless the Christakis and Fowler study could eliminate the potential variables in category (c), for example, then it would be impossible to distinguish confounding from social influence. In general, these three explanations (social influence, homophily, and confounding) are (almost) impossible to distinguish in observational network studies. How, then, are the social sciences to advance knowledge in this area?

Fortunately there have been a handful of recent advances in the realm of sensitivity analysis that allow researchers to evaluate the potential role of unmeasured confounders in changing the perceived empirical results of their work when they are handling network data. These techniques, long employed in the service of observational data, were some of the first to demonstrate the causal link between smoking and lung cancer, for example. In particular, VanderWeele (2011) proposed a sensitivity analysis technique to assess the extent to which an unmeasured factor responsible for homophily or confounding would have to be related to both the ego's and the alter's state to substantially alter qualitative and quantitative conclusions. This work was extended by VanderWeele, Ogburn, and Tchetgen (2012) and indicates that there are reasonable conditions to use the kinds of models that Fowler and Christakis advance. Substantively, it appears that the Fowler and Christakis results are fairly robust to the skepticism about selection biases. In general network tools can be employed while accounting for this kind of endogeneity. Sensitivity analyses are also possible when network characteristics are used as explanatory variables in regression contexts.

Although the substantive findings of the obesity study emerge basically unscathed from the critiques of selection bias, there remained a significant push to study the effects of networks experimentally. I explore this possibility in the next subsection.

4.2 Experimental Approaches

A common suggestion when observational data is faced with some threat of selection bias is for the researcher to conduct a randomized field experiment. This is incredibly complicated in the context of social networks because most of the experimental subjects are understood to be socially connected to others. As a consequence, if the experimenter wishes to randomly assign some of the population to receive a treatment and the rest of the population to be considered a control condition, it becomes difficult to isolate a control group that is unconnected to a treatment group. Two primary experimental options exist. First, it is possible to randomly assign some members of the network to receive a stimulus and see how that percolates through the network. In this case, the researcher needs to carefully consider who is randomly assigned to the control condition and in particular to ensure that those assigned to the control condition are socially isolated from those assigned to treatment. Second, it is possible to randomly assign a new network structure – to assign new social ties, for example. This kind of study is best illustrated by the "dorm room" experiments, where undergraduate freshmen are randomly assigned to roommates. Yet, this type of experiment is complicated by homophily: if the subjects fail to comply with the new network structure – that is, to make new friends who are very different from themselves – then it is impossible to evaluate whether or not there are network effects. This is the paradox of homophily – it is the presence of homophily that generates such concerns about observational studies, but homophily also makes it very difficult to randomly assign a new network structure. The fundamental component of any experiment is to find a way to stimulate something truly exogenous into the network.

Field experimentalists have long been concerned about spillover from within social networks. Randomized field experiments frequently take place in concentrated geographic regions. Many subjects in those experiments are then exposed to multiple other individuals in both the treatment and control groups, so if the treatment is something that is contagious – information, for example – subjects can be exposed to the treatment indirectly. If this happens, then estimates of the direct effect of the experiment (the local average treatment effect) may be biased. Yet, subject to certain restrictions or assumptions, it is possible to estimate the direct effect without bias. These include making the heroic assumption of the stable unit treatment value (Holland 1986), designing the experiment to estimate and account for spillover within specified hierarchical groups (Sinclair et al. 2012; Hudges and Halloran 2008), or limiting the exposure possibilities (Aronow and Samii 2013). In this chapter we explore the second option in greater depth.

In a classic randomized experiment, individual subjects are assigned to treatment and control. The central problem with the classic experiment is indirect exposure: either a treated subject could communicate with an untreated subject (and thus indirectly treat someone in the control condition), or else a treated subject could communicate with another treated subject (and thus amplify the treatment effect). The solution to this kind of design is simply to have a control group that is sufficiently isolated from the treatment group via a multilevel randomization. For example, Sinclair et al. (2012) conducted a voter mobilization campaign where registered voters were randomly assigned to treatment and control conditions based on their households and zipcodes. In this framework, then, it is possible to compare the average outcome of three types of individuals: one who is treated but lives in a household and a zip code where no one else is treated, one who is not treated but lives in a household where someone else is treated and in a zip code where no one else is treated, and finally one who is not treated and lives in a household and zip code where no one else is treated. If we assume that the social network of transmission is based on geography and is limited by zip code, then we can legitimately compare these three individuals: by comparing the turnout decision of the treated individual to the person who is not treated (and has no one around him treated), we can estimate the direct effect of the experiment, and by comparing the turnout decision of the untreated individual who lives in a treated household to the person who is not treated (and has no one around her treated), we can then also estimate the indirect effect of network transmission. Other experimentalists have employed similar approaches to try to isolate individuals who are eligible to be both directly and indirectly treated based on a model of network transmission (Nickerson 2008; Bond et al. 2012). This approach requires some assumptions about the network structure, as well as the ability to know something about the network itself, but it also implicitly allows the researcher to test whether this is a good network model if the treatment is something that is known to have a modest transmission rate.

4.3 Modeling Approaches

Network analyses tend to be ones that impose serious limitations on what can be estimated. This is because network data quickly becomes "big data" once you consider the potential number of relationships that may influence outcomes. For a study with N individuals, for example, they may be connected to 2^N others where those relationships create additional parameters to be estimated in any kind of networked model. This quickly increases the computational complexity of the conventional analytical models. In the field of networked data, there are two primary types of modeling approaches, and I discuss only one briefly in this subsection. First, spatial statistical models assume that links are more likely between nodes closer in latent space. These spatial models incorporate not only a latent trait but also include spatial parameters in the error term. These are fundamentally additional modeling approaches that draw causal inferences to respond to the kinds of critiques made about the Christakis and Fowler work (2007), but are particularly useful in more limited data frameworks. Second, exponential random graph models (ERGM) allow researchers to specifically model the network (Cranmer and Desmarais 2010). It is this later topic that I explore in more depth in this subsection, because it employs a slightly different approach to drawing different kinds of inferences.

Imagine that the outcome variables of interest are alliance-ties between county-pairs. The primary motivation for ERGM is to provide a model whereby we can explain those ties as a function of the characteristics of the network. In this sense, ERGM is very similar to regression where the network ties are the outcome variable, but it does not require assumptions of independence. ERGM, unlike regression, does not require the researcher to assume that each state decides its alliance portfolio independent of all other decisions made by all other states and moreover that decisions even within a state's alliance portfolio are independent – assumptions that seem heroic by most standards. Instead, ERGM models the probability of observing that network of alliance relationships over the other networks we could have observed. It does make the assumptions that there is no omitted variable bias and that the particular realization of the outcome variable is drawn from a multivariate distribution based on a particular structure of the network. A reasonable intuition is to think of ERGM as analogous to a logistic regression that accounts for the network dependencies properly. ERGM models are appropriate in a limited range of circumstances – for example, they will fail to converge if there are too many covariates in the model and moreover will converge only in the context of thin networks, where nodes are more frequent than edges. They are also not equipped to handle nonbinary edges, networks that change over time, or missing data. Finally, they fundamentally require a very strong assumption about the presence of the appropriate set of covariates: the researcher must include those covariates that are theorized to affect the formation of a network tie (but not excess covariates of the model that may fail to converge) or else the model is subject to omitted variable bias. That said, this is an exceptionally practical tool when the researcher wishes to explain the formation of a network based on the presence of covariates.

TABLE 4.2. *ERGM on Florentine Marriages*

	Estimate	Std. Error	*p*-value
Edges	−2.30	0.40	≤1e-04***
Abs Diff Wealth	0.015	0.006	0.0131*

To illustrate the capacity of an ERGM, let us return to the example of the Florentine marriages. Here suppose that we believed that the Florentine marriages were to be explained by both the degree centrality of a family (the total number of other families they were already connected to by marriage) and by a difference in relative wealth between families. That is, this would provide some evidence of strategic marriages – marriages that took place between families could be explained by a strategic incentive to "marry up" in terms of wealth or in terms of connection. Table 4.2 illustrates the coefficients from this estimation procedure.[6]

These results indicate that there is little to suggest that the network in general is formed as a consequence of the total number of edges for each family: the degree centrality is in fact a negative and statistically significant predictor for the formulation of the network. Yet the absolute difference in wealth is a weakly positive and statistically significant predictor. This would suggest that in fact the entire network is not based on the kinds of strategic marriages the Medici are theorized to have orchestrated – which in part explains why the Medici were so successful with their innovation.

5 CONCLUSION

What tools from network analysis are most useful to social scientists? Networks emerge as both areas of interest and empirical complications, and in data as small as the ruling families of Florence to the enormity of Facebook. Visualization of networks, quantification of networks, and community detection have both strengths and limitations in partnering with traditional social science hypothesis testing. These tools are best employed in conjunction with randomized field experiments and modeling approaches.

Some of the most standard tools that are employed to quantify networks illustrate what we can see when conceptualizing individuals as part of a network and subsequently quantifying some of those network's characteristics. By evaluating the centrality of the Medici in terms of marriages, for example, we can understand their rise to power during the Renaissance. By appropriately defining the network, these network parameters provide summary statistics that can be quite revealing about the distribution of power and influence within a network. As demonstrated with the example of the karate club, they can also be predictive of vulnerabilities in an organization.

Yet, although these network tools are interesting, they are only truly useful to social sciences when paired with some kind of statistical test. Network inference is best conducted with either sensitivity analyses, experimental approaches, or direct modeling approaches (which have the disadvantage of requiring some very strong assumptions). These three areas are being actively developed by methodologists and statisticians.

Substantively we observe consistent evidence that networks do influence a panoply of outcomes. A growing body of research documents the influence of context on voter turnout – the extent to which citizens' experiences are affected by their experiences of race and poverty, for example (Hersh and Nall 2015), or the participation choices of their friends (Bond et al. 2012). With the rise of big data, we can now observe this kind of association, but it requires extensive computing: simply to illustrate what is needed, Hersh and Nall (2015) analyze 73 million geocoded registration records to determine the relationship between racial context and turnout and Bond et al. (2012) analyze 61 million Facebook users' participation choices. The most exciting frontier in this line of research is to pair many of these network tools with these large data sets to allow for new kinds of hypothesis testing. Community detection algorithms appear prime candidates for such a marriage.

Human beings are part of a social environment. We typically characterize people as atomistic actors, yet the most basic actions (health choices, the decision to turn out to vote) are decisions that are associated with each person's social network. Thus social networks lead to particular outcomes of interest. Studying networks allows us to deepen our understanding of individual behavior and attitudes and to formalize the relationships across political institutions. In the end, we are all connected to each other, and the tools of network analysis help us understand our susceptibilities to each other, as well as our capabilities to effect real change in our own environment.

Notes

1. Indeed there is rising interest in the field of political networks, resulting in a new American Political Science Association section founded in 2009. Yearly membership dues are $8.00.
2. This example is drawn from Seth Masket's lecture "But Is It a Network?" presented during the IGNITE talks at Boulder PolNet 2012. The lecture is available online: http://www.youtube.com/watch?v=hv6wfR5WU4I.
3. In terms of visualizing a network, it is easiest to use the igraph R package. It enables both static and dynamic network graphs, and input data can be either a two-column edge list or an n × n adjacency matrix. Plotting your data allows you to make sense of the network so long as it is not too big, particularly in the case where the network changes over time. A wonderful example of a dynamic network is one where re-tweets are plotted over time, available through http://youtu.be/XX9he5lkNSo.
4. Social scientists who study networks use this data so frequently that they have developed an award, called the "Karate Club Award," for the first person at a conference to use this data: http://networkkarate.tumblr.com/.

5. Much of what is analyzed in this chapter is conducted using the igraph package in R. There are very good alternative options as well, including UCINET (https://sites.google.com/site/ucinetsoftware/home), Pajek (http://vlado.fmf.uni-lj .si/pub/networks/pajek/), and Siena (http://www.stats.ox.ac.uk/~snijders/siena/). Data is also available from Mark Newman's Network Data (http://www-personal.umich.edu/~mejn/netdata/) and the Stanford Large Network Data set Collection (http://snap.stanford.edu/data/).
6. Practically speaking this is the result of merely 20 iterations.

References

Albert, Reka, Hawoong Jeong, and Albert-Laszlo Barabasi. (1999) "The Diameter of the World Wide Web." *Nature* 401: 130–135.

Alvarez, R. Michael and Betsy Sinclair. (2012) "Electoral Institutions and Legislative Behavior: The Effects of the Primary Processes." *Political Research Quarterly* 65(2).

Aronow, Peter M. and Cyrus Samii. (2013) "Estimating Average Causal Effects under Interference between Units." http://arxiv.org/abs/1305.6156.

Barbera, Pablo. (2015) "Birds of the Same Feather Tweet Together: Bayesian Ideal Point Estimation Using Twitter Data." *Political Analysis* 23(1): 76–91.

Berardo, Ramiro. (2009) "Processing Complexity in Networks: A Study of Informal Collaboration and its Effect on Organizational Success." *Policy Studies Journal* 37(3): 521–539.

Bond, Robert M., Christopher J. Fariss, Jason J. Jones, Adam D. I. Kramer, Cameron Marlow, Jamie E. Settle, and James H. Fowler. (2012) "A 61-Million-Person Experiment in Social Influence and Political Mobilization." *Nature* 489: 295–298.

Bonica, Adam. 2014. "Mapping the Ideological Marketplace." *American Journal of Political Science* 58(2): 367–387.

Christakis, Nicholas A. and James H. Fowler. (2007) "The Spread of Obesity in a Large Social Network over 32 Years." *New England Journal of Medicine* 357: 370–379.

Christakis, Nicholas A. and James H. Fowler. (2009) *Connected: The Surprising Power of Our Social Networks and How They Shape Our Lives*. Little, Brown.

Cranmer, Skyler and Bruce A. Desmarais. (2010) "Inferential Network Analysis with Exponential Graph Models." *Political Analysis* 19: 66–86.

Fenno, Richard. 1978. *Home Style: House Members in their Districts*. Little, Brown.

Fowler, James H. (2006) "Legislative Cosponsorship Networks in the U.S House and Senate." *Social Networks* 28(4): 454–465.

Franzese, Robert and Jude Hayes. (2007) "Spatial-Econometric Models of Cross-Sectional Interdependence in Political-Science Panel and Time-Series-Cross-Section Data." *Political Analysis* 15(2): 140–64.

Gailmard, S. and J. W. Patty. (2013) Learning while Governing: Expertise and Accountability in the Executive Branch. Chicago, University of Chicago Press.

Girvan M. and Newman M. E. J. (2002) "Community Structure in Social and Biological Networks." *Proceedings of the National Academy of Sciences* 99: 7821–7826.

Hersh, Eitan and Clayton Nall. (2015) "The Primacy of Race in the Geography of Income-Based Voting: New Evidence from Public Voting Records." *American Journal of Political Science*. Forthcoming.

Holland, P. (1986) "Statistics and Causal Inference." *Journal of the American Statistical Association* 81: 945–970.

Hudges, Michael G. and M. Elizabeth Halloran. (2008) "Towards Causal Inference with Interference." *Journal of the American Statistical Association* 103(482): 832–843.

Katz, Daniel Martin, Joshua R. Gubler, Jon Zelner, Michael J. Bommarito II, Eric Provins, and Eitan Ingall. (2011) "Reproduction of Hierarchy? A Social Network Analysis of the American Law Professoriate." *Journal of Legal Education* 61(1): 1–28.

Krebs, Valdis E. (2002) "Uncloacking Terrorist Networks." *First Monday* 7(4): 1–15.

McClurg, Scott and J. K. Young. (2011) "Political Networks" *PS: Political Science and Politics* 44(01): 39–43.

Milgram, Stanley. (1967) "The Small World Problem." *Psychology Today* 60–67.

Newman, M. E. J. (2004) "Modularity and Community Structure in Networks." *Proceedings of the National Academy of Sciences* 103(23): 8577–8582.

Nickerson, David W. (2008) "Is Voting Contagious? Evidence from Two Field Experiments." *American Political Science Review* 102: 49–57.

Padgett, John F. (1993) "Robust Action and the Rise of the Medici, 1400–1434." *American Journal of Sociology* 98: 1259–1319.

Porter, Mason A., Peter J. Mucha, M. E. J. Newman, and Casey M. Warmbrand. (2005) "A Network Analysis of Committees in the U.S. House of Representatives." *Proceedings of the National Academy of Sciences* 102(20): 7057–7062.

Shalizi, Cosma and Andrew C. Thomas. (2011) "Homophily and Contagion Are Generically Confounded in Observational Social Network Studies." *Sociological Methods and Research* 40: 211–239.

Sinclair, Betsy. (2012) *The Social Citizen: Peer Networks and Political Behavior.* University of Chicago Press.

VanderWeele, T. J. (2011) "Sensitivity Analysis for Contagion Effects in Social Networks." *Sociological Methods and Research*, 40: 240–255.

VanderWeele, T J., E. L. Ogburn, and E. J. Tchetgen. (2012) "Why and When "Flawed" Network Analyses Still Yield Valid Tests of No Contagion." *Statistics, Politics, and Policy* 3: 1–11.

Wasserman, Stanley and Katherine Faust. (1994) *Social Network Analysis: Methods and Applications.* Cambridge University Press.

Zachary, Wayne W. (1977) "An Information Flow Model for Conflict and Fission in Small Groups." *Journal of Anthropological Research* 32(4): 452–473.

5

Ideological Salience in Multiple Dimensions

Peter Foley

Analytics Media Group

People care about different things in politics, and when they are asked a question, each individual may process it differently or call on different memories and ideas when formulating their response. In the political science literature, this heterogeneity is usually described as *salience*: memories, ideas, considerations, or choice features that an individual is likely to apply in his or her decision are considered more salient.

In the universe of spatial ideal point models of ideology, salience takes on a more specific meaning: the weights that people apply to various preference dimensions when making their choices. To the extent that memories and ideas drive people's positions on these dimensions and the likelihood that they will use a particular dimension when making a political choice, the spatial model definition meshes reasonably nicely with the more general definition.

Formal models of voter choice and party strategy capture salience is a very compact and high-level way. Individuals have ideal points in a policy space, they are faced with possible outcomes in the policy space, and their utility of each outcome depends on the salience-weighted distance between their ideal point and the policy of interest. See Hinich and Munger (1997) for a more extensive discussion. Unfortunately, the existing techniques for spatial ideal point estimation are poorly suited to the analysis of survey data, and existing techniques for modeling salience do not operate in the same latent space as salience in formal models.

In applied research on voter choices, salience is almost always related to very specific ideas, considerations, or features of a model. For example, Transue (2007) emphasizes racial identity and examines how that affects issue preferences. Gerber et al. (2010) emphasizes party identity in a field experiment and examines how that influences attitudes. In the related literature on latent moral preferences, Rosenblatt et al. (1989) demonstrate that mortality salience affects how people punish others who violate norms.

140

These applications are extremely specific and do not relate directly to high-level summaries of political ideology. The disconnect is apparent in the conclusion of Transue (2007), where the author attempts to connect the policy-specific findings to more general psychological and political theories. That connection is desirable, because it is much easier for us to think about a few dimensions of ideology, rather than the thousands of possible policy dimensions, but so far, there has been no way to connect observable outcomes to the salience of these dimensions to individuals or groups.

Spatial ideal point estimation procedures almost never allow for individual variation in the underlying space (Clinton et al., 2004; Poole and Rosenthal, 1985; Martin and Quinn, 2002; Peress, 2009), though the study by Lauderdale (2010) is a recent exception that lets legislators vary in their consistency with the latent space as a whole, but not with specific dimensions or along diagonals. Very few estimation methods allow for demographic predictors of ideal points that are extremely important for analyzing voter behavior where we have a limited number of observations per individual and are primarily interested in group-level effects (though see Martin et al., 2011, for a one-dimensional exception).

Other researchers have looked at voter heterogeneity directly, but have taken the latent space as fixed. Rivers (1988) uses voters' self-reported ideology and partisanship and rank-ordered ratings of politicians as inputs and then examines how voters vary in how they appear to weight partisanship versus ideology. The downsides of this analysis are that the salience parameterization requires no interaction between ideology and partisanship, and it does not produce a latent space that is at all comparable to legislative models (which were still in their infancy in 1988); therefore, there is no way to link the results of Rivers (1988) with legislative behavior. More recently, Glasgow (2001) has examined British voter choices among multiple parties given fixed and known ideal points, but allows voter heterogeneity through random coefficients on the impact of social class. As with the examples of salience research described earlier, the heterogeneity is extremely structured and limited.

This chapter attempts to bridge the gap between the estimation of ideal points and ideological space and the estimation of salience in that ideological space. I build on constructions of ideology from the formal literature and also on the ideal point estimation techniques from the legislative and judicial voting literatures to produce an intuitively interpretable and reasonably practical (though computationally intensive) method for simultaneously estimating ideal points and salience with hierarchical predictors from survey data. Unlike the existing ideal point estimation models, I allow the latent space to be "warped" by an individual's salience matrix, and because the focus is on demographic groups rather than specific individuals, I also include hierarchical predictors of both ideal points and salience. Unlike past literature on voter heterogeneity, the model does not require an a priori fixed structure on the latent space or that individual ideal points be known with certainty.

TABLE 5.1. *Model notation*

s	index of the "subject" or person
q	index of a specific question or choice
ϕ_s	s's ideal point in the latent ideological space
y^*_{sq}	s's ideal response on the single-dimensional choice line for question q
y_{sq}	s's actual response or choice on question q, indexed from 1
J_q	the number of possible responses to question q minus 1, which is the number of cutpoints in an ordinal model
ζ_{qj}	the position of the jth cutpoint on the single-dimensional choice line for question q
λ_q	a nonzero vector that maps the ideal points onto question dimensions
A_s	the salience weighting matrix for subject s
ϵ_{sq}	the question-specific random noise used by subject s when answering question q

In the end, the procedure developed here produces group- and individual-level estimates of ideal points and salience that can drop directly into formal models such as those in Hinich and Munger (1997). This allows researchers to finally test some of the models' predictions, and to the extent that the formal models hold, this procedure opens up new empirical avenues for understanding how parties select platforms, decide what to emphasize, choose whom to target, and react to changes in voter preferences.

1 BUILDING UP A STATISTICAL MODEL WITH SALIENCE

The aim of this chapter is to develop a link between formal models of issue salience and measureable data. The primary consideration is minimizing changes required at each end of the link: finding a construction of the statistical model that not only varies as little as possible from standard estimation techniques but also produces parameters that can drop cleanly into formal models.

There is some variation in the notation used for item response theory (IRT) models in political science, so to avoid confusion, Table 5.1 defines the basic IRT notation that I use. In most multidimensional IRT models of political choices, each question has a direction vector λ and a set of cutpoints ζ, and each individual has an ideal point ϕ. The ordinal answers are given by y, and a linear latent term is given by y^*. The basic decision process follows like this[1]:

$$y^* = \phi\lambda + \epsilon, \qquad\qquad \epsilon \sim \text{Normal}(0,1) \qquad (1)$$

$$\text{or equivalently} \quad y^* = \left(\phi + \frac{\epsilon}{\|\lambda\|}\right)\lambda, \qquad \epsilon \sim \text{MVN}(0, I) \qquad (2)$$

$$\text{and then} \quad y = 1 + \sum_j \{y^* < \zeta_j\} \qquad (3)$$

The equivalence of steps 1 and 2 is shown in more detail in Appendix A.1. The intuition behind this model is that a low-dimensional ideological space summarizes basic patterns of policy preferences in the population. A particular individual has an ideal "summary" policy bundle represented by a point in this low-dimensional space. Their answers to particular question are based on their summary policy plus some question-specific variation that is not captured by the summary policy.

Note that in this construction, everyone employs the same summary space when considering policies, and question-specific variation is highly constrained – independent and homoskedastic – and those constraints may not reasonably capture political thought.

1.1 Linking IRT and Formal Models

The most basic formal models that employ spatial voter preferences treat ideal points as common knowledge, use a common policy space shared by everyone, and treat the voter choices as perfect optimizations based on Euclidean distance in the policy space – meaning that voters have discrete or intentionally mixed strategies, but they do not have any random noise added in to their decisions.

Policy Space

Importantly, the "common policy space" in the formal models is predefined. There is no uncertainty in the spatial parameters. In the statistical domain, this corresponds to confirmatory factor analyses that define a few policy dimensions, assign questions to each dimension, and then try to fit ideal points and other parameters into the predefined space. However, the assignment of policy dimensions is always somewhat ad hoc (or it would be exploratory factor analysis) and subject to biases on the part of the analyst.

Because there is generally too little information available to preassign the policy dimensions to questions, the legislative and judicial voting literatures have tended toward exploratory models that do not constrain the policy space more than needed for statistical identification. I view this as a wise choice, and so the linkage between formal and statistical models I develop here is based more on exploratory and less on confirmatory factor analyses.

Hyperplanes versus Outcome Positions

The next hurdle to be addressed is the nature of voter choices. Formal models of voter choice usually define options as outcome positions in policy space, and voters want to obtain the policy outcome closest to their ideal point.

Formally, those models define outcomes v_{qj} that fall along a line defined by vectors α_q^v and λ_q, with $\alpha_q^v \cdot \lambda_q = 0$ and positions on that line defined by scalars γ_{qj}^v:

$$j \in \{1, \ldots, J_q + 1\} \tag{4}$$

$$v_{qj} = \alpha_q^v + \lambda_q \gamma_{qj}^v \tag{5}$$

$$y = \underset{j \in \{1, \ldots, J_q + 1\}}{\arg \min} (x_{sq} - v_{qj})^{\mathsf{T}} (x_s - v_{qj}) \tag{6}$$

IRT models, in contrast, use hyperplanes to split the space into groups with different question-specific preferences $x_{sq} = \phi_s + \frac{\epsilon_{sq}}{\|\lambda_s\|}$. These formulations can be observationally equivalent for binary and ordinal choices with up to four options – meaning that given a set of hyperplanes, we can construct policy outcomes such that the voters between two hyperplanes are closer to the corresponding outcome position than to any other outcome position.

When the number of choices is five or higher – meaning there are four or more hyperplanes – it is possible to have hyperplanes that split the cloud of voter preferences in ways that are impossible to obtain from outcome positions alone.[2] We can, however, represent a model that uses ordered outcome positions with a hyperplane construction by constructing hyperplanes perpendicular to the line of outcome positions that intersect the line at the midpoints between neighboring outcomes.

Thus, any data that can be represented by outcome positions can be represented equally well, if not better, by hyperplanes, and so I use a hyperplane representation in the modeling. To the extent that the model's fitted parameters can be represented by outcome positions, if we want to analyze questions in terms of their outcome positions, it is possible to translate fitted hyperplanes into a set of policy outcomes for each question. So when the policy outcome construction is reasonable in light of observed data, we can calculate the outcome positions, but when the data is inconsistent with outcome points, the model is not constrained.

Before moving on, I should note that with choice-specific utility noise, it is possible to represent any set of hyperplanes, but that nearly doubles the degrees of freedom per choice and greatly complicates identification. Such a setup might be useful in ex-post conversion from hyperplanes to ideal points, but it is not helpful within the model itself.

Noise Parameterization

Formal models usually ignore, random variation in voter choices, or that variation usually enters as outcome-specific biases that behave like the noise term in multinomial logit. In binary and ordinal IRT models, noise enters the voter choice as a bias on the question-specific latent term (y^* in this chapter's notation). In the MNL-style formal models, if we hold all other parameters fixed, increasing the amount of noise in the model will shift all outcome probabilities monotonically toward a uniform distribution. In ordinal probit models used in IRT, extremely high levels of noise will shift the outcome probabilities toward the extreme values and away from middle options, but at moderate levels of noise, the impact on outcome probabilities is non-monotonic. As noise variance increases, nearby interior options can rise in probability at first, but then fall as the variance increases enough to shift all the probability toward the extreme options.

In the models developed here, I base the noise parameterization on a traditional ordinal IRT construction and only modify when necessary to introduce salience into the model. This is the standard method used in the limited literature on political ideal point estimation with ordinal data, but there is no principled reason to assume that the IRT construction of noise is superior to MNL-style biases. Optimal noise parameterization is an empirical question that merits further research, but it is outside the scope of this chapter, and so I stick to the standard, though possibly imperfect, parameterization.

1.2 Adding in Salience

In formal models that use outcome policy positions, salience enters in the distance calculation. For a positive definite salience matrix A_s, ideal point ϕ_s, and policy outcomes $v_1, \ldots, v_{J_q}$, we just make a slight tweak to Equation 6:

$$v_{qj} = \alpha_q^v + \lambda_q \gamma_{qj}^v$$

$$y = \underset{j \in \{1, \ldots, J_q+1\}}{\arg\min} \ (x_s - v_{qj})^\mathsf{T} A_s (x_s - v_{qj}) \tag{7}$$

As we have discussed, when $A = I$, the parameterization in terms of outcome policies v is a constrained version of a hyperplane model. We do not want to force those constraints just so that we can model salience, so we must instead find a parameterization of salience that works in the hyperplane representation. To do this, I first parameterize 7 in terms of hyperplanes and then see what adjustments (if any) need to be made so that the hyperplane version can be unconstrained.

Let us look at the simplest case for optimization. We have two outcomes points, v_1 and v_2, and we want to find the hyperplane that splits the space of x_s according to their optimal outcome. For simplicity, I drop some constant subscripts in this derivation. The values on the hyperplane z satisfy

$$(z - v_1)^\mathsf{T} A(z - v_1) = (z - v_2)^\mathsf{T} A(z - v_2), \tag{8}$$

and since A is positive definite, we can find a square root matrix with the same eigenvectors using an eigendecomposition:

$$A = Q \Lambda Q^\mathsf{T} \tag{9}$$

$$B = Q \Lambda^{1/2} Q^\mathsf{T} \tag{10}$$

where Q is an orthonormal matrix, Λ is a diagonal matrix of positive eigenvalues, and $\Lambda^{1/2}$ is a diagonal matrix of the square roots of the eigenvalues.[3] Then B is positive definite and has the property that

$$A = B^\mathsf{T} B = B B^\mathsf{T}. \tag{11}$$

We substitute $B^\mathsf{T} B$ for A in equation 8 to get

$$(z - v_1)^\mathsf{T} B^\mathsf{T} B(z - v_1) = (z - v_2)^\mathsf{T} B^\mathsf{T} B(z - v_2) \tag{12}$$

$$(Bz - Bv_1)^\mathsf{T} (Bz - Bv_1) = (Bz - Bv_2)^\mathsf{T} (Bz - Bv_2), \tag{13}$$

which is straightforward to solve in terms of Bz:

$$Bz = \frac{Bv_1 + Bv_2}{2} + C \tag{14}$$

where

$$C \cdot (Bv_1 - Bv_2) = 0. \tag{15}$$

Since $v_1 - v_2$ is proportional to λ as defined in Equation 5, $(Bv_1 - Bv_2)$ is proportional to $B\lambda$, and so the hyperplanes must be of the form

$$z^\mathsf{T} B\lambda = \text{constant}. \tag{16}$$

To find the constant, all we have to do is calculate the value under the z for which $C = 0$ in Equation 14, which I denote by z^0:

$$z^0 = B^{-1}\left(\frac{Bv_1 + Bv_2}{2}\right) \tag{17}$$

$$= \frac{v_1 + v_2}{2}, \tag{18}$$

and we can then punch in z^0 to solve for the constant in 16:

$$(z^0)^\mathsf{T} B\lambda = \left(\frac{v_1 + v_2}{2}\right)^\mathsf{T} B\lambda \tag{19}$$

$$= \left(\frac{\alpha + \lambda\gamma_1 + \alpha + \lambda\gamma_2}{2}\right)^\mathsf{T} B\lambda \tag{20}$$

$$= \left(\alpha + \lambda\frac{\gamma_1 + \gamma_2}{2}\right)^\mathsf{T} B\lambda. \tag{21}$$

Note that the α term cannot be reduced away; while $\alpha^\mathsf{T}\lambda = 0$ by definition, it is not generally true that $\alpha^\mathsf{T} B\lambda = 0$. And since the B terms vary between individuals, the "constant" on the right-hand side is not the same for each individual.

This highlights the fact that nonuniform salience removes the "perpendicular shift invariance" property described in Appendix A.2. That means that, except for any parameters that determine A_s itself, we double the number of parameters associated with each question. Now rather than just having a direction, each question has a direction and an origin.

But we can simplify this slightly. $(\alpha + \lambda\frac{\gamma_1 + \gamma_2}{2})$ can just be written as $(\alpha + \lambda * \eta_j)$ with scalar η for each cutpoint (which is now a point in latent space, rather than a point on the real line). Much like the outcome points, these cutpoints fall on a line in the latent space, but the cutpoint construction again offers more flexibility in the positioning of slicing hyperplanes just as they did in the version without salience.

The final task is to translate back from hyperplanes into a model structure like equations 2 and 3:

$$y_{sq}^* = \left(\phi_s + \frac{\epsilon_{sq}}{\|\lambda\|}\right) B_s \lambda_q, \qquad \epsilon_{sq} \sim \text{MVN}(0, I) \qquad (22)$$

$$\text{and then} \quad y_{sq} = 1 + \sum_j \left\{ y_{sq}^* < (\alpha_q + \lambda_q * \eta_{qj})^\top B_s \lambda_q \right\} \qquad (23)$$

1.3 Noise Parameterization

Most IRT models assume homoskedastic latent errors, but the salience construction described earlier introduces structured heteroskedasticity that needs to be examined before we move forward. Equation 22 can be rewritten as

$$y_{sq}^* = \phi_s B_s \lambda_q + \frac{\epsilon_{sq} B_s \lambda_q}{\|\lambda\|}, \qquad \epsilon_{sq} \sim \text{MVN}(0, I), \qquad (24)$$

and then the noise term is distributed as

$$\frac{\epsilon_{sq} B_s \lambda_q}{\|\lambda\|} \sim \text{Normal}\left(0, \frac{\lambda^\top B_s^\top B_s \lambda}{\|\lambda\|^2}\right) \qquad (25)$$

$$\sim \text{Normal}\left(0, \frac{\lambda^\top A_s \lambda}{\|\lambda\|^2}\right), \qquad (26)$$

and the cutpoint transformation can be expanded similarly:

$$(\alpha_q + \lambda_q * \eta_{qj})^\top B_s \lambda_q = \underbrace{\alpha_q B_s \lambda_q}_{\text{shift}} + \underbrace{\lambda_q^\top B \lambda_q}_{\text{scaling}} \eta_{qj}. \qquad (27)$$

We want to compare the scaling term in Equation 27 with the variance in 26, both of which are scalars. In the simplest case, where A_s is the identity matrix, the variance in 26 equals 1, and the scaling term in 27 is equal to $\|\lambda\|^2$. As we move away from $A_s = I$, the variance of the noise in 26 increases proportionally with the A_s-weighted length of λ_q. The scale term increases proportionally to the B_s-weighted length of λ_q. Even though the eigenvectors of A_s and B_s are the same by construction, there is not a simple linear relationship between $\lambda_q^\top A \lambda_q$ and $\lambda_q^\top B \lambda_q$.

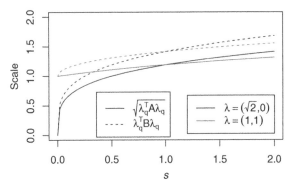

FIGURE 5.1. Changes in error standard deviation and cutpoint scaling terms as the salience matrix moves away from the identity matrix.

To illustrate this, examine a simple two-dimensional case with

$$A = \begin{pmatrix} s & 0 \\ 0 & 1 \end{pmatrix} \qquad B = \begin{pmatrix} \sqrt{s} & 0 \\ 0 & 1 \end{pmatrix}$$

$$\lambda_1 = \begin{pmatrix} 1 \\ 1 \end{pmatrix} \qquad \lambda_2 = \begin{pmatrix} 1 \\ 0 \end{pmatrix} \qquad \lambda_3 = \begin{pmatrix} 0 \\ 1 \end{pmatrix}$$

where s is an extra term to illustrate what happens as A moves away from I. As s increases, the scaling terms $\lambda_q^\mathsf{T} A \lambda_q$ and $\lambda_q^\mathsf{T} B \lambda_q$ vary as shown in Figures 5.1 and 5.2.

To a very rough approximation, increases in salience in the direction of or perpendicular to λ_q do not have a large impact on the noise in the question-specific ordinal model. When λ is in between parallel and perpendicular to the salience changes, movement away from I acts like a very slight increase in the noise of the question-specific ordinal model, but the effect is only apparent

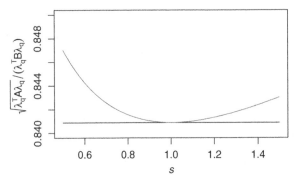

FIGURE 5.2. Change in ratio of error standard deviation to cutpoint scaling terms as the salience matrix moves away from the identity matrix.

at rather extreme salience weights. That does not mean that salience has no impact on the model, but just that its primary effect will often be through the shift term in Equation 27.

If additional flexibility is desired in the model, a natural place to add it is in this noise parameterization term – although the parameterization in this chapter does not substantially vary the ordinal model's noise term, we might want it to. For example, if we think that people near extremes on particular dimensions would collect more information relating policies to those dimensions, then they might have very clear opinions on policy questions that lie on their 'favorite' dimension and would have lower noise in their question-specific ordinal model. That sort of extension is left for future work, however, and this chapter focuses on developing the basic model.

1.4 Hierarchical Modeling of Salience Matrices

With a relatively small number of noisy observations per individual, non-hierarchical estimates of ideal points can be quite noisy, and individual-level estimates of salience are even more disconnected from actual observable data. Furthermore, since we are more interested in group-level and population-level variation than in the positions of specific survey repspondents, we need a hierarchical structure to determine what patterns of salience exist in the population as a whole.

Unfortunately, there are no directly applicable models for us to use here. Other fields that use hierarchical models of positive definite matrices usually focus on shrinking submatrices toward a shared "parent" matrix or a particular global structure. Here our problem is different: we want to use a set of continuous variables to predict an individual's salience matrix, but we do not have a nested structure to our data or other parent matrix that might apply. So, we need to design our own modeling technique for positive definite matrices.

The first place to start is in determining what properties we need from a hierarchical model of salience matrices:

- Salience matrices should be positive definite.
- Reordering demographic predictors should have no impact on the resulting salience matrices.
- Removing a demographic predictor from the model should have the same impact as having a "zero" parameter for that predictor, where zero remains to be defined.
- Demographic predictors should not have an impact on the same set of eigenvectors, and so forth.
- Demographic predictors should be able to increase or decrease salience in any direction.

Order invariance is a particularly difficult property to obtain because very few operations on matrices are commutative. Matrix addition does commute, but the sum of positive definite salience matrices has strictly greater salience on all dimensions than any of its components, and so simple addition of matrices will not let demographic predictors decrease salience on a specific dimension. Yet order invariance is one of the most important elements of this model. Without it, we have no simple way of interpreting the results, because the interpretation of each demographic's effects depends on the effects of all the other demographics in the model and the sequence in which they are included in the model. It also greatly complicates the construction of priors because priors that are reasonable when only one demographic is included in the model may have very different meanings when other demographics are added.

For example, one naive approach to combining positive definite matrices is to simply multiply them. Here, that means we would construct positive definite matrices for the effect of each demographic on each individual and multiply all of an individual's matrices to obtain the final salience matrix. Unfortunately, if the eigenvectors of all of these matrices are not identical, the second and later demographic variables are effectively operating on a rotated version of the ideal point space, rather than simply a scaled one. At the extreme, if the demographic matrices have multiplied together to rotate the space significantly, a demographic that appears to increase salience on one axis – for example, a diagonal matrix with a value of 2 at $(1, 1)$ and 1 on the rest – may actually be increasing the salience of a completely different axis.

The order invariance, eigenvector variation, increase/decrease, and zero parameter properties are all simple to satisfy if we can just operate on the space of real symmetric matrices rather than positive definite ones. If we can aggregate the demographic effects in a symmetric matrix space and transform that into a space of positive definite matrices, then we can satisfy all the desired properties fairly easily.

Conveniently for us, the eigendecomposition-based matrix exponential gives a straightforward transformation from real symmetric matrices to positive definite ones. The transforms (Equation 28) give an straightforward and almost one-to-one mapping between the space of real square matrices and positive definite matrices.[4] B is a positive definite matrix, and E is its counterpart in the space of symmetric matrices.

$$A = Q\exp(\Lambda)Q^{\mathsf{T}}$$
$$E = Q\Lambda Q^{\mathsf{T}}$$
(28)

where Λ is a diagonal matrix and $[\exp(\Lambda)]_{ij} = \exp(\Lambda_{ij})$.

This gives a natural way to aggregate the effects of different demographic variables. Each individual's E can simply be a sum of demographic matrices weighted by the individual's demographic parameters: weighted sums of matrices have a natural zero term (the zero matrix), they are commutative, and they do not require that the component matrices share eigenvectors.

So, given a length-v vector of demographic covariates Z_s, we can use the exponential transformation to construct their salience matrix as follows. First we draw their individual-specific noise according to some distribution over symmetric matrices:

$$\tilde{E}_s \sim F. \tag{29}$$

Then we calculate a weighted sum of the $k \times k$ demographic parameter matrices plus the individual-specific noise:

$$E_s = \tilde{E}_s + \sum_v Z_{sv} \cdot E_s^v \tag{30}$$

take its eigendecomposition so that we can construct a square root matrix with the same eigenvectors

$$E_s = Q_s \Lambda_s Q_s^\mathsf{T}, \tag{31}$$

and finally calculate the salience matrix and its square root:

$$A_s = Q_s \exp(\Lambda_s) Q_s^\mathsf{T} \tag{32}$$

$$B_s = Q_s \exp\left(\tfrac{1}{2}\Lambda_s\right) Q_s^\mathsf{T}. \tag{33}$$

1.5 Identification of Salience Matrices

Once the scale, rotation, and reflection of the latent space are identified by any of numerous standard methods (see Rivers (2003) for a summary of options), all that remains for identification is to ensure that the scale of salience in each dimension is standardized.

In particular, multiplication of all A_s matrices by a positive definite matrix can be counteracted by appropriate shifts in that λ and η terms, so we need to pin down its scale. One way to do this is to pin down the mean of all the E_s terms, which is easy to do by centering the matrix of hierarchical predictors Z and ensuring that Z does not include a column of constants. To aid in interpretation, it is also helpful to scale the columns of Z to unit variance, though this is not absolutely necessary.

2 FINAL MODEL SPECIFICATION

In this chapter, I have discussed a variety of modeling options, but for clarity, I write everything down in one place here. The model uses only two latent dimensions of ideology.

$$y_{sq}^* = \phi_s B_s \lambda_q + \epsilon_{sq}, \qquad \epsilon_{sq} \sim \text{Logistic}(0,1) \tag{34}$$

$$y_{sq} = 1 + \sum_j \left\{ y_{sq}^* < (\alpha_q + \lambda_q * \eta_{qj})^\mathsf{T} B_s \lambda_q \right\} \tag{35}$$

$$\phi_s \sim \text{MVN}(Z\beta^\phi, I) \tag{36}$$

$$B_s = Q_s \exp(\Lambda_s) Q_s^\mathsf{T} \tag{37}$$

$$Q_s \Lambda_s Q_s^\mathsf{T} = E_s \tag{38}$$

with demographic predictors on the E_s terms

$$E_s = \sum_v (Z_{sv} D^v) + \tilde{E}_s, \tag{39}$$

with the following weakly informative priors. Note that $\tilde{E}_s$ and D^v are constrained to be symmetric, so the priors apply to only the upper triangle, and the subdiagonal terms are constrained to the transpose of the superdiagonal terms:

$$(\tilde{E}_s)_{ij} \sim \text{Normal}(0, \sigma^h) \tag{40}$$

$$D_{ij}^v \sim \text{Normal}(0, \sigma^d) \tag{41}$$

$$\lambda_q \sim \text{MVN}(0, \sigma^\lambda I) \tag{42}$$

$$\alpha_q \sim \text{MVN}(0, \sigma^\alpha I). \tag{43}$$

The main alteration from this discussion is that an ordinal logit model is used for the final stage, rather than ordinal probit. This is done to take advantage of efficient ordinal logit code in Stan that does not have an ordinal probit counterpart. However, ordinal logit and probit are rarely very different in practice, so the change is unlikely to be substantively important.

The normal priors over each term in the matrices $\tilde{E}_s$ and D^v are admittedly somewhat ad hoc, but there is no literature on the distributions of logs of covariance matrices. In principle, I could have put a Wishart prior on $\exp(\tilde{E}_s)$ and $\exp(D^v)$, but that would have added an additional $n + k$ eigendecomposition to the likelihood calculation, which would significantly slow an already computationally demanding model.[5]

For $\sigma = 1$ and 2 dimensions, the priors on $\tilde{E}_s$ and D^v produces matrices that, when exponentiated, qualitatively approximate an inverse Wishart distribution with an identity scale matrix and 3 degrees of freedom, which is a fairly common choice of prior over positive definite matrices. Smaller values of σ shrink the resulting $\exp(\tilde{E}_s)$ and $\exp(D^v)$ toward the identity matrix.

3 APPLICATION

I apply this model to a subset of the common content from the 2010 Cooperative Congressional Election Survey (CCES). The CCES is an Internet survey composed of a number of "team" modules from various universities and groups, plus a core set of common questions asked to all respondents. The survey is administered by Polimetrix on a representative sample of U.S. voters. The full common content file has more than 50,000 respondents, but I use a sample of 1,000 respondents from California (CA). I do this for two reasons: the full sample is too large for efficient computation (the CA sample takes about a day to run, even with Hamiltonian Monte Carlo), and so long as the data must be subsampled, it is helpful for interpretation to have a relatively coherent political environment across the sample. California has distinct regional politics, but there is much less variation than across the United States as a whole.

The model is estimated in Stan (Stan Development Team, 2013a,b) from R 2.15.3 (R Core Team, 2012). Stan samples from the posterior using Hamiltonian Monte Carlo, which speeds the estimation of this particular model by an order of magnitude, and it includes functionality for calculating the eigendecompositions used in this model.

4 RESULTS

I ran two models: one without variable salience, and a second with salience included in the model. The first model gives a baseline for comparing how introducing salience changes the demographic effects on ideal points and the factor loadings of survey questions.

4.1 Model without Salience

For the first model, I alter the specification from Section 2 to fix all the B_s terms to the identity matrix. This turns it into a simple ordinal IRT model with hierarchical predictors of ideal points.

The model was run in Stan with an iterative tuning procedure to get close to the posterior mode before tuning the Hamiltonian Monte Carlo parameters for the final sampling run. I ran 4 chains starting near the posterior mode for 50 tuning iterations followed by 100 sample draws, for a total of 400 points in the posterior.

Because the purpose of this model is to serve as a baseline for comparison with the salience model, I do not deeply analyze the parameter estimates. Instead I highlight a few features that will be important for comparison.

The factor loadings in Figure 5.4 show that most of the questions in the survey loaded primarily on the first latent dimension (the dimensions were rotated so that P1 had the most variation in loadings). There is still a good amount of spread along P2, though none of the questions loaded on P2 exclusively. The

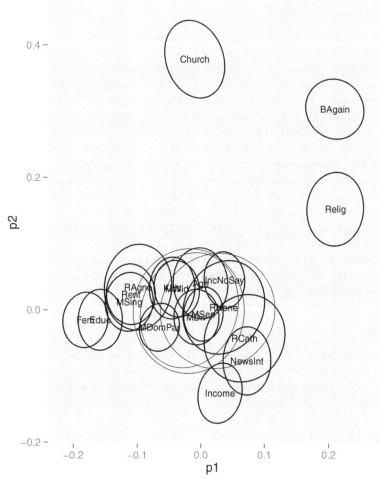

FIGURE 5.3. Effects of demographic parameters on political ideal points in model with uniform salience. Ellipses are the 40% confidence ellipse for the effect estimates (roughly comparable to 1 standard deviation).

dimensions are scaled by individual-level variation in ideal points, so this scaling occurs partly because the ideal points along P2 had more individual-specific variation relative to the demographic effects.

The weak demographic effects on P2 are somewhat visible in Figure 5.3, where many of the demographic effects lie close to 0 on the P2 dimension. There are exceptions, particularly for Church, Income, BAgain, and Relig. These four variables, along with Fem, MSing, and Educ, are discussed in more detail later. The lack of questions along P2 makes estimation of ideal points

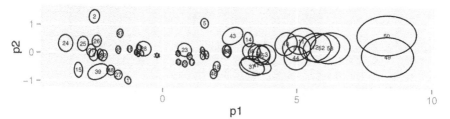

FIGURE 5.4. Loadings of the questions on each political dimension in the model with uniform salience. Ellipses are the 40% confidence ellipse for the effect estimates (roughly comparable to 1 standard deviation).

noiser along P2, as the confidence ellipse shown in Figure 5.5 demonstrates. The uncertainty on P2 is much greater than on P1, so the confidence ellipse is stretched vertically.

4.2 Model with Salience

The salience model was also run in Stan with an iterative tuning procedure to get close to the posterior mode before tuning the Hamiltonian Monte Carlo parameters for the final sampling run. I ran 4 chains starting near the posterior mode for 50 tuning iterations followed by 100 sample draws, for a total of 400 points in the posterior.

The salience model has somewhat different question loadings (Figure 5.7) than the uniform model. The handful of highly predictable questions high on the P1 scale are bent downward somewhat to load on the P2 scale as well, though the ratio in this tail is still around 5:1 loading on P1:P2. Most of the other questions are in generally similar positions. There are a few loadings that shift around, particularly in questions such as 24, 39, and 15 that had noisy salience estimates, but the overall picture is very similar aside from the bend at the high end of P1.

The parameter estimates (Figure 5.6) are also generally similar to those for the uniform model (Figure 5.7) – variables shift a bit, but none are switching directions or moving wildly. BAgain and Relig shift a bit to the right on P1, and MSing shifts slightly to the left, but there is very little other variation on P1. On P2, BAgain and Relig both become even more positive, whereas Church moves toward 0 and Income becomes slightly more negative.

In terms of individual point estimates (Figure 5.8), the uncertainty on P1 is similar to before, whereas the uncertainty on P2 decreases slightly. The figure overstates the decrease slightly, however, because the variation in the mean P2 estimates increases as noise decreases, and so the scale of the P2 axis in Figure 5.7 is slightly expanded from that in Figure 5.4. The decrease is still there, but is just not quite so large as the figure makes it appear.

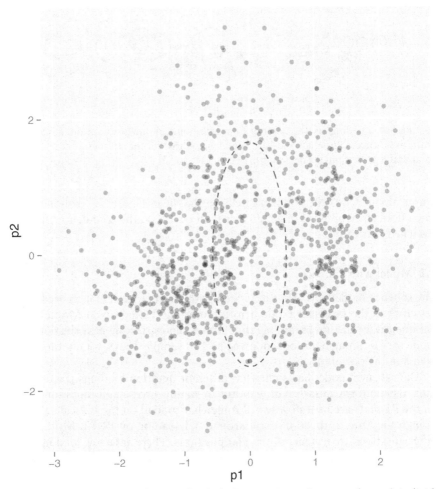

FIGURE 5.5. Distribution of a sample of ideal points (posterior mean for each individual) from the model with uniform salience. The dotted ellipse is a 95% credible ellipse for a representative individual at the origin.

Now that we have seen that the changes to the latent space are relatively mild – demographic effects and question loadings are not wildly different from the previous model – we can move into the meat of the salience model: the demographic effects on salience, examples of individual salience ellipses and noise, and fitted indifference curves for individuals.

I visualize salience ellipses using level curves for a multivariate normal distribution with the salience matrix included as its covariance term. When an ellipse is stretched in one direction, the individual or group is affected more by

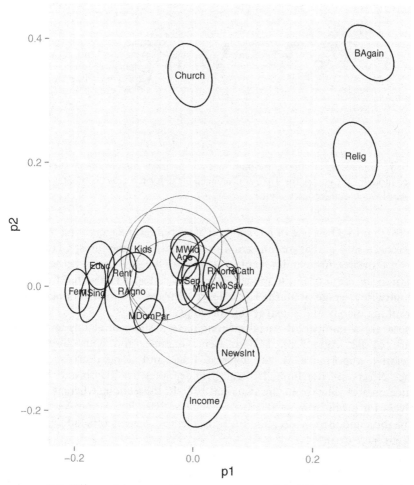

FIGURE 5.6. Effects of demographic parameters on political ideal points in the variable salience model. Ellipses are the 40% confidence ellipse for the effect estimates (roughly comparable to 1 standard deviation).

variation along that direction, and when the ellipse is compressed in a direction, they do not care as much about that variation. I find this more intuitive than the usual visualization of centered indifference curves, though indifference curves are helpful when also visualizing individuals' ideal points.

The demographic effects are each small on their own, but they build on each other to produce a substantial amount of variation in individual salience estimates. For visualization, I look at the effects of having values of 10 on each (centered and scaled) demographic variable and 0 on all other variables and

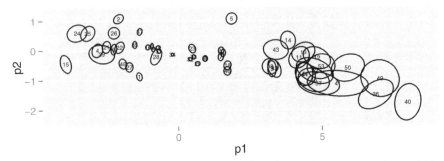

FIGURE 5.7. Loadings of the questions on each political dimension in the variable salience model. Ellipses are the 40% confidence ellipse for the effect estimates (roughly comparable to 1 standard deviation).

compare that to a baseline of having 0 on all variables. Exaggerating the effect by 10 is necessary so that we can actually see variation in the ellipses. Figure 5.9 shows the mean ellipse and a sample of drawn ellipses to get a sense for the estimation uncertainty in the model. The mean ellipse is calculated by taking the pointwise average of all the log salience matrices and then exponentiating the resulting matrix and constructing the ellipse.

There are a number of variables that have a substantial impact on the salience of P2. Age, Fem, MWid, Rent, Income, and Kids all increase the relative importance of P2, whereas Educ and Relig decrease it. The salience effects are not limited to the primary axes, so RCath and RaceNo produce greater salience in the diagonal (P2−P1) direction, whereas BAgain and NewsInt produce more relative salience on (P1+P2). Some factors such as education and income decrease overall salience, whereas others like BAgain and Rent increase it.

The salience estimates are closely related to the demographic effects on ideal points. BAgain increases salience in a roughly (P1+P2) direction, and the BAgain ideal point effect is shifted out along this axis in the salience model compared to the uniform model. Salience affects how parameters move between the uniform and salience models, but it is not strictly connected to the actual parameters.

One of the more interesting effects of salience occurs when the ideal point parameter and axes of the salience ellipse are roughly 45°. In party strategy models, this allows a candidate to capture more of a certain group by moving perpendicularly to the group's ideal point. We see roughly this pattern for Relig. Relig shifts ideal points in a (P1+P2) direction, but it increases salience only along P1. So more religious people are in the upper right of the latent space, but care about movement along P1. A candidate at the origin could then boost support among religious people by shifting slightly *downward* to the right, which is closer along P1, but not closer in the latent space overall.

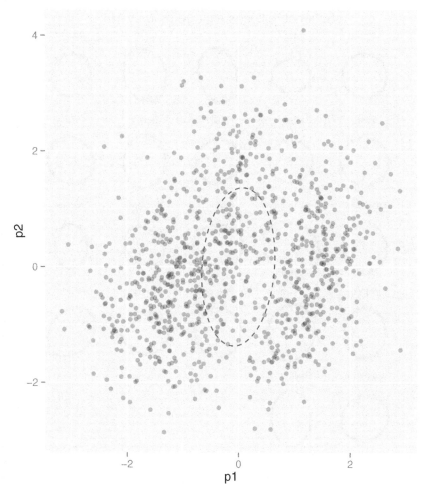

FIGURE 5.8. Distribution of a sample of ideal points (posterior mean for each individual) from the variable salience model. The dotted ellipse is a 95% credible ellipse for a representative individual at the origin.

Similar effects can occur on cross-terms – for example, between RCath and Fem – where the salience impact of RCath and the ideal point impact of Fem are neither parallel nor perpendicular. A campaign trying to target religious voters might want to tune its messages differently for males and females, because religious males and females can be swayed by different shifts. This is a huge simplification, because there are many other variables to consider, but it shows the utility of modeling salience at a group level.

In terms of individual estimates, the model produces noisy but moderately informative posteriors on the individual-specific salience noise. The thick

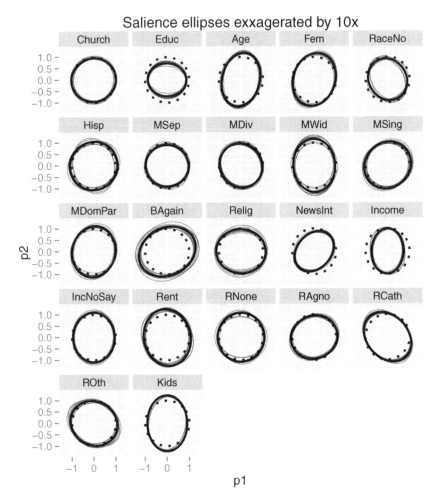

FIGURE 5.9. Salience ellipses for individuals with a value of 10 on each of the variables and 0 on all other demographics. The demographic variables are scaled to mean 0 and variance 1, so this extreme value is unrealistic and just helps with visualization. The dotted unit circle provides a "no effect" reference.

ellipses in Figure 5.11 for ellipses drawn for a single individual are tighter together than the thin black ellipses for a sample across individuals. Some of this is because the thick ellipses include demographic information about the individual, whereas the black ones are drawn from across the population. However, when we strip away demographic effects and look just at an individual's noise term (Figure 5.10, for a different individual), the thick ellipses are still tighter together than the black ones, and so we can estimate individual-specific variation in this model, albeit noisily.

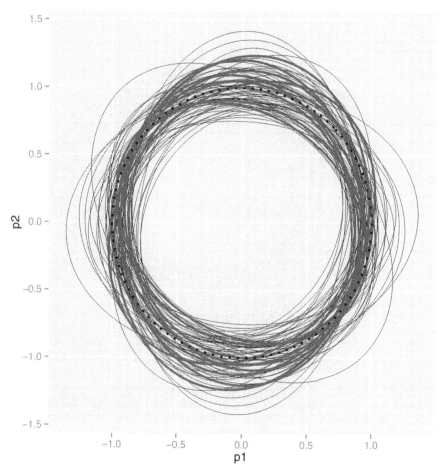

FIGURE 5.10. Example of individual-specific salience noise for a sample of individuals (thin) and multiple draws from a single individual (thick). The dotted unit circle provides a "no effect" reference.

Finally, to visualize how salience actually affects the ideal points and indifference curves of voters, Figure 5.12 displays a sample of mean ideal points and mean indifference curves: level curves for a multivariate normal distribution centered at the ideal point with covariance equal to the inverse of the salience matrix. The key result is that we see a substantial amount of variation in the salience across the population. Some of the ellipses are much larger than others, some are nearly circular while others are highly stretched, and throughout the distribution of ideal points, we see variation in salience. Individuals who have similar ideal points may still behave quite differently as a result of their salience differences.

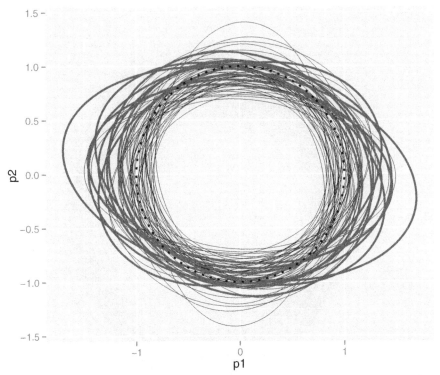

FIGURE 5.11. Example of individual salience ellipses (combination of demographic factors and individual variation) for a sample of individuals (thin), and multiple draws from a single individual (thick). The dotted unit circle provides a "no effect" reference.

5 CONCLUSIONS

The technique developed here offers a way to simultaneously estimate ideal points and salience on multiple dimensions from the types of survey data that we commonly have in political science, and in doing so, it opens up a new set of modeling options for researchers, particularly those doing experimental work related to political ideology.

Estimates of ideal points and salience can be input directly into formal models to understand where political parties should be moving in order to maximize votes, or the demographic parameters can be used to simulate possible distributions of ideal points and salience independent of the peculiarities of the survey sample used for estimation. This method provides the necessary inputs for actually testing formal models of party strategy under heterogeneous salience and, if the models survive the test, for making new predictions of party and voter behavior.

Thanks to the hierarchical design, researchers can include treatment variables in the model and estimate their impact on broad ideological dimensions

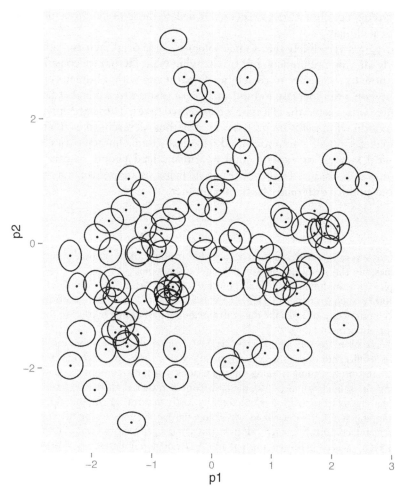

FIGURE 5.12. Mean ideal points and indifference curves for a sample of individuals from the variable salience model.

rather than examining single issues in isolation or constructing ad hoc scales that vary from paper to paper and lab to lab. They can examine how treatments change salience over broad dimensions such as social or economic policies as a whole, rather than just looking at how direct manipulations on a specific dimension change specific outcomes.

In the world of political campaigns, changing *how* a voter thinks about an issue is sometimes easier than changing *what* he or she thinks about it – adjusting salience is easier than shifting an ideal point – and this method provides a way for campaigns and parties to test how their messages are affecting not only preferences but also how people translate those preferences into specific political choices.

Similarly, it is very likely that some biological and social factors operate by not directly altering preferences, but by changing what factors we consider: for example, how likely we are to remember empathizing with a homeless person when voting on a tax increase to fund shelters or instead to remember how the city's money was wasted the last time we increased taxes. Those are impacts on salience, not direct impacts on preferences, and thus hierarchical estimation of salience makes it possible to understand what individual characteristics, genes, physiological factors, or experimental treatments lead people to care about certain issue dimensions. In looser terms, it helps us figure out why people think about politics differently from one another.

Notes

1. There are several other decision processes that produce observationally equivalent outcomes, but this notation will simplify later discussions.
2. Example: with unidimensional space, put cutpoints at -1.1, -1, 1, and 1.1. There is no point ζ such that $\|\zeta - (-1)\| < 0.1$ and $\|\zeta - 1\| < 0.1$, so there is no way that distance minimization can make the central region wide enough relative to the width of the neighboring regions.
3. A more common "matrix square root" is the Cholesky decomposition, but it is not positive definite, nor does it preserve eigenvalues, so it can rotate and skew the space rather than simply scaling it along set dimensions. Also, the computations involved in fitting the model primarily calculate A from B rather than the reverse, so this particular eigendecomposition is not actually costly in terms of computation.
4. The mapping is one to one whenever B has unique eigenvalues or the computational eigendecomposition method gives the same eigenvectors for $Q\Lambda Q^{-1}$ as for $Q\exp(\Lambda)Q^{-1}$ where Q is orthonormal and Λ is a diagonal matrix.
5. Another option would be to separate the priors over the correlation and marginal variance components of the covariance matrices, which could allow the scale of the demographic's effects on salience to vary more while keeping the correlation components constrained. That method offers more flexibility, but unfortunately still requires an additional layer of $n + k$ eigendecompositions to calculate the matrix logs needed by the likelihood calculation.

References

J. Clinton, S. Jackman, and D. Rivers. The Statistical Analysis of Roll Call Data. *American Political Science Review*, 98(2):355–370, 2004.

A. S. Gerber, G. A. Huber, and E. Washington. Party Affiliation, Partisanship, and Political Beliefs: A Field Experiment. *American Political Science Review*, 104(4):720–744, 2010.

G. Glasgow. Mixed Logit Models for Multiparty Elections. *Political Analysis*, 9(1):116–136, 2001.

M. J. Hinich and M. C. Munger. *Analytical Politics*. Cambridge University Press, 1997.

B. E. Lauderdale. Unpredictable Voters in Ideal Point Estimation. *Political Analysis*, 18(2):151–171, 2010.

A. Martin and K. Quinn. Dynamic Ideal Point Estimation via Markov Chain Monte Carlo for the US Supreme Court, 1953–1999. *Political Analysis*, 10(2):134–153, 2002.

A. D. Martin, K. M. Quinn, and J. H. Park. MCMCpack: Markov Chain Monte Carlo in R. *Journal of Statistical Software*, 2011.

M. Peress. Small Chamber Ideal Point Estimation. *Political Analysis*, 17(3):276, 2009.

K. T. Poole and H. Rosenthal. A Spatial Model for Legislative Roll Call Analysis. *American Journal of Political Science*, 29(2):357–384, 1985.

R. Core Team. *R: A Language and Environment for Statistical Computing*. R Foundation for Statistical Computing, Vienna, Austria, 2012.

D. Rivers. Heterogeneity in Models of Electoral Choice. *American Journal of Political Science*, 32(3):737–757, 1988.

D. Rivers. Identification of Multidimensional Spatial Voting Models. Technical report, July 2003.

A. Rosenblatt, J. Greenberg, S. Solomon, T. Pyszczynski, et al. Evidence for Terror Management Theory: I. The Effects of Mortality Salience on Reactions to Those Who Violate or Uphold Cultural Values. *Journal of Personality and Social Psychology*, 57(4):681–690, 1989.

Stan Development Team. *Stan Modeling Language*, 1.3 edition, 2013a.

Stan Development Team. *Stan: A C++ Library for Probability and Sampling*, 1.3 edition, 2013b.

J. E. Transue. Identity Salience, Identity Acceptance, and Racial Policy Attitudes: American National Identity as a Uniting Force. *American Journal of Political Science*, 51(1):78–91, 2007.

APPENDIX A

Proofs Related to Salience Models

A.1 EQUIVALENCE OF TRADITIONAL AND HYPERPLANE-BASED CONSTRUCTIONS

The two model constructions for ordinal IRT with multiple latent dimensions are

- Traditional

$$y^* = \phi\lambda + \epsilon, \qquad \epsilon \sim \text{Normal}(0, 1) \tag{A.1}$$

$$y = 1 + \sum_j \{y^* < \eta_j\} \tag{A.2}$$

- Hyperplane-based

$$y^* = \left(\phi + \frac{\epsilon}{\|\lambda\|}\right)\lambda, \qquad \epsilon \sim \text{MVN}(0, I) \tag{A.3}$$

$$y = 1 + \sum_j \{y^* < \eta_j\} \tag{A.4}$$

In Equation A.3, note that variation in ϵ perpendicular to λ has no impact on y^*. Since the distribution of ϵ is spherical, we can rotate it into a space that has $\lambda/\|\lambda\|$ as the first basis vector, call the rotated variable ϵ', and just look at the marginal distribution along that $\lambda/\|\lambda\|$ dimension. The transformed mean and variance of ϵ' are still 0 and I, and since the marginal distribution of any dimension of a standard multivariate normal is simply a standard normal, the distribution of $\epsilon' \cdot \frac{\lambda}{\|\lambda\|}$ is Normal$(0, 1)$, and so if we define a final variable $\epsilon'' = \epsilon' \cdot \frac{\lambda}{\|\lambda\|}$, that is equivalent to the ϵ term in A.1.

A.2 CHOICE MODEL INVARIANCE TO PERPENDICULAR SHIFTS UNDER UNIFORM SALIENCE

We begin with a spatial choice model parameterized in terms of outcome policy positions with ideal point ϕ, question direction vector λ, question- and individual-specific noise ϵ, individual-specific salience matrix A, and cutpoints ζ:

$$y^* = \left(\phi + \alpha + \frac{\epsilon}{\|\lambda\|}\right)\lambda, \qquad \epsilon \sim \text{MVN}(0, I) \tag{A.5}$$

$$y = 1 + \sum_j \{y^* < \eta_j\}, \tag{A.6}$$

and without loss of generality, assume that $\alpha \cdot \lambda = 0$ so that α captures shifts perpendicular to the question direction vector.

Since $\alpha\lambda = 0$, the manipulations to A.5 that make α disappear are trivial.

$$y^* = \phi\lambda + \alpha\lambda + \frac{\epsilon\lambda}{\|\lambda\|} \tag{A.7}$$

$$= \phi\lambda + \frac{\epsilon\lambda}{\|\lambda\|} \tag{A.8}$$

$$= \left(\phi + \frac{\epsilon}{\|\lambda\|}\right)\lambda \tag{A.9}$$

And so the distribution of observable outcomes y conditional on ϕ and λ are not affected by shifts in ϕ perpendicular to λ.

6

Random Forests and Fuzzy Forests in Biomedical Research

Daniel Conn and Christina M. Ramirez

Department of Biostatistics, UCLA Fielding School of Public Health

1 INTRODUCTION

With the advent of high-throughput technologies such as multicolor flow cytometry and next-generation sequencing, high-dimensional data has become increasingly common in biomedical research. In many applications such as proteomics, genomics, and immunology, the data has become increasingly wide. That is, we know a great deal about a small number of subjects. In these applications, the number of features greatly exceeds the number of observations. This "large p, small n" problem gives rise to a number of well-known statistical issues.

For example, a researcher may be interested in discovering a certain single nucleotide polymorphism (SNP) that is associated with a particular disease outcome. Note that a nucleotide is a subunit of the DNA molecule, and each nucleotide consists of either an A (adenine), T/U (thymine/uracil), G (guanine), or C (cytosine), with base pairs formed between the former and latter two nucleotides. A SNP is a single base pair such that the nucleotides differ between members of a population.

For example, 99% of patients may carry two A alleles, AA. One percent of the population may have different nucleotides on one or more alleles, say AG or GG at this particular base pair. In this case, A would be the common allele. The feature corresponding to this SNP may count the number of rare alleles (0, 1, or 2). Alternatively, the features may record whether an observation has alleles AA, AG, or GG. This is achieved with two dummy variables. In this case, there are two features corresponding to each SNP.

In many cases, there may be hundreds of thousands of potentially important SNPs and only a few hundred subjects. To further complicate matters, these SNPs may be highly correlated with one another. The SNPs may be more or less variable across members of the population. Some SNPs may be missing for a significant portion of the observations. Additional demographic features, such as gender or race, may confound the relationship between a SNP and a disease outcome. In many of these applications, prediction may be secondary to feature selection. That is, a researcher may want to know the top variables of interest for further study.

Classical regression methods such as linear regression or logistic regression are highly unstable if p is comparable to n, and they altogether fail to yield a result if p is larger than n. Despite the failure of these classical methods, progress is possible. One solution is to conduct a separate univariate test of significance for each feature. When p is large, procedures such as Bonferroni's method for controlling the family-wise error rate are too conservative. It is more common to control the false discovery rate using the methods of Benjamini and Hochberg (1995) and Storey (2003).

While conducting a series of univariate tests is often useful, these procedures have a number of drawbacks. First of all, univariate tests fail to control for important demographic confounders. Second, if the correlation between biological features is high, as is often the case in biomedical applications, the effects of the features cannot be disentangled from one another. Third, these univariate tests may miss important interactions among the features or fail to capture important nonlinear relationships between the features and the outcome.

High-dimensional regression methods are required to overcome these various difficulties. High-dimensional linear variable selection methods, such as the LASSO (Tibshirani, 1996) or SCAD (Fan & Li, 2001), are commonly used to select important features. These linear variable selection methods can account for common demographic features and can perform quite well if the correlation between features is not too high Raskutti et al. (2010) and Van De Geer et al. (2009). Unfortunately, these linear models can miss important interactions, and they can be misleading if the true relationship is nonlinear.

Great energy has also gone into developing nonparametric regression methods designed to handle high dimensions. Random forests (RFs) (Breiman, 2001) and support vector machines (Cristianini & Shawe-Taylor, 2000) are examples of nonparametric regression methods designed to handle high-dimensional data. These methods are able to detect interactions as well as nonlinear structure.

The increased flexibility of these high-dimensional regression methods comes at a price. First, statistical inference via these methods is much more challenging. While recent progress has been made in developing a significance test for the LASSO (Lockhart et al. , 2014), significance tests derived from methods such as this as well as random forests are known to suffer serious statistical drawbacks (Strobl & Zeileis, 2008). Second, unless careful measures are taken to control the complexity of the model, these methods will mistake noise for signal and overfit the data. Even in low dimensions, the flexibility of the nonparametric regression methods can lead to overfitting. In this chapter, we first introduce RFs and then describe the method's extensions in detail.

2 RANDOM FORESTS APPLIED TO BIOMEDICAL RESEARCH

Biomedical research often has many more predictors than observations, which is often referred to as the "small n, large p problem." This problem becomes even more intractable when many of the parameters are highly correlated. The lack of independence violates the underlying assumptions of many standard statistical models. Further, many biological systems involve complex correlation patterns, including high-order interactions and network effects. When the parameter space is large, it is not feasible to prespecify the interactions a priori, and many of these interactions may be unknown. In many genomic studies, there may be only a small number of variables that are actually important to the phenotype; therefore, there may be a large number of noise parameters relative to the important variables. Thus, some sort of variable selection and parameter reduction is desirable.

The two most widely used machine learning algorithms in medical science are random forests (RFs) and support vector machines (SVMs) (Goldstein et al., 2011). Both have high predictive accuracy, but only RFs are discussed here. The popularity of RFs is due to their relative computational efficiency, robustness to outliers, and invariance to mixed variable types. Moreover RFs are relatively hard to overfit, are nonparametric, and naturally handle interactions and variable importance. RFs have been described as the best "off-the-shelf" algorithm, and they enjoy good predictive accuracy and widespread use. There are a number of widely available software packages to implement RFs (Liaw & Wiener, 2002; Hothorn et al., 2010; Zhang et al., 2009; Schwarz et al., 2010).

Random forests have been used in many applications, such as genomics and proteomics (Somorjai et al., 2003; Bureau et al., 2005; Sampson et al., 2011; Lunetta et al., 2004; Sun et al., 2007; Chang et al., 2008; Jiang et al., 2009; Reif et al., 2009). The response is usually a phenotypic trait, such as disease status, and the predictors are often genetic markers, such as SNPs or gene expression levels. RFs have also been used for prediction in a wide variety of settings such as HIV replication capacity (Segal et al., 2004), protein-protein interactions (Lin et al., 2004; Šikić et al., 2009), protein and RNA binding sites (Wu et al., 2009), binding affinity (Ballester & Mitchell, 2010), glycosolation sites (Hamby & Hirst, 2008), and drug sensitivity (Riddick et al., 2011). Several packages have been developed to use RF specifically to handle genomic data. For example, Willows was specifically designed to efficiently create tree-based models for SNPs (Zhang et al., 2009), whereas Random Jungle was developed for fast implementation of RFs for SNP data (Schwarz et al., 2010).

Due to the nonparametric nature of the trees, interactions do not need to be specifically modeled, but are included in the underlying tree structure. These interactions are accounted for in the variable importance rankings. Several studies have shown that variable importance scores are more stable than other approaches for variable interactions (Lunetta et al., 2004; McKinney et al., 2006; Nicodemus et al., 2007; García-Magariños et al., 2009; Qi et al., 2006), including gene × environment (Cordell, 2009) and gene × gene (Maenner et al., 2009). Random forests examine interactions in a nonparametric manner and one that is computationally feasible because it examines random subsets of parameters.

Using marginal *p*-values as a dimension reduction tool can lead to biased results. This strategy also does not consider interactions. Random forests have been suggested as an alternative strategy for variable (feature) reduction and have been widely used in a variety of applications from gene expression to QSAR modeling; see Cordell (2009); Lunetta et al. (2004); Chang et al. (2008); Svetnik et al. (2003); Díaz-Uriarte & De Andres (2006); and Mansiaux & Carrat (2014). Random forests have also been used for unsupervised learning (Shi et al., 2005), imputing missing data (Stekhoven & Bühlmann, 2012), and detecting outliers (Shi & Horvath, 2006).

3 CLASSIFICATION AND REGRESSION TREES

To understand RFs, we first discuss the base learner, which is the classification and regression tree (CART). CART, popularized by Breiman et al. (1984), is a nonparametric regression method well known for its ability to detect inter-actions and interpretability. CART uses a binary tree to recursively partition the feature space. The method extends naturally to the case of multicategory classification problems. It has also been extended to handle censored data in the form of survival trees (Ishwaran et al., 2008). CART also handles missing data; see Hapfelmeier et al. (2014); Stekhoven & Bühlmann (2012); and Breiman et al. (1984).

In CART it is typical to denote the outcome as Y and the jth feature by X_j ($j = 1, \ldots, p$). At the top of the binary tree, the root node contains all obser-vations. The root node is then split into two child nodes. If X_j is continuous, the left node contains all observations such that $X_j \leq c$, whereas the right node contains all observations such that $X_j > c$. Each child node is then split further, each by its own splitting rule. If X_j is categorical and takes values in the discrete set A, the splitting rule is determined by a subset A^*. All observations with X_j in A^* fall into one child node. Likewise, all observations with X_j outside of A^* fall into the other child node.

This process is continued until various stopping criteria are met. In partic-ular, the depth of the tree is limited by the sample size, n. If a node contains a single observation it cannot be further subdivided. A node that has not been split and does not have children is called a terminal node. Ideally, the obser-vations that fall within the same terminal node should, with high probability, have similar outcomes to one another. Each internal node is associated with a splitting rule. This splitting rule can be represented as a pair of the form $r = (X_j, c)$ or $r = (X_j, A^*)$. Each terminal node is associated with its own conditional distribution.

Algorithms for fitting CART models are distinguished by how they use the data to construct the tree. We quote Breiman et al. (1984): "three elements are necessary to determine a tree:

1. A way to select a split at every intermediate node.
2. A rule for determining when a node is terminal.
3. A rule for assigning a value $y(t)$ to every terminal node t"

where $y(t)$ represents the predicted outcome within node t. Regardless of the type of outcome (numeric, categorical, ordinal, or censored) the general principles for tree construction are as just stated, which in part explains why tree-based models have proven to be easily extensible.

We now describe the algorithm presented in Breiman et al. (1984) for fitting regression trees. This algorithm is implemented in the **R** package **rpart**. Suppose we are to split an internal node t. Denote the left and right nodes obtained using the splitting rule r by $t_L^{(r)}$ and $t_R^{(r)}$, respectively. The best splitting rule r^* for t is determined by finding the splitting rule that minimizes $p_L s^2(t_L^{(r)}) + p_R s^2(t_R^{(r)})$, where p_L and p_R are the probabilities that an observation falls into node t_L and t_R, respectively. Similarly, $s^2(t_L^{(r)})$ and $s^2(t_R^{(r)})$ are the variances in the left and right nodes, respectively.

The criterion $p_L s^2(t_L) + p_R s^2(t_R)$ can be thought of as a measure of the heterogeneity of outcomes within the resultant children nodes after applying a particular splitting rule. Classification trees are similar to regression trees, although they use a different measure of node impurity. For classification, the most common measure of node impurity is the Gini index: $\phi(t) = 2\hat{p}(1 - \hat{p})$, where $\hat{p}$ is the estimated probability an observation in node t takes the value 1. The Gini index is maximized when $p = 0.5$. In other words, the Gini index is maximized if a node is as impure as possible. Given a node t, the optimal splitting rule is the one that minimizes the weighted average of node impurities in its children: $p_L \phi(t_L) + p_R \phi(t_R)$.

In the case of both classification and regression, a node is split unless it contains less than a prespecified number of observations. The prediction $y(t)$ for observations falling into terminal node t is often taken to be the average in the case of regression and the majority vote within the node for classification.

4 RANDOM FORESTS (RFs)

It is well known that classification and regression trees are prone to overfitting. The resulting predictions can be highly unstable. RFs, the popular machine learning algorithm introduced by Breiman (2001), compensates for this instability by combining the predictions of multiple trees. Each tree produces a jagged, highly nonlinear estimate of the true regression surface. Averaging the predictions from multiple trees serves to provide a smoother fit to the data (Hastie et al., 2009).

The random forests algorithm proceeds as follows:

1. Draw a large number of bootstrap samples. Refer to the number of bootstrap samples as *ntree*.
2. For each bootstrap sample, a tree is constructed. However, the procedure for splitting nodes is now partially randomized. At each node t, randomly select a subset of the original p features. The number of features selected is commonly referred to as *mtry* ($mtry \leq p$). Split the given node using the optimal splitting rule that can be derived from the randomly selected *mtry* features.
3. In the case of regression trees, predictions are derived by averaging the predictions of the individual trees. For classification, the prediction is majority vote of all the trees.

Thus, as the name suggests, the RF algorithm involves averaging the predictions of an ensemble of randomly generated trees. The randomness in random forests is derived from two sources. The first source is the result of growing an ensemble of trees on multiple bootstrapped data sets. This algorithm is known as bootstrap aggregating or "bagging." Bagging was introduced in Breiman (1996). The procedure for determining the splitting rule at each node is also partially randomized in the RF algorithm, which is the second source of randomness. When $mtry = p$, the RF algorithm is equivalent to bagging.

Low values of *mtry* will lead to better prediction if many of the features have a small effect on the outcome (Hastie et al., 2009). High values of *mtry* will perform well if only a few features have a large effect on the outcome. Hastie et al. (2009) liken using random forests with low *mtry* to ridge regression. High values of *mtry* allow the individual trees to zone in on the most important features. This is desirable if only a few features are highly important.

The two sources of randomness improve on the predictive ability of classification and regression trees by reducing the variance of the resulting predictions. The bootstrapping produces a smoother, more stable estimate of regression surface. The randomness induced by the random selection of *mtry* features further reduces the variance by reducing the correlation between the ensemble of trees (Hastie et al., 2009). Low values of *mtry* are associated with higher bias and lower variance (Breiman, 2001). High values of *mtry* are associated with higher variance and lower bias.

For each bootstrap sample, approximately one-third of the observations are left out of the sample. These left-out observations are referred to as "out of bag" or OOB. These out-of-bag samples provide an internal estimate of the test set error. The OOB error rate is defined as the mean squared prediction error obtained by using trees grown on the bootstrap samples to estimate the outcome from OOB samples. The OOB error rate can be used to select the optimal value of *mtry* (Hastie et al., 2009).

The **R** package **randomForest** implements random forests using the classification and regression tree algorithms of Breiman et al. (1984). The **R** package **party** constructs random forests using conditional inference trees under the unbiased recursive partitioning framework.

5 RANDOM FOREST VARIABLE IMPORTANCE MEASURES

The enhanced predictive abilities of RFs come at the price of decreased interpretability (Breiman et al., 2001). Despite their seemingly black box nature, RFs can still be used for variable selection. A number of variable importance measures (VIMs) are available to determine which features are important for predicting the outcome.

We first introduce the permutation VIM for regression. For the ith tree grown on the ith bootstrap sample, the variable importance of feature j is computed as followed. First, the mean squared prediction error for the OOB samples, $error OOB_i$, is calculated. Then, the values of feature j are permuted, and the prediction error $error OOB_i^*$ is recalculated. The permutation variable importance is defined as

$$\frac{1}{ntree} \sum_{i=1}^{ntree} error OOB_i^* - error OOB_i. \tag{1}$$

If feature j is important we would expect the mean squared prediction error after permutation to be much higher. We expect that features that are vital for prediction would have high permutation variable importance. Randomly permuting feature j should diminish any relationship between feature j and the outcome.

In the case of classification, $error OOB_i$ is the misclassification rate calculated using the ith tree to predict the classes of the individual OOB observations. Likewise, $error OOB_i^*$ is the misclassification rate after permuting the levels of feature j. The expression for the permutation variable importance is then identical to (1).

For classification trees, there is a second common VIM called the Gini importance. Each time feature j is used to split a node t, the reduction in the Gini index is recorded. Denote this reduction in the Gini index on the ith tree, at node t, by $\Delta_i(t,r) = \phi(t) - p_L \phi(t_L^{(r)}) - p_R \phi(t_R^{(r)})$, where r represents a splitting rule of the form (X_j, c). The Gini importance is the sum of such decreases in node impurity:

$$\sum_{i=1}^{ntree} \sum_{t} \Delta_i(t,r). \tag{2}$$

The inner summation is taken over all splits that involved feature j.

Classification and regression trees yield another naive estimate of variable importance. A feature's importance may be measured by the number of times it has been used to split an internal node. This measure of variable importance extends naturally to random forests. A feature's importance would be the average number of times it has been used to split an internal node. The objection to this measure of variable importance is that not all splits are equally important. Some splits lead to large decreases in node impurity, some less so. Splits near the top of the tree may also be considered more important. The aforementioned measures of variable importance naturally take into account the importance of a split.

6 SOURCES OF BIAS FOR RANDOM FOREST VARIABLE IMPORTANCE MEASURES

6.1 Gini Importance

Gini importance is biased against categorical features with a small number of levels and is biased in favor of continuous features or categorical features with many levels. A categorical feature leads to $2^K - 1$ possible splitting rules, where K is the number of levels that the feature takes. A continuous feature yields $n - 1$ possible splitting rules. Given two unimportant features, the feature with more possible splitting rules will, by chance, find its way into more trees and come out with a higher Gini importance.

Boulesteix et al. (2012a) note that the Gini importance also favors balanced categorical features over unbalanced categorical features. This is particularly troubling in biomedical applications. Boulesteix et al. (2012a) discuss this issue in the context of discovering important SNPs. Despite these troubles with the Gini importance, Boulesteix et al. (2012b) point out circumstances in which it outperforms the permutation variable importance. In particular, the Gini importance is effective in classification problems where one of the outcomes is particularly rare.

6.2 Bootstrapping versus Subsampling

In the algorithm proposed by Breiman (2001) randomness is introduced by growing trees on bootstrapped data sets. It is also possible to introduce randomness by growing trees on random subsamples of the data. The distinction here is between sampling n subjects with replacement (bootstrapping) and sampling a random subset $\lfloor fraction * n \rfloor$ of the data, where *fraction* is commonly taken to be 0.632.

Strobl et al. (2007) compare the VIMs obtained by bootstrapping and subsampling. They found that bootstrapping induced a bias in favor of categorical variables with many levels. This bias is the result of general issues pertaining to the bootstrap and hypothesis tests (Bickel & Ren, 2001). As a result of this bias, the default setting in the package **party** is to sample without replacement.

6.3 Correlated Features

Correlation among features is a common problem. For example, in the context of linear regression, correlation among the features is known as multicollinearity. Although it may not have an adverse effect on the predictive performance of random forests, the effects of correlation on VIMs may be quite severe. Again, this is similar to how multi-collinearity may result in highly unstable estimates of particular regression coefficients without affecting predictive performance.

Suppose two important features are correlated with one another. Intuitively, correlation makes it difficult to disentangle the effects of one feature from another. However, for the purposes of prediction, one variable can be used as a surrogate for the other. Therefore, predictive accuracy will remain largely unaffected if only one of the two important features is selected.

Though the problem of correlated features is not particular to RFs, they are particularly prone to it. This is because RFs are constructed by examining a sequence of marginal effects. Consider the process of splitting the root node. In general, the feature with the highest marginal association is selected to split the root node. Thus, important features that are correlated with one another are generally selected at the top of the tree. As the tree is grown out, the value of the correlated features within each node becomes homogeneous, and the independent features have a chance to enter the tree. Unfortunately, if the sample size is small, the independent features may not make it into the tree at all.

Nicodemus et al. (2010) found this behavior in a series of simulations investigating how random forests behave in the presence of correlated features. Their simulation assumed a linear model with $n = 2,000$ and $p = 12$. They found that correlated features were selected toward the top of the tree and that the permutation VIM was biased in favor of correlated features. The bias was more pronounced for lower values of *mtry*, although the variance of the VIMs increased.

A number of simulation studies have been carried out to determine the effects of correlation on random forests (Strobl et al., 2008; Nicodemus & Malley, 2009; Archer & Kimes, 2008; Gregorutti et al., 2013). Strobl et al. (2008) propose an alternative "conditional" variable importance measure that appears in simulations to eliminate the bias in favor of correlated features. Conditional variable importance measures are computed by permuting observations only within levels of the tree-induced partition. The calculation of conditional variable importance measures is computationally intensive and precludes its use in large data sets.

7 FUZZY FORESTS: AN EXTENSION OF RANDOM FORESTS TO HANDLE CORRELATED FEATURES

In this section, we discuss the fuzzy forests algorithm introduced by Conn et al. (2015). Fuzzy forests were specifically developed to counter the aforementioned biases observed in random forests. We then compare fuzzy forests (FFs) to random forests in a simulation.

The FF algorithm first partitions the features into distinct groups, such that the variables within groups are highly correlated with one another while variables in different groups are roughly independent. A separate recursive feature elimination RF is then applied to each group. The features that have not been screened out by this recursive feature elimination are then combined, and a final recursive feature elimination is carried out to select the top k features, where k is user specified.

Fuzzy forests are implemented in the **R** package **fuzzyforest**. Note that **fuzzyforest** has specific functions to allow for the easy use of weighted genetic co-expression network analysis (WGCNA) in partitioning the features (Zhang & Horvath, 2005). See Conn et al. (2015) and Fromentin et al. (2015) for further details on the motivation and implementation of fuzzy forests.

To demonstrate the performance of random forests and fuzzy forests in the high dimensions with correlated features, we carry out the following simulation. In the first setting, we set $n = 100$ and $p = 100$. The features were divided into four groups of size 25. Features within each group had multivariate normal distribution. Within the first three groups, the correlation between all features was 0.8. Within the last group, the correlation between features was 0. All features had mean 0 and variance 1.

Outcomes, Y, were generated by the following distribution:

$$Y = f(X) + \epsilon, \tag{3}$$

where $\epsilon_i \sim N(0, 0.1)$ and

$$f(X) = 5X_1 + 5X_2 + 2X_3 + 5X_{76} + 5X_{77} + 2X_{78}. \tag{4}$$

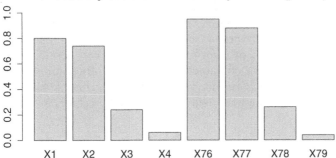

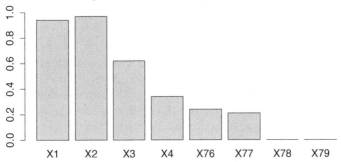

FIGURE 6.1. Results of simulation with $n = 100$, $p = 100$.

Here X_1, X_2, and X_3 were highly correlated with one another, whereas X_{76}, X_{77}, and X_{78} were independent. The coefficients of all other features were set to 0. For each random forest, *mtry* was set to the square root of the number of features.

We generated 100 data sets. To evaluate the performance of random forests we recorded the percentage of times the significant features obtained a VIM in the top 10. Similarly for fuzzy forests, we recorded the percentage of times important variables were selected in the top 10. In addition to the significant features, we also recorded the same information for features X_4 and X_{79} so that we could examine whether either algorithm falsely selected unimportant features. The results are seen in Figure 6.1.

For random forests, the probability of selection is biased in favor of the correlated features, and the important independent variables are largely ignored. Note that the unimportant feature X_4 has a higher average VIM and probability of selection than the most important uncorrelated important features. The

Probability of Selection for Fuzzy Forests (*p*=1,000)

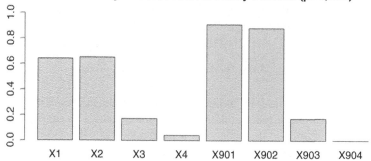

Probability of Selection for Random Forests (*p*=1,000)

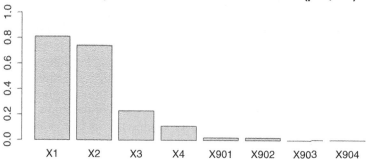

FIGURE 6.2. Results of simulation with $n = 100$, $p = 1,000$.

FF algorithm appears to be slightly biased in favor of the uncorrelated features, although it manages to select the important correlated features at a reasonably high rate.

We carried out a similar simulation with $n = 100$ and $p = 1,000$. In this simulation, there were 10 groups of features, each containing 100 features. The features once again had multivariate normal distribution with 0 mean and marginal variance 1. For 9 of the 10 groups of features, the correlation among features was 0.8. The 10th group of features was independent. Once again, the outcomes were generated as $Y = f(X) + \epsilon$ where $\epsilon \sim N(0, .1)$ and

$$f(X) = 5X_1 + 5X_2 + 2X_3 + 5X_{901} + 5X_{902} + 2X_{903}. \tag{5}$$

The results of the simulation are similar to the case with $p = 100$ although more pronounced (Figure 6.2).

In this case, RFs essentially ignore the uncorrelated features, whereas FFs still manage to consistently select the correct uncorrelated features. The selection probabilities for the correct features are still high even in the presence of so many extra noise features. In the last simulation the number of noise parameters is roughly 10 times the sample size, and yet FFs are still able to pick up on the signal.

8 SURVIVAL FORESTS

RFs are an attractive method in biomedical applications because of their ability to handle censored or missing data. Censored data arises often arises in studies where the outcome is the time until a particular event. In biomedical applications, this outcome is often time until recurrence of disease or death. As is traditional in the field of survival analysis, we refer to the outcome of interest as failure or death, though it is, of course, important to note that censored data appears in a wide variety of contexts. For example, the event of interest could be time until marriage or time until an unemployed individual is employed again.

Associated with each subject, we have a failure time, T, and a censoring time C. A subject i is said to be right censored if the failure time, T_i is greater than the censoring time C_i ($T_i > C_i$). In other words, we have incomplete information on the censored subjects. We know that they survived to some time point greater than or "to the right of" C_i. In a study of fixed length τ, a subject will have censoring time $C_i = \tau$ if he or she survives to the end of the study. Other censoring schemes are possible. For example, a subject is said to be interval censored if we know that the subject died at some time point after L_i and before R_i. In this chapter, our focus is on right-censored data.

If the failure times were observed for every subject, we would be able to use the standard methods for regression to analyze such data. Unfortunately, in the case of right-censored survival data, we only observe $Y_i = min(T_i, C_i)$. Specialized methods are required to analyze right-censored data and to evaluate the performance of a given model. For each subject i, we observe an outcome of the form (Y_i, δ_i) and a feature vector X_i. Here, Y_i is as above and δ_i takes the value 1 when $Y_i = T_i$ and 0 when $Y_i = C_i$. In other words, $\delta_i = 1$ if the subject i was observed until failure, and $\delta_i = 0$ if subject i was censored.

A common quantity of interest in survival analysis is the survival function: $1 - F(t) = P(T > t) = S(t)$. In the presence of censoring, the famed Kaplan-Meier method is used to estimate $S(t)$ (Kaplan & Meier, 1958). The log-rank test can be used to compare the survival profiles of two (or possibly more) groups. The Kaplan-Meier method is a univariate method. The log-rank test can only be used to compare discrete subpopulations of subjects. Regression methods are required when one of the features is continuous or when p is moderate to large.

A common parametric regression method for analyzing right-censored data is to assume a linear model on the log scale and then make a parametric assumption about the distribution of the error term. We assume $log(T_i) = X_i'\beta + \epsilon_i$, where ϵ_i might have a normal or extreme value distribution. Maximum likelihood estimation would then be used to estimate β.

Perhaps the most popular regression method for survival analysis is the Cox proportional hazards model. Given a continuous positive random variable T, the hazard function is defined as $h(t) = f(t)/(1 - F(t))$, where T has probability density function $f(t)$ and cumulative density function $F(t)$. The hazard function is interpreted as the instantaneous risk of failure at time t.

The Cox proportional hazards model assumes that the hazard function for the ith individual is of the form $h(t) = h_0(t)exp(X_i'\beta)$. This model is a semi-parametric model because the baseline hazard $h_0(t)$ is left unspecified. The parameter β is estimated by maximizing the partial likelihood. On the one hand, the Cox proportional hazards model allows for a great deal of flexibility by leaving the baseline hazard unspecified. On the other hand, its assumption of proportional hazards is quite restrictive and may fail in practice.

Both survival models discussed here have been extended to the case of $p > n$ by introducing penalties of the same form used in ridge regression, LASSO, or SCAD. Unfortunately, both the parametric linear model and the Cox proportional hazards model may fail to capture important interactions.

Survival forests (SFs) have been proposed as a nonparametric alternative to the aforementioned models. As with RFs for regression or classification, SFs are an ensemble method that combines the predictions of multiple survival trees. Tree-based models for survival data were first introduced in early papers by Ciampi et al. (1981), Marubini et al. (1983), and especially Gordon and Olshen (1985). Survival trees were extended to RFs soon after the introduction of RFs for regression. Breiman (2003) released a guide for implementing SFs. SF methodology has been developed further by Ishwaran et al. (2004), Hothorn et al. (2006), Ishwaran et al. (2008), Ishwaran and Kogalur (2010), and Zhu and Kosorok (2012). An extensive review is given in Bou-Hamad et al. (2011).

We now describe the process of generalizing classification and regression trees to censored data. As the sample standard deviation is undefined in the presence of censoring, a new criterion for determining when to split a node is required. In general, a test statistic is used to compare the survival profiles in the two daughter nodes. The optimal splitting rule is then defined as the splitting rule that maximizes the test statistic. The test statistic may be a likelihood ratio test statistic from a parametric survival model, or it may be taken from a nonparametric test such as the log-rank test statistic. Stopping criteria for survival trees are often defined by the number of uncensored individuals in a node. Ishwaran et al. (2008) and Zhu and Kosorok (2012) prespecify a minimum number of uncensored individuals as the criterion for determining when a node is too small to be split. The survival experience of individuals in a terminal node may be summarized by the median survival time derived from a Kaplan-Meier estimator (Segal, 1988).

The survival forest methodology is a current area of methodological research. We describe the algorithm of Ishwaran et al. (2008) and then that of

Hothorn et al. (2006). These procedures are on the face quite different from one another and are implemented in the **R** packages **randomSurvivalForestSRC** and **party**, respectively.

As in the usual RF algorithm, multiple trees are grown on bootstrapped data sets, and the selection of features to split on at a given node is random. For each tree k, a subject with feature vector X_i will have a corresponding estimated cumulative hazard, $\hat{H}_b^*(t|X_i)$, where $\int_0^\infty h(t)dt = H(t)$ is called the cumulative hazard. The ensemble cumulative hazard is defined as

$$\hat{H}_e^*(t|X_i) = \frac{1}{ntree} \sum_{b=1}^{ntree} \hat{H}_b^*(t|X_i). \tag{6}$$

Similarly, the OOB ensemble cumulative hazard for X_i is defined as

$$\hat{H}_e^{**}(t|X_i) = \frac{\sum_{b=1}^{ntree} I_{i,b} \hat{H}_b^*(t|X_i)}{\sum_{b=1}^{ntree} I_{i,b}}, \tag{7}$$

where $I_{i,b} = 1$ if subject i was not selected in the bth bootstrap sample and 0 otherwise.

In the case of regression, the average mean square prediction error on the out-of-bag samples was used to assess the performance of RFs. Because the true survival time, T_i, is unobserved, the OOB cannot be directly calculated. Instead of the mean square prediction error, Ishwaran et al. (2008) use the C-index of Heagerty and Zheng (2005) to assess predictive ability. Briefly, the C-index measures the extent to which a predictive survival analysis model correctly predicts which of two observations will have a longer survival time. Given two observations i and j, i is defined to have a smaller predicted survival time than j if

$$\sum_{l=1}^{m} \hat{H}_e^{**}(t_l^0|X_i) > \sum_{l=1}^{m} \hat{H}_e^{**}(t_l^0|X_j), \tag{8}$$

where $t_1^0, \ldots, t_m^0$ are prespecified time points (often simply the observed survival times). The C-index, C, is defined as the percentage of such pairs that are correctly classified. A model with a high C-index has high predictive performance. The prediction error is defined as $PE = 1 - C$.

For RFs in the context of regression, the variable importance was defined as the increase in OOB error after permuting the values of each feature. Again, the OOB error cannot be directly calculated in the presence of censoring. The variable importance for feature j is calculated by sending OOB observations down the tree. Each time a node is split with feature j, the observation is sent right or left at random. The prediction error, PE^*, obtained using this noised-up tree is then calculated. The variable importance is defined as $PE^* - PE$.

In contrast to the approach taken in Ishwaran et al. (2008), Hothorn et al. (2006) utilize the framework of Molinaro et al. (2004). Letting Y_i now represent $\log(T_i)$, the objective is to find the function f that minimizes the expected loss: $E_{Y,X}L(Y, f(X))$, where L is a loss function. A common choice for L is squared loss $L(Y, f(X)) = (Y - f(X))^2$. Without censoring, we would usually parametrize f by a set of parameters ψ and estimate ψ by finding

$$min_{\psi \in \Psi} \sum_{i=1}^{n} L_{\psi}(Y_i, X_i), \tag{9}$$

where Ψ is the parameter space of ψ.

In the presence of censoring, Y_i is generally not fully observed. Let $\tilde{Y}_i$ represent $min(Y_i \log(C_i))$, $\tilde{T}_i = min(T_i, C_i)$, and let $G(C|X)$ be the survivor function of C. It can be shown that

$$E_{Y,X}L(Y, f(X)) = E_{Y,X}\left[L(\tilde{Y}, \psi(X))\frac{\delta}{G(\tilde{T}|X)}\right]. \tag{10}$$

Therefore, although the minimization of (9) cannot be solved, it instead suffices to find

$$min_{\psi \in \Psi} \sum_{i=1}^{n} L_{\psi}(\tilde{Y}_i, X_i)\frac{\delta_i}{\hat{G}(\tilde{T}_i|X)}, \tag{11}$$

where $\hat{G}(\tilde{T}_i|X)$ may be derived using the Kaplan-Meier estimator. The inverse probability of censoring is used to weight the uncensored observations.

We denote the vector of weights by **w**. Note that censored observations have weight 0. The SF algorithm proposed in Hothorn et al. (2006) is similar to the usual algorithm for regression with a few exceptions. Again multiple bootstrap samples are taken, but the number of times each subject appears in the bootstrap sample is distributed as a multinomial with parameters n and $(\sum_{i=1}^{n} w_i)^{-1}w$.

9 APPLICATION TO HEALTH POLICY DATA SETS

Policy makers as well as medical researchers depend on health surveys to understand the health of the population. The California Health Interview Survey (CHIS) is the largest health survey of its kind in the nation. The survey is an ongoing biennial survey that was constructed to be representative of California's diverse population and provides detailed information on the health status, health care needs, access to care, utilization of health care, health-related behaviors, as well as insurance coverage for Californians. The 2011–2012 public data set contains 42,935 observations on adults and has approximately 185 potential predictor variables. We used the constructed variable RBMI as our

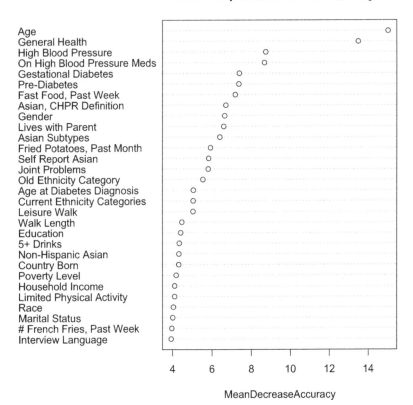

FIGURE 6.3. Graph of variable importance measures.

outcome variable. This variable has four levels based on BMI values and mirrors the guidelines set by the World Health Organization. If BMI < 18.5 then the variable is coded as 1 for underweight, 2 for normal BMI, 3 for overweight (BMI between 25 and < 30), and 4 for obese (BMI > 29.99). The results presented here are not meant to be the definitive analysis of the data set, but do illustrate the usefulness of random forests in variable selection. In many surveys, the number of parameters can be daunting, especially if one considers interactions. Surveys also often use both Likert scales and continuous measures as potential features. Data sets that have this "mixed" type of data can often prove problematic in variable selection.

To show the utility of machine learning in these situations, we first conducted a random forests analysis and used the permutation variable importance to choose the top 30 variables (see Figure 6.3). Note that to account for the survey structure, we used a weighted bootstrap for the random forest. The run time was approximately 11.1 seconds for 50,000 trees. We tried many values of

TABLE 6.1. *Variables Selected by Both Forwards and Backwards Selection*

Name	Description
AB1	General health condition
AB16	Limitation of activities due to joint pain
AB22	Doctor told had diabetes
AB30	Rx for blood pressure
AB51	Type I/II diabetes
AB99	Doctor told pre-diabetes
AC31	# times ate fast food
AD13	Currently pregnant
AD37W	Walked 10 minutes for transport
AD40W	Walked 10 minutes for leisure
AD57	Condition limits physical activity
AE15	Smoked 100+ cigarettes limetime
AE15A	Smokes everyday
AG11	Spouse usually works
AH43A	Live with parent
AH50_P	Name of medicare HMO plan
AJ103	How often get appointment in 2 days
AJ109	Used internet to find med info/year
AJ110	Confidence to complete online application on own
AJ113	How often Dr explains clearly to you
AJ29	Felt nervous past 30 days
AK22_P	Household total annual income
AL7	Currently on WIC
AM2	How often couldn't afford to eat balanced meals
HGHTL_P	Height inches
HHSIZE_P	Household size
INSPR	Covered by plans purchased on own
LATIN9TP	Latin/Hispanic – 9 levels
OFFTK_S	Job offers insurance
OMBSRASO	Self-report non-Hispanic Asian
PCTLF_P	Percent life in the US
SRAA	Self-report African American

mtry with similar results. We then analyzed the data using a more conventional approach. We performed a multinomial logistic model that includes the survey weights and used both backward and forward selection to determine the important variables, using SAS version 9.3. These procedures were computationally intensive, and each run took approximately three hours on a Mac-Book Pro with 2.7-GHz Intel Core i7 processors. We then took all the variables that each model selected as important via p-values that were <0.0001. Table 6.1 lists the important variables that were selected by both the forward and backward

TABLE 6.2. *Variables Uniquely Selected by Backward Selection*

AB108	Confidence to control asthma
AB109	Visit to ER for diabetes in past 12 months
AB110_P	Visit to ER for diabetes because unable to see own Dr
AB40	Still has asthma
AB41	Asthma attack last 12 months
AB43	Health professional gave asthma plan
AB81	Gestational diabetes
AB98	Written copy of asthma plan
AC6	Dr told had a stoke
AC7	Fallen more than one year
AD19	Abnormal mammogram
AD51	Cognitive difficulties
AG20	Language speak with friends
AH13A	ER visit for asthma last 12 months
AH22	Delay in medical care last 12 months
AH33NEW	Born in US
AH75	Tried to find healthcare on own
AI45	Main reason spouse not in employers health plan
AJ10	Need someone else to help understand Dr
AJ33	Feel everything an effort past 30 days
AKWKLNG	Time at main job
AL2	Receiving TANF or Calworks
BINGE12	Binge drinking past 12 months
DSTRS12	Likely had psychological distress last 12 months
DSTRS30	Likely had psychological distress last month
FSLEVCB	Food security states (binary)
INS12M	Months covered by insurance last year
INSEM_S	Spouse covered by employer plan
INSPS_S	Spouse covered by plan purchased on own
INTVLANG	Interview language
MAM_SCRN	Mammogram last year
MARIT	Marital status (3 categories)
MARIT2	Marital status (4 categories)
SERVED	Time on active duty
SRASO	Self-report other Asian group
SRH	Self-report Hispanic
SRKR	Self-report Korean
SRVT	Self-Report Vietnamese

selection model. Tables 6.2 and 6.3 list the important variables that are unique to forward and backward selection models, respectively.

It is interesting to note which variables are common to all the models and which ones are absent from both forward and backward selection models. All

TABLE 6.3. *Variables Uniquely Selected by Forward Selection*

AB17	Doctor told had asthma
AB64	Doctor told arth/gout/lupus
AD41W	# times walked for leasure/week
AE3	# times ate fries/week
AE50	Recommended mammogram by Dr
AG21	Language of tv/radio/paper
AH102_P	# nights in hospital/month
AI25NEW	RX coverage edited for Medi-Cal
AK3	# hours worked/wk
AM21	People in neighborhood can be trusted
DIAMED	Taking insulin or pills
HMO	HMO status
IHS	Covered by Indian Health Services
MARIT_45	Marital status >45 years old
RACEDOF	Ethnicity
SRAGE_P	Self-reported age
UR_RHP	Rural and urban

three models found that general health, being on high blood pressure medication, being prediabetic, eating fast food, living with parents, joint problems, walking for leisure, being a non-Hispanic Asian, household income, limits on physical activity, and marital status were all important in the prediction of BMI categories. Backward selection selected variables such as binge drinking and ER visits, whereas forward selection selected variables such as asthma and lupus. A subset of variables was found to be important by RFs that was ignored by either the forward or backward selection models. This subset included age, diagnosis of high blood pressure, gestational diabetes, binge drinking, and number of times French fries were eaten in the last week. Several variables that were determined to be important by RF were ignored by both forward and backward selection models and included gender, education, country born, poverty level, specific Asian subtypes, fried potatoes in the past month (note this includes hash browns as well as French fries), age of diabetes diagnosis, walk length, and the language spoken during the interview. It is interesting to note that both forward and backward selection procedures did not include gender and education. Large studies have found an association between gender, education, and BMI (Maddah et al., 2003; Hermann et al., 2011; Molarius et al., 2000). However, sometimes this relationship is not an additive one, but is seen only through interactions. For example the CDC found that college-educated women are less likely to be obese than less educated women, but there was no similar trend for men (Ogden et al., 2010). This suggests that there is an interaction between gender and education, something that could be missed using forward and backward selection.

Random forests are nonparametric and are inherently nonlinear, thus freeing the investigator from having to make assumptions that may not be justifiable. In all models we assumed all variables were equally likely a priori and did not explicitly code for any interactions. Random forests are able to detect interactions, including high-order interactions. These interactions are taken into account in the variable importance measures. Random forests are also fast. The set of the top 30 variables was also stable – where we define stability as the inclusion of the same set of variables in each run – when we ran the analysis with different values of *mtry* and different random seeds. This method has the advantage of being fast and can aid policy makers and researchers in defining the important variables that they should focus on when determining health outcomes. As data sets become bigger and bigger, this benefit will become increasingly important. Using methods such as forward and backward selection can be time intensive and becomes infeasible when interactions are also considered. As our data becomes increasingly large, it is possible to miss important variables and interactions with more traditional methods. Assuming an additive model can lead to highly misleading results if there are large interactions between variables. Ignoring such interactions can lead to incorrect policy decisions. Thus, policy makers and researchers in the social and political sciences, as well as the medical sciences, should consider utilizing machine learning techniques for variable selection, such as random forests and their offshoots.

10 CONCLUSION

The world is becoming increasingly data driven. With our ever-increasing ability to digitize every aspect of our lives, the quantified self is fast becoming the new reality. Indeed Apple's ResearchKit has the potential to revolutionize medicine; these same tool kits will be used to better quantify how we shop, travel, and vote. However, even though our ability to generate data is ever increasing, it is of paramount importance to expand our capability to analyze and interpret that data. Only through analytics, not simply the generation of data, will we be able to answer policy questions and arrive at informed solutions. Incorrect analysis can lead to biased and poor decision making. Data sets are only going to become bigger and more complex, as has been seen in many fields from medicine to astrophysics to political science. Classical statistical methods are struggling to keep pace with the nature of the data being generated. These older methods are also not computationally feasible in very large data sets. In many fields, not just genetics, we are realizing that interactions are vitally important to prediction. When one considers all possible interactions, the parameter space becomes so large that transitional methods fail. Although many new methods are being developed, random forests and their offshoots offer a convenient and fast way to examine the data.

Our discussion of random forests has only scratched the surface. Random forests are an exciting area of research. We only touched on various extensions to random forests to better handle correlated features and censoring; however, there are a wide variety of improvements to random forests. Verikas et al. (2011) give an overview of many of the latest developments in RF methodology with an eye toward machine learning and data mining.

In recent years, a number of great advances have also been made toward understanding the theoretical underpinnings of random forests. While a general proof of consistency for Breiman's originally proposed algorithm proves to be elusive, consistency has been shown for a variety of simplified versions of random forests. Consistency of single trees has been proven when the number of observations within terminal nodes goes to infinity; however, random forests are traditionally constructed so that the number of observations in the terminal nodes is small.

See Lin and Jeon (2006), Hastie et al. (2009), and Scornet (2015) for illuminating discussions of the connections between random forests and adaptive nearest neighbor regression methods. Biau et al. (2008) investigate the consistency of bagging and two variants of random forests. They also shed light on how the greedy nature of the tree-growing algorithm used in Breiman's algorithm can lead to inconsistent estimates. Biau (2012) and Denil et al. (2013) introduce further variants of random forests for which consistency can be demonstrated. Scornet et al. (2014) investigate the consistency of the original algorithm in the context of additive regression models and shed light on how random forests excels when p is larger than n.

Although random forests are commonplace in certain biomedical and genetics applications, we believe they remain underutilized in the social sciences and health policy decision making. As the physical, medical, and social sciences become more data driven, they are also becoming more interdisciplinary. To fully understand the complex systems in our world, a researcher or policy maker must understand aspects of many diverse fields to make sense of the data. Too much time and effort are spent reinventing what is already known in other fields. Machine learning is one tool that should be included in the analytic toolbox across disciplines. Traditional model selection methods such as backward selection, forward selection, and best subsets selection may be highly unstable, biased, and computationally infeasible as the number of parameters and possible interactions increases. We believe random forests offer one solution to this problem and are particularly useful in the analysis of complex survey data sets, which are commonly used in the social sciences.

As our ability to generate very wide data sets grows, we will need to improve methods to efficiently harness the information contained in the data. Random forests and their offshoots give some of the best "off-the-shelf" and approachable algorithms for prediction as well as feature selection. RFs are computationally efficient because of their embarrassingly parallel nature. However, a random forest is not an *enchanted forest*, and care must still be taken in modeling and interpretation of the output. There are no panaceas, and the researcher must use the method that is best suited for his or her own data needs. One needs to take into account the source of the data to ensure that there is no selection bias. Even the best of algorithms do not allow the researcher to ignore factors such as confounders and selection bias. Care must still be taken to ensure that the results are generalizable even though the method does not seem to overfit. This is especially true in the case where the parameters greatly outnumber the observations.

References

Archer, Kellie J., & Kimes, Ryan V. 2008. Empirical characterization of random forest variable importance measures. *Computational Statistics & Data Analysis*, 52(4), 2249–2260.

Ballester, Pedro J., & Mitchell, John B. O. 2010. A machine learning approach to predicting protein–ligand binding affinity with applications to molecular docking. *Bioinformatics*, 26(9), 1169–1175.

Benjamini, Yoav, & Hochberg, Yosef. 1995. Controlling the false discovery rate: A practical and powerful approach to multiple testing. *Journal of the Royal Statistical Society. Series B (Methodological)*, 289–300.

Biau, Gérard. 2012. Analysis of a random forests model. *Journal of Machine Learning Research*, 13(1), 1063–1095.

Biau, Gérard, Devroye, Luc, & Lugosi, Gábor. 2008. Consistency of random forests and other averaging classifiers. *Journal of Machine Learning Research*, 9, 2015–2033.

Bickel, Peter J., & Ren, Jian-Jian. 2001. The bootstrap in hypothesis testing. *Lecture Notes-Monograph Series*, 91–112.

Bou-Hamad, Imad, Larocque, Denis, Ben-Ameur, Hatem, et al. 2011. A review of survival trees. *Statistics Surveys*, 5, 44–71.

Boulesteix, Anne-Laure, Bender, Andreas, Bermejo, Justo Lorenzo, & Strobl, Carolin. 2012a. Random forest Gini importance favours SNPs with large minor allele frequency: Impact, sources and recommendations. *Briefings in Bioinformatics*, 13(3), 292–304.

Boulesteix, Anne-Laure, Janitza, Silke, Kruppa, Jochen, & König, Inke R. 2012b. Overview of random forest methodology and practical guidance with emphasis on computational biology and bioinformatics. *Wiley Interdisciplinary Reviews: Data Mining and Knowledge Discovery*, 2(6), 493–507.

Breiman, L. 2003. How to use survival forests. *Department of Statistics, UC Berkeley*.

Breiman, Leo. 1996. Bagging predictors. *Machine Learning*, 24(2), 123–140.

Breiman, Leo. 2001. Random forests. *Machine Learning*, 45(1), 5–32.

Breiman, Leo, Friedman, Jerome, Stone, Charles J., & Olshen, Richard A. 1984. *Classification and Regression Trees*. CRC press.

Breiman, Leo, et al. 2001. Statistical modeling: The two cultures (with comments and a rejoinder by the author). *Statistical Science*, 16(3), 199–231.

Bureau, Alexandre, Dupuis, Josée, Falls, Kathleen, Lunetta, Kathryn L., Hayward, Brooke, Keith, Tim P., & Van Eerdewegh, Paul. 2005. Identifying SNPs predictive of phenotype using random forests. *Genetic Epidemiology*, 28(2), 171–182.

Chang, Jeffrey S., Yeh, Ru-Fang, Wiencke, John K., Wiemels, Joseph L., Smirnov, Ivan, Pico, Alexander R., Tihan, Tarik, Patoka, Joe, Miike, Rei, Sison, Jennette D., et al. 2008. Pathway analysis of single-nucleotide polymorphisms potentially associated with glioblastoma multiforme susceptibility using random forests. *Cancer Epidemiology Biomarkers & Prevention*, 17(6), 1368–1373.

Ciampi, A., Bush, R. S., Gospodarowicz, M., & Till, J. E. 1981. An approach to classifying prognostic factors related to survival experience for non-Hodgkin's lymphoma patients: Based on a series of 982 patients: 1967–1975. *Cancer*, 47(3), 621–627.

Conn, Daniel, Ngun, Tuck, Li, Gang, & Ramirez, Christina M. 2015. *Fuzzy Forests: A New WGCNA Based Random Forest Algorithm for Correlated, High-Dimensional Data*. Tech. rept. UCLA SPH, Biostatistics.

Cordell, Heather J. 2009. Detecting gene–gene interactions that underlie human diseases. *Nature Reviews Genetics*, 10(6), 392–404.

Cristianini, Nello, & Shawe-Taylor, John. 2000. *An Introduction to Support Vector Machines and Other Kernel-Based Learning Methods*. Cambridge University Press.

Denil, Misha, Matheson, David, & De Freitas, Nando. 2013. Narrowing the gap: Random forests in theory and in practice. *arXiv preprint arXiv:1310.1415*.

Díaz-Uriarte, Ramón, & De Andres, Sara Alvarez. 2006. Gene selection and classification of microarray data using random forest. *BMC Bioinformatics*, 7(1), 3.

Fan, Jianqing, & Li, Runze. 2001. Variable selection via nonconcave penalized likelihood and its oracle properties. *Journal of the American Statistical Association*, 96(456), 1348–1360.

Fromentin, Remi, Ramirez, Christina M., Khoury, Gabriela, Sinclair, Elizabeth, Hecht, Frederick M., Deeks, Steven G., Lewin, Sharon R., Sékaly, Rafick P., & Chomont, Nicolas. 2015. Immunological markers associated with HIV persistence during ART identified by iterated conditional random forests analysis. *International AIDS Society*.

García-Magariños, Manuel, López-de Ullibarri, Inaki, Cao, Ricardo, & Salas, Antonio. 2009. Evaluating the ability of tree-based methods and logistic regression for the detection of SNP-SNP interaction. *Annals of Human Genetics*, 73(3), 360–369.

Goldstein, Benjamin A., Polley, Eric C., & Briggs, Farren. 2011. Random forests for genetic association studies. *Statistical Applications in Genetics and Molecular Biology*, 10(1), 1–34.

Gordon, L., & Olshen, R. A. 1985. Tree-structured survival analysis. *Cancer Treatment Reports*, 69(10), 1065–1069.

Gregorutti, Baptiste, Michel, Bertrand, & Saint-Pierre, Philippe. 2013. Correlation and variable importance in random forests. *arXiv preprint arXiv:1310.5726*.

Hamby, Stephen E., & Hirst, Jonathan D. 2008. Prediction of glycosylation sites using random forests. *BMC Bioinformatics*, 9(1), 500.

Hapfelmeier, Alexander, Hothorn, Torsten, Ulm, Kurt, & Strobl, Carolin. 2014. A new variable importance measure for random forests with missing data. *Statistics and Computing*, 24(1), 21–34.

Hastie, Trevor, Tibshirani, Robert, and Friedman, Jerome, Hastie, T., Friedman, J., & Tibshirani, R. 2009. *The Elements of Statistical Learning*. Vol. 2. Springer.

Heagerty, Patrick J., & Zheng, Yingye. 2005. Survival model predictive accuracy and ROC curves. *Biometrics*, **61**(1), 92–105.

Hermann, Silke, Rohrmann, Sabine, Linseisen, Jakob, May, Anne M., Kunst, Anton, Besson, Herve, Romaguera, Dora, Travier, Noemie, Tormo, Maria-Jose, Molina, Esther, et al. 2011. The association of education with body mass index and waist circumference in the EPIC-PANACEA study. *BMC Public Health*, **11**(1), 169.

Hothorn, Torsten, Bühlmann, Peter, Dudoit, Sandrine, Molinaro, Annette, & Van Der Laan, Mark J. 2006. Survival ensembles. *Biostatistics*, **7**(3), 355–373.

Hothorn, Torsten, Hornik, Kurt, Strobl, Carolin, & Zeileis, Achim. 2010. *Party: A laboratory for recursive partytioning.*

Ishwaran, Hemant, Blackstone, Eugene H., Pothier, Claire E., & Lauer, Michael S. 2004. Relative risk forests for exercise heart rate recovery as a predictor of mortality. *Journal of the American Statistical Association*, **99**(467), 591–600.

Ishwaran, Hemant, & Kogalur, Udaya B. 2010. Consistency of random survival forests. *Statistics & Probability Letters*, **80**(13), 1056–1064.

Ishwaran, Hemant, Kogalur, Udaya B., Blackstone, Eugene H., & Lauer, Michael S. 2008. Random survival forests. *Annals of Applied Statistics*, 841–860.

Jiang, Rui, Tang, Wanwan, Wu, Xuebing, & Fu, Wenhui. 2009. A random forest approach to the detection of epistatic interactions in case-control studies. *BMC Bioinformatics*, **10**(Suppl 1), S65.

Kaplan, Edward L., & Meier, Paul. 1958. Nonparametric estimation from incomplete observations. *Journal of the American Statistical Association*, **53**(282), 457–481.

Liaw, Andy, & Wiener, Matthew. 2002. Classification and regression by random-forest. *R News*, **2**(3), 18–22.

Lin, Yi, & Jeon, Yongho. 2006. Random forests and adaptive nearest neighbors. *Journal of the American Statistical Association*, **101**(474), 578–590.

Lin, Nan, Wu, Baolin, Jansen, Ronald, Gerstein, Mark, & Zhao, Hongyu. 2004. Information assessment on predicting protein-protein interactions. *BMC Bioinformatics*, **5**(1), 154.

Lockhart, Richard, Taylor, Jonathan, Tibshirani, Ryan J., & Tibshirani, Robert. 2014. A significance test for the LASSO. *Annals of Statistics*, **42**(2), 413.

Lunetta, Kathryn L., Hayward, L. Brooke, Segal, Jonathan, & Van Eerdewegh, Paul. 2004. Screening large-scale association study data: exploiting interactions using random forests. *BMC Genetics*, **5**(1), 32.

Maddah, M., Eshraghian, M. R., Djazayery, A., & Mirdamadi, R. 2003. Association of body mass index with educational level in Iranian men and women. *European Journal of Clinical Nutrition*, **57**(7), 819–823.

Maenner, Matthew J., Denlinger, Loren C., Langton, Asher, Meyers, Kristin J., Engelman, Corinne D., & Skinner, Halcyon G. 2009. Detecting gene-by-smoking interactions in a genome-wide association study of early-onset coronary heart disease using random forests. *BMC Proceedings*, vol. 3, p. 588. BioMed Central Ltd.

Mansiaux, Yohann, & Carrat, Fabrice. 2014. Detection of independent associations in a large epidemiologic data set: a comparison of random forests, boosted regression trees, conventional and penalized logistic regression for identifying independent factors associated with H1N1pdm influenza infections. *BMC Medical Research Methodology*, **14**(1), 99.

Marubini, E., Morabito, A., & Valsecchi, M. G. 1983. Prognostic factors and risk groups: Some results given by using an algorithm suitable for censored survival data. *Statistics in Medicine*, 2(2), 295–303.

McKinney, Brett A., Reif, David M., Ritchie, Marylyn D., & Moore, Jason H. 2006. Machine learning for detecting gene-gene interactions. *Applied Bioinformatics*, 5(2), 77–88.

Molarius, Anu, Seidell, Jacob C., Sans, Susana, Tuomilehto, Jaakko, Kuulasmaa, Kari, et al. 2000. Educational level, relative body weight, and changes in their association over 10 years: An international perspective from the WHO MONICA Project. *American Journal of Public Health*, 90(8), 1260–1268.

Molinaro, Annette M., Dudoit, Sandrine, & Van der Laan, Mark J. 2004. Tree-based multivariate regression and density estimation with right-censored data. *Journal of Multivariate Analysis*, 90(1), 154–177.

Nicodemus, Kristin K., & Malley, James D. 2009. Predictor correlation impacts machine learning algorithms: Implications for genomic studies. *Bioinformatics*, 25(15), 1884–1890.

Nicodemus, Kristin K., Malley, James D., Strobl, Carolin, & Ziegler, Andreas. 2010. The behaviour of random forest permutation-based variable importance measures under predictor correlation. *BMC Bioinformatics*, 11(1), 110.

Nicodemus, Kristin K., Wang, Wenyi, & Shugart, Yin Y. 2007. Stability of variable importance scores and rankings using statistical learning tools on single-nucleotide polymorphisms and risk factors involved in gene x gene and gene x environment interactions. *BMC Proceedings*, vol. 1, p. S58. BioMed Central Ltd.

Ogden, Cynthia L., Lamb, Molly M., Carroll, Margaret D., & Flegal, Katherine M. 2010. Obesity and socioeconomic status in adults: United States 1988–1994 and 2005–2008. NCHS data brief no 50. National Center for Health Statistics. Hyattsville, MD.

Qi, Yanjun, Bar-Joseph, Ziv, & Klein-Seetharaman, Judith. 2006. Evaluation of different biological data and computational classification methods for use in protein interaction prediction. *Proteins: Structure, Function, and Bioinformatics*, 63(3), 490–500.

Raskutti, Garvesh, Wainwright, Martin J., & Yu, Bin. 2010. Restricted eigenvalue properties for correlated Gaussian designs. *Journal of Machine Learning Research*, 11, 2241–2259.

Reif, David M., Motsinger-Reif, Alison A., McKinney, Brett A., Rock, Michael T., Crowe, J. E., & Moore, Jason H. 2009. Integrated analysis of genetic and proteomic data identifies biomarkers associated with adverse events following smallpox vaccination. *Genes and Immunity*, 10(2), 112–119.

Riddick, Gregory, Song, Hua, Ahn, Susie, Walling, Jennifer, Borges-Rivera, Diego, Zhang, Wei, & Fine, Howard A. 2011. Predicting in vitro drug sensitivity using random forests. *Bioinformatics*, 27(2), 220–224.

Sampson, Dayle L., Parker, Tony J., Upton, Zee, & Hurst, Cameron P. 2011. A comparison of methods for classifying clinical samples based on proteomics data: A case study for statistical and machine learning approaches. *PloS One*, 6(9), e24973.

Schwarz, Daniel F., König, Inke R., & Ziegler, Andreas. 2010. On safari to Random Jungle: A fast implementation of Random Forests for high-dimensional data. *Bioinformatics*, 26(14), 1752–1758.

Scornet, Erwan. 2015. Random forests and kernel methods. *arXiv preprint arXiv:1502.03836*.

Scornet, Erwan, Biau, Gérard, & Vert, Jean-Philippe. 2014. Consistency of random forests. *arXiv preprint arXiv:1405.2881*.

Segal, Mark Robert. 1988. Regression trees for censored data. *Biometrics*, 35–47.

Segal, Mark R., Barbour, Jason D., & Grant, Robert M. 2004. Relating HIV-1 sequence variation to replication capacity via trees and forests. *Statistical Applications in Genetics and Molecular Biology*, 3(1), 1–18.

Shi, Tao, & Horvath, Steve. 2006. Unsupervised learning with random forest predictors. *Journal of Computational and Graphical Statistics*, 15(1).

Shi, Tao, Seligson, David, Belldegrun, Arie S, Palotie, Aarno, & Horvath, Steve. 2005. Tumor classification by tissue microarray profiling: Random forest clustering applied to renal cell carcinoma. *Modern Pathology*, 18(4), 547–557.

Šikić, Mile, Tomić, Sanja, & Vlahoviček, Kristian. 2009. Prediction of protein–protein interaction sites in sequences and 3D structures by random forests. *PLoS Computational Biology*, 5(1), e1000278.

Somorjai, Ray L., Dolenko, B., & Baumgartner, Richard. 2003. Class prediction and discovery using gene microarray and proteomics mass spectroscopy data: Curses, caveats, cautions. *Bioinformatics*, 19(12), 1484–1491.

Stekhoven, Daniel J., & Bühlmann, Peter. 2012. MissForest – non-parametric missing value imputation for mixed-type data. *Bioinformatics*, 28(1), 112–118.

Storey, John D. 2003. The positive false discovery rate: A Bayesian interpretation and the q-value. *Annals of Statistics*, 2013–2035.

Strobl, Carolin, Boulesteix, Anne-Laure, Zeileis, Achim, & Hothorn, Torsten. 2007. Bias in random forest variable importance measures: Illustrations, sources and a solution. *BMC Bioinformatics*, 8(1), 25.

Strobl, Carolin, Boulesteix, Anne-Laure, Kneib, Thomas, Augustin, Thomas, & Zeileis, Achim. 2008. Conditional variable importance for random forests. *BMC Bioinformatics*, 9(1), 307.

Strobl, Carolin, & Zeileis, Achim. 2008. Danger: High power! – exploring the statistical properties of a test for random forest variable importance. *Proceedings of the 18th International Conference on Computational Statistics*.

Sun, Yan V., Cai, Zhaohui, Desai, Kaushal, Lawrance, Rachael, Leff, Richard, Jawaid, Ansar, Kardia, Sharon L. R., & Yang, Huiying. 2007. Classification of rheumatoid arthritis status with candidate gene and genome-wide single-nucleotide polymorphisms using random forests. *BMC Proceedings*, vol. 1, p. 562. BioMed Central Ltd.

Svetnik, Vladimir, Liaw, Andy, Tong, Christopher, Culberson, J., Christopher, Sheridan, Robert P., & Feuston, Bradley P. 2003. Random forest: A classification and regression tool for compound classification and QSAR modeling. *Journal of Chemical Information and Computer Sciences*, 43(6), 1947–1958.

Tibshirani, Robert. 1996. Regression shrinkage and selection via the Lasso. *Journal of the Royal Statistical Society. Series B (Methodological)*, 267–288.

Van De Geer, Sara A., Bühlmann, Peter, et al. 2009. On the conditions used to prove oracle results for the Lasso. *Electronic Journal of Statistics*, 3, 1360–1392.

Verikas, Antanas, Gelzinis, Adas, & Bacauskiene, Marija. 2011. Mining data with random forests: a survey and results of new tests. *Pattern Recognition*, 44(2), 330–349.

Wu, Jiansheng, Liu, Hongde, Duan, Xueye, Ding, Yan, Wu, Hongtao, Bai, Yunfei, & Sun, Xiao. 2009. Prediction of DNA-binding residues in proteins from amino acid sequences using a random forest model with a hybrid feature. *Bioinformatics*, **25**(1), 30–35.

Zhang, Bin, & Horvath, Steve. 2005. A general framework for weighted gene co-expression network analysis. *Statistical Applications in Genetics and Molecular Biology*, **4**(1).

Zhang, Heping, Wang, Minghui, & Chen, Xiang. 2009. Willows: A memory efficient tree and forest construction package. *BMC Bioinformatics*, **10**(1), 130.

Zhu, Ruoqing, & Kosorok, Michael R. 2012. Recursively imputed survival trees. *Journal of the American Statistical Association*, **107**(497), 331–340.

PART 2

COMPUTATIONAL SOCIAL SCIENCE APPLICATIONS

7

Big Data, Social Media, and Protest

Foundations for a Research Agenda

Joshua A. Tucker, Jonathan Nagler, Megan MacDuffee Metzger, Pablo Barberá, Duncan Penfold-Brown, and Richard Bonneau*

1 INTRODUCTION

The past decade has witnessed a rapid rise in the use of social media around the globe.[1] For political scientists, this is a phenomenon begging to be understood. It has been claimed repeatedly – usually in the absence of solid data – that these social media resources are profoundly shaping participation in social movements, including protest movements (see Bond, Fariss, Jones, Kramer, Marlow, Settle, & Fowler 2012; Cha et al. 2010; Jungherr, Jurgens, & Schoen 2012; Lynch 2011; Shirky 2011). Social media are often assumed to affect an extremely wide range of individual-level behaviors, including communicating about politics to friends and family members, donating or soliciting money for political campaigns and causes, voting, and engaging in collective forms of protest. In truth, however, the research community knows remarkably little about whether (*and especially how*) the use of social media systematically affects political participation.

Perhaps nowhere is this lack of knowledge more clear than in the matter of political protest. In recent years, the use of social media has been linked to the spread of political protests in cities around the world, including Moscow, Kiev, Istanbul, Ankara, Cairo, Tripoli, Athens, Madrid, New York, and Los Angeles. Obviously, social protest itself is far from new, but the fact that it is possible for potential protest participants, as well as geographically removed observers, to access real-time accounts of protest behavior documented and

* The authors are all members of the New York University Social Media and Political Participation laboratory (smapp.nyu.edu). The writing of this article was supported by the INSPIRE program of the National Science Foundation (Award # SES-1248077) and Dean Thomas Carew and the Research Investment Fund (RIF) of New York University. We thank John Jost for his contributions to an earlier version of this manuscript.

archived through micro-blogging (e.g., Twitter) and social media (e.g., Facebook) websites is a novel phenomenon. Protest activities are flagged by participants themselves with distinctive hashtags on Twitter.[2] As political scientists, then, the question of how these activities on social media actually affect the decision of individuals to participate in protests would seem to be a subject ripe for research, as too is the macro question of how social media changes the nature of protest itself.

As is often the case in both popular and scholarly commentary, new phenomena inevitably engender a counternarrative, claiming that the phenomenon is either not new or not important. The rise of social media – and the concurrent level of fascination accorded to it across the media spectra – and its relationship to mass protests movements have been no exception in this regard. As we illustrate in more detail in Section 2, critics have suggested, in turn, that social media was not actually all that new, not all that prevalent, not all that relevant, or some combination of all three.

As time has passed, however, it has become increasingly difficult to sustain the idea that social media use is completely unrelated to mass protests as we observe politicians flocking to Twitter to rally supporters (Munger 2014), tens of millions of tweets using hashtags related to protest events (Barberá and Metzger 2013), Facebook pages organizing movements that generated hundreds of thousands of likes *per day* at the height of protests (Tucker et al. 2014a), and surveys showing that majorities of participants in protests were there at least in part because they had received invitations or information on social media (Onuch 2014).

With this in mind, the goal of this chapter is twofold. First, we lay out some basic, empirically observable characteristics of social media use during protests that could be said to be *necessary* criteria for us to believe that social media could have affected participation in political protest. To be clear, we are not at this time ready to provide causal evidence of an effect for social media on individual level decisions to join protests. Instead, we want to identify patterns of social media usage that would be *inconsistent* with social media usage being related to protest participation. By systematically showing that these conditions do not hold, we are arguing that we cannot reject the contention that social media usage may have affected participation in these protests and thus that the subject warrants future study. Second, we demonstrate that the empirical and methodological tools already exist using *publicly available data* to assess some of these criteria by providing evidence from the 2013 Turkish Gezi Park protests and the 2013–2014 Ukrainian Euromaidan protests, and that both movements do indeed qualify as protests in which social media could well have played an important role.[3] We then conclude the chapter by briefly laying out a micro-level research framework for future analysis regarding the means by which individual use of social media could hinder or facilitate participation in mass protests.

2 SOCIAL MEDIA AND PROTEST

Social media has been used as a tool of protest almost since it became popular as a tool for social interaction, with some contending that it has played a vital role in spreading basic information during such events. Lysenko and Desouza (2012) have suggested that Twitter was especially helpful in internationalizing the Moldovan protests and broadcasting information about mass demonstrations. At the same time, claims such as these were challenged by Morozov (2009a), who concluded that there were too few Twitter users in Moldova at the time to produce such effects.[4]

Since Moldova there have been a rash of protests, revolutions, and uprisings that have been heralded as "social media" revolutions. From the Occupy Movement in the United States to the Green Revolution in Iran to the Indignados Movement in Spain, popular understanding has been that social media has had a substantial impact on the way that social movements are organized, emerge, and are carried out. At the same time, scholars and media pundits continue to argue about the importance of social media and about what role it specifically plays. In general, skeptics point to the lack of concrete behavioral evidence demonstrating that citizens' online involvement directly shapes offline events; they conclude that the use of social media is neither a necessary nor sufficient condition of protest (Aday et al. 2010; Gladwell 2010; Lynch 2011; Schwartz 2011). Further, scholars such as Hale (2013) have argued that it was the reality of events on the ground that caused the "revolution" and not the use of social media. Perhaps the most widely recognized of these critiques is Malcolm Gladwell's 2010 article in *The New Yorker*, eye-catchingly titled "Small Change: Why the Revolution Will Not Be Tweeted."[5] Gladwell argued that the types of social networks that are facilitated by Twitter or Facebook involve "weak" (rather than "strong") social ties, in the language of Granovetter (1983). As a result, he concluded that they are unlikely to motivate the types of commitment and sacrifice required to sustain a protest movement. Social media usage, according to Gladwell, may support certain varieties of "slacktivism" (defined by the online "urban dictionary" as "the act of participating in obviously pointless activities as an expedient alternative to actually expending effort to fix a problem"), but they pose very little threat to existing political regimes.

The largest scale target of these criticisms is the Arab Spring Revolutions in 2011. Again, there was an initial excitement that social media had been an enormous motivating factor. Indeed, the U.S. State Department apparently regarded Twitter as sufficiently important in promoting regime opposition that it asked the company to postpone scheduled maintenance tasks to avoid disruption of service.[6] This excitement was followed, however, by an enormous level of criticism that the real work was happening offline. Morozov (2011) pointed out that cyber-activists were meeting in person to strategize. Other scholars (Tufekci & Wilson 2012) have argued that many of the activists working online knew each other in person (i.e., their connection was not generated by weak ties online). Other scholars pointed out that English-language tweets dominated the primary hashtags (Wilson & Dunn 2011). Still others (Bruns et al. 2013) have found seemingly less domination of the overall social media conversation by English-language participation, and yet even these relatively positive accounts suggest that more activity was in English than in Arabic in the Egyptian case, and that much of the activity came from outside of the country.

Bennet and Segerberg (2012), however, contend that it is not necessarily the case that new approaches to protest are ineffective, as Gladwell implies; rather, it is just that their putative effectiveness is difficult to understand on the basis of familiar, traditional models of collective action. These authors suggest that a new form of organization, which they term "connective action," has emerged in response to the new opportunities afforded by digital technology and the use of social media. In contrast to Gladwell, they claim that the relatively decentralized, diffuse nature of organization in these social movements constitutes their basis for success rather than a sign of failure. Using the 15M protests in Spain in 2011–2012 as an example, they argue that given "its seemingly informal organization, the 15M (or Indignado) mobilization surprised many observers by sustaining and even building strength over time, using a mix of online media and offline activities that included face-to-face organizing, encampments in city centers, and marches across the country" (Bennet & Segerberg 2012, p. 741).

The problem with many of these debates is that those who think social media matters for protest and those who tend to argue that it does not are talking around one another more than they are talking to each other. Many of the criticisms made by, for example, Morozov, are true. It is clear that organizers continue to engage in traditional forms of organization and that, in the case of the Arab Spring, strong ties played important roles. This is doubtless true in the case of other protest movements, and yet this does not preclude the fact that social media may be changing the dynamics of mobilization. Activists can employ different strategies at the same time, and new strategies can shape the old (and vice versa).

Further, there seems to be a very narrow understanding in some work of what it would mean for social media to actually "matter," suggesting that what we need is to understand in more precise ways what social media is doing during protest. Thus the purpose of this chapter is to create a foundation from which future work can be built by establishing as a baseline the necessary conditions that must be met to suggest that social media *might* be doing something new in terms of organizing protests. Establishing this foundation is essential. Before we can show *what* social media is doing, we must first show *that* social media is doing something new at all.

To explore these questions we use data from two recent cases: the Gezi Park protests in Turkey in the summer of 2013 and the Euromaidan protests in Ukraine during the winter of 2013–2014. The Turkish protests began as relatively small, primarily environmentally driven protests in opposition to the proposed destruction of Gezi Park in the center of Istanbul to build a shopping mall. After the police entered the park and burned the tents of the small group of activists camped in the square – an action that was viewed as a massive, violent overreaction to a calm, peaceful protest – hundreds of thousands of people joined the protests in Gezi Park. During the first few days of these events, as the protests grew in size, the mainstream media in Turkey failed to cover the protests. At the same time, activity on social media related to the protests was widespread and reached seemingly unprecedented levels in days.

The result was a remarkable quasi-natural experiment pertaining to information diffusion through online social networks. In the first month of the protest alone, more than 30 million tweets citing the most salient hashtags were transmitted; most of these were sent in Turkish from inside the country. These figures were significantly higher than those observed in earlier social movements, such as the Egyptian revolution of 2011, where less than 30% of the tweets originated in Egypt (Starbird 2012). Furthermore, almost a half-million of the Turkish tweets were geolocated, with over 80% inside Turkey.

The protests in Ukraine exhibited a similar dynamic whereby a small, seemingly limited event quickly gave way to much larger protest against the regime more generally. Protests in Ukraine were triggered initially by the failure of Ukrainian president Viktor Yanukovych to sign an association agreement with the European Union that had been in the works for a number of months. Yanukovych backed out of the agreement just as he was scheduled to sign it. In response, opposition leaders and activists took to Twitter and Facebook and called on citizens to converge on Independence Square in Kiev to protest the decision. The protests quickly grew into the largest ones in Ukraine since the Orange Revolution, eventually culminating in Yanukovych's ouster, as well as leading to the annexation of Crimea by Russia and the ongoing separatist conflict in Eastern Ukraine.

In the following sections we outline a set of minimal conditions necessary to demonstrate the value of continued research into the role of social media in protest, before exploring whether and how these conditions are met in our two key cases.

3 CONDITIONS TO REJECT SKEPTICISM

We turn now to elucidating a set of characteristics of social media use that can be said to lay out our "minimal thresholds" (or necessary conditions) for holding open the possibility that social media could have played a role worth investigating in a protest movement.[7] We propose five such criteria: (1) the content of messages on social media must contain details about the protests; (2) social media usage should track developments on the ground in predictable ways; (3) social media use related to the protest must at least in part be taking place among people in the country in which the protest takes place;[8] (4) social media use related to the protest must at least in part be taking place in the primary language(s) used by people in the county in which the protest takes place; and (5) when protest participants are asked how they came to participate in the protest, nontrivial numbers must report having received information about the protests or invitations to participate in the protests through social media.[9]

First, we suggest that the contents of social media messages should transmit important details about the protests, including information about when and where a given demonstration is taking place, as well as what happens once the demonstration begins. This would suggest that protest activity could, in principle, be facilitated by information that is disseminated through social media. Ideally, machine learning techniques will be developed to code (and quantify) messages automatically in terms of their organizational content. In the meantime, we are relying on a different technique, which is to monitor the popularity over time of public Facebook pages that provide detailed information about protests. We also identify and follow hashtags that are most clearly related to the organization of protest activity and observe (qualitatively) messages from political elites and organizations that are related to the protests.

Our second condition is that social media usage should closely track developments on the ground as they unfold. That is, we should observe dynamic spikes in social media use that coincide with major events related to protest activity and regime responses to that activity.

Third, at least some of the social media messages related to protests should originate from within the country in which the protests are taking place, which would indicate that social media was not merely serving as a vehicle for spreading international news and commentary. The most reliable way to do this is to examine "geo-tagged" tweets, which have metadata associated with the tweet that reports the location of the poster when the post was made. These locations are highly accurate, but only a small number of people choose to geo-tag posts. On Twitter, the percentage has historically been in the 1–2% range (although it is increasing and, as we note later, it was significantly higher than that in the Turkish case). Nonetheless, even this relatively small proportion of users provides an opportunity to explore trends in the data.

A fourth condition is that a significant proportion of tweets about the protests should be written in the primary language(s) used by citizens in the country of protest. Language classification of tweets is relatively easy and accurate using off-the-shelf language detection programs. To be clear, our expectation is never that all protest-related tweets will be written in a native language. Social media provide excellent opportunities and incentives for protesters to attract international attention to what is happening in their country. However, if social media posts were being made more or less exclusively in a foreign language, then skeptics would be warranted to doubt that social media was directly facilitating protest participation in the country of interest.

All four of these conditions can be assessed by analyzing social media data. However, traditional survey analysis also remains an extremely valuable tool for learning about the relationship between social media use and political behavior. Thus our final criterion is simply that, if we have access to surveys of protest participants, we would want to see respondents mentioning social media when directly asked about why or how they managed to take part in the protest.

4 EMPIRICAL EVIDENCE: TURKEY AND UKRAINE

4.1 Background and Data

With these conditions in mind, the next step is to examine the evidence from Turkey and Ukraine. We followed a similar Twitter data collection strategy in both cases. First, we developed a list of keywords and hashtags related to the protests. We selected these terms from observing sample posts, our own knowledge of events on the ground, and in consultation with locals and experts.[10] We then used a python package we developed for collecting tweets in real time to collect all tweets that contained any of these keywords or hashtags (this package is available at https://github.com/SMAPPNYU/TweetCollector).[11] Our data, then, contains almost every tweet sent using any of our keywords or hashtags during the collection period. Although we may have missed some relevant tweets without hashtags or any of our keywords, overall our collection should represent a significant portion of the tweets sent about the events under study. In the Turkish case, the data analyzed in this chapter was collected from May 31, 2013, to June 30, 2013, and contains 29,901,410 tweets. In Ukraine, the data was collected from November 25, 2013, through February 28, 2014, and contains 10,918,931 tweets.[12]

In both countries, we also scraped public Facebook pages dedicated to the protests.[13] The data collection process for Facebook is different than for Twitter. At any time, we can scrape all of the information that is available on any public Facebook page, meaning that unlike in the case of Twitter we are able to scrape data ex post.[14] However, a crucial limitation to analyzing Facebook data is that only public pages can be scraped. Whereas the vast majority of Twitter accounts are public, the vast majority of Facebook accounts are not. Public Facebook pages typically include the pages of politicians, organizations, and public figures. Additionally, often pages are created to coordinate resources or activities during protests or simply to promote the protests themselves, and it is these that we examine in this chapter.[15] These pages certainly represent only a small portion of total Facebook activity about the protests, but nonetheless can give us some insight into one of the ways individuals use the platform during protest.

4.2 Content of Messages and Details about Protest

In the first 24 hours alone of our Turkish Twitter data collection, the most popular protest hashtag, #direngeziparki (in its various spellings), appears in more than 1.5 million tweets. This was a dramatic increase from previous protests in which social media was reported to be important. To put this starkly, this was more tweets than the most important hashtag from the Egyptian revolution *for the entirety of the revolution* (Wilson & Dunn 2011). Some of this is undoubtedly related to different dynamics in terms of the use of hashtags more generally, but it is nonetheless startling. Throughout the protest, we continue to see high levels of activity on Twitter (see Figure 7.2 in Section 4.3). Due to the fact that the tweets in our data set contain hashtags and keywords explicitly connected to the protests themselves, as opposed to general terms that might be related to the protest but could be used for other purposes, we have good evidence that people are talking about protest online.

This inference is further reinforced by a qualitative examination of a sample of the tweets.[16] Among the tweets, we find calls for blood donations of certain blood types to local medical centers to assist injured protestors, advice on how to wash one's face if exposed to tear gas, and resources for getting legal assistance if arrested, along with general pro-protest conversation. We even observe a tweet directed at a particular user to get out of a café and come join the protests.

In the Ukrainian case, Twitter activity was, overall, lower than in Turkey. Particularly in the beginning of the protests, we see comparatively low levels of Twitter use. For comparison, the most common Ukrainian hashtag #Euromaidan (and its Russian and Ukrainian equivalents) was tweeted only 120,000 times in the first six days of data collection. Over time, however, we observe these overall rates increase dramatically in the Ukrainian case. As in the Turkish case, a qualitative examination suggests that our data includes tweets with links to maps of where to get coffee and tea for free, tweets from politicians and activists about the protests, and tweets about levels of violence. One of the leaders of the opposition, Arseniy Yatsenyuk, even took to Twitter to reject a deal presented by the government (see Figure 7.1).

We also find additional evidence that social media was being used to disseminate information that was directly related to participating in the protests from Facebook. A number of Facebook pages were started that related to the protests in both Turkey and Ukraine. Tables 7.1 and 7.2 show a breakdown of some of the key pages in each case. These pages were explicitly geared toward providing information about the protests and about what was happening in the protests. These pages were particularly important in Ukraine, where activity

Arseniy Yatsenyuk
@Yatsenyuk_AP

No deal @ua_yanukovych, we're finishing
what we started. The people decide our
leaders, not you. #Євромайдан

RETWEETS   FAVORITES
459   146

3:41 PM - 25 Jan 2014

FIGURE 7.1. Tweet by opposition leader Arseniy Yatsenyuk on January 25, 2014.

on Facebook was very high, despite comparatively low levels of activity on
Twitter. For example, the main Euromaidan Facebook page was started on
November 21, at the very beginning of the protests, and quickly grew in popularity so that by less than two weeks into the protests, it already had 126,000
likes (Barberá and Metzger 2013).[17] Other pages focused on topics such as
organizing medical care and carpools to the protests.

4.3 Social Media Use and Offline Developments

Next, we examine whether social media use was responsive to key events on the
ground. Most significantly, we would expect increases in activity when important events are taking place, and less activity when things on the ground are
relatively stable. Figure 7.2 shows the overall level of activity on Twitter using
our keywords and hashtags across the first 30 days of the protests in Turkey,
with several key events annotated.[18] We can observe increases in activity corresponding with a number of key events during the protests. The highest density
of activity is associated with May 31/June 1, which is the beginning of our
data set and coincides with the use of police force, including tear gas and water
cannons against protesters, as well as the initial call for people to come to join
the protests. After this initial burst of Twitter usage, levels of activity diminish,
although it is important to note that there is still a good bit of activity throughout the protest period. We see another spike in activity around June 11 when
police make an attempt to clear the square, and yet another when the square
is successfully cleared by the police. All together, this provides strong evidence
to support the conclusion that our second condition is met in the Turkish case.
Activity on social media seems to vary with key events on the ground in ways

TABLE 7.1. *Key Facebook Pages: Ukraine*

Page	Purpose	# of Likes	Date Started
www.facebook.com/ EuroMaydan	Main page	290,000	11/21/2013
www.facebook.com/ EvromaidanSOS	Organizing Resources (legal, social, and journalistic) for victims of violence and protest participants	102,000	11/30/2013
www.facebook.com/ EnglishMaidan	News about Euromaidan in English	40,860	11/30/2013
www.facebook.com/ maidanmed	Coordinating volunteer medical care	5,221	12/02/2013
www.facebook.com/ maidanhelp/	Coordinating help of a variety of types for those on the Maidan	5,804	12/06/2013
www.facebook.com/ helpgettomaidan	Organizing carpools to the protests	12,375	12/10/2013
www.facebook.com/ RESOURSES.maidan	Similar to Euromaidan SOS	1,561	01/24/2014
http://vk.com/ antimaydan	Anti-Maidan vKontakte page	484,440 (followers)	

we would expect, and as activity on the ground diminishes, so do social media conversations about protest. To be clear, this pattern does not conclusively demonstrate that social media is being used to organize participation in the protests or that it is being used to report on the protests to outside audiences

TABLE 7.2. *Key Facebook Pages: Turkey*

Page	Purpose	# of Likes	Date Started
www.facebook.com/ TaksimDayanismasi	Taksim Solidarity Movement Page; Started Before Protests	82,683	02/15/2012
www.facebook.com/ geziparkidirenisi/	Most Popular Occupy Gezi Page	643,951	05/31/2013
www.facebook.com/ TaksimDiren	Another Occupy Gezi Page	55,854	05/31/2013
www.facebook.com/pages/ Diren-Gezi-Park	Another Turkish Occupy Gezi Page	25,136	06/01/2013
www.facebook.com/ OccupyGezi/	Mostly English Occupy Gezi Page	65,215	05/31/2013

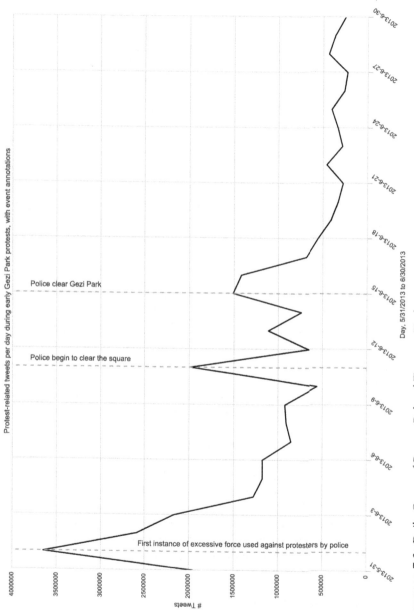

Protest-related tweets per day during early Gezi Park protests, with event annotations

Police clear Gezi Park

Police begin to clear the square

First instance of excessive force used against protesters by police

Day. 5/31/2013 to 6/30/2013

Tweets

FIGURE 7.2. Daily Count of Protest Related Tweets – Turkey.

as or after they occur, but it does hold open the possibility that either and/or both of these are occurring.

Figure 7.3, which shows the same data for Ukraine, reveals a similar pattern of correspondence between key events on the ground and levels of activity on social media. We can see an initial spike in activity after protestors are beaten by police in the early days of the protests, and then additional spikes in response to other violent incidents. We see a huge uptick in relation to the first fatalities of the protests and then an absolutely enormous uptick in activity associated with the resurgence of violence in February. The increase in activity in relation to the anti-protest laws is not as dramatic as that associated with instances of violence, which is perhaps not entirely surprising. Nonetheless, we see a responsiveness on the part of Twitter users to the passing of these laws, which preceded increased protest activity and violence.

We find similar trends if we look at data from Facebook (Figures 7.A1 and 7.A2 in the Online Appendix).[19] In the Turkish case, there was no single page associated with protest organizers, so we present data from the two most widely liked Facebook pages related to the protest. TaksimDayanismasi ("Taksim Solidarity") is the Facebook page for the movement that started the original initial environmental protests. As such, this page existed before the protests, but we observe a huge increase in activity on this page related to the increase in size of the protests and the intervention of the police in the protests. We can also see spikes here around June 11 and 16, when the police attempted to clear the square, as we saw with the Twitter activity described earlier, and finally a return to relatively low levels of activity once the main protest period is over. Geziparkidirenisi (whose name on the page is Diren Gezi Parki, which loosely translates as "Resist Gezi Park") is the most-liked page started specifically in response to the protests. Again, we can see similar increases in activity in response to events on the ground, although activity on this page is higher overall, with likes reaching a million during the height of the protests.

In the Ukrainian case, there was a more clearly centralized main page, the Euromaidan page. If we observe activity on this page over time, we see similar trends to those found in Turkey. There are high levels of activity throughout the main protest periods, with a lull during the relatively calm, quiet period around New Year's Day and subsequent upticks in activity as the situation becomes tense again in January. Further, we see spikes corresponding with key events, as we saw on Twitter. For example, there is a huge uptick on January 15 corresponding with the anti-protest law, as well as a continuing increase as the situation grows violent in response.

Finally, we find some evidence in our data that people actually join social media in response to protest events. Figures 7.A3 and 7.A4 in the Online Appendix (www.cambridge.org/CSSonlineappendix) show the distribution of account creation dates for users who tweeted at least once in our data set. What we find is a relatively uniform distribution over dates preceding the protests in

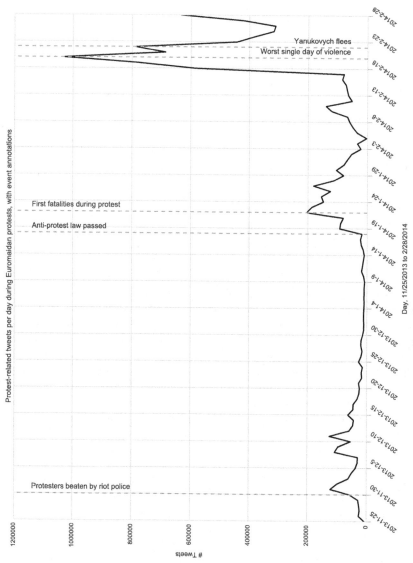

Protest-related tweets per day during Euromaidan protests, with event annotations

First fatalities during protest

Anti-protest law passed

Protesters beaten by riot police

Yanukovych flees

Worst single day of violence

Tweets

Day, 11/25/2013 to 2/28/2014

FIGURE 7.3. Daily Count of Protest Related Tweets – Ukraine.

211

both the Ukrainian and Turkish cases, but a spike in accounts created during the very first days of the protests. Although some of this increased activity is, no doubt, associated with the creation of accounts *about* the protests, the total number of accounts created is too high for this to be the primary explanation for the phenomenon. In Ukraine, where the protests continued over a longer period, we also see spikes corresponding to subsequent increases in protest activity. All of this strongly suggests that users may be joining Twitter precisely because it is an avenue to receive and/or share information concerning the protests.

Taken together, activity on social media seems to be highly responsive to key events on the ground in both cases: as activity on the ground diminishes, so too do social media conversations about protest. Furthermore, not only were people who were already on Twitter varying the quantity of their discussion of protest-related events in accordance with developments on the ground, but the data also suggest that people were joining Twitter in response to offline protest-related developments.

4.4 Location of Social Media Usage

One of the major critiques of the role of social media during the Arab Spring Revolutions was that much of the seemingly high levels of activity witnessed on social media during these events actually originated outside of the region, or was in English rather than Arabic, or both (Aday et al. 2010; Wilson & Dunn 2011). In Section 2, we suggested that this critique may not be so much an objection to social media's role in the protests as an observation that social media can play a number of different roles during a protest. However, even if one role of social media is to publicize events to the international community, if this is the *only* way that the protests are being discussed on social media, it might indicate that social media were not playing such a key role in influencing individual participation in those protests. Our data from Turkey, however, suggests that not only was a nontrivial portion of the activity on social media coming from within Turkey and written in the local language, but in fact the majority of it was.

Ideally, we would like to be able to see where all online activity related to the protests originated. Unfortunately, this is not possible. Although we can use the location that individual users declare on their accounts, this is an imperfect measure of where people are actually located at a given moment in time. As discussed earlier, however, a small proportion of Twitter users geolocate their tweets.[20]

When we observe the tweets from the data set that contain geolocation information in the Turkish case, we find that these tweets were overwhelmingly originating from within Turkey, and thus represented a striking departure from the patterns recorded during the Arab Spring. Of the tweets in our data set that are geocoded, more than 80% originated in Turkey. The map in Figure 7.4 shows the location of tweets sent with geographic information.[21] The darker

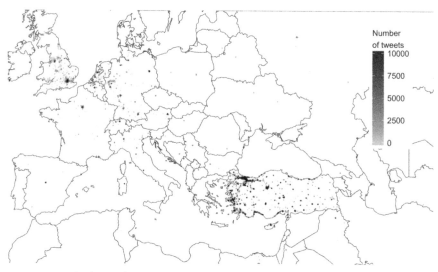

FIGURE 7.4. Geolocated Tweets: Turkey.

the color of the dot in a location, the more tweets were sent from that location. Here, we can see how dense the concentration of tweets coming from within Turkey was, as well as high concentrations in regions with large Turkish populations, such as around Berlin and London. The concentration in Istanbul and in other major Turkish cities that experienced protests is particularly dense. Even in other major cities and areas with expat communities from Turkey, we do not see nearly the concentration of activity that we see from within Turkey, and especially in major Turkish cities. All of this suggests that the bulk of activity that we saw on Twitter was local.

In the Ukrainian case, the situation is somewhat different. Over the course of the protests, only 46% of geocoded tweets originated in Ukraine. Looking at a map of these geolocated tweets (Figure 7.5), we find a lower concentration of tweets in Ukraine during the Euromaidan protests than in Turkey during the Turkish protests. Nonetheless, 46% still is a significant portion of activity and certainly suggests a strong domestic component in addition to an international one. This finding is still in line with our condition that there be a significant amount of social media activity within the country where the protests occur, but it suggests differences in the character of the activity on Twitter between the Turkish and Ukrainian cases. One clear question for future research is to understand how different patterns of social media use emerge in different contexts. Of note is that, due to the geopolitical situation in Ukraine vis-a-vis Russia, the international community was much more engaged with the Ukrainian protests than the Turkish protests (especially as Russian figures became more vocal near the end of the protest period). This suggests that the international community would be more likely to be more involved and might

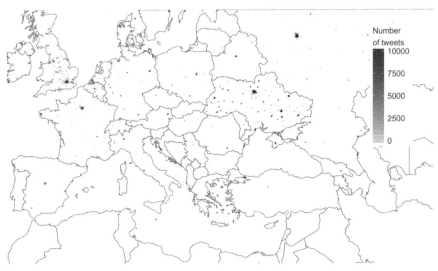

FIGURE 7.5. Geolocated Tweets: Ukraine.

explain the difference in local versus international tweets. Alternatively, there might be different patterns among people who choose to geo-code their tweets than among those who did not.

4.5 Condition 4: Language of Social Media Use

Language use is important not only as a marker of whether activity is local but also as a means of indicating whether activity is directed to other local people or toward the international community. We can imagine a scenario, for example, in which the majority of activity about the protest originates in Turkey or Ukraine, but if this activity is entirely in English, it would not suggest convincingly that it was directed at those participating in the protest or those in communities experiencing protest.[22]

Looking at the first 30 days of the protest in Turkey, we find that 74% of tweets sent during this time were written in Turkish. The majority of the remainder were in English, with a few in other languages. However, a more relevant indication of tweets sent in Turkish may be obtained by examining the language of tweets sent by users whose accounts were registered with a Turkish-language preference. Figure 7.6 shows the proportion of tweets in each language over time sent from accounts registered with a Turkish-language preference. What this figure shows is that not only are the overwhelming majority of tweets in Turkish but also that for each single day the majority of tweets are in Turkish. Although we might expect that tweets written in English could be aimed toward outsiders, Tweets written in Turkish are most likely primarily

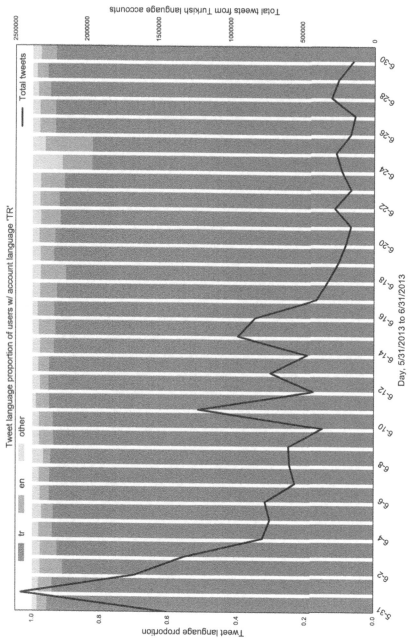

FIGURE 7.6. Daily Language Use in Turkey by Turkish-preferred Twitter Accounts.

215

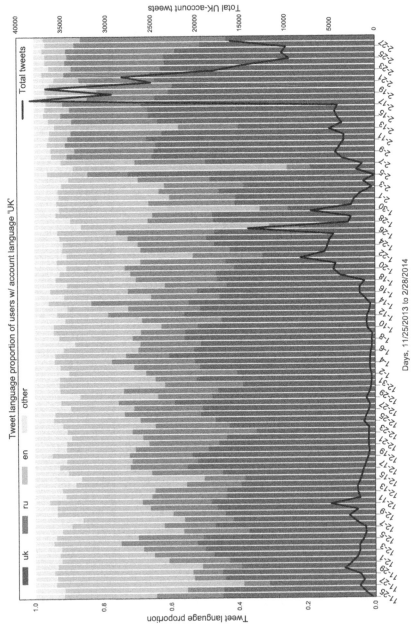

FIGURE 7.7. Daily Language Use in Ukraine by Ukrainian-preferred Twitter Accounts.

aimed at domestic audiences, with a secondary audience being expat communities outside of Turkey. Further, the conversation is clearly not being driven primarily by international news media, which would tend to be in languages other than Turkish.[23]

In the Ukrainian case, the situation is less clear. Figure 7.7 shows the proportion of tweets by language each day for users who registered their accounts in Ukrainian.[24] Here, what we can see is that even for these Ukrainian-language users, a large proportion of their tweets are in English (or Russian), sometimes nearing 50% of tweets on a single day. What this finding suggests is that even though we see high levels of activity in English, it does not suggest that the tweets are coming from outside the country. A nontrivial proportion of that activity is likely originating from local language users. Thus even without being able to locate users geographically via geotagging, we can make some inferences about where tweets are originating from.[25]

Taken together, we find that across both protests a significant proportion of activity is taking place in the local language. Nonetheless, this examination also suggests different patterns of language use in the two cases. In Ukraine, English was a heavily used language among Twitter users, whereas in Turkey the vast majority of activity on Twitter was taking place in Turkish. These data suggest that in both cases Twitter was used by the native population, primarily for communicating with other in-country compatriots. But the substantial use of English by users whose registered language was Ukrainian suggests that Twitter was also used to attract international attention.

4.6 Surveys of Protesters

Our fifth condition is harder to investigate, because we do not yet have good survey data from participants in the Turkish protests, although work to this effect is underway. Initial in-depth interviews conducted in the summer of 2014, however, suggest promising evidence in this regard. Of 16 individuals interviewed about their participation in the protests, all but 2 initially heard about the protests on social media. Of those who did not learn about the protests on social media, one was abroad when the protests first began and saw the news on TV, and the other does not have a social media account. Although this is obviously a very small sample size, it at least points in the direction of social media playing an important role in informing people about protests.

Some initial survey evidence from Ukraine strengthens this conclusion. In a survey conducted during the protests, Onuch (2014) finds that when participants were asked how they learned about the protests, 37.2% mentioned Facebook, and 12.8% vKontakte, a Russian-language social media platform similar to Facebook.[26] Although this suggests that people learned about the protests in other ways as well, it is also evidence that a substantial proportion of protestors learned of the protests through social media.

5 CONCLUSION

One goal of this chapter has been to establish a set of criteria that, taken together, augur for the possibility of an important role for social media in either the individual-level decision to participate or not participate in a protest and/or the overall trajectory of the protest movement itself.

The second goal of this chapter was to apply these criteria to two recent protest events that captured international attention: the Turkish Gezi Park protests of spring 2013 and the Ukranian Euromaidan protests of winter 2013–2014. Although there are some potentially interesting areas of variation in the results of our analysis, the overall finding is similar: across both cases, we find consistent evidence in line with the conditions we have laid out. Unlike – perhaps – earlier protest movements, the recent Turkish and Ukrainian protests do not seem to be susceptible to the types of critiques leveled at those who questioned the importance of social media in pre-2013 protest movements.[27]

With a wealth of evidence suggesting a potentially important role for social media in affecting protest behavior and development in both Turkey and Ukraine, we can move on to the interesting causal questions of how it is that social media encourages individual-level participation.[28] We present such a theoretical outline in much greater details elsewhere (Jost et al. 2014), but for now we highlight three important avenues for future theoretical development and empirical research.

First, political science has long pointed to the importance of **information** about the potential costs and benefits of participating in protests (Kuran 1989, 1991; Lohmann 1994; Tucker 2007). Implicit in models such as these is the assumption that participation requires being able to calculate the anticipated benefits of various potential outcomes (such as shifts in policy or leadership) and to compare them with the anticipated costs of participation (such as injury or arrest) and making some determination that the former outweighs the latter. Social media could certainly supply information about both the potential costs and benefits of participation. Such information is not limited to information about specific protests: social media posts can be a source of information about policy positions by candidates or parties and a whole array of politically relevant topics. Moreover, if social media increases the sheer quantity of information to which an individual is exposed – a supposition that seems quite likely to us, but that still needs to be demonstrated empirically – then it could also play an important role in reducing an individual's level of uncertainty about factors related to the decision to join a protest.[29] And if it is uncertainty that often prevents people from joining protests, then we can envision a direct path from more access to social media to more individuals choosing to join protests or participate by voting or making campaign contributions.

Social psychology, in contrast, calls our attention to the role of **motivation** to participate in protest through factors such as anger at perceived injustice (i.e., moral outrage), group belonging and shared interests (i.e., social identification), and beliefs about group empowerment (i.e, group efficacy).[30] Social media might well deliver a large number of messages that stress perceptions of injustice, social identity, and group empowerment. Although technically challenging, we should in time be able to develop machine learning tools that enable us to measure the extent that these types of messages are prevalent in online conversations related to specific protests and whether the prevalence (or lack thereof) of such messages has an impact on individual-level decisions to join protests.

Finally, it seems crucially important to take account of the **networked** component of social media data. The fact that social media are transmitted through networks into which individuals have self-selected (e.g., from friends on Facebook or people an individual has chosen to follow on Twitter or Google +) means that both information and potential sources of motivation may be given added credence above and beyond what an individual would normally attach to such a message were she simply to encounter it in a neutral environment (for example, on a flyer or on the evening news). Furthermore, posts on social media are also pre-vetted: we learn not simply that there is a protest (or that there is moral outrage fueling the desire for a protest), but that our friends, relatives, or respected colleagues have endorsed this particular course of action or share this sense of moral outrage.

All three of these factors – information, motivation, and social networks – offer rich opportunities for developing hypotheses about the relationship between social media and protest and other political activity. Testing these hypotheses will be technically challenging and computationally intensive. That being said, we now have data that we can draw on to test these hypotheses, the likes of which we could only have dreamed of as little as a decade ago. Furthermore, it is not just our access to data that has changed, but rather the world itself. The evidence presented in this chapter suggests there is very good reason to think that if we really want to understand why individuals participated in the Gezi Park or Euromaidan protests, we need to understand the role of social media in the individual decision-making process. The theories, tools, and method to do so therefore represents an extremely exciting path for future developments in the study of political behavior.

Notes

1. As of June, 2015, Facebook reports 1.49 billion monthly users, which means that more than one out of every five people in the entire world uses Facebook monthly (http://newsroom.fb.com/company-info/, accessed 10/8/15). As of October, 2015, Twitter reports 316 million monthly users, with approximately 500 million tweets sent daily (https://about.twitter.com/company, accessed 10/8/15).
2. Widely used hashtags include #OWS = Occupy Wall Street; #Jan25 = protests in Egypt; #Dec24 = protests in Russia; #direngezipark = protests in Turkey; and #Euromaidan = protests in Ukraine.

3. These analyses build on research conducted by the NYU SMaPP lab in real time and previously written up in *Al Jazeera English, The Monkey Cage, The Huffington Post*, and as part of our SMaPP Data Reports series (http://smapp.nyu.edu/reports/turkey_data_report.pdf; http://smapp.nyu.edu/reports/Ukraine_Data_Report.pdf).

4. Writing only a few days later, Morozov (2009b) urged critics not to lose sight of the larger picture: "The fact that so few [Twitter users] actually managed to keep the entire global Twittersphere discussing an obscure country for almost a week only proves that Twitter has more power than we think."

5. http://www.newyorker.com/reporting/2010/10/04/101004fa_fact_gladwell.

6. See http://blog.twitter.com/2009/06/down-time-rescheduled.html.

7. We define social media as web-based applications that allow users to contribute content, modify content already posted by others, and to share content that can be viewed by others. Furthermore, social media allow users to join in communities with other people to whose content they will be exposed. The paramount examples of social media are sites such as Facebook, Twitter, Instagram, and Google +.

8. Although as we discuss in more detail elsewhere (Tucker et al. 2014a, Tucker et al. 2014b), one strategic use of social media during protests is precisely to spark discussion of events in the international community, and therefore *outside* of the country in question.

9. The fifth condition is obviously not a condition about social media use per se, but is the most obvious verification condition that we can state. Note that these are criteria for social media to have a direct effect on protest participation; we set aside for now the possibility that information spread through social media created the conditions for protest to occur.

10. Key words and hashtags included in the collections are available in the Online Appendix at https://dataverse.harvard.edu/dataverse/smapp.

11. Twitter generously makes all tweets available for searching and downloading in real time. Provided that one's search terms does not yield a collection of tweets greater than 1% of the total tweets at any given time, you will receive every single tweet that meets your critera. On the occasions when you hit the "rate limit" of 1% of all tweets, you are notified by Twitter that this is occurring. Tweets based on keyword searches from the past, however, must be purchased, thus putting a premium on quick decisions about starting Twitter collections. During the collection period for Turkey we did hit this limit on a few occasions, leading us to lose a small number of tweets that would otherwise be in the collection.

12. Both collections started several days later than the events themselves, reflecting the time it took us to become aware of the protests and to start our collections, which means we do not have the very earliest Twitter activity from the protests included in our analysis.

13. We did this using R.

14. One limitation here is that if users have deleted their posts, we have no way to know whether this happened, and the post will not appear in our data. Nonetheless, it is relatively rare for users to go back and delete posts they have made, so we do not feel that for the particular data we are studying this is a significant issue at this time.

15. For each of these pages we are able to collect all posts, all likes on posts, and all comments on posts. We are able to see the number of likes the page itself has

received, but not the names of those individuals. Thus, we are able to see how users are interacting with some of the key public pages related to the protests.

16. We examined, of course, only a tiny fraction of the tweets we collected. But we did select them randomly, and given that we found so many tweets related to the protests, that gave us added confidence that we were getting tweets related to the protests generally in the data set.

17. On Facebook, if you "like" a public page, it means you will see some of its posts on your homepage in the future. So in this sense, it is equivalent to following another user on Twitter.

18. One important note about the timeline of the Turkish protests is that the bulk of the protest activity was centered around the period of time before the first clearing of the square, which began on June 15. Protest activity continued at a low level throughout the country after this time, but the primary protest period is the period preceding this event.

19. When observing Facebook activity, we report on three separate indicators of activity by *users* of the page (i.e., not the people posting on the page): comments made on posts, "likes" given to posts, and "shares" of the posts. Recall as well that we can only observe activity on *public* Facebook pages, and most personal users keep their pages private and only accessible to their Facebook "friends." Thus any estimate of the importance of Facebook from analyses made with publicly available data should be considered a lower bound. Most Twitter accounts, by contrast, are public.

20. In the data on the Turkish protests we analyze here, only 1.8% of tweets are geocoded. Of the tweets on the Ukrainian protests we analyze, only 1% are geocoded. Although this is a relatively small proportion of users, we have no reason to believe that the types of users who would choose to use this function would be more likely to be at the location of protests than other users. In fact, if we believe that people might be afraid of being arrested for protest activities, we might expect users closer to the scene of the action to be less likely to use this feature.

21. There are other ways to estimate the location of Twitter users by relying on user supplied biographical information. For the current analysis, however, we rely solely on the more reliable – albeit less frequently available – geo-tagged location data.

22. There are two ways that we can analyze language use on Twitter: the language in which the account is registered (i.e., the language in which the user interacts with Twitter), and Twitter's automatic language classification of the tweet itself. The registration language of the account give us a best estimate of a user's preferred (and most likely native) language, while the language of the tweet shows a choice as to what language was used at that particular moment. More work remains to be done to clear some noise out of these data. For example, we do not know how Twitter handles tweets with hashtags in multiple languages. We also need to get a better sense of the cases in which one might prefer to interact with Twitter in a language that is not one's native language (Wilson 2014). For now, the proper way to interpret the data presented in this section are as being based on the assumptions that a declared language is a user's preferred language and that Twitter is accurately classifying the language of tweets.

23. Figure 7.A5 in the Online Appendix shows a similar language breakdown for all tweets, not only those sent by users registered with a Turkish-language preference.

24. Although Wilson (2014) suggests that some Ukrainian speakers might have registered for Russian-language Twitter accounts for technical reasons, there is no reason to suppose anyone would register for a Ukranian-language Twitter account who did not prefer interacting with Twitter in Ukrainian. So these are undoubtedly the accounts of Ukrainian speakers.

25. The caveat here is that we need to be willing to assume that Twitter activity is not dominated by the local-language expat community, which seems reasonable given the relative number of Ukranian speakers inside as opposed to outside Ukraine.

26. In addition, 4.1% of respondents reported their source as a Facebook message from a student group, 3.7% reported receiving a Facebook message from a social movement organization, and 1.1% reported receiving a Facebook message from a political party. Note that respondents could give multiple answers, so it is worth noting that the most popular answer was still radio/TV, which 52.3% of protesters listed. See Onuch (2014), figure 3.

27. As for the meta-level critique that social media fueled protests are incapable of lasting change, the course of recent history in Ukraine refutes that argument.

28. This should not be taken as implying the findings in this chapter are not particularly exciting by themselves. Ten years ago there was no Facebook and no Twitter, let alone vKontakte, Instagram, FourSquare, Google +, and other social media platforms we have not considered here. After fits and starts of protest movements that may or may not have incorporated social media in important ways, we may have now arrived at a point where it is impossible to consider a serious protest movement without a social media component to it, especially in wealthier countries. We see the evidence presented in this chapter as fairly conclusive in showing that this moment has indeed arrived.

29. E.g., Do I share the goals of the protesters? Where are protests taking place? Is participation dangerous? How is the regime responding?

30. See for example Barbalet 1998; Drury & Reicher 2009; Tausch et al. 2011a, b; McGarty et al. 2013.

References

Aday, Sean, Henry Farrell, Marc Lynch, John Sides, John Kelly, and Ethan Zuckerman. 2010. *Blogs and Bullets: New Media in Contentious Politics.* Washington, DC: U.S. Institute for Peace.

Aday, Sean, Henry Farrell, Marc Lynch, John Sides, and Dean Freelon. 2012. *Blogs and Bullets II: New Media and Conflict after the Arab Spring.* Washington, DC: U.S. Institute for Peace.

Applebaum, Anne. 2009. "In Moldova, the Twitter Revolution That Wasn't." *Washington Post.* Accessed at http://www.washingtonpost.com/wp-dyn/content/article/2009/04/20/AR2009042002817.html.

Barbalet, J. 1998. *Emotion, Social Theory, and Social Structure: A Macrosociological Approach.* Cambridge: Cambridge University Press.

Barbera, Pablo. 2014. Access to Facebook API via R. R package version 0.4. http://CRAN.R-project.org/package=Rfacebook.

Barbera, Pablo & Metzger, Megan M. 2013. "How Ukrainian Protestors are Using Twitter and Facebook." *Monkey Cage Blog.* Accessed at http://www.washingtonpost.com/blogs/monkey-cage/wp/2013/12/04/strategic-use-of-facebook-and-twitter-in-ukrainian-protests/.

Bennett, Lance and Segerberg, Alexandra. 2012. "Digital Media and the Personalization of Contentious Politics." *Information, Communication and Society* 15(5): 739–768.

Bond, Robert, Fariss, Christopher, Jones, Jason, Kramer, Adam, Marlow, Cameron, Settle, Jaime, and Fowler, James. 2012. "A 61-Million-Person Experiment in Social Influence and Political Mobilization." *Nature* 489: 295–298.

Bruns, Axel, Hieghfield, Tim, & Burgess, Jean. 2013. "The Arab Spring and Social Media Audiences: English and Arabic Twitter Users and Their Networks." *American Behavioral Scientist* 70 (7): 871–898.

Cha, Meeyoung, Haddadi, Hamed, Benevenuto, Fabricio and Gummadi, Krishna. 2010. "Measuring User Influence in Twitter: The Million Follower Fallacy." *Proceedings of the Fourth International AAAI Conference on Weblogs and Social Media* 10–17.

Drury, J. & Reicher, S. D. 2009. "Collective Psychological Empowerment as a Model of Social Change: Researching Crowds." *Journal of Social Issues* 67: 707–726.

Gladwell, Malcolm. 2010. "Small Change: Why the Revolution Will Not Be Tweeted". *The New Yorker*. Accessed at www.newyorker.com/magazine/2010/10/04/small-change-malcolm-gladwell.

Granovetter, Mark. 1983. "The Strength of Weak Ties: A Network Theory Revisited." *Sociological Theory* 1: 201–233.

Hale, Henry. 2013. "Regime Change Cascades: What We Have Learned from the 1848 Revolutions to the 2011 Arab Uprisings." *Annual Review of Political Science* 16: 331–353.

Jost, John T., Barberà, Pablo, Metzger, Megan M., Nagler, Jonathan, Sterling, Joanna, & Tucker, Joshua A. 2014. "Digital Dissent: Informational and Motivational Pathways to Political Protest Through Social Media." Unpublished manuscript.

Jungherr, Andreas, Jurgens, Pascal, and Schoen, Harald. 2012. "Why the Pirate Party Won the German Election of 2009 or the Trouble with Predictions: A Response to 'Predicting Elections with Twitter: What 140 Characters Reveal about Political Sentiment.'" *Social Science Computer Review* 30(2): 229–234.

Kuran, Timur. 1989. "Sparks and Prairie Fires: A Theory of Unanticipated Political Revolution." *Public Choice* 61(1): 41–74.

Kuran, Timur. 1991. "Now out of Never: The Element of Surprise in the East European Revolutions of 1989." *World Politics* 44: 7–48.

Lohmann, Suzanne. 1994. "Dynamics of Informational Cascades: The Monday Demonstrations in Leipzig, East Germany, 1989–1991." *World Politics* 47: 42–101.

Lynch, Mark. 2011. "After Egypt: The Limits and Promises of Online Challenges to the Authoritarian Arab State." *Perspectives on Politics* 9(2): 301–310.

Lysenko, Volodymyr and Desouza, Kevin. 2012. "Moldova's Internet Revolution: Analyzing the Role of Technologies in Various Phases of the Confrontation." *Technological Forecasting and Social Change* 79(2): 341–361.

McGarty, C., Thomas, E. F., Lala, G., Smith, L. G., & Bliuc, A. M. 2013. "New Technologies, New Identities, and the Growth of Mass Opposition in the Arab Spring." *Political Psychology* 1–16.

Morozov, Evgeny. 2009a. "Moldovas Twitter Revolution." *Foreign Policy*. Accessed at http://neteffect.foreignpolicy.com/posts/2009/04/07/moldovas_twitter_revolution.

Morozov, Evgeny. 2009b. "Moldova's Twitter Revolution Is NOT a Myth." *Foreign Policy*. Accessed at http://foreignpolicy.com/2009/04/10/moldovas-twitter-revolution-is-not-a-myth/.

Morozov, Evgeny. 2011. "Whither Internet Control?" *Journal of Democracy* 22: 63–74.

Munger, Kevin. 2014. "Tweets, Elites and Feets on the Streets: Measuring Regime Response to Protest Using Social Media." Unpublished manuscript.

Onuch, Olga. 2014. "Euromaidan Protests in Ukraine: Social Media versus Social Networks." Paper presented at the Comparative Workshop on Mass Protests, London.

Schwartz, Elizabeth. 2011. "The Impact of Social Network Websites on Social Movement Involvement". Unpublished Manuscript. Accessed at http://cbsmpapers.web.unc.edu/files/2011/08/SchwarzSNSSocialMovements.pdf.

Shirky, Clay. 2011. "The Political Power of Social Media: Technology, the Public Sphere and Political Change". *Foreign Affairs*. Accessed at https://www.foreignaffairs.org/articles/2010-12-20/political-power-social-media.

Starbird, Kate and Palen, Leysia. 2012. "(How) Will the Revolution Be Retweeted? Information Diffusion and the 2011 Egyptian Uprising." *Proceedings of the ACM 2012 Conference on Computer Supported Cooperative Work.*

Tausch, N. Becker, J., Spears, R., Christ, O., Saab, R., Singh, P., & Siddiqui, R. N. 2011a. "Explaining Radical Group Behavior: Developing Emotion and Efficacy Routes to Normative and Non-Normative Collective Action." *Journal of Personality and Social Psychology* 101: 129–148.

Tucker, J. 2007. "Enough! Electoral Fraud, Collective Action Problems, and Post-Communist Colored Revolutions." *Perspectives on Politics* 3: 535–551.

Tucker, Joshua A., Metzger, Megan M., Penfold-Brown, Duncan, Bonneau, Richard, Jost, John, & Nagler, Jonathan. 2014a. "Protest in the Age of Social Media: Ukraine's #Euromaidan." Carnegie Reporter, 7(4): 8–20.

Tucker, Joshua A., Metzger, Megan M., Penfold-Brown, Duncan, Bonneau, Richard, Jost, John, & Nagler, Jonathan. 2014b. "Social Media and the #Euromaidan Protests." Paper presented at the Comparative Workshop on Mass Protests, London.

Tufekci, Zeynep & Wilson, Christopher. 2012. "Social Media and the Decision to Participate in Political Protest: Observations from Tahrir Square." *Journal of Communication* 62: 363–379.

Wilson, S. 2014. "Networks, Protest and Euromaidan: Social Media Networks and the Ukrainian Protests." Working Paper.

Wilson, Christopher & Dunn, Alexandra. 2011. "Digital Media in the Egyptian Revolution: Descriptive Analysis from the Tahrir Data Sets." *International Journal of Communication* 5: 1248–1272.

8

Measuring Representational Style in the House

The Tea Party, Obama, and Legislators' Changing Expressed Priorities

Justin Grimmer
Stanford University

1 INTRODUCTION

Communication is a central component of representation (Mansbridge, 2003; Disch, 2012). Legislators invest time and resources in crafting speeches in Congress, composing press releases to send to newspapers, and distributing messages directly to their constituents (Yiannakis, 1982; Quinn et al., 2010; Lipinski, 2004; Grimmer, 2013). Indeed, the primary problem in studying the role of communication in representation is that legislators communicate so much that analysts are quickly overwhelmed. Traditional hand-coding is simply unable to keep pace with the staggering amount of text that members of Congress produce each year.

In this chapter I use a *text as data* method and a collection of press releases to measure how legislators present their work to constituents (Grimmer and Stewart, 2013). Specifically, I measure legislators' expressed priorities: the attention they allocate to topics and issues when communicating with constituents (Grimmer, 2010). Using the measures of legislators' expressed priorities, I characterize how Republicans respond to the drastic change in institutional and electoral context after the 2008 election. Not only did the Republican party lose the White House but also the Tea Party movement mobilized and articulated conservative objections to particularistic spending. Replicating a finding from Grimmer, Westwood, and Messing (2014) with alternative measures, I show that Republicans abandon credit claiming. Instead, Republicans articulate criticisms of the Democratic party, the Obama administration, and Democratic policy proposals. In contrast, Democrats embrace credit claiming and defend Democratic policies – though less vocally than Republicans criticize those same proposals. In spite of the shifts in rhetoric, though, I demonstrate that there is a strong year-to-year relationship in legislators' presentational styles. So, although legislators are responsive at the margin to changing conditions, the basic strategy remains the same.

This chapter contributes to a growing literature that examines legislative speech using automated methods for text analysis (Hillard, Purpura, and Wilkerson, 2008; Monroe, Colaresi, and Quinn, 2008; Quinn et al., 2010; Grimmer, 2013; Cormack, 2014). This literature has demonstrated how computational tools can be successfully used to examine the content of legislation and how the types of bills passed over time have changed (Adler and Wilkerson, 2012). Other studies have demonstrated how text analysis can be used to provide nuanced measures of legislators' ideal points (Gerrish and Blei, 2012). Still other studies have demonstrated how legislators use communication to create an impression of influence over expenditures (Grimmer, Westwood, and Messing, 2014).

As in these prior studies, I exploit a large collection of congressional text to study what legislators say and why it matters for representation. I use a collection of nearly 170,000 House press releases: every press release, from each House office, from 2005 to 2010. There is increasing evidence that press releases are a reliable and useful source for capturing how legislators communicate with their constituents. Grimmer (2013) shows that press releases contain politically relevant content not found in floor speeches and have a direct effect over the content of newspaper stories and constituent evaluations. This particular collection of press releases is also useful because it covers a tumultuous time in American history that included the wars in Iraq and Afghanistan, a financial and mortgage crisis that precipitated the deepest recession in a generation, and changes in party control of the Congress and presidency.

To examine the content of the press releases, I apply a model that estimates a hierarchy of topics and how legislators allocate their attention to each level of topics (Blaydes, Grimmer, and McQueen, 2015). To construct the hierarchy of topics, the model nests, or classifies, a set of granular topics into a set of coarse topics. This modeling strategy builds on pachinko allocation models that allow for a nesting of topics, while contributing a model that relies on a different distribution that allows for fast inferences (Li and McCallum, 2006). The model is useful both substantively and statistically. Substantively, it provides an automatic classification between more position taking, credit claiming, and advertising press releases. Previous versions of topic models applied to congressional communication required a second manual step to perform this classification (Quinn et al., 2010; Grimmer, 2013). This second step can be useful, but also can make analysis cumbersome and adds another layer of interpretation to the analysis.

Statistically, the model helps address concerns about selecting the number of topics in a model. One of the most consequential assumptions made when applying topic models is deciding how many topics to include in the analysis. Determining the number of topics is a particularly vexing problem for social scientists, because our goals when using unsupervised methods are often difficult to quantify (Grimmer and King, 2011) and because different types of analysis imply that different numbers of topics are ideal (Chang et al., 2009). The model in this chapter addresses this problem by providing two sets of topics. One set of topics is granular, or more specific, and is intended to capture legislators' attention to specific policy debates and actions that are discussed in the press releases. The second set of topics is coarse, or more broad, and captures broad differences in the types of language that legislators use when communicating with constituents. By providing two types of topics, I show how the model facilitates an analysis of who discusses specific issues with constituents, while also facilitating broad comparisons in what legislators say to constituents.

Together, the model and data make possible new measures that help answer long-standing questions about how political representation works in American politics (Mayhew, 1974; Fenno, 1978). As I discuss in the conclusion, this chapter provides a demonstration of how large-scale analysis of text can facilitate deeper and broader insights into how representation occurs in American politics.

2 TOPIC MODELS FOR SOCIAL SCIENCE

To analyze the collection of House press releases I use a topic model that estimates both coarse and granular topics. Topic models are an increasingly popular tool for studying large collections of texts (Blei, Ng, and Jordan, 2003; Quinn et al., 2010). They are an unsupervised tool that discovers the salient issues, or topics, in a collection of documents and then measures how attention to topics varies across documents or, actors, or over time. Part of the reason for the popularity of topic models is that they exploit a hierarchical structure that is easily extended to include different features of the documents, the authors of the model, and when the documents were written (Blei and Lafferty, 2006; Quinn et al., 2010; Grimmer, 2010; Mimno and McCallum, 2008; Grimmer and Stewart, 2013). Exploiting this extensibility, Roberts, Stewart and Airoldi (2014a) introduce the *structural topic model* (STM): a general model that allows users to flexibly include a wide array of covariates to better understand how attention to topics varies and how different types of speakers discuss the same basic topic (see also Mimno and McCallum, 2008).

Models like STM condition on a user-provided set of characteristics. Other topic models, however, learn about groups from the analysis. For example, Grimmer (2013) introduces a model that groups legislators who dedicate similar attention to topics when communicating with constituents, while simultaneously estimating the topics of discussion and legislators' attention to those topics (see also Wallach, 2008). The clustering of legislators has methodological benefits by facilitating more accurate smoothing across individual senators. The clustering also provides substantive insights by creating coarse summaries of how legislators engage their constituents.

A closely related set of models groups together topics that place similar emphasis on the same set of words. Models such as pachinko allocation estimate a hierarchy of topics (Li and McCallum, 2006). At the top of the hierarchy are general topics that capture broad emphases in the texts. At the bottom of the hierarchy are more granular topics about narrower content in the documents. Like the clustering of authors based on their attention to topics, this grouping provides methodological advantages, ensuring that information is borrowed from topics that emphasize similar words.

The nesting of topics also helps address one of the major challenges in utilizing topic models in applied research. Like other unsupervised learning methods, topic models require users to set the number of topics that are used in the model. And determining how many components to include in a model remains one of the biggest challenges in applying topic models for social scientific research. Some methods attempt to avoid this assumption and use nonparametric priors to estimate the number of topics (Teh et al., 2006). But nonparametric priors are no panacea. Instead, models that make use of nonparametric priors substitute an explicit assumption about the number of topics to include in the model with an implicit assumption based on the properties of the particular nonparametric prior used (Wallach et al., 2010). This implicit assumption arises because nonparametric priors are not explicitly attempting to estimate the "correct" number of components to include in an unsupervised model, but instead they are attempting to estimate an underlying density. This is problematic, because Wallach et al. (2010) show that strong assumptions in the nonparametric priors determine the number of estimated components.

Alternatively, scholars have increasingly used task-specific tests to determine the number of topics (Chang et al., 2009; Roberts et al., 2014b; Grimmer and Stewart, 2013). For example, it is common to select the number of topics that have the best predictive performance, but methods that perform well in prediction might have poor substantive properties (Chang et al., 2009). Other scholars have suggested methods that quantify the coherence of the topics, tying the evaluation closer to the way social scientists use topic models (Bischof and Airoldi, 2012; Roberts et al., 2014b; Grimmer, 2010).

These tests are useful, but still limit the application of any one instance of a topic model. This limitation occurs because the optimal number of topics in any application depends on how the model and estimates from the model will be applied. When studying how legislators communicate with constituents, for example, more granular topics are useful when examining who participates in debates around policies or who claims credit for specific kinds of spending in districts. For other questions, however, a more coarse classification might be useful. For example, when making broad comparisons across legislators' styles, it may be useful to compare their attention to credit claiming to their rates of position taking, regardless of what legislators claim credit for securing or what topics they articulate positions about.

Rather than estimate a single set of topics, this chapter uses a model first introduced in Blaydes, Grimmer, and McQueen (2015) that estimates two different sets of topics, similar to the nesting of topics in pachinko allocation (Li and McCallum, 2006). The model that I use here has a two-layer hierarchy and nests granular topics into a set of coarse topics. The nesting allows us to naturally define subsets of topics that use broadly similar language or language that accomplishes a similar substantive goal. Although the nesting of topics actually increases the number of parameters to set when estimating the model, it also makes the final model fit more broadly applicable – ensuring that the same model can be used to assess granular differences in the specific debates in which legislators participate, while also making coarse comparisons across documents.

3 A MODEL FOR NESTED TOPICS

To apply statistical models to the collection of press releases, I first pre-process the texts, representing its content as numbers. I do this using a standard set of techniques, though I slightly vary the recipe to account for idiosyncratic features of congressional press releases (Grimmer and Stewart, 2013). I first make the most common, and perhaps most counterintuitive, assumption and discard word order (commonly referred to as the bag of words assumption). I also discarded punctuation and capitalization and stemmed the words, mapping words that refer to the same basic content to a common stem. I then removed words that occurred in less than 0.5% of the press releases, words that occurred in more than 90% of the press releases, stopwords, and proper nouns that refer to specific congressional districts, members of Congress, or U.S. cities. Removing this set of words ensured that I do not obtain a set of region or congressperson-specific topics.

The result of the process is that for each legislator-year i ($i = 1, \ldots, 2,587$) I represent each press release j ($j = 1, \ldots, N_i$) as a $W = 2,727$ element-long count vector $\mathbf{y}_{ij} = (y_{ij1}, y_{ij2}, \ldots, y_{ij2727})$.[1] Each y_{ijw} counts the number of times token w occurs in document j from legislator i. Like Grimmer (2010), I model the collection of legislators' press releases as a mixture of von Mises-Fisher distributions, a distribution on a hypersphere, using vectors that have (Euclidean) length 1 (Banerjee et al., 2005; Grimmer, 2010; Gopal and Yang, 2014). To utilize the distribution, I work with a normalized version of the count vector, $\mathbf{y}_{ij}^* = \frac{\mathbf{y}_{ij}}{\sqrt{\mathbf{y}_{ij}' \mathbf{y}_{ij}}}$.

To construct the model, I suppose that in each year, each representative in the House of Representatives, i, divides attention over a set of K topics π_i, where π_{ik} represents the proportion of the representative's press release allocated to topic k. Throughout the analysis I treat π_i as a measure of legislators' *expressed priorities*: the issues legislators emphasize when communicating with constituents. It is a priority because the model does not identify a particular policy position legislators might take in their public statements. And it is expressed because the emphasis legislators give in their press releases to issues might differ from the time they spend working on those topics in the institution or from their own personal priorities.[2]

The attention to topics is assumed to stochastically control the frequency of each topic in the collection of press releases. Each press release j from a legislator in a year is assumed to have one *granular* topic, which I represent with the indicator vector τ_{ij}. We assume that $\tau_{ij} \sim \text{Multinomial}(1, \pi_i)$. Given the granular topic, a document's content is drawn from a corresponding von Mises-Fisher distribution. That is, $y_{ij}^* | t_{ijk} = 1 \sim$ von Mises-Fisher(κ, μ_k), where κ is a concentration parameter – analogous to the variance in a normal distribution – and μ_k is a $2,727$ element-long vector that describes the center of the topic.[3] If an entry of μ_k, μ_{kw} has a large weight, it implies that the token w is particularly prevalent in the topic.

To construct a hierarchy of topics I assume that the granular topics are nested in the coarse topics. Equivalently, the model simultaneously clusters documents into a set of granular topics and clusters granular topics into coarse topics. For each of the K granular topics I suppose that each granular topic belongs to one of C coarse topics. Let σ_k be an indicator vector for granular topic k: if $\sigma_{kc} = 1$ then granular topic k is assigned to coarse topic c. I suppose that $\sigma_{kc} \sim \text{Multinomial}(1, \beta)$ where β is a C element-long vector that describes the proportion of granular topics assigned to each of the coarse topics. Given σ_k, I then draw the granular topic from a von Mises-Fisher distribution with a center at the corresponding coarse topic. Specifically, $\mu_k | \sigma_{kc} = 1 \sim$ von Mises-Fisher(κ, η_c). One of the virtues of using the von Mises-Fisher distribution is that it is conjugate to itself (Banerjee et al., 2005; Gopal and Yang, 2014), facilitating the hierarchy of topics.[4]

I follow Grimmer (2010) and set priors on π_i, β, and η_m to limit their influence on the parameters. The data-generating process and priors imply the following hierarchical model:

$$\pi_i \sim \text{Dirichlet}(0.01)$$

$$\eta_c \sim \text{vMF}(\kappa, \frac{1}{\sqrt{2727}})$$

$$\beta \sim \text{Dirichlet}(1)$$

$$\sigma_k \sim \text{Multinomial}(1, \beta)$$

$$\mu_k | \sigma_{mk} = 1 \sim \text{vMF}(\kappa, \eta_m)$$

$$\tau_{ij} | \pi_i \sim \text{Multinomial}(1, \pi_i)$$

$$y_{ij}^* | \tau_{ijk} = 1, \mu_k \sim \text{vMF}(\kappa, \mu_k),$$

which implies the following posterior distribution:

$$p(\pi, \eta, \beta, \sigma, \mu, \tau | Y) \propto \prod_{m=1}^{C} c(\kappa) \exp\left(\kappa \eta_m' \frac{1}{\sqrt{2727}}\right)$$

$$\times \prod_{m=1}^{C} \prod_{k=1}^{K} \left[\beta_m c(\kappa) \exp\left(\kappa \mu_k' \eta_m\right)\right]^{\sigma_{m,k}}$$

$$\times \prod_{i=1}^{2,727} \left[\prod_{k=1}^{K} \pi_{ik}^{-0.99} \times \prod_{j=1}^{N_i} \left[\pi_{ik} c(\kappa) \exp\left(\kappa y_{ij}^* \mu_k\right)\right]^{\tau_{ijk}}\right] \quad (1)$$

where $c(\kappa)$ is a normalizing constant for the von Mises-Fisher distribution.

To approximate the posterior I use the variational approximation described in Blaydes, Grimmer, and McQueen (2015).[5]

To apply this model (and other topics models), I have to assume the number of granular and coarse topics in the model. I select 44 granular topics – a number used in previous studies of Congressional communication – and 8 coarse topics. The number of coarse topics was determined after initial experiments with a subset of documents, but because the estimation is fully Bayesian, the model may do automatic model selection and select fewer topics. This occurs in this application, in which only seven of the coarse topics are assigned granular topics.

4 VALIDATING THE TOPICS AND LEGISLATORS' EXPRESSED PRIORITIES

As Quinn et al. (2010) argue, unsupervised models require less work initially – to estimate the topics of discussions – but then require more substantial investment to interpret their content. To begin interpreting the model output, Table 8.1 presents the coarse topics – between the horizontal lines – and the corresponding granular topics. The left-hand column contains a short description of each topic that I created after reading a random sample of press releases assigned to the category, the middle column provides the eight words that best distinguish the topic from the other topics, and the right-hand column presents the proportion of press releases that fall into the particular category.

Table 8.1 demonstrates that the model is able to both identify distinct granular topics in the press releases and that the coarse topics identify substantively interesting groups of press releases. Consider, for example, the *Credit Claiming* coarse topic, which identifies press releases that legislators use to receive credit for expenditures that occur in their district (Mayhew, 1974; Grimmer, Westwood, and Messing, 2014). The granular topics assigned to the credit claiming

TABLE 8.1. *The Coarse and Granular Topics in House Press Releases*

Topic	Keywords	Value
Pos. Taking/Advertising	hous,tax,state,busi,vote,student,school,act	0.416
Committee Position	hous,committe,member,congress,repres,chairman,republican,democrat	0.046
Sponsored Leg.	act,legisl,law,protect,feder,hous,pass,introduc	0.043
International Disputes	state,unit,govern,israel,iran,intern,right,human	0.039
Taxes	tax,incom,relief,famili,credit,taxpay,increas,deduct	0.029
Health Leg.	health,care,insur,reform,cost,coverag,american,afford	0.028
Finance/Mortgage Crisis	financi,credit,mortgag,taxpay,consum,market,card,bank	0.027
Unemployment	job,unemploy,economi,econom,creat,american,stimulu,worker	0.026
Art Contests	school,student,high,art,district,competit,congression,educ	0.024
Office Hours/Internships	offic,district,congressman,constitu,staff,congression,hour,servic	0.023
Vote Explained	vote,right,congress,hous,elect,act,member,amend	0.02
Student Loans	student,educ,colleg,loan,program,school,higher,univers	0.02
Child. Issues	children,health,program,schip,care,insur,famili,child	0.017
Small Businesses	busi,small,job,tax,loan,sba,owner,econom	0.016
Prescription/Illicit Drugs	medicar,drug,senior,prescript,plan,enrol,beneficiari,benefit	0.016
Farming	farm,agricultur,farmer,program,produc,crop,food,usda	0.012
Trade	trade,agreement,china,worker,market,american,job,free	0.012
Service Academies	academi,nomin,student,school,militari,servic,high,appoint	0.011
Women's Issues	women,cancer,pay,equal,violenc,act,diseas,awar	0.008
Credit Claiming	fund,grant,water,program,feder,commun,project,airport	0.187
Stimulus Funding	fund,program,million,appropri,provid,billion,feder,help	0.035
Transportation Funds	project,fund,transport,million,improv,counti,feder,highway	0.034
Municipal Grants	commun,grant,develop,fund,counti,program,announc,rural	0.03
Fire Grants	grant,depart,firefight,program,equip,assist,announc,fund	0.025
FEMA/Disaster	disast,fema,assist,flood,feder,emerg,counti,hurrican	0.02
Health Spending	health,care,center,servic,medic,hospit,provid,commun	0.019
Water Grants/Resources	water,lake,project,river,great,resourc,fund,clean	0.017
Airport Grants	airport,grant,aviat,fund,faa,improv,runway,transport	0.007

Topic	Keywords	Value
Military Support/Budget	research,statement,budget,defens,militari,servic,famili,today	0.115
Statements	statement,today,datelin,fed,famili,peopl,death,pass	0.029
Veteran Service	servic,honor,militari,famili,serv,member,veteran,medal	0.027
Budget	budget,spend,fiscal,deficit,cut,tax,billion,year	0.025
Military Issues	defens,militari,forc,air,base,million,armi,nation	0.023
Research Support	research,cell,stem,scienc,univers,fund,diseas,develop	0.011
National Politics	presid,american,earmark,iraq,court,safeti,statement,congress	0.107
National Holidays	american,peopl,america,congress,nation,wage,work,day	0.027
Pres. Attack/Defend	presid,obama,bush,statement,address,american,union,congress	0.027
Iraq	iraq,troop,war,iraqi,presid,militari,forc,statement	0.025
Judiciary	court,suprem,right,decis,judg,rule,law,justic	0.013
Cons./Employee Safety	safeti,food,product,fda,consum,drug,recal,children	0.01
Earmarks	earmark,egregi,week,spend,republican,project,appropri,reform	0.005
District Positions	veteran,energi,new,oil,va,price,fuel,increas	0.091
Oil and Gas	energi,oil,price,fuel,renew,effici,increas,product	0.042
Veterans Care	veteran,va,care,affair,servic,benefit,militari,medic	0.028
Ribbon Cutting	new,citi,state,facil,said,site,region,area	0.021
National Security	secur,nation,border,immigr,illeg,homeland,social,law	0.068
National Park	nation,park,guard,histor,land,area,forest,preserv	0.025
Homeland Security	secur,social,homeland,port,terrorist,nation,attack,protect	0.024
Immigration	immigr,border,illeg,secur,law,enforc,alien,reform	0.02
District Meetings	meet,hall,town,counti,constitu,congressman,district,street	0.016
District Meetings	meet,hall,town,counti,congressman,constitu,district,street	0.016

coarse topic each claim credit for different kinds of expenditures. For example, Stephanie Herseth (D-S. D.) (later Herseth-Sandlin) issued a press release that "announced $3 million in appropriations funding for a new water well at Ellsworth Air Force Base" (Herseth, 2006), and Rep. Rodney Alexander (R-LA) "and Sen. David Vitter announced today that Evangeline Parish will receive a federal grant in the amount of $74,980 to purchase and install equipment to improve the water system" (Alexander, 2007). Other legislators claim credit for grants to airports, such as Bart Stupak (D-MI) who "announced three airports in northern Michigan have received grants totaling $726,409 for airport maintenance and improvements" (Stupak, 2010). Still other legislators claim credit for grants to fire departments in their district, such as Brian Higgins (D-NY) who "announced Bemus Point Volunteer Fire Department will receive $43,966 in federal Homeland Security funding" (Higgins, 2006). Although these legislators are claiming credit for different types of expenditures, they are all engaging in the same activity: ensuring they receive credit for spending in the district. To do this, the legislators use distinct language that the coarse topic identifies: *announcing funds* for *projects* in their district. The hierarchical model, then, is able to identify a category of political action that previous qualitative scholarship had identified (Mayhew, 1974; Fenno, 1978) and that other applications of topic models had to manually categorize after the model was run (Grimmer, 2013). Other coarse topics identify distinct ways that legislators discuss their work with constituents. The most prevalent coarse topic identifies positions legislators take, positions they hold in Washington, or services that they perform for constituents. Other coarse topics identify debates about national politics, support for the military, and national security. Rather than requiring an ad hoc second step or manual labeling, then, the coarse topics identify substantively interesting groups of topics automatically from the collection of press releases.

Within the coarse topics the granular topics identify areas of salient policy disputes. For example, the granular *Iraq* topic, nested in the *National Politics*, coarse topic, identifies press releases about the second Gulf war. In 2007 Michael Capuano, a liberal Democrat from Massachusetts, explained that he "pushed for a vote on a course of action that would have gotten us out of Iraq much sooner and stipulated that all funding go toward drawing down troops" (Capuano, 2007), whereas Jerry Lewis, a conservative Republican from California, criticized a supplemental spending bill for the war, arguing that "this legislation does not accurately reflect the will of the American public ... but rather the desires of Speaker Pelosi and the Abandon Our Troops Caucus within the Democratic Party" (Lewis, 2007). Other topics identify press releases about a wide range of substantive topics – such as the financial crisis, rising unemployment, farming, and immigration – and discuss ways legislators directly engage constituents, including district meetings, congressional art contests, service academy nominations, and internships in congressional offices.

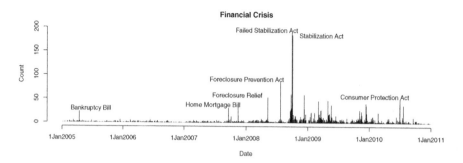

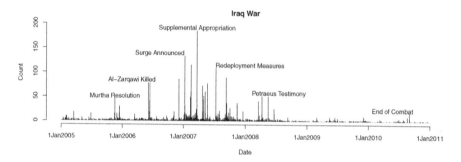

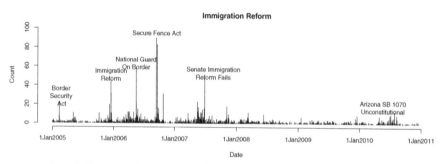

FIGURE 8.1. Spikes in topics correspond with real world events. This figure shows that large spikes in attention to topics corresponds with salient events that drive Congressional attention. This is evidence that the granular topics are valid.

Although it is not feasible to validate each of the individual topics in this single chapter, I can examine over-time variation in the prevalence of topics as a measure of face validity of the topics (Quinn et al., 2010). Figure 8.1 shows the daily count of press releases from the financial crisis (top plot), the Iraq War (middle plot), and immigration reform (bottom plot). Each plot shows that spikes in attention to each topic corresponds with major events. For example, the days with the most press releases about the financial crisis correspond with the congressional debate and initial inaction at the height of the financial crisis. There are similar spikes in attention to the Iraq War as legislators debated supplemental spending bills that redeployed U.S. troops and at the end of combat in Iraq. The large increases in attention that correspond with actual events are evidence that the granular topics are valid – that they estimate the content I claim they are estimating.

However, not only do I have to demonstrate that the estimated topics are valid – capturing the types of rhetoric I claim that they are – but I also have to demonstrate that my measures of legislators' expressed priorities accurately capture how legislators explain their work in Washington to constituents. Figure 8.2 presents evidence that the model is accurately estimating how legislators divide their attention in press releases. As Grimmer and Stewart (2013) argue, one of the most stringent convergent validity checks for an unsupervised learning method is to compare its output to estimates from hand-coded documents that are intended to measure the same topic or concept. The left-hand plot in Figure 8.2 carries out this comparison for a subset of the model. Its vertical axis shows the estimated number of credits claiming press releases from each legislator in each year from the unsupervised model used in this chapter. Its horizontal axis shows the estimated number of credit-claiming press releases from a model explicitly designed to identify credit-claiming press releases. Specifically, the estimates are from Grimmer, Westwood, and Messing (2014), who used a team of well-trained coders to hand-code 800 press releases as credit claiming or not. Then, they used an ensemble of supervised learning techniques to classify the remaining press releases. The black line is a 45-degree line, where the points would align if there were a perfect relationship between the two measures. The tight clustering of points along the line provide visual evidence for the strong correlation of 0.93. This strong correlation remains if I compare the proportion of press releases allocated to credit claiming (0.79).

The strong correlation between supervised and unsupervised credit claiming provides evidence that our model is accurately estimating how legislators portray themselves to constituents. As a second validity check I examine whether expected variation in legislators' behavior manifests in our measures. A reasonable expectation is that legislators will discuss more often prominent industries located in their district (Adler and Lapinski, 1997). As a simple assessment of this expectation, I regressed the proportion of press releases in the farming category on the proportion of employed constituents who work in farming. This reveals that legislators who represent farming districts discuss agriculture more often. Indeed, representatives from districts at the 90th percentile of farm employment allocate 1.4 percentage points more of their press releases to agriculture than colleagues with few farm jobs in the district (95% confidence interval [0.01, 0.02]).

Legislators' position in the institution is another likely predictor of how they present their work to constituents. For example, one might expect that members of the Appropriations Committee would focus more on credit claiming than other legislators. The measures from the model suggest they do. Members of the

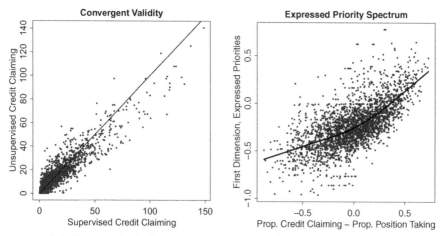

FIGURE 8.2. Expressed priority measures converge with previous measures and display similar variation. The left-hand plot shows that the measure of credit claiming from the unsupervised model is closely related to measures of credit claiming from a supervised model, as presented in Grimmer, Westwood, and Messing (2014). The right-hand plot shows that the primary variation underlying legislators' expressed priorities is a position taking-credit claiming spectrum.

Appropriations Committee allocate 5.9 percentage points more of their press releases to credit claiming than other representatives (95% confidence interval, [0.04, 0.07]). Similarly, one might expect that congressional leaders would focus less on claiming credit for expenditures and more on broad national issues – an expectation that manifests in our measured credit claiming. Party leaders in the House allocate 4.0 percentage points fewer of their press releases to credit claiming (95% confidence interval [−0.07, −0.01]) and 6.2 percentage points more to the national issues topic (95% confidence interval [0.04, 0.08]).

My estimates of House members' presentational styles also exhibit variation that is consistent with other well-validated measures of presentational styles. Grimmer (2013) shows that legislators' expressed priorities lies on a credit claiming – position taking spectrum. The right-hand plot in Figure 8.2 shows that this same variation underlies House members' press releases. It plots the principal component of legislators' expressed priorities against the proportion of press releases that claim credit, less the proportion of press releases where legislators articulate positions. There is a strong correlation between the two measures of 0.65, as well as a correlation of 0.71 between legislators' credit claiming rates and the principal component underlying the expressed priorities. Like senators, House members must decide how to balance claiming credit for spending that happens in their district with position taking.

And like senators, who House members represent is correlated with how they balance credit claiming and position taking. Grimmer (2013) demonstrates that senators who misaligned with their districts focus more on credit claiming, whereas aligned legislators articulate more positions. House members from marginal districts allocate 5.4 percentage points more of their press releases to credit claiming than their more aligned colleagues (95% confidence interval [0.04, 0.07]), whereas more aligned representatives 5.0 percentage points more of their press releases to national topics (95% confidence interval [0.04, 0.06]) and 3.8 percentage points more to articulating positions and advertising (95% confidence [0.03, 0.05]).

The unsupervised model is able to accurately identify both coarse and granular topics and to reliably estimate legislators' credit claiming propensity. In the next section I use the estimated priorities to show how members of the Republican Party shift their attention after Barack Obama's election toward criticism and away from claiming credit for expenditures in their district.

5 STABILITY AND CHANGE IN LEGISLATORS' EXPRESSED PRIORITIES

The collection of press releases used in this chapter covers six volatile years in American history and in Congress, reflecting change in who held institutional power in Congress and the electoral pressure that representatives, particularly Republicans, felt from their base. Republicans held the House majority in 2005, but lost that majority in the 2006 elections. The Republicans were then routed in both the 2008 congressional and presidential elections. Not only did they lose the White House but they also surrendered seats in both the House and Senate, bolstering the Democratic Party's majority. And as the newly elected Congress and Obama passed stimulus measures and began considering health reform, a mass movement of conservatives – the "Tea Party" – articulated frustrations with stimulus spending, health care reform, and Obama administration policies (Skocpol and Williamson, 2011). The conservative movement pressured Republican members of Congress to reject particularistic expenditures and to lower taxes and threatened those who failed to do so with primary challenge.

In response to the changing electoral and institutional pressures, Republicans altered how they presented their work to constituents. The left-hand plot in Figure 8.3 replicates a plot from Grimmer, Westwood, and Messing (2014), but uses the unsupervised measures of credit claiming to show that after Obama's election Republicans allocated a much smaller percentage of their press releases to credit claiming than in previous years. In 2005 Republican legislators claimed credit for spending in 23.2% of their press releases, whereas Democrats claimed credit in 23.5% of theirs. By 2010, however, Republicans allocated only 9% of their press releases to credit claiming – a 5.5 percentage point decline from 2010. The shift in Republican credit claiming is primarily due to conversion: from 2009 to 2010 Republicans decreased their credit-claiming rate 6.7 percentage points (95% confidence interval [−0.09, −0.05]). In contrast to the Republican aversion to credit claiming, Democratic

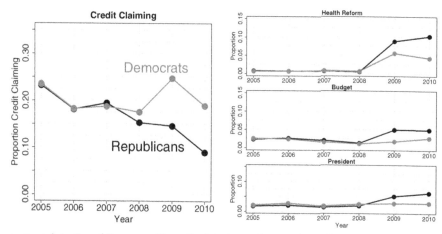

FIGURE 8.3. Republicans avoid credit claiming and instead attack presidential policies.

credit claiming spiked in 2009, when Democrats allocated 24.7% of their press releases to claiming credit for spending.

Instead of claiming credit, Republicans amplified criticism of the Obama administration and Democratic policies. The top plot in the right-hand side of Figure 8.3 shows the proportion of press releases Republicans (black line) and Democrats (gray line) allocated to health care reform. As the legislation that would eventually become the Affordable Care Act worked its way through Congress, both Democrats and Republicans increased the frequency of press releases about health care reform, but Republican House members were especially focused on this topic. In 2009 Republican House members allocated 3.3 percentage points more of their press releases to health reform than Democrats (95% confidence interval [0.02, 0.05]), and this difference grew to 6.0 percentage points in 2010 (95% confidence interval [0.04, 0.08]).

When Republicans discussed health care reform they were critical both of the content of the legislation and the legislative procedure to pass it. For example, Adam Putnam (R-FL) expressed skepticism about the potential benefits of health care reform, because "despite the president's very rosy view of cost savings, I think most Americans have learned through hard experience to be skeptical of such claims" (Putnam, 2009). Ralph Hall (R-TX) offered a similar condemnation of the legislation, arguing, "We need health care reform, but the Democrats' radical plan is not the prescription for reform that the American people want or deserve" (Hall, 2010). Republicans also expressed dismay that Democrats decided "to break their promise of open and informed debate over Health Care" (Linder, 2010) and warned their constituents that "in Washington, we're witnessing... Pelosi Madness... as the Speaker attempts to push through this health care legislation, regardless of cost, the desire of the American people and transparency." (Sensenbrenner, 2010). Even after the legislation passed, Republicans, such as Tom Price (R-GA), criticized the law, arguing that "Democrats ignored the Constitution in order to pass a law that would put Washington in control of your personal health care, while curtailing access to quality, affordable health care" (Price, 2010).

The growing Tea Party movement also conveyed dismay about particularistic expenditures (Skocpol and Williamson, 2011). The middle right-hand plot in Figure 8.3 shows that, consistent with Tea Party rhetoric, Republicans also attacked Obama and Democrats on particularistic expenditures in the stimulus aid and in spending more generally. In 2008, both Republicans and Democrats allocated about the same attention to discussing the federal budget: in their press releases, Republicans allocated 1.4% of their press releases to budget issues, only slightly more than the 1.2% of press releases allocated by the Democrats. By 2009, however, a large difference emerged: Republicans allocated 5.0% of their press releases to the budget, a 3.6 percentage point increase from 2008 and 3.2 percentage points more than Democratic House members. And Republicans maintained their focus on the budget in 2010, allocating 5.1% of their press releases to the budget and spending issues.

Just as in the health care debates, Republicans were sharply critical of the Obama administration when discussing the budget. For example, Todd Akin (R-MO) argued that the American Recovery and Reinvestment Act "places an additional $800 Billion on top of historic levels of debt, and without the realistic promise of actual job creation" (Akin, 2009). Eric Cantor (R-VA) criticized a budget proposal because "the President's budget spends more than any other in history, creates the largest deficits in history, and imposes the largest tax increases in history – at a time when our country can least afford it" (Cantor, 2010). And Mary Bono-Mack alleged that "the passage of the state bailout bill is yet another example of the Democrats' tax and spend policies which are compromising our nation's future and the futures of our children and grandchildren" (Bono-Mack, 2010). The differences are evident in more quantitative comparisons of Republican and Democratic language when discussing the stimulus. Republicans used words like *spend, govern, democrat, taxpayer,* and *trillion* at a much higher rate than Democrats, who used words like *budget, cut,* and *education* more often than Republicans. The bottom plot in Figure 8.3 shows a similar increase in Republican criticism of the president.

The shift in rhetoric is evidence that legislators' expressed priorities are responsive to changing conditions in districts and oppositions. Yet, there remains stability in legislators' expressed priorities from year to year. One way to measure this is to assess the correlation across years in the proportion of press releases legislators allocate to the coarse topics, given that legislators remain in Congress. Overall, there is a year-to-year correlation of 0.81 in legislators' expressed priorities. This strong correlation is found in credit claiming (0.60) and is particularly strong in noncredit-claiming coarse topics (0.83). Yet, the stability is not found only in the year-to-year measurse of legislators' expressed priorities. The strong correlation is even present over the entire six-year period studied here. The correlation between House members' expressed priorities in 2005 and expressed priorities in 2010 is 0.72.

Even though Republicans and Democrats shift their rhetoric as different policy proposals are considered or in response to pressure from the base, legislators maintain largely the same style over the six years. This provides insight into the origins of legislators' presentational styles. Using one of the most volatile time periods in recent political history, we see evidence that legislators adjust how they discuss their work with constituents in response to changing electoral and institutional conditions. But the response is on the margin and is a deviation from a longer run strategy that legislators develop over the course of their career (Grimmer, 2013). As a result, there remains a strong over-time relationship in legislators' expressed priorities.

6 CONCLUSION

A growing literature shows how legislators use communication to shape their relationship with constituents. This chapter contributes to this literature, providing new measures of how House members' expressed priorities respond to tumultuous changes in institutional and electoral contexts. To measure the expressed priorities, I use a large collection of House press releases and a statistical topic model that estimates granular and coarse topics, along with legislators' attention to those topics. The model provides two different types of topics, facilitating granular analysis of legislators' attention to more specific policy areas and of more general behavior, such as credit claiming.

Using the measures from the model, I show that Republican House members abandon credit claiming after Obama's election, whereas Democratic House members amplify their credit claiming. In place of claiming credit for projects in their districts, Republican House members criticize the Affordable Care Act, stimulus expenditures, and more generally the Obama administration. Even though there is a shift in rhetoric after the 2008 elections, I show that legislators' attention to the coarse topics is broadly stable over time. This demonstrates legislators' ability to respond to changing institutional and electoral conditions, but this response is a change on the margin from their persistent strategies.

Computational tools make it possible to study how legislators directly engage their constituents and how this engagement matters for representation. Models that are developed to better understand how Congress works can contribute to many other substantive areas. Consider, for example, how we understand the relationship between legislators' work in Washington and what they say about that work to constituents. Currently, measures are developed in individual areas and related to each other in a second-stage analysis. A more productive model might link the activities in a single model, allowing creation of a comprehensive measure of how legislators approach diverse areas of their work (Bernhard, Sulkin, and Sewell, 2014). Such a model would be useful in any setting where scholars wanted to link text with nontext data to facilitate inferences.

Computational tools could also be useful in understanding the effects of legislators' statements on constituents. For example, Grimmer, Westwood, and Messing (2014) use text analysis tools to motivate experiments that demonstrate these effects. To do this they had to determine the most salient features of the credit claiming messages to vary. But pairing random assignment with machine learning methods could facilitate *discovery* of the features of messages that are likely to have the largest effect on constituent response. In general, there is a need to better understand how to understand causal inference and text analysis methods (Roberts et al., 2014b).

Expanded resources and models also facilitate inferences that were previously impossible. For example, previous work has analyzed how legislators are covered in local newspapers and how legislators try to alter that coverage (Arnold, 2004). Yet, technological limitations limited the scope of what we could learn about how legislators were covered. Computational tools and digital collections of news, facilitate insights into how legislators are covered across diverse outlets and over extended time periods. Likewise, we know little about what constituents say when communicating with their legislators (Butler, 2014; Grose, Malhotra, and Van Houweling, 2014). And although it is unlikely that congressional offices will provide access to letters from constituents, social media provides an opportunity to study how members of the public pressure representatives in public settings.

A common theme in this future work is that a combination of new digital records of text and statistical tools for analyzing the large collections will provide deep insights into how representation occurs in American politics.

Notes

1. There are 23 legislator years where I have no press releases from some legislators in a given year.
2. Grimmer (2013) shows that there is a correlation between how legislators behave in the institution and what they say to constituents.
3. One might be concerned that the vMF distribution is inappropriate here, because of the zeros in the document. While this is a technical concern, in the actual application of the model the zeros, matter little, because there are many other plausible assumptions in the data-generation process.
4. Indeed, I could continue the hierarchy and create a nesting of the coarse topics. My experience has been, however, that in this setting another layer of topic clustering provides few insights and fairly noisy summaries of the texts.
5. Because I fix the prior on π_i we are able to avoid maximizing the Dirichlet hyperparameters.

References

Adler, E. Scott and John S. Lapinski. 1997. "Demand-Side Theory and Congressional Committee Composition: A Constituency Characteristics Approach." *American Journal of Political Science* 41(3):895–918.

Adler, E. Scott and John Wilkerson. 2012. *Congress and the Politics of Problem Solving.* Cambridge University Press.

Akin, Todd. 2009. "Rep. Akin Opposes Big Government Spending Plan." Representative Press Release.

Alexander, Rodney. 2007. "Rep. Alexander, Sen. Vitter Announce Grant Funding for Evangeline Parish." Representative Press Release.

Arnold, R. Douglas. 2004. *Congress, the Press, and Political Accountability.* Princeton University Press.

Banerjee, Arindam, Inderjit S. Dhillon, Joydeep Ghosh, and Suvrit Sra. 2005. "Clustering on the Unit Hypersphere Using von Mises-Fisher Distributions." *Journal of Machine Learning Research* 6:1345–1382.

Bernhard, William, Tracy Sulkin, and Daniel Sewell. 2014. "Legislative Style." University of Illinois Mimeo.

Bischof, Jonathan and Edoardo Airoldi. 2012. "Summarizing Topical Content with Word Frequency and Exclusivity." In *International Conference on Machine Learning,* ed. John Langford and Joelle Pinelle. pp. 201–208.

Blaydes, Lisa, Justin Grimmer, and Alison McQueen. 2014. "Mirrors for Princes and Sultans: Advice on the Art of Governance in the Medieval Christian and Islamic Worlds." Stanford University Mimeo.

Blei, David and John Lafferty. 2006. "Dynamic Topic Models." *Proceedings of the 23rd International Conference on Machine Learning* 23.

Blei, David, Andrew Ng and Michael Jordan. 2003. "Latent Dirichlet Allocation." *Journal of Machine Learning and Research* 3:993–1022.

Bono-Mack, Mary. 2010. "Congress Needs to End Its Tax Spend Policies." Representative Press Release.

Butler, Daniel. 2014. "The Discriminating Politician." Washington University Mimeo.

Cantor, Eric. 2010. "Rep. Cantor on Fiscal Year 2011 Budget." Representative Press Release.

Capuano, Michael. 2007. "Rep. Capuano Issues Statement on Iraq, H.R. 1591: The Iraq Accountability Act of 2007." Representative Press Release.

Chang, Jonathan, Jordan Boyd-Graber, Sean Gerrish, Chong Wang, and David Blei. 2009. "Reading Tea Leaves: How Humans Interpret Topic Models." In *Neural Information Processing Systems.*

Cormack, Lindsey. 2014. "Sins of Omission: Legislator (Mis)Representation in Constituent Communications." New York University Mimeo.

Disch, Lisa. 2012. "Democratic Representation and the Constituency Paradox." *Perspectives on Politics* 10(3):599–616.

Fenno, Richard. 1978. *Home Style: House Members in their Districts.* Addison-Wesley.

Gerrish, Sean and David Blei. 2012. "How They Vote: Issue-Adjusted Models of Legislative Behavior." In *Neural Information Processing Systems.*

Gopal, Siddharth and Yiming Yang. 2014. "Von Mises-Fisher Clustering Models." *Journal of Machine Learning Research* 32(1):154–162.

Grimmer, Justin. 2010. "A Bayesian Hierarchical Topic Model for Political Texts: Measuring Expressed Agendas in Senate Press Releases." *Political Analysis* 18(1):1–35.

Grimmer, Justin. 2013. *Representational Style: What Legislators Say and Why It Matters*. Cambridge University Press.

Grimmer, Justin and Gary King. 2011. "General Purpose Computer-Assisted Clustering and Conceptualization." *Proceedings of the National Academy of Sciences* 108(7):2643–2650.

Grimmer, Justin and Brandon M. Stewart. 2013. "Text as Data: The Promise and Pitfalls of Automatic Content Analysis Methods for Political Texts." *Political Analysis* 21(3):267–297.

Grimmer, Justin, Sean J. Westwood, and Solomon Messing. 2014. *The Impression of Influence: Legislator Communication, Representation, and Democratic Accountability*. Princeton University Press.

Grose, Christian, Neil Malhotra, and Robert P. Van Houweling. 2014. "Explaining Explanations: How Legislators Explain their Policy Position and How Citizens React." Stanford University Mimeo.

Hall, Ralph. 2010. "Rep. Hall Urges Democrats to Drop Plans for Government Takeover of Health Care." Representative Press Release.

Herseth, Stephanie. 2006. "Rep. Herseth Announces $3 Million for Ellsworth Water Well." Representative Press Release.

Higgins, Brian. 2006. "Higgins Announces Federal Grant for Bemus Point Fire Department." Representative Press Release.

Hillard, Dustin, Stephen Purpura, and John Wilkerson. 2008. "Computer-Assisted Topic Classification for Mixed-Methods Social Science Research." *Journal of Information Technology & Politics* 4(4):31–46.

Lewis, Jerry. 2007. "Rep. Lewis Denounces Supplemental Spending Bill That Lets Politicians Micromanage Troop Decisions." Representative Press Release.

Li, W. and A. McCallum. 2006. "Pachinko Allocation: DAG-Structure Mixture Models of Topic Correlations." In *International Conference on Machine Learning*. pp. 577–584.

Linder, John. 2010. "Linder Statement on C-Span Call for Transparency." Representative Press Release.

Lipinski, Daniel. 2004. *Congressional Communication: Content and Consequences*. University of Michigan Press.

Mansbridge, Jane. 2003. "Rethinking Representation." *American Political Science Review* 97(4):515–528.

Mayhew, David. 1974. *Congress: The Electoral Connection*. Yale University Press.

Mimno, David and Andrew McCallum. 2008. "Topic Models Conditioned on Arbitrary Features with Dirichlet-Multinomial Regression." *Conference on Uncertainty in Artificial Intelligence*. Plenary Presentation.

Monroe, Burt, Michael Colaresi, and Kevin Quinn. 2008. "Fightin' Words: Lexical Feature Selection and Evaluation for Identifying the Content of Political Conflict." *Political Analysis* 16(4):372.

Price, Tom. 2010. "Rep. Price Issues Statement on Court Ruling that Obamacare Is Unconstitutional." Representative Press Release.

Putnam, Adam. 2009. "Rep. Putnam Issues Statement on President Obama's Health Care Speech." Representative Press Release.

Quinn, Kevin et al. 2010. "How to Analyze Political Attention with Minimal Assumptions and Costs." *American Journal of Political Science* 54(1).

Roberts, Margaret E., Brandon M. Stewart, and Edoardo M. Airoldi. 2014a. "Structural Topic Models." Harvard University Mimeo.

Roberts, Margaret E et al. 2014b. "Structural Topic Models for Open-Ended Survey Responses." *American Journal of Political Science* 58(4):1064–1082.

Sensenbrenner, James. 2010. "March Madness... Washington Style." Representative Press Release.

Skocpol, Theda and Vanessa Williamson. 2011. *The Tea Party and the Remaking of Republican Conservatism*. Oxford University Press.

Stupak, Bart. 2010. "Rep. Stupak Announces $726,409 for Airports in Alpena, Delta, Chippewa Counties." Represenative Press Release.

Teh, Yee Weh, Michael Jordan, Matthew Beal, and David Blei. 2006. "Hierarchical Dirichlet Processes." *Journal of the American Statistical Association* 101(476):1566–1581.

Wallach, Hanna. 2008. "Structured Topic Models for Language." PhD thesis, University of Cambridge.

Wallach, Hanna, Lee Dicker, Shane Jensen, and Katherine Heller. 2010. "An Alternative Prior for Nonparametric Bayesian Clustering." In *Proceedings of the Thirteenth International Conference on Artificial Intelligence and Statistics (AISTATS)*. Vol. 9.

Yiannakis, Diana Evans. 1982. "House Members' Communication Styles: Newsletter and Press Releases." *Journal of Politics* 44(4):1049–1071.

9

Using Social Marketing and Data Science to Make Government Smarter

Brian Griepentrog, Sean Marsh, Sidney Carl Turner, and Sarah Evans
Fors Marsh Group

It is generally agreed that the most important single function of government is to secure the rights and freedoms of individual citizens. Adam Smith, the eighteenth-century philosopher, was restrictive in his view of these rights, limiting them essentially to three basic government functions: protection of the nation, administration of law and order, and the provision of certain public functions (e.g., infrastructure and education; Smith, 1976). Although the role of government and the process by which it is executed vary greatly, the benefits provided to the citizens of countries with well-managed government systems are clear. Countries with more effective governments are more likely to obtain better credit ratings, attract more investment, offer higher quality public services, encourage higher levels of human capital accumulation, effectively utilize foreign aid resources, accelerate technological innovation, and increase the productivity of government spending (Burnside & Dollar, 2000; Baum & Lake, 2003). Further, countries with more effective governments have better educational systems and more efficient health care (Lewis, 2006; Baldacci, Clements, Gupta, & Cui, 2004).

In the past when government agencies have wanted to institute change or influence citizen behavior, they often relied on a common set of educational or policy initiatives. These tools rely on a broad-brush approach aimed at developing knowledge, reinforcing desired behaviors through funding initiatives and/or tax incentives, or requiring change through the development of new regulatory measures or laws. Although these uniform, rational, and compliance methods have their place, technological and societal shifts have required and provided opportunities for government and public policy to adapt. Society has increasingly pushed for government to become more goal-oriented, aiming for measurable results that can be achieved with some degree of immediacy (Geurts, 2010). Furthermore, technological changes have created opportunities for agencies to rely more heavily on advanced statistical methods with social marketing[1] principles to seamlessly integrate targeted communication efforts with their more traditional tools to bring about behavioral change.

At the core of the government's ability to effectively shift to more targeted, efficient, and outcome-oriented initiatives is the exponentially increasing amount of administrative- and/or survey-based information available in electronic format. This information has taken on the general moniker of "big data" as a singular definition, but the respects from which it can be big vary meaningfully, affecting how it can be approached and its ultimate utility. One common differentiator is the degree to which data are "tall" or "fat." Data can be tall such that it may have millions of observations, allowing for the estimation of parameters of interest that, under certain assumptions, can be meaningfully generalizable to a population of interest and robust to sampling variability. Alternatively, data can be fat, meaning that it has information on a large number of potentially relevant predictors of the outcome of interest, allowing for the estimation of better identified and better fitting models. Although the term "big data" is used quite frequently, the reality is that agencies much less often have at their disposal data that is truly big, being both tall and fat.

The wide variety of U.S. government agencies have responded to this environmental shift by embracing advanced analytic techniques that are able to address big data. In our own work with the U.S. government, we have dealt with many of these tall and fat data projects and their unique outgrowths. In this chapter, we address two such projects that fall within the social marketing umbrella, yet deal with the unique data analytic challenges presented by the different types of big data. The first example is a project with the Animal and Plant Health Inspection Service (APHIS) that involves developing and identifying high-risk traveler segments using border inspection data to prevent pest introduction into the U.S. This project details some of the unique challenges involved in constructing, analyzing, and interpreting a tall data set. The second example is a project with the Federal Voting Assistance Program (FVAP) that involves a model-based method for estimating the population of U.S. citizens abroad to increase their likelihood of voting success. For this example, we detail the unique challenges of model building, testing, and validation relying on a fat data set in which there are lots of variables but few cases (i.e., countries).

PREVENTING RISK TO U.S. AGRICULTURAL HEALTH AND NATURAL RESOURCES

APHIS is the division of the U.S. Department of Agriculture (USDA) charged with protecting animal and plant resources from agricultural diseases and pests such as the Mediterranean fruit fly and Asian long-horned beetle. These pests and diseases can harm native species of plants and animals, the economy, and human health. Further, pests enter the U.S. and cross state lines in several preventable ways, such as on commercial shipments (e.g., wooden pallets); by hitchhiking on vehicles, fruits, plants, seeds, or animals; and coming with travelers who bring prohibited fruits, plants, seeds, animals, and other items back from other countries. International travelers play a key role in the introduction, spread, and prevention of invasive species; however, they hardly think twice about these issues. In an effort to change their behavior, APHIS has increasingly looked to educational and social marketing approaches to complement existing enforcement approaches. These proactive approaches seek to increase awareness of the threat of invasive species and reduce the number of people who attempt to bring prohibited food or plant items into the U.S.

One of the key steps in the communication and social marketing process is identifying the population segments to target with messaging. International travelers, particularly those most germane to the APHIS mission, represent a relatively small portion of the entire population and have unique interests and demographic characteristics. Grouping the population into segments allows for more efficient strategies to reach them and more effective use of resources. One basic axiom of effective communications is that when a program is developed for too broad an audience, no group is effectively reached. Tailored communication, however, increases the likelihood the target audience will be reached and that its members will pay attention to the message (Weinreich, 2010). Although this sounds like a rather simple strategy, the difficulty is identifying what defines a segment, where members of a particular segment are located, what tools are most effective in reaching that target segment, and what message is likely to most strongly influence that segment's behavior. Following our general best practice, our research team set out to address these questions through a multimethod approach involving both qualitative and quantitative techniques. In this instance, this involved archival data analysis of Agricultural Quarantine Inspection Monitoring (AQIM) data, qualitative interviews with agents and travelers, and cross-sectional surveys of departing travelers. We focus our attention on the archival analysis because it best represents some of the big data challenges discussed throughout this book.

Data Set Construction

A common big data challenge we worked through at the onset of the initiative was identifying, compiling, merging, and prioritizing the large amount of data available. The main source in the study was the AQIM data. When travelers enter the U.S. from international points of origin, they are subject to inspection for items of agricultural interest (e.g., fruits, meats, wooden handicrafts). The AQIM data catalogs all inspection cases, including those with no restricted items found, those with restricted items that were cleaned or treated, those with restricted items that were inspected and released, and those with seized items. No personally identifiable information (PII) is collected or retained in the AQIM data, making the external sharing and disclosure of this data of minimal privacy risk. For researchers working with government data, these privacy concerns can significantly affect the timing and ultimately viability of a project. Although timing and viability of the current project were not affected by privacy concerns, it is rather interesting given our project that the main risk listed by USDA in its privacy impact analysis (PIA) is time-related – "the availability of the information and the length of time it would take for users to perform data mining activities due to the breadth of data."[2] In other words, the AQIM data represents tall challenges.

We first faced questions regarding how the scope of the analysis should be defined. Though this data is collected for travelers entering the U.S. through a variety of pathways (i.e., air, land, and maritime), the decision was made to restrict analyses to air and land pathways due to the scope of the ultimate communication effort that would be developed from the results. The air pathway included both international origins and predeparture origins. Predeparture inspections of passenger baggage are conducted when travelers enter the continental U.S. from Hawaii and Puerto Rico. Next, a reasonable period of time was selected – determined to be three years – based on average volume of data for a one-year period. Data from October 2008 to September 2011 was pulled for each of the primary travel pathways: air ($n = 351,746$), land ($n = 624,794$) and predeparture ($n = 79,592$).[3]

Next, to supplement the AQIM data, we sought additional data sources that identified seized items, but did not differentiate further in terms of relative risk. In other words, our segments would have been prioritized by volume alone if solely examining the AQIM data. However, different commodities carry different risks, and with limited resources, it would be essential to prioritize segments that posed the greatest risk for initial outreach efforts. Ultimately, we supplemented AQIM data with commodity risk weights (risk of each specific agricultural item; for example, an orange) and country risk weights (agricultural risk by country of origin) that were provided by the Center for Plant Health Science and Technology (CPHST). These weights existed in internal reports separate from the AQIM data and were able to be incorporated through interdepartmental coordination.

With data sources identified, the next step in identifying meaningful segments was to develop a master data set by joining records from all pathways, years, and ports – and appending commodity and country risk information. Before analyzing this data, we examined the distributions to inform later data manipulations and recoding. In general, we applied simple data manipulations to facilitate subsequent analyses. For example, we aggregated variables that pertained to an item or items associated with a passenger so that each was represented by a single value per passenger. Other variables, such as risk weight associated with an item (commodity risk weight multiplied by country risk), were summed at the passenger level so that a single risk indicator was associated with a case regardless of the number of items of interest. Therefore, a single high-risk item could carry as much weight as multiple lower risk items.

Analytic Method

Several analytic techniques could have been applied to identify relevant segments or clusters in the USDA APHIS data, including cluster analysis (also called segmentation analysis or taxonomy analysis), discriminant function analysis, multinomial logistic regression, Q-mode factor analysis, and latent class analysis. We selected cluster analysis for the current study after preliminary analysis of the available data. Cluster analysis seeks to identify homogeneous subgroups of cases in a population. This class of tools finds the most significant solution possible, but does not focus on null hypothesis significance testing. Unlike discriminant function analysis, it does not require that group membership be prespecified for each case by the researcher.

Within cluster analysis, the appropriateness of specific methods of clustering depends largely on the nature of the predictor data and the size of the analysis sample. Hierarchical clustering is appropriate for smaller samples (<250) and uses data that are interval or true dichotomies. K-means clustering is generally preferred when data sets are large (>1,000) and also uses data that are interval or are true dichotomies. However, the researcher must specify the number of clusters in advance.

Our chosen method, two-step clustering, creates preclusters and then clusters those using hierarchical methods. This method also handles large data sets, but it accommodates categorical as well as continuous predictor data, an advantage given the nature of the APHIS data. Using this approach, predictors such as country of origin and point of entry may be used to predict a violation (i.e., an attempt to enter the continental U.S. with a restricted agricultural item) or type of violation. Each cluster analysis yielded a set of unique segments of the population that are likely to move specified restricted/prohibited materials unknowingly or not through air, land, or predeparture pathways and through particular sites (e.g., San Francisco).

Results

Initial analysis for each pathway using all data (cases with no item found, items that were cleaned or treated, items that were inspected and released, or seized items) did not provide meaningful cluster results and did not allow for proper identification of restricted-item-carrying segments at the site level (i.e., clusters were distinguished by whether an item was seized). Therefore, separate cluster analyses were conducted for the subset of seized items for each pathway in the final analysis. Results by pathway that included data with only cases of seized or cleaned agricultural items provided strong clusters. The land cluster analysis yielded a two-cluster solution (group 1, $n = 9{,}314$; group 2, $n = 11{,}790$); the air cluster analysis yielded a four-cluster solution (group 1, $n = 3{,}053$; group 2, $n = 5{,}137$; group 3, $n = 6{,}199$; group 4, $n = 3{,}602$); and the predeparture cluster analysis yielded a four-cluster solution (group 1, $n = 1{,}087$; group 2, $n = 687$; group 3, $n = 1{,}228$; group 4, $n = 1{,}166$).

Interpretation

With analysis completed, we worked through a challenge inevitable when dealing with data science in the government space – subjective interpretation of the meaning of the results. Because these results were to inform the development of a campaign that would not exist in a vacuum but instead would be implemented in a mix of policy, political, and budgetary influences, the final solution could not be determined by machine-based analysis of the results alone. Rather, there was a significant human component that ultimately would be required for the effort to result in applicable findings and recommendations. This human influence is first seen in the definition of potential audience segments, identified from the clusters described in the results section. Although the clusters are computationally driven, they are meaningless (practically speaking) without the interpretation of the researcher(s). With the clusters as a starting point, we translated the results into homogeneous segments that would be appropriate for tailored communication. These segments were identified by examining demographic and behavioral characteristics that distinguished each cluster. Namely, we described segments based on similarities in traveler origin, traveler destination (land only), travel reason, type of restricted agricultural item seized or cleaned, and port of entry.

An overall risk then was assigned to each segment by the multiplication of three terms. The segment n (number with a specific commodity, travel site, country of origin, and travel reason) was multiplied by commodity risk and the country risk for the plant or animal item. The number of observations accounted for the quantity of a specific commodity product that was brought to or through each site, the commodity risk was used to account for the risks associated with different types of food based on the types of foreign species they can carry and the unique agricultural products produced in the U.S., and the country risk was used to take into account where diseases of concern are located.

The process of prioritizing segments, however, did not end with a simple ranking of risk. Rather, a subjective element again played an essential role in maximizing the potential impact of the results by injecting procedural and budgetary realities necessary to garner widespread organizational buy-in. That is, several client-provided insights guided prioritization of the segments. Specifically, animal and plant products were to be represented, as were a variety of entry pathways (i.e., air, land, and predeparture all represented). The result was a tiered approach in which top segments in each category rose to the top. A

TABLE 9.1. *Selected Segments by Site, Type of Product, Segment Description, and Travel Pathway*

Site	Segment Description	Pathway
ANIMAL PRODUCTS		
San Francisco	People traveling for family visits, tourism, and business from China with beef and poultry	Air
Miami	People traveling for family visits from South America (Colombia, Ecuador, and Peru) with pork	Air
San Ysidro	People traveling for any reason from Mexico to California with pork or eggs	Land
PLANT PRODUCTS		
San Ysidro	People traveling for business and family visits from Mexico to California with apples, pears, and citrus	Land
Lihue	People traveling for home from Hawaii with apples, pears, citrus, and tropical fruit	Predeparture
Miami	People traveling from Jamaica with tropical fruit	Air

prioritized list of segments was then reviewed by APHIS experts who integrated our ranking with their knowledge of agricultural disease and production areas within the U.S. (items of high risk coming into the U.S. regions with limited agricultural production) to determine the five most risky plant and animal item segments. The end result was data-driven segments that represented a variety of priorities and stakeholders. The selected segments are shown in Table 9.1.[4]

Conclusion

This APHIS initiative provides one example of how data science is providing a foundation on which a government agency can build a social marketing effort. Changing behavior is not simply about educating people about what is (or is not) in their best interest – people engage in behaviors they know could be detrimental every day. Successful behavior change initiatives begin with a deep understanding of the underlying beliefs and motivations that drive an audience's behavior and then put the motivation for the behavior change in terms that are meaningful to that audience. Identifying and prioritizing audience segments are of critical importance for governmental (and nongovernmental) social marketing initiatives.

The data challenges of this project were largely addressed through a logical progression of steps, which reduced the size and scope of an unwieldy data set. Our approach highlights the role of the analyst and subject matter expert in focusing in on specific research questions. For example, the decision to restrict analyses to air and land pathways was made in collaboration with APHIS based on the scope of the ultimate communication effort that would be developed from the results. This approach allows big data analysis to take place with more traditional computing resources, while also ensuring collaboration between agency experts and decision makers in planning the research, interpreting the findings, and actually using the research to make decisions.

This effort was designed and implemented in a variety of ways that have made APHIS smarter. First, APHIS has been able to be more cost efficient by focusing its outreach efforts on particularly high-risk groups, with media budget allocations made based on salient segment characteristics (e.g., traveler location, travel destination). Second, the segmentation solution has been the foundation for follow-on research to identify key messages and channels relevant to each of the prioritized segments. This has allowed APHIS not only to know where to communicate but also to identify how and when to communicate with similar precision. The integration of data science and subjective interpretation by agency experts has garnered widespread support for the effort internally and confidence in the evolving strategy. These segmented communication efforts began fielding in early 2015, with a formal evaluation planned for the summer of 2015.

PREDICTING OVERSEAS CITIZENS

The APHIS example discusses some of the challenges and opportunities of working with, constructing, and interpreting a tall data set, but an equally vexing challenge is working with fat data sets with few cases and many predictors. A recent project we conducted with the Federal Voting Assistance Program (FVAP) is a great example of some of these challenges. FVAP works to ensure that members of the U.S. military, their eligible family members, and overseas citizens are aware of their right to vote and have the tools and resources to successfully do so – from anywhere in the world. Therefore, it is critical that FVAP knows where and how many U.S. citizens are located abroad to direct its services. Unfortunately, analyzing the population of U.S. citizens abroad is complicated by the lack of available data for many (particularly developing) countries, the diverse motivations for U.S. citizens traveling and living overseas, and the economic and institutional environments of many of the countries in which U.S. citizens reside. Consequently, attempts to estimate this population face necessary tradeoffs between breadth (i.e., the number of countries that can be estimated) and depth (i.e., the accuracy and detail of the estimates that can be made). Currently, there are several estimates of the number of citizens living abroad (varying from one million to seven million) that academics, government organizations, nongovernmental organizations, and private industry use to plan and implement programs targeted to the overseas U.S. citizen population. Unfortunately, these estimates vary wildly and have often been accompanied by little documentation, used varying definitions of the population of U.S. citizens abroad, and been criticized for having problematic and/or unclear methods.

To help confront this challenge, we partnered with the National Opinion Research Center (NORC) at the University of Chicago and Lightbox Analytics to develop an enumeration system that relied on information that is available to help estimate information that is missing with the goal of creating as complete a count as possible. The first step was developing a robust model that accurately predicts the available estimate for the overseas U.S. citizen population for the subset of countries in which estimates are provided by the host country. This subset provided great utility, because these countries not only provide a Foreign Government Estimate (FGE) for the U.S. population but also a host of other variables that have been found or have been theorized to be correlates or predictors of this estimate. Once developed, this model was used to project the number of U.S. citizens for every country that lacked an FGE, as well as to adjust the estimates for countries that use alternative definitions of overseas U.S. citizens.

Given the relatively few number of existing country estimates and virtually limitless data for each country, our data set was considerably overweight. One of the biggest risks in situations like these is overfitting the data such that the preferred model explains both the signal and the noise, consequently resulting in weak predictive performance and thus poor estimates. The following sections describe (1) model development, (2) calibrating model estimates, (3) robustness testing, and finally (4) the resulting model estimates.

Model Development

The first step in our project was identifying and collecting FGEs using several different sources of data:

- The Organization for Economic Cooperation and Development (OECD) International Migration Database, which provided data on the number of U.S. citizens during the years 2000 to 2010 for most OECD countries.
- The individual countries or directly from their national statistical agencies. Links for the websites of foreign government statistical agencies were identified using the U.S. Census Bureau webpage titled "International Collection of the U.S. Census Bureau Library."[5] Estimates obtained from countries' websites were usually from their most recent census.
- Specific reports on migration commissioned by the national government. These estimates were obtained from foreign government censuses and immigrant registries.
- FGEs available in a U.S. Census Bureau internal document titled "Estimating Native Emigration from the U.S." (Schachter, 2008), which was compiled as part of a project to estimate U.S. net emigration. Although this document included estimates for a period that roughly covered the

years 1990 to 2008, we included only estimates from post-1999 (to avoid complexity introduced by the large number of border changes that occurred in the 1990s).

Predictor Variables

The number and type of potential variables that are available for many countries are staggering. One of the first ways in which we minimized the potential of overfitting the model was to only include variables for which we had explicit justification. This justification most often was in the form of past theoretical work and empirical findings. Although working with any type of big data can and often is approached as a "data-mining expedition," this approach poses real risk when working with fat data sets. A great deal of time could be dedicated to this stage and the process by which variables were included or excluded in particular. However, for the sake of time and space, only three broad classes of categories are provided here:

1. Administrative: Counts of the number of particular subpopulations of U.S. citizens living in a given country ("count" variables) available from administrative records (e.g., number of Social Security beneficiaries published by the Social Security Administration).
2. Theoretical: Noncount variables that have a theoretical relationship with bilateral migration. Theoretical variables have been theoretically and empirically identified as correlates of bilateral migration stocks and flows for samples, including all origin countries for which data is available. It is worth noting that for many of the variables included, it was unclear to what degree they are associated with migration by U.S. citizens.
3. Measurement: Measurement variables are used to adjust the predictions of the model such that they reflect a consistent definition for the size of the population of interest, U.S. citizens.

Although additional variables such as State Department consulate registrations could have been included, these data were not publicly available due to security considerations. As a result, including this data in the analysis would have precluded outside researchers from reproducing the results and thus undermined the transparency of the analysis. Further, the inclusion of sensitive data into our models would bring into play a whole host of additional concerns related to data acquisition, storage, use, and sharing not originally envisioned for this work.

Calibrating Model Estimates

Estimating the overseas U.S. citizen population is complicated by uncertainty about which predictors should be used to model this population and the resulting risk of overfitting the model. To address these uncertainties, we used a variant of a method called ensemble Bayesian model averaging (EBMA), which has been found to yield more accurate out-of-sample predictions than using a single model. It has been used successfully in such applications as armed conflict prediction and forecasting the outcome of presidential campaigns (Montgomery, Hollenbach, & Ward, 2012). The general approach of EBMA is to take predictions from multiple models (i.e., ensembles) and create an average of all the estimates weighted by each model's fit to the data and correlation or redundancy with predictions derived from other models.

The estimate is found to be more accurate than estimates derived from any single model because it minimizes the effects of overfitting caused by individual model specifications. At the same time, this method allows the final estimate to incorporate as much information as possible from the predictor variables. The model space from which this average prediction is derived takes the form of all possible combinations of predictor variables. For k predictors, the number of models, N, equals $2^{\hat{}}(k)$. As applied to the estimation of overseas U.S. citizens, the approach is not likelihood based, and therefore it is not Bayesian. Instead, it is based on root mean square error (see the later discussion). Consequently, the modeling approach is simply ensemble model averaging (EMA).

The N models take the following form:

$$FGE_{it}^{m} = \beta C_{it} + \beta X_{it}^{m} + \gamma 1 REGISTRY_{it} + \gamma 2 CITIZEN_{it} + \gamma 3 DUAL_{it} + \gamma 4 (DUAL_{it} * CITIZEN_{it}) + e_{it}^{m},$$

where FGE is the foreign government estimate representing the count of the U.S. citizen population in country i in year t; C is a vector of variables indicating the size of specific subpopulations of an overseas U.S. citizen population that are common to every model; X is a vector of predictor variables derived from the academic international migration literature that might explain variations in the U.S. citizen population of country i included in model m (and thus will vary from model to model); $REGISTRY$ is a dummy variable that takes a value of 1 if the country's FGE is based on a registry count; $CITIZEN$ is a dummy variable that takes a value of 1 if the FGE pertains to the number of U.S. citizens in the country, and 0 otherwise; $DUAL$ is a dummy variable that takes a value of 1 if the country allows dual citizenship with the U.S.; $DUAL * CITIZEN$ is an interaction variable that takes a value of 1 if the country both allows dual citizenship and has an FGE that counts U.S citizens, and 0 otherwise; and e is an error term. Because the FGE is bounded at 0, each model was estimated using the poisson pseudo-maximum likelihood estimator, following Santos Silva and Tenreyro (2006). Observations were weighted by the inverse of the estimated probability that a country would have an FGE. For more information concerning the collection of FGEs in the previous round of research, please consult the 2013 OCE Report (FVAP 2013) https://www.fvap .gov/uploads/FVAP/Reports/OCE_Technical_Report.pdf.

The measurement variables (i.e., those not included in vectors C or X) are included to control for differences in how foreign governments estimated their

U.S. population and whom they decided to count. When generating predictions from a model, $\gamma 1$ is set to 0, $\gamma 2$ is set to 1, and $\gamma 4$ is set to 0. The prediction therefore represents the estimated number of citizens the country would report if it had used a census. We assume this to be more likely to capture most U.S. citizens in a country than a registry-based instrument. We set the interaction coefficient to 0 to account for the tendency of countries allowing dual citizenship to singularly classify U.S. citizens as citizens of the host country. By modeling the effect of the government's choice of measurement instrument and whom the government chose to count for the size of the FGE, we are able to incorporate useful information contained in FGEs that may affect how similar the estimates are across countries.

The final estimate of the overseas U.S. citizen population for a country in each year is a weighted average of the estimates for that country-year generated by a model set defined by all possible combinations of the theoretical variables. The specification weight in this case is a function of both the out-of-sample predictive performance of the specification and the degree to which the model's predictions are correlated with the predictions of other models. We measured the out-of-sample predictive performance using the inverse of the mean squared error (MSE). The out-of-sample MSE is determined through K-fold cross-validation (Stone, 1977), where each observation in the sample is randomly assigned to one of K subsamples, the model is estimated using the $K-1$ subsamples, predictions are estimated for the excluded validation sample, and the MSE (weighted by the selection bias weight α_i, from above) is generated for that subsample. The cross-validation procedure is repeated K times, with each subsample acting as the validation sample in turn. The cross-validation step is then repeated S times, with the average of the $S * K$ MSEs used as the model MSE. In this application, it set $K = 5$ and $S = 10$. The other component of the specification weight captures the degree to which the predictions generated by a model are not redundant with predictions generated by other models; it is measured using the mean inverse correlation between a given model and all other models in the model set. The metric w^m is larger when models simultaneously (1) make relatively accurate out-of-sample predictions, as measured by the inverse of the MSE, and (2) are uncorrelated or not redundant with predictions made from other models.

Thus, each model's contribution to the final estimate is determined by its out-of-sample predictive ability (minimizing error that could result from determining model performance based on an in-sample fit only) and the model's unique predictive power. This process is all in place to minimize overfitting such that its predictive power is more likely due to variation in the U.S. citizen populations and not to random measurement error (Hawkins, 2004; Ward, Greenhill, & Bakke, 2010), while also being sure to include a diverse set of model specifications rather than just minor variations of the same model. The proposed validation metric thus rewards accuracy, penalizes redundancy, and improves the likelihood of cross-validation.

Robustness Testing

In addition to model averaging using cross-validated based weights, we considered three other estimation methodologies. One model estimation approach considered was Bayesian model averaging (BMA), a model averaging routine very similar to the chosen method, but one that uses an alternative model weighting scheme based on the Bayesian information criterion (BIC). The other two model estimation approaches considered were random forests and additive regression imputation. Random forests are a machine-learning algorithm that uses heuristic rules to search the model space in a manner that is potentially more efficient than the model averaging methods. Additive regression, by contrast, is similar to a generalized linear model except that it fits some function of each predictor to the data in predicting the outcome. Even though the EMA, BMA, and random forests performed similarly, we preferred the EMA approach given the difficulties with specifying the "correct" anti-logged BIC weight and the fact that the cross-validated model weights used by EMA directly test for model overfitting and correlation.

Model Estimates

Aggregates of the estimates resulting from the EMA methodology are provided in Table 9.2 by State Department regions.[6] The estimates show that the number of U.S. citizens living overseas has grown steadily from 2000 to 2013, increasing 60% overall during that period. These estimates also show that the majority of the population of U.S. citizens abroad is located in the Western Hemisphere and Europe, and this remained the case throughout the period of 2000–2010.

There is a tendency for regions with initially small estimated U.S. citizen populations to see greater growth. Although the estimated population of U.S. citizens in Europe is relatively high, that region also saw the lowest rates of growth over the period of 2000–2010. By contrast, Africa, the Middle East, and Southern Asia, while having the lowest totals throughout the period, saw the fastest growth. This is consistent with a change in the geographic distribution of the population of U.S. citizens abroad, with U.S. citizens becoming less concentrated over time and the population of lagging regions beginning to converge with the higher population regions.

Conclusion

The goal of this effort was to develop an estimate of the population of U.S. citizens abroad that would allow FVAP to allocate resources more effectively and efficiently and target its voter assistance outreach to the greatest number of Uniformed and Overseas Citizen Absentee Voting Act (UOCAVA) voters. Although no estimate should ever be considered final, the EMA approach we employed allowed for precise predictions with small samples. Our model did so

TABLE 9.2. *Estimate of the Population of U.S. Citizens Abroad by Global Region, 2000–2010*

Year	Africa	East Asia & Pacific	Europe & Eurasia	Near East	South & Central Asia	Western Hemisphere	Global Total
2000	52,763	370,009	923,066	119,414	33,259	1,203,359	2,701,869
2001	54,852	380,651	948,868	119,358	33,112	1,223,450	2,760,291
2002	54,298	392,833	969,335	112,028	39,512	1,261,526	2,829,533
2003	58,033	416,567	1,002,806	127,111	45,102	1,317,421	2,967,039
2004	62,538	438,368	1,048,491	149,712	53,070	1,383,127	3,135,305
2005	69,460	462,839	1,089,428	162,078	61,763	1,455,999	3,301,566
2006	67,516	518,835	1,123,249	169,325	65,897	1,507,595	3,452,418
2007	77,297	578,090	1,176,333	189,119	78,893	1,781,450	3,881,182
2008	89,888	603,188	1,179,756	203,939	85,259	1,953,433	4,115,463
2009	91,470	601,856	1,109,921	211,874	95,017	2,018,579	4,128,716
2010	100,052	626,189	1,071,890	234,552	107,732	2,189,973	4,330,387
% Change, 2000–2010	90%	69%	16%	96%	224%	82%	60%
Average Annual Growth Rate	6.61%	5.40%	1.51%	6.98%	12.47%	6.17%	4.83%

Note: Totals are rounded to the nearest person. The sum of the region totals consequently does not equal the global totals.

by representing weighted averages of predictions from multiple models defined from subsets of theoretically grounded predictor variables. The weights were then determined by the predictive accuracy of the model that generates the prediction and its lack of redundancy with other models. This enabled the incorporation of relevant information for a large number of predictors while mitigating the risk of overfitting.

The big data estimates provided in this report help provide a picture of the size and geographic distribution of the population of U.S. citizens abroad, as well as its change over time. The changing geographic distribution of the overseas U.S. citizen population revealed in this analysis has strong implications for how FVAP will allocate resources in the future. Specifically, although the estimates indicate that the U.S. citizen population is to a large extent concentrated in Europe and the Western Hemisphere and has remained so throughout the 2000–2010 period, there are substantial differences in the estimated rate of growth between countries and regions that suggest an increase in the geographic dispersion of U.S. citizens. This represents an improvement in the state of knowledge about the overseas U.S. citizen population prior to this project, which could only draw on population counts produced by a subset of foreign governments or estimates produced by federal and international agencies that were either subject to security restrictions or based on decades-old data.

FVAP has already become smarter, using the results of this analysis to target its limited marketing budget in those countries with the largest estimated populations of U.S. citizens. In addition, the estimates allow FVAP to anticipate changes in the geographic distribution of the overseas U.S. citizen population, permitting the government to plan ahead and adapt to a potential rise in the number of U.S. citizens in Africa, Asia, and the Middle East. Finally, the estimates, along with total vote counts obtained from state and local election officials and more detailed subpopulation data obtained from the OECD, may in the future allow FVAP to obtain estimates of expected and observed voting rates by country. These rates will, in turn, allow FVAP to further refine its marketing and outreach efforts to target overseas U.S. citizens whose location may represent an impediment to electoral participation. This advancement will ultimately allow for the development of outreach to address specific challenges of specific populations in specific parts of the world.

OVERALL CONCLUSION

Data sciences, social marketing, and government policy are all currently in the midst of incredible changes and advances. At the root of this change is technology. Because of advances in technology, we not only have the ability to collect, aggregate, and store more information than ever before but we are also able to analyze and interpret the patterns that exist in a much wider and varied manner. These shifts are only beginning; every day businesses and government are gaining access to more and more information and detail about U.S. citizens.

This shift is having a profound impact on how the U.S. government is thinking and planning for the future. In January 2014, President Obama asked for a review of big data and the implications it would have for the U.S. In May 2014, this White House review was released to the public. It identified a myriad of ways that big data can be used to grow our economy, improve health and education, and make our nation safer and more energy efficient. According to the review, "Big data technologies will be transformative in every sphere of life."[7] Clearly, there is great excitement about big data. However, there is also trepidation. One concern often mentioned and already being discussed in great detail in the public policy arena deals with how the government should use big data. It is increasingly being recognized that the technological and analytical tools available pose real risk to long-standing civil rights protections in how personal information is used in housing, credit, employment, health, education, and the marketplace.

In the two examples we provide in this chapter, there is a strong common undercurrent of this balance between privacy and the need to obtain results that benefit and/or protect U.S. citizens. On the surface, these efforts seem relatively innocuous. In our work with FVAP, we are trying to help U.S. citizens, no matter where they live, exercise their democratic right to vote. In our work with APHIS, we are trying to preserve America's ecological security. In both of these examples, however, there is a real risk of gathering or creating a great deal of personal information. "Who is traveling?" "Where are they going?" "How long are they going to be out of the U.S.?" "What are they doing while on travel?" "Do they intend to come back to the U.S., when, and with what?" All of this potential information if gathered and tracked by the government would raise questions related to civil rights and authority.

In working with the government, it is extremely important that all parties involved are cognizant of these types of limitations and of this risk, and avoid gathering or creating this personal information. At its foundation, effective marketing relies on getting the right information to the right person at the right time. In our examples, all parties involved in the work were in clear agreement that we would not be answering the question "Who?" Rather, our data sets, analytic approaches, and research outcomes were focused on answering the question "Where?" Where should FVAP (i.e., which foreign country) and APHIS (i.e., which departure origin and pathway of travels) focus their resources and outreach efforts? With this focus, we were able to clearly answer the questions posed while also complying with our responsibility to not gather or create information about specific people or to push government authority. Effectively, the methodologies employed in our two examples represent the government becoming smarter with respect to its ability to extract audience-relevant information from limited data

A second theme that we have found working with big data, highlighted by these examples, is that not all big data is created equal. We have provided two characterizations, fat and tall, to reflect these differences. Whereas fat data is characterized by a large number of predictors relative to the number of observations, tall data is typically characterized by a large number of observations relative to the number of predictors. The methodology employed to analyze data will differ depending on the degree to which the data is fat or tall. Specifically, when the analyst has access to data for many potential predictors but few observations, model specification becomes critical due to the potential for overfitting in small samples.

In our FVAP example, we employed theory to select a subset of the models for estimation and model averaging to extract useful information captured by the models in this still large subset. The computational challenges presented by fat data relative to tall data will thus depend heavily on the strength of the analyst's priors with respect to what characteristics of the unit of observation are likely to predict the outcome of interest. Analysts of fat data with strong priors can reduce the computational requirements of their analysis substantially while simultaneously improving the accuracy of their estimates by restricting the number of models estimated. These priors will, in turn, be a function of analyst's experience in the policy area and familiarity with the relevant academic literature. By contrast, model selection was far less of a concern in our APHIS example where the number of observations far outweighed the number of model variables. In this instance, we focused more on the memory and processing requirements necessary for analyzing millions of records as well as the need for analyst and agency collaboration to build, analyze, and interpret of findings.

"Fatness/tallness" is just one possible dimension of the data, of which we are sure there are many, many more. Regardless, the type and format of big data available have a profound impact, affecting directly how to initially set up the data file for analysis, how to address or fill in missing data and/or cases, the analysis plan, how to apply certain data analytic techniques, and the computational resources needed. Most important, it affects the appropriateness of the conclusions to be drawn and provides real bounds on the actionability of the findings. This is particularly true in settings, such as when working with federal government agencies, where the importance placed on quality and the cost of incorrect interpretations can be so high. There is not a single set of best practices, software solutions, or analytic models that we have found to be best (or even appropriate) across all potential scenarios. Big data provides tremendous opportunity to derive actionable recommendations from information, but it requires real versatility and training from those working with it.

A final theme worth highlighting, related to the previous ones, is the important role of the decision maker and the analyst. The increasing prominence of big data in the commercial and government space has also resulted in a proliferation of an ever-growing set of data analytic and data mining tools. Some are commercially available from such organizations as HP, IBM, and SAS, and dozens of open-sourced software programs are available at a nominal fee if not altogether free. These are powerful tools that open up a myriad of possibilities to a data analyst; however, many are designed in a way that they require little training or knowledge of statistical theory. This provides great potential but also creates real concern. The role and requirements for the analyst, we hope we have made clear, are increasing because of big data, not decreasing. From a modeling perspective, the analyst must carefully consider what variables to include, what models to use, and how best to ensure that the answers he or she provides are replicable and generalizable. Simply feeding all the information you have available into a program and running a set of scripts or routines on that data is a terribly irresponsible practice, but is becoming increasingly common in our experience. The analyst team must also become increasingly involved in the operation of the agency and the total set of information available to them. The potential amount of data that can be included in the modeling work is growing every day. The usefulness of this information, however, is limited if it is not collected and stored in the proper way and cannot be linked to some unit of interest (geography, etc.). Without this, how big the data that is available will always be less than what is possible. Finally, as was made clear in the APHIS example, even with big data, working side by side with agency experts and decision makers to plan the research, interpret the findings, and actually use the research to make decisions is, and always has been, the best way that research and data can improve business or government outcomes.

In closing, we must mention one last point. Too frequently, in the government setting, we are beginning to hear conversation about how big data and the tools associated with it can be used to replace more traditional research efforts such as probability surveys, focus groups, and experimental tests. In an environment where budget reduction is at the forefront of everyone's mind, this is not surprising given the costs of some of these efforts. But we feel we must proceed very carefully. Basing government decisions and policy recommendations on only administrative records would represent a huge leap backward. Instead of replacing these traditional tools, we urge all of our clients and everyone else operating in the government arena to consider how best to conduct these studies so they can be integrated into other information already in the agency's possession. In the end, it is through creating better integration of all the information available that we will be able to distinguish those efforts that are duplicative or unnecessary from efforts that add to our knowledge and result in an improved and more informed government.

Notes

1. Social marketing is an umbrella term for a type of communication effort that borrows heavily from traditional marketing, but emphasizes nontangible products (e.g., ideas, attitudes, behaviors). Social marketing principles are especially well suited for translating complex behavior change techniques into products that can be more easily and effectively promoted to the population segment(s) of interest (Lefebvre & Flora, 1988). These products are promoted through a wide range of communication

channels and use a variety of communication tools ranging from traditional media to the increasingly popular social media options, depending on the preferences and usage patterns of the target segment(s).

2. Retrieved on December 14, 2014 from http://www.usda.gov/documents/APHIS_AQAS_PIA.pdf.

3. Additional pathways exist within the AQIM, but were determined to be less valuable for this analysis because of their low numbers and lack of a source location.

4. The San Ysidro segments were combined because of their similarities in traveler origin and destination, appropriate regardless of travel group. The San Francisco segment is actually a combination of five sites (San Francisco, Los Angeles, Newark, Seattle, and New York (JFK)), with San Francisco being the site with the most cases of seized or cleaned items.

5. Links to foreign government statistical office websites were retrieved from http://www.census.gov/population/international/links/stat_int.html.

6. State Department region definitions were retrieved from http://www.state.gov/countries/.

7. Retrieved on December 14, 2014, from http://www.whitehouse.gov/sites/default/files/docs/big_data_privacy_report_may_1_2014.pdf.

References

Baldacci, E., Clements, B., Gupta, S., & Cui, Q. (2004). *Social spending, human capital and growth in developing countries: Implications for achieving the MDGs* (International Monetary Fund Working Paper 04/217).

Baum, M. A., & Lake, D. A. (2003). The political economy of growth: Democracy and human capital. *American Journal of Political Science, 47*, 333–347.

Burnside, C., & Dollar, D. (2000). Aid, policies and growth. *American Economic Review, 90*(4), 847–868.

Geurts, T. (2010). *Public policy making: The 21st century perspective.* The Netherlands: Be Informed. Retrieved from http://www.beinformed.com/BeInformed/webdav-resource/binaries/pdf/publications/public-policy-making.pdf?webdav-id=/Be%20Informed%20Bibliotheek/0000%20WEBDAV/WebDAV%20StatContent.bixml.

Hawkins, D. M. (2004). The problem of overfitting. *Journal of Chemical Information and Computer Sciences, 44*(1), 1–12.

Lefebvre, R. C., & Flora, J. A. (1988). Social marketing and public health intervention. *Health Education Quarterly, 15*(3), 299–315.

Lewis, M. (2006). *Governance and corruption in public health care systems* (Working Paper 78). Washington, DC: Center for Global Development.

Montgomery, J. M., Hollenbach, F. M., & Ward, M. D. (2012). Improving predictions using ensemble Bayesian model averaging. *Political Analysis, 20*(3), 271–291.

Santos Silva, J. M. C., & Tenreyro, S. (2006). The log of gravity. *Review of Economics and Statistics, 88*(4), 641–658.

Schachter, J. (2008, December 24). *Estimating native emigration from the United States.* Memorandum developed during contract work for the U.S. Census Bureau.

Smith, A. (1776). *An inquiry into the nature and causes of the wealth of nations.* London: W. Strahan.

Stone, M. (1977). Asymptotics for and against cross-validation. *Biometrika*, 64(1), 29–35.

Ward, M. D., Greenhill, B. D., & Bakke, K. M. (2010). The perils of policy by *p*-value: Predicting civil conflicts. *Journal of Peace Research*, 47(4), 363–375.

Weinreich, N. K. (2010). *Hands-on social marketing: A step-by-step guide to designing change for good.* Thousand Oaks, CA: Sage Publications.

10

Using Machine Learning Algorithms to Detect Election Fraud

Ines Levin
University of Georgia

Julia Pomares
Centro de Implementacion de Politicas Publicas para la Equidad y el Crecimiento (CIPPEC)

R. Michael Alvarez
California Institute of Technology

1 INTRODUCTION

For more than a decade, increased scrutiny has been placed on the administration and integrity of democratic elections throughout the world (Levin and Alvarez 2012). The surge of interest in electoral integrity seems to be fueled by a number of different factors: an increase in the number of nations conducting elections, more concerns about election administration and voting technology, the increased use of social media, and a growing number of scholars throughout the world who are interested in the study of integrity and the possible manipulation of elections (Alvarez, Hall, and Hyde 2008).

Although there are many ways that the integrity of elections can be assessed – for example, by studying the opinions of voters about their confidence in the conduct of elections (Alvarez, Atkeson, and Hall 2012) or through election monitoring (Bjornlund 2004; Hyde 2007, 2011; Kelley 2013) – many methodologists, statisticians and computer scientists have contributed to the new and growing literature on "election forensics". This body of research involves the development of a growing suite of tools – some as simple as looking at the distributions of variables, such as turnout in an election, and others that use more complex multivariate statistical models – to sift through observational data from elections to detect anomalies or outliers as potential indicators for election fraud and manipulation (Levin et al. 2009; Alvarez et al. 2014).

The literature on election forensics now has advanced a somewhat dizzying array of methods for detecting election anomalies, without providing guidance

266

for when particular methods might best be utilized by analysts. That is, when is it best to look for anomalies in distributions of voter turnout? When should digit tests (such as Benford's Law) be applied? What about the use of regression models to detect outliers, either in single or multiple contests? How much statistical power do distributional tests have in common settings where you want to try to detect election outliers? These questions have motivated some of our recent research and have led us to consider the use of new techniques, such as machine learning, for the detection of election manipulation in nations like Venezuela (Alvarez et al. 2014).

Machine learning procedures use statistical tools to find patterns in the data that reveal new and relevant information that may prove useful for performing an action or task. In this chapter we focus on the use of machine learning algorithms for detecting voter fraud. We explain and illustrate how machine learning can be used to detect anomalies in election returns and to learn about the likelihood of electoral manipulation at individual polling locations. Machine learning techniques have seen only limited use for the detection of election fraud, and we believe that this is an important new application for these tools (Alvarez et al. 2014; Cantu and Saiegh 2011).

We introduce readers to both unsupervised and supervised learning procedures. Unsupervised learning algorithms sort polling locations into *clusters* based on similarity, leaving it up to the analyst to decide – *after* the classification process is complete – whether group-specific electoral attributes (for example, characteristics of the distribution of voter turnout and vote shares) are indicative of known types of fraud. The supervised approach, instead, automatically classifies polling locations into clean and tainted *classes* depending on their resemblance to hypothetical clean and tainted cases.

2 USING LEARNING ALGORITHMS TO DETECT VOTER FRAUD

Preparing the Data

We start by downloading election results measured at different levels of aggregation, for example: national, district, municipal, polling place, or precinct. Electoral data sets typically consist of spreadsheets containing information about the number of votes received by each party or candidate (or the electoral alternative in the case of referenda), the number of invalid and blank votes, and often also the number of eligible or registered voters for each electoral unit. Before proceeding to the data analysis, data sets can be augmented by computing other electoral quantities based on published election results (such as vote shares and voter turnout) and then merging these data with information from other sources (such as census data and historical election returns).

Subsequently, we create a synthetic data set that can be used for evaluating and comparing the performance of different classification procedures and for *training* supervised machine learning algorithms on discrepant patterns in clean and tainted data. The process of creating this training data set first involves the generation of synthetic *clean* data and then the manipulation of the clean data in known ways (typically in ways resembling common forms of voter fraud, such as vote stealing or ballot box stuffing) in order to create synthetic *tainted* data. For instance, we may simulate vote stealing by transferring a proportion of votes from the opposition to the incumbent, or ballot box stuffing by inflating turnout and allocating manufactured votes to the incumbent party.

Once the data augmentation and generation processes are complete, we apply a series of machine learning algorithms, described next. The main goal of machine learning algorithms is to form clusters of electoral locations and to label them based on qualitative knowledge or on their resemblance to hypothetical clean and tainted cases. Specifically, if the distribution of electoral variables within a cluster is consistent with what we expect if the data were clean, then this cluster will usually be labeled as clean (with the labeling being carried out by the analyst after cluster assignments are complete, or automatically by the algorithm). If, instead, the distribution of electoral variables within the cluster resembles what we expect if the data had been manipulated in a certain fashion, then the cluster will usually be labeled as tainted.

A Menu of Learning Algorithms

This section introduces readers to a number of machine learning algorithms that can be used to classify electoral units into clean and tainted classes based on the distribution of electoral variables such as voter turnout and vote shares.[1] The first algorithm (k-means classifier) is *unsupervised*, since it makes no use of a priori knowledge about the impact of voter fraud on electoral variables entering into the classification procedure. Instead, the algorithm builds clusters of electoral units exhibiting common patterns in a number of electoral variables and leaves it up to the analyst to label the clusters (as clean or tainted, for instance) based on the characteristics of its component units. All other algorithms described in this section are *supervised*, since they incorporate information about what fraud "looks like" (that is, about the expected distribution of electoral indicators in clean and tainted locations) and automatically assign meaningful labels to electoral units using a two-stage procedure: first, they model the relationship between values taken by electoral indicators and the occurrence of fraud in a training data set (often a synthetic one containing simulated electoral data); second, they use the model estimated in the first stage to predict the occurrence of fraud in unlabeled locations in the test data (that is, in the actual electoral data).

K-Means Classifier

Electoral locations are classified into k clusters, such that values taken by electoral variables whose distributions would be distorted by the occurrence of voter fraud (such as voter turnout and vote shares obtained by large and minor parties) are as similar as possible for locations assigned to the same cluster, and as dissimilar as possible for locations assigned to different clusters. In contrast to supervised learning algorithms, the unsupervised k-means algorithm is not guided by information about what fraud looks like (i.e., it is not told what specific patterns to look for in the data) and does not automatically assign meaningful cluster labels. Instead, it freely explores the data and forms clusters based on patterns that might not be a priori known to exist, constrained only by the total number of clusters and other initial conditions imposed by the analyst. It is within the discretion of the analyst to assign meaningful cluster labels after cluster assignments are finalized. The classification procedure generally works as follows.

First the analyst selects an appropriate number of clusters k. This can be based on qualitative knowledge about the possible types electoral fraud and which parties could be responsible for the manipulation. Alternatively, if qualitative knowledge is incomplete (for instance, if unknown forms of fraud could be taking place that distort the data in distinct ways, potentially leading to a larger-than-expected number of clusters), then the analyst can select k based on information contained in the data by increasing k up to a point where further increments no longer contribute to making clusters more homogeneous (a procedure known as the Elbow Method).

Next, the algorithm (or the analyst) selects k initial cluster *centers*. Typically, k units are selected at random from the entire data set, and values taken by electoral variables at these locations are used as initial cluster centers. Then, all other units in the data set are assigned to the cluster corresponding to the nearest cluster center. The most common metric used to calculate proximity to cluster centers is the Euclidean distance, which can be computed using the following formula:

$$d(e,n) = \sqrt{\sum_{\forall f \in F} (e_f - n_f)^2}$$

where $d(e,n)$ denotes the distance between location e and neighbor location n, f denotes a given electoral variable whose values are associated with the occurrence of fraud, and F denotes the entire set of measured electoral variables (predictors of the occurrence of fraud).

In subsequent stages, the algorithm updates the location of cluster centers and cluster assignments until within-cluster homogeneity has been maximized. Specifically, after the initial assignment is complete, cluster centers are reset to the mean value of electoral variables among all units within the cluster. After that, the procedure continues recursively – with units being reassigned to nearest clusters and cluster centers being recalculated following each reassignment – until no further adjustments are possible (nor necessary since within-cluster homogeneity has been maximized).[2]

Once cluster assignments are finalized, the analyst can inspect the character-istics of the different clusters and label them based on substantive knowledge. For instance, she may first identify those clusters where the distribution of electoral variables looks typical and, for the remaining apparently anomalous clusters, try to identify patterns in the relationship between electoral variables that might be indicative of the occurrence of known types of voter fraud.

K-Nearest Neighbors (kNN) Classifier

Electoral units are again classified into *k* grouping or clusters. However, in con-trast to the unsupervised k-means method, kNN incorporates a priori informa-tion about what fraud looks like and automatically assigns meaningful labels to all locations in the test data set. The procedure begins by calculating, for each electoral location in the test data set, the percentage of units labeled as tainted over the *k* nearest units in the training data set (that is, the percentage of tainted units is calculated within a *neighborhood* of size *k*), where proximity is assessed by a metric calculated in terms of a given number of input variables (such as incidence of outliers in voter turnout and voter shares). Similar to the k-means algorithm, the most commonly used metric to calculate proximity is Euclidean distance. Subsequently, each electoral unit is assigned the label corresponding to the most common class (i.e., clean or tainted) in the size-*k* neighborhood.

K-nearest neighbors classifiers are considered *lazy learners*, because they only use local information (from as many as k neighboring electoral units) to learn about the likelihood of fraud in any given electoral location. We move now to introduce readers to machine learning algorithms that make more efficient use of the available information, because they make predictions about the occurrence of fraud in any electoral location based on values taken by electoral variables in all electoral units in the training data set.

Bayes Classifiers

Contingency tables and Bayes theorem are used to compute the posterior prob-ability of fraud conditional on values taken by electoral indicators in clean and tainted locations, using the information contained in the training data set. Sub-sequently, estimated posterior probabilities are used to predict the occurrence of fraud for electoral locations in the test data set.

For instance, suppose an analyst was interested in using a single categorical electoral variable – an indicator of whether voter turnout was low (L), medium (M), or high (H) – to classify electoral locations into clean (C) and tainted (F) classes. In that case, Bayes theorem could be used to compute the posterior probability of fraud using the following rule:

$$P(F|T) = \frac{P(T|F)\,P(F)}{P(T)}$$

where P(T|F) is the likelihood of turnout level T conditional on the occurrence of fraud (where T can take values L, M, or H); $P(F)$ is the prior probability of fraud (based on analyst beliefs); and $P(T)$ is the unconditional probability that turnout level equals T (used as a normalizing constant to ensure that the posterior probabilities of fraud add up to 1). To illustrate this rule, suppose that we observed the following relationship between the occurrence of fraud and turnout for 1,000 electoral locations in the training data set:

Turnout (T)

		Low (L)	Medium (M)	High (H)	Total
Electoral Unit	Clean (C)	50	800	50	900
	Tainted (F)	25	25	50	100
	Total	75	825	100	1,000

The likelihood of observing different levels of voter turnout conditional on the occurrence of voter fraud – that is, P(T|F) – can be computed by dividing table cells by row totals. The marginal probabilities of fraud and levels of voter turnout, in turn, can be computed by dividing row and column totals by the total number of locations. In this example, the probability of fraud conditional on medium turnout equals P(F|M) = P(M|F) P(F)/P(M) = (25/100) * (100/1,000)/(825/1,000) = 0.03. The probability of fraud conditional on high turnout, in turn, equals P(F|H) = P(H|F) P(F)/P(H) = (50/100) * (100/1,000)/(100/1,000) = 0.50. Lastly, the probability of fraud conditional on low turnout equals P(F|L) = P(L|F) P(F)/P(L) = (25/100) * (100/1,000)/(75/1,000) = 0.33. These results suggest that the likelihood of fraud is about 17 and 11 times larger when turnout is high or low, respectively, than when there is a medium level of voter turnout. This hypothetical situation is consistent with ballot box stuffing (leading to high turnout levels) and vote stealing where a proportion of stolen votes is transferred to the incumbent party and the rest is destroyed (leading to low turnout levels).

Using Bayes rule to detect voter fraud becomes more complicated when the training data set contains numerous continuous electoral variables (such as turnout rates and vote shares obtained by multiple parties). When that happens, analysts can take steps to simplify the application of Bayes rule (Lantz 2013). They can do so by discretizing electoral variables in order to build contingency tables like the ones shown earlier, and employing "naïve" **Bayes classifiers** that simplify the calculation of posterior probabilities by assuming that electoral indicators are (1) equally important for learning about the occurrence of fraud and (2) independent conditional on class assignment. However, taking these simplifying steps can be problematic, because discretizing electoral variables implies losing information, and it might be unrealistic to assume that electoral indicators are equally important for predicting the occurrence of fraud or that they are conditionally independent. Turnout, for instance, might be more informative about the magnitude and type of fraud than vote shares, and vote shares obtained by different parties might fail to satisfy the conditional independence assumption.[3]

Tree-Based (Divide-and-Conquer) Classifiers

Similar to the previous algorithm, in this fourth type of algorithm electoral locations are classified into clean or tainted classes in two stages. In the first stage, the training data set is used to create a *decision tree* – a set of logical decision rules expressed as if-then-else conditional statements that must be applied in a given order – that can be used to classify electoral locations in the actual test data. Decision rules are generated using a *divide-and-conquer* strategy by recursively splitting the training data set based on values taken by electoral indicators, beginning with the indicator with the greater predictive power. Features used to split the data at each tree node are selected as to create increasingly homogeneous partitions – that is, partitions where there is a greater concentration of either clean or tainted locations than in the preceding data segment.

In the second stage, rules comprising the decision tree are used to classify electoral locations by applying them from top to bottom to the test data.[4] For instance, suppose that splitting the training data based on levels of voter turnout produced relatively homogeneous partitions, with all units in the medium turnout partition being clean, and most units in the low or high turnout partitions being tainted. Suppose further that splitting low and medium turnout partitions based on vote share obtained by the incumbent party led to perfectly homogeneous subpartitions, with all units in subpartitions where the incumbent obtained medium or small vote shares being clean, and all units in subpartitions where the incumbent obtained high vote shares being tainted (due to the occurrence of vote stealing for low-turnout locations and ballot box stuffing for high-turnout locations). If this were the case, the analyst could use the information in the training data set to construct the decision tree depicted in Figure 10.1.

The hypothetical decision tree shown in Figure 10.1 can be used to classify electoral locations in the test data by answering questions related to the level of voter turnout and incumbent vote share, in the following order: (1) Is voter turnout low, medium, or high? If the level is medium, classify it as clean. Otherwise, if the level is low, ask: (2) Is the incumbent vote share medium or small, or large? If it is medium or small, classify it as clean; otherwise, classify it as tainted due to the occurrence of vote stealing. Similarly, if the level of voter turnout is high, ask: Is the incumbent vote share medium or small, or large? If

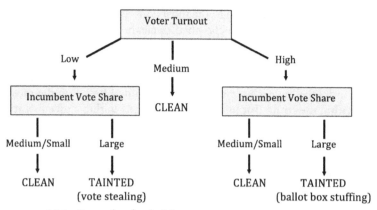

FIGURE 10.1. Example of a decision tree.

it is medium or small, classify it as clean; otherwise, classify it as tainted due to the occurrence of ballot box stuffing.

Rule-Based (Separate-and-Conquer) Classifiers

Similar to tree-based classifiers, rule classifiers split the data into homogeneous partitions using previously learned logical decision rules. In contrast to tree-based learners (which develop rules using a divide-and-conquer strategy), rule-based learners develop rules using a *separate-and-conquer* strategy. Specifically, rule learners start by identifying an antecedent condition (expressed as ranges of values in one or more electoral variables) covering a homogeneous group of electoral units in the training data set (that is, a group of units labeled as either clean or tainted), and then separate units satisfying this condition from the rest of the data. After that, they proceed recursively by identifying additional antecedent conditions covering subsets of the remaining units in the training data set, and then setting those subsets aside, until all electoral units have been covered by an antecedent condition. The pairing of an antecedent condition with the class label associated with units satisfying this condition gives rise to an if-then decision rule – for instance, "if turnout is larger than 90% and the vote share obtained by the incumbent party exceeds 50%, then label as tainted due to the occurrence of ballot box stuffing; else if . . . " – that can subsequently be used to classify unlabeled units in the test data set. An advantage of rule-based learners, compared to decision trees, is that the set of rules is easier to understand and can be applied more directly: the data does not need to be passed through a decision tree.

The simplest rule-based algorithm is called **ZeroR**, for it develops no rule. Instead, it simply determines the most common label in the training data and then assigns the corresponding class to every unlabeled unit in the test data. In the context of fraud-detection applications, if most electoral units in the training data are clean, then ZeroR would lead to the most conservative solution where all unlabeled units in the test data are classified as clean. Another simple rule-based classifier is called **OneR** because it develops a single rule. In the context of fraud-detection applications, OneR would proceed as follows: first, stratifying the training data in terms of values taken by electoral variables predictive of voter fraud; second, labeling each strata as clean or tainted based on the most common label within the strata (for instance, if most units within a given strata are clean, then the strata is labeled as clean); third, developing a single rule based on values taken by electoral variables in strata labeled as clean and tainted; and fourth, classifying unlabeled units in the test data set based on the rule developed in the previous stage. In this chapter, we apply a more sophisticated rule-based classifier called **RIPPER** (Repeated Incremental Pruning to Produce Error Reduction) that is capable of capturing more complex patterns in the data (Cohen 1995).

Tree- and rule-based classifiers are *greedy learners*, because they pass on segments of the data to the different rules in order of arrival. Although these algorithms have the advantage of being resource efficient, they are not guaranteed to find the optimal solution (i.e., the classification leading to the greatest within-group homogeneity with the minimum number of rules). The reason is that, although greedy algorithms find local optima (optimal solutions given the order in which rules were applied), they do not necessarily find global optima, because the order in which rules are applied may bias the final result.

Ensemble Methods

Predictions produced by different algorithms are combined together to produce a more accurate prediction of the occurrence of fraud. If algorithms included in the ensemble have complementary strengths and weaknesses (such as distinct biases that cancel out when combined together), then the aggregation process is likely to lead to stronger and less biased inferences. Two common ensemble procedures applied in this chapter are **bagging**, where bootstrapping is used to pass on random subsets of the data to algorithms in the ensemble, and then a final classification is arrived at by a majority vote among predictions produced by individual algorithms; and **boosting**, where subsets of the data passed on to individual algorithms in the ensemble are not selected entirely at random, but are more likely to include previous misclassifications. A third ensemble procedure applied in this chapter is termed **random forests**, an algorithm involving bagging of decision trees, where both random subsets of the data and random subsets of predictive features (in our case, subsets of electoral variables that are predictive of the occurrence of fraud) are passed on to individual trees in the ensemble, and then a final classification is arrived at by a majority vote among predictions produced by individual decision trees.

3 APPLICATION: GREATER BUENOS AIRES, ARGENTINA, 2013

Electoral Context

We study the Argentine case, in particular the area around the capital city of Buenos Aires, for a number of reasons. After a history of systematic manipulation of election results during the first decades of the 20th century – in particular the "infamous decade" analyzed by Cantu and Saiegh (2011) – a long period of regime instability that coexisted with the electoral exclusion of the largest party (the Peronist Party). Since the return to democracy in 1983 after a cruel dictatorship, no outcome of a national election has been contested by losing parties. However, after several highly competitive provincial elections over the last several years, claims about fraud gained saliency again in public opinion. These concerns about electoral manipulation take place against a background of high fragmentation of the party system (Calvo and Escolar 2005) and claims from small opposition parties who find it difficult to safeguard their ballots on Election Day. Partly as a response to these claims, there have been various efforts to reform the procedures and technology of elections in the country, which have received a good deal of scrutiny and analysis from academics and scholars in Argentina and abroad.[5]

We study the most recent data from Argentina in this chapter, focusing on the province of Buenos Aires, the largest electoral district and the most salient election. In 2013, Argentines went to the polls to renew half of the lower chamber and a third of the Senate, as well as provincial and local legislative seats. It was the final midterm election before the end of Cristina Fernandez de Kirchner's second and last term in office. On August 11, 2013, voters in the province of Buenos Aires went to the polls to select candidates for four races (national deputies, provincial deputies, provincial senators and city councils), and a general election was held on October 27. Since 2011, parties are obliged to nominate candidates for the presidency and for the legislative chambers by competing in open primaries. Even if there is no internal competition, all parties and electoral coalitions must participate in the primaries and exceed the threshold of 1.5% of the votes to get to the general election. These elections are funded by the state and are compulsory for voters.

Although the incumbent Frente para la Victoria (FPV) party got a third of the votes for both chambers and was able to maintain the largest bloc in Congress, it lost the election in the four largest districts of the country, including the province of Buenos Aires. In Buenos Aires, the challenger Frente Renovador (FR) party led by Sergio Massa (former chief of cabinet during the preceding Kirchner administration) ended up first in the primary elections, anticipating his victory in the general election (see election results for the district of Buenos Aires in Table 10.1). FR is a newly created faction within the Peronist Party (the party of the president that controls 17 of 24 governorships). Except for

TABLE 10.1. *Vote Shares in Primary and General Elections (% of total votes)*

Party List or Electoral Coalition	Province of Buenos Aires	
	Primary Election	General Election
FPV (List supported by Cristina Fernandez de Kirchner)	29.6	32.3
FR (Peronist faction, not aligned with FPV)	35.0	44.0
FPCS (Center-left opposition)	11.2	11.7
ULT (Center-right opposition)	10.5	5.4
Leftist Coalition (Workers Party, among others)	3.9	5.0
Others	5.0	1.6

a very small electoral option (earning 1% of the votes in the primary and not getting to the general contest), all party lists in the province of Buenos Aires had no internal competition for national races so open primaries for those races were perceived by the public opinion as a massive pre-election poll.

Data Analysis

In this section we illustrate the application of the different machine learning algorithms introduced in Section 2, using data from the August 2013 primary election for national deputies' candidates, focusing on 11,449 *mesas*[6] in the Greater Buenos Aires area.[7] The electoral variables included in our analysis are voter turnout rates; vote shares received by the only contenders controlling municipal governments in the Conurbation, the *Frente para la Victoria* (FPV) and *Frente Renovador* (FR); vote shares received by the center-left *Frente Progresista Civico y Social* (FPCS) and center-right *Unidos por la Libertad y el Trabajo* (ULT); and the sum of vote shares obtained by other minor parties (accounting for 5% of the vote).

Before proceeding to the classification stage, we generated synthetic clean and tainted data to assess the performance of the different machine learning algorithms by comparing true clusters in the synthetic data with estimated clusters in the synthetic data; we also used the synthetic data to train supervised machine learning algorithms before applying them to the actual electoral data. To preserve the natural relationship between electoral variables that would exist in the absence of fraud, we generated clean data by using a multilevel regression approach to model electoral features incorporated into the analysis – including voter turnout and vote shares – allowing model intercepts to vary by municipality,[8] and then using the estimated model coefficients to predict clean turnout rates and vote shares. After that, to complete the generation of the synthetic data we selected a random subset of the clean synthetic data and manipulated it in ways consistent with the following two hypothetical situations:

1. **Vote stealing (VS):** where one of the parties steals votes from other parties; with a proportion of stolen votes being destroyed and the rest being transferred to the party carrying out the manipulation[9]
2. **Ballot box stuffing (BBS):** where one of the parties adds manufactured votes to the ballot box or inflates final vote counts in its own favor

Our analysis of anomalies focuses on the FR and FPV for two reasons. First, the FR and FPV were the only lists controlling municipal governments, and they gathered around 75% of the votes in a tight election (a margin of victory of 5 points), with the rest of the votes being distributed among several small options. Second, according to an analysis conducted on Election Day, the FR and FPV were the only lists able to secure high coverage of party monitors throughout the Greater Buenos Aires area (Pomares and Page 2014). Since in Argentina political parties are responsible for disseminating ballots and replacing them on voting booths, party monitors play a key role in safeguarding ballots.

Of the two types of fraud listed, the first type of fraud (vote stealing) should result in relatively small turnout rates, large vote shares for the perpetrator, and small vote shares for other parties. The second type of fraud (ballot box stuffing) should result in relatively large turnout rates, large vote shares for the perpetrator, and typical vote shares for other parties. These expectations were taken into account in generating synthetic electoral indicators in the training data set. The exact amount of fraud (the proportion of votes stolen from other parties in the case of vote stealing and inflation of the turnout rate in the case of ballot box stuffing) is not held fixed for tainted *mesas* in the training data set, but varies in a random manner. In *mesas* tainted with vote stealing (VS), the proportion of stolen votes varies between 0.31 and 0.68, as does the proportion of votes transferred to the perpetrator. In *mesas* tainted with ballot box stuffing (BBS), in turn, the proportion of abstention counted as votes in favor of the perpetrator varies between 0.50 and 1.00.

Assumptions made in generating synthetic clean and tainted *mesas* lead to distinct distributions of electoral variables in the training data set depending on the class label (see Figure 10.2). For instance, whereas the distribution of voter turnout is centered at 80% among clean locations, it is centered at 95% among locations tainted with ballot box stuffing and 72% in *mesas* tainted with vote stealing (where a proportion of votes cast for opposition parties is assumed to be destroyed). The distribution of vote shares (measured as a percentage of the eligible electorate) obtained by the two largest electoral alliances (FPV and FR) also varies considerably depending on the type of anomalies: whereas the distribution in clean data is centered around 31% and 22% for the FR and FPV, respectively, the distribution in synthetic tainted data is bimodal.[10] Lastly, since it is assumed that ballot box stuffing only affects the total vote count and

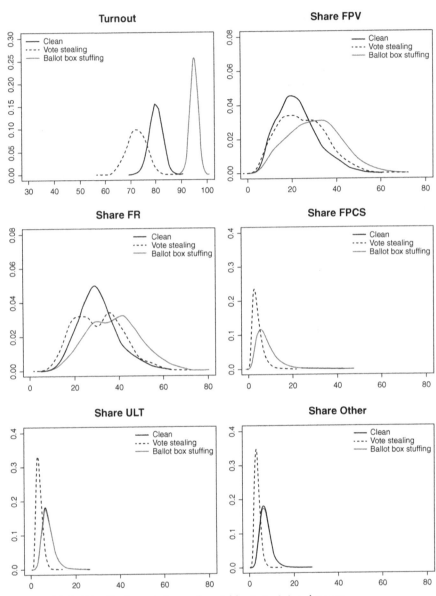

FIGURE 10.2. Distribution of electoral variables in training data set.

the number of votes received by the perpetrator, and since vote shares are measured as a proportion of the eligible electorate (not as a proportion of the total number of votes cast), vote shares obtained by other parties (including the FPCS and ULT) follow the same distribution in clean data as in data tainted

TABLE 10.2. *Performance of Unsupervised Learning Algorithm (k-means clustering)*

Cluster Characteristics and Ex-Post Labels, Training Data

Cluster	Turnout	Share FPV	Share FR	Share FPCS	Share ULT	Share Other	N	Label (assigned ex-post)
1	0.75	0.15	0.41	0.05	0.04	0.04	2,500	VS (FR)
2	0.95	0.40	0.28	0.08	0.08	0.07	1,960	BBS (FPV)
3	0.95	0.21	0.47	0.08	0.08	0.07	1,955	BBS (FR)
4	0.72	0.34	0.22	0.04	0.04	0.04	2,265	VS (FPV)
5	0.80	0.22	0.29	0.09	0.08	0.08	2,769	Clean

Performance of Unsupervised Learning Algorithms in Training Data

		Predicted Class				
		Clean	VS (FPV)	BBS (FPV)	VS (FR)	BBS (FR)
	Clean	**0.71**	0.08	0.03	0.18	0.00
	VS (FPV)	0.00	**0.89**	0.00	0.10	0.00
True Class	BBS (FPV)	0.00	0.00	**0.81**	0.00	0.19
	VS (FR)	0.01	0.12	0.00	**0.87**	0.00
	BBS (FR)	0.00	0.00	0.16	0.00	**0.84**

with ballot box stuffing (centered around 7–8% in all cases). The distribution of vote shares obtained by other parties, however, is centered at considerably lower values (around 4% in all cases), when either the FPV or FR hypothetically benefit from vote stealing.

Unsupervised Learning

After generating the training data set, we proceeded to apply a k-means unsupervised machine learning algorithm using R. First, we implemented it on the training data to determine whether the algorithm was capable of recovering the five clusters known to exist in the synthetic data – clean; VS by FPV; BBS by FPV; VS by FR; and BBS by FR. The upper table in Table 10.2 gives mean values of electoral variables for the center of each cluster found by the k-means algorithm. These statistics suggest that the algorithm was successful in finding clusters with characteristics similar to those known to exist on true clusters in the training data. For instance, cluster 1 contains *mesas* where the turnout rate was relatively low compared to other clusters (an average of 0.75), where the vote share corresponding to the FR was relatively high, and where vote shares corresponding to other parties were relatively small; we labeled

TABLE 10.3. *Predictions of Unsupervised Learning Algorithm (k-means clustering)*

Cluster Characteristics, Test Data, Five Clusters

Cluster	Turnout	Share FPV	Share FR	Share FPCS	Share ULT	Share Other	N
1	0.79	0.14	0.31	0.15	0.09	0.07	2,077
2	0.80	0.29	0.27	0.05	0.07	0.07	2,917
3	0.80	0.15	0.45	0.05	0.06	0.05	1,513
4	0.79	0.20	0.31	0.09	0.08	0.08	3,958
5	0.80	0.45	0.17	0.03	0.05	0.06	984

Cluster Characteristics, Test Data, Eight Clusters

Cluster	Turnout	Share FPV	Share FR	Share FPCS	Share ULT	Share Other	N
1	0.79	0.17	0.28	0.16	0.09	0.08	1,215
2	0.78	0.10	0.36	0.13	0.11	0.06	796
3	0.80	0.48	0.15	0.02	0.05	0.06	702
4	0.80	0.23	0.28	0.09	0.09	0.08	2,207
5	0.81	0.15	0.48	0.04	0.05	0.05	943
6	0.79	0.17	0.36	0.09	0.07	0.07	1,782
7	0.81	0.34	0.24	0.04	0.07	0.07	1,654
8	0.79	0.24	0.32	0.05	0.07	0.07	2,150

this cluster as one consistent with VS by FR. We continued in a similar manner for the remaining clusters, labeling them based on our knowledge of the data-generating process.

Following the ex-post assignment of cluster labels, we created a *confusion matrix* showing the relationship between true and predicted cluster labels (see lower section of Table 10.2). Results from the synthetic data indicate that the algorithm correctly identified 71% of clean cases (in other words, the false-positive rate equaled 29%); 87% and 89% of cases tainted with VS by FPV and FR, respectively; and 81% and 88% of cases tainted with BBS by FPV and FR, respectively. Misclassifications of tainted *mesas* rarely involved false negatives (that is, tainted *mesas* incorrectly classified as clean) or misclassified fraud type (that is, VS classified as BBS and vice vesa); most usually, they involved wrong guesses as to the identity of the party benefiting from the anomalies (this happened between 10% and 12% of the time in the case of VS, and between 16% and 19% of the time in the case of BBS).

The previous assessment suggests that if similar clusters exist in the actual data as in the training data, then the k-means algorithm should do a fairly good job in classifying unlabeled *mesas* in the test data into the anticipated clusters. The topmost section of Table 10.3 contains the results found after

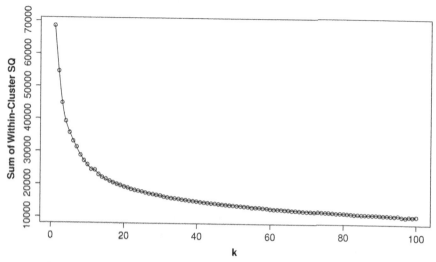

FIGURE 10.3. Relationship between number of clusters (k) and overall within-cluster heterogeneity.

applying a k-means algorithm with five clusters. Similar to the topmost section of Table 10.2, it gives mean values of electoral variables for the center of each cluster found by the k-means algorithm. According to these statistics, the largest cluster in the test data (number four) looks similar to the cluster labeled as clean in the training data. Clusters 3 and 5, in turn, are ones where vote shares corresponding to FR and FPV are high and where vote shares for other parties (especially FPCS) are particularly small, a pattern consistent with the occurrence of vote stealing. The fact that turnout rates are not atypically low in these *mesas*, however, suggests that if vote stealing is taking place, then most votes are being transferred to the party carrying out the manipulation (i.e., votes are not being systematically destroyed). Clusters 1 and 2, lastly, exhibit unexpected patterns that are not consistent with those prevailing in hypothetical clusters in the training data.

Although the synthetic training data is known to have five clusters, it is possible that the actual test data has more or less than five clusters. If this is the case, then imposing $k = 5$ could lead to invalid inferences (such as biased cluster characteristics and assigning *mesas* to incorrect or inexistent clusters). To deal with this issue, we repeatedly applied the algorithm for values of k ranging between 1 and 100. Subsequently, we plotted the relationship (shown in Figure 10.3) between k and the sum of within-cluster sum of squares (a measure of overall within-cluster heterogeneity) to determine the value of k after which further increases in the number of clusters produced little informational gains. Results depicted in Figure 10.3 indicate that the optimal number of clusters (suggested by the "elbow" in the curve) lies around eight. The lower section of Table 10.3 gives mean values of electoral variables at cluster centers after the number of clusters is increased from five to eight. We find that clusters 3, 4, and 5 are relatively similar (in terms of mean values of electoral variables) to clusters 3, 4, and 5 when k was set to five. Furthermore, although FPV's vote share is relatively high in cluster 7 and FR's vote share is relatively high in clusters 2 and 6, patterns in clusters 2, 6, and 7 are not wholly consistent with the ones we anticipated for *mesas* tainted with either BBS or BS. Thus, these results show that allowing for variation in the number of clusters proves to be a valuable strategy.

Supervised Learning

In the second stage of our analysis, we applied a number of supervised machine learning algorithms where, instead of allowing algorithms to freely search for patterns in the data, we asked them to search for patterns in voter turnout and vote shares that could be indicative of specific types of anomalies (specifically, vote stealing or ballot box stuffing benefiting either the FPV or the FR). The six supervised machine learning procedures applied in this section are: k-nearest neighbors, implemented using the *class* R package (Venables and Ripley 2002); naïve Bayes, implemented using the *e1071* R package (Meyer et al. 2014); RIPPER rule learner, implemented using the *RWeka* R package (Hornik, Buchta, and Zeileis, 2009); bagged decision trees, implemented using the *ipred* R package (Peters and Hothorn 2013); and random forest, implemented using the *randomForest* R package (Liaw and Wiener 2002). As explained in Section 2, each of these algorithms is implemented in two stages: first, a predictive model (or set of rules) is estimated using the training data, and second, the model is used to classify unlabeled *mesas* in the actual test data.

Similar to how we proceeded during the application of the k-means algorithm, we again first assessed the predictive accuracy of the different methods. We did so by training each procedure on a random subsample of the training data (containing 90% of the synthetic training *mesas*) and then using estimates to predict class assignments among the remaining training *mesas*. Table 10.4 gives a series of *confusion matrices* showing the relationship between true and predicted class labels for each of the six procedures in the portion of the synthetic training data that was not used during the training stage.

Diagonal elements in confusion matrices specify the proportion of correctly classified cases for each class. These numbers suggest that all procedures are successful in minimizing the incidence of false positives (i.e., the proportion of clean *mesas* classified as tainted). The algorithm producing the largest number of false positives is the naïve Bayes classifier, where 4% of clean *mesas* are classified as vote stealing by FR – a proportion that is still considerably lower than the 29% incidence of false positives produced by the k-means unsupervised

TABLE 10.4. *Performance of Supervised Learning Algorithms in Training Data (relationship between true class and predicted class; proportions)*

k-Nearest Neighbors

		Predicted Class				
		Clean	VS (FPV)	BBS (FPV)	VS (FR)	BBS (FR)
	Clean	1.00	0.00	0.00	0.00	0.00
	VS (FPV)	0.01	0.95	0.00	0.04	0.00
True Class	BBS (FPV)	0.00	0.00	0.87	0.00	0.13
	VS (FR)	0.02	0.02	0.00	0.97	0.00
	BBS (FR)	0.00	0.00	0.16	0.00	0.84

Naïve Bayes

		Predicted Class				
		Clean	VS (FPV)	BBS (FPV)	VS (FR)	BBS (FR)
	Clean	0.96	0.00	0.00	0.04	0.00
	VS (FPV)	0.01	0.90	0.00	0.10	0.00
True Class	BBS (FPV)	0.00	0.00	0.82	0.00	0.18
	VS (FR)	0.02	0.08	0.00	0.90	0.00
	BBS (FR)	0.00	0.00	0.16	0.00	0.84

C5.0 Decision Tree (w/boosting and costly mistakes)

		Predicted Class				
		Clean	VS (FPV)	BBS (FPV)	VS (FR)	BBS (FR)
	Clean	0.99	0.01	0.00	0.00	0.00
	VS (FPV)	0.01	0.96	0.00	0.04	0.00
True Class	BBS (FPV)	0.00	0.00	0.88	0.00	0.12
	VS (FR)	0.02	0.02	0.00	0.97	0.00
	BBS (FR)	0.00	0.00	0.15	0.00	0.85

RIPPER Rule Learning

		Predicted Class				
		Clean	VS (FPV)	BBS (FPV)	VS (FR)	BBS (FR)
	Clean	0.98	0.00	0.00	0.02	0.00
	VS (FPV)	0.01	0.93	0.00	0.06	0.00
True Class	BBS (FPV)	0.00	0.00	0.87	0.00	0.13
	VS (FR)	0.04	0.02	0.00	0.95	0.00
	BBS (FR)	0.00	0.00	0.21	0.00	0.79

(continued)

283

TABLE 10.4. *(continued)*

Bagged Decision Trees

		Predicted Class			
	Clean	VS (FPV)	BBS (FPV)	VS (FR)	BBS (FR)
True Class Clean	1.00	0.00	0.00	0.00	0.00
VS (FPV)	0.01	0.97	0.00	0.03	0.00
BBS (FPV)	0.00	0.00	0.87	0.00	0.13
VS (FR)	0.03	0.01	0.00	0.96	0.00
BBS (FR)	0.00	0.00	0.17	0.00	0.843

Decision Tree Forests

		Predicted Class			
	Clean	VS (FPV)	BBS (FPV)	VS (FR)	BBS (FR)
True Class Clean	1.00	0.00	0.00	0.00	0.00
VS (FPV)	0.01	0.96	0.00	0.03	0.00
BBS (FPV)	0.00	0.00	0.89	0.00	0.11
VS (FR)	0.03	0.01	0.00	0.96	0.00
BBS (FR)	0.00	0.00	0.16	0.00	0.84

learning algorithm (see the lower section of Table 10.2). Additionally, off-diagonal elements in the first column of each matrix suggest that all algorithms are also successful in minimizing the occurrence of false negatives (i.e., the proportion of tainted *mesas* classified as clean). The algorithm producing the largest incidence of false negatives is the RIPPER rule learner, where 4% of *mesas* tainted with VS by FR are classified as clean. Similar to what we found for the k-means algorithm, the most common mistake is the misclassification of the party perpetrating the manipulation, with the incidence of this type of mistake being particularly high for BBS. The naïve Bayes classifier and RIPPER rule learner exhibit the highest incidence of the latter type of mistake.[11]

After completing the evaluation, we applied the different procedures to the actual electoral data. Results discussed in the previous paragraph indicate that, if clean and tainted *mesas* in the test data exhibit patterns in electoral variables that are similar to those prevailing within classes in the synthetic training data set, then all of the supervised machine learning procedures should prove useful for detecting anomalies. Table 10.5 gives the percentage of actual *mesas* in the test data classified as clean and tainted by each type of fraud (VS and BBS), as well as the percentage of *mesas* where detected anomalies increase the vote share of either the FPV or the FR. Except for the k-nearest neighbors algorithm, all other procedures produce relatively consistent results, with the percentage of clean *mesas* ranging between 75.3% and 82.0%, the percentage of *mesas* exhibiting patterns consistent with BBS ranging between 17.2% and 23.1%, and the percentage of *mesas* exhibiting patterns consistent with VS ranging between 0.6% and 1.5%. Also, with the exception of the RIPPER rule learner, all procedures detect larger percentages of anomalies committed by the FR than of anomalies committed by the FPV.

After completing the grouping step, we used the classification done by the random forests algorithm to study the distribution of electoral variables among *mesas* assigned to clean classes and among *mesas* assigned to classes tainted with VS and BBS (see Figure 10.4). The visual inspection of the distribution of electoral variables allows us to determine whether within-class patterns are consistent with those observed within the corresponding hypothetical classes in the training data set (presented earlier, in Figure 10.2). Although distributions in the actual electoral data are centered at different levels compared to distributions in the training data, it is still the case that turnout is considerably higher among *mesas* classified as tainted with BBS (with voter turnout averaging about 84%) than among *mesas* classified as clean (with voter turnout averaging about 79%). Moreover, consistent with expectations, FPV and FR vote shares in *mesas* tainted with BBS exhibit bimodal distributions, with the higher mode corresponding to instances where the party itself seems to be responsible for the manipulation. For instance, whereas the average FR vote share stands at 27% in situations consistent with BBS by the FPV, it stands at 36% in situations consistent with BBS by the FR itself. Moreover, results are consistent with the assumption that BBS only affects the total vote count and the number

TABLE 10.5. *Proportion of Clean and Tainted Mesas in Test Data* (%)

Learning algorithm	Clean	Tainted	Vote stealing hypothesis			Ballot box stuffing hypothesis		
			Total	by FPV	by FR	Total	by FPV	by FR
k-Nearest Neighbors	41.1	58.9	0.3	0.2	0.1	58.5	22.0	36.5
Naïve Bayes	81.1	18.9	1.2	0.2	1.0	17.7	5.7	12.0
C5.0 Decision Tree (w/adaptive boosting and costly mistakes)	78.1	21.9	0.6	0.3	0.3	21.2	5.5	15.7
RIPPER Rule Learning	75.3	24.7	1.5	0.5	1.1	23.1	14.7	8.4
Bagged Decision Trees	82.0	18.0	0.7	0.5	0.2	17.2	6.6	10.7
Decision Tree Forests	80.9	19.1	0.7	0.4	0.3	18.4	6.5	11.9

N = 11,449.

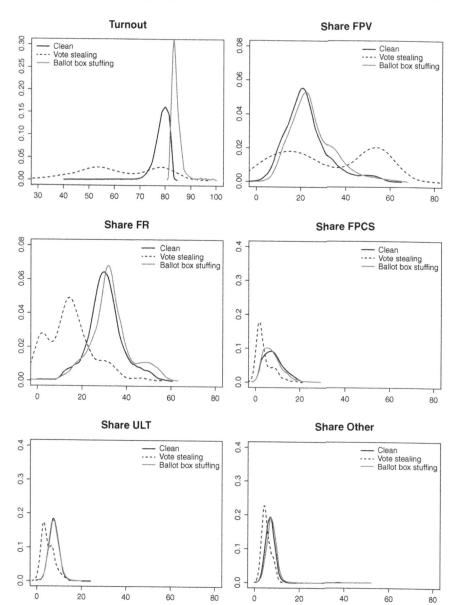

FIGURE 10.4. Distribution of electoral variables in test data set (learning algorithm: random forest).

of votes for the perpetrator, since the distribution of vote shares obtained by other parties (measured as a fraction of the eligible electorate) is almost the same for *mesas* classified as clean class as for *mesas* classified as tainted with BBS. The prevalence of BBS over VS could be explained for two reasons. First, since voting is compulsory in Argentina, very low levels of turnout at certain polling stations might be more suspicious than higher ones. Second, it is very risky to steal ballots from the urn during voting hours (taking advantage of the possible absence at some points of the day of party monitors). By contrast, it might be easier to commit ballot box stuffing during voting hours by adding ballots from voters who have not shown up (impersonation).

The distribution of electoral variables in the actual electoral data set is less smooth (compared to the distribution in the training data set) in the case of VS, since fewer *mesas* were classified as tainted with vote stealing. However, results are also mostly consistent with expectations: the distribution of vote shares among the two large parties is again bimodal (with modes determined by the identity of the party responsible for the manipulation), and in particular, vote shares obtained by other parties are considerably smaller than in *mesas* classified as clean. For instance, whereas the average FPCS vote share is 8% among clean *mesas*, it equals 3% and 4% in *mesas* tainted with VS by FPV and FR, respectively.

Relationship between Identified Anomalies and Contextual Variables

In the third and final stage of our analysis, we studied the relationship between identified anomalies and contextual variables potentially associated with the occurrence of voter fraud. We did so by first computing the proportion of *mesas* classified as clean, tainted with VS, and tainted with BBS for each of the 24 municipalities in Buenos Aires's Conurbation; we subsequently looked at (1) the relationship between the proportion of tainted *mesas* and an aggregate indicator of unsatisfied basic needs (see Figure 10.5)[12] and (2) the spatial distribution of the proportion of units classified as tainted with BBS by each party, of partisan support, and of the index of unsatisfied basic needs (see Figure 10.6).[13]

Results presented in Figure 10.5 suggest that the incidence of anomalies (measured as the proportion of *mesas* classified as tainted within the municipality) is systematically higher in municipalities where more households are leaving under duress (that is, where the index of unsatisfied basic needs takes higher values). Results presented in Figure 10.6, in turn, suggest that the distribution of the two most common types of anomalies detected by the random forest algorithm (BBS by FPV and BBS by FR) is closely related to the distribution of partisan support across municipalities: anomalies favoring FR are more common in municipalities controlled by the FR, and anomalies favoring FPV are more common in municipalities controlled by the FPV. Another revealing finding is that the incidence of tainted *mesas* is usually higher in

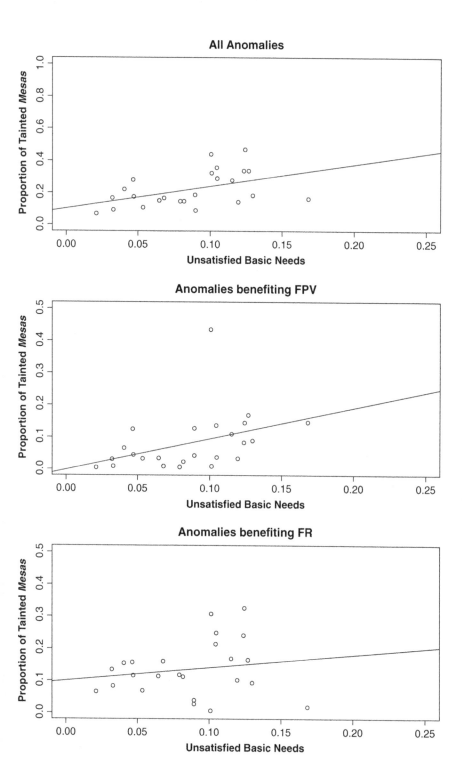

FIGURE 10.5. Relationship between Anomalies and unsatisfied basic needs (24 munici-palities of Buenos Aires's Conurbation; learning algorithm: random forests). *Note:* Each point corresponds to one municipality.

**Spatial distribution of Ballot Box
Stuffing (Anomalies
benefiting FPV)**

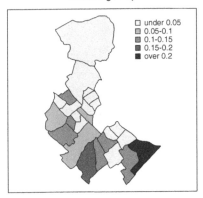

**Spatial distribution of Ballot Box
Stuffing (Anomalies
benefiting FR)**

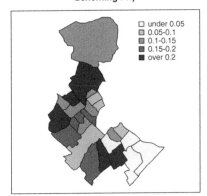

**Spatial Distribution of Partisan Support
(Incumbent party in municipal government)**

Spatial Distribution of Unsatisfied Basic Needs

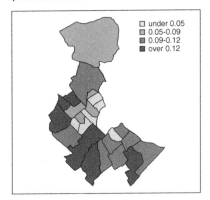

FIGURE 10.6. Spatial distribution of anomalies and contextual variables (24 municipalities of Buenos Aires's Conurbation; learning algorithm: random forest).

municipalities located farther away from the City of Buenos Aires (lying right next to the center-east of the Conurbation), especially those located in the northwest, southwest, and south of the Conurbation, where it is also the case that more households have unsatisfied basic needs. This finding is consistent with the fact that election monitoring by parties in the second ring around the city is harder to guarantee and surveys showed that coverage of party monitors there was smaller than in the first ring around the city (Pomares and Page 2014).

In sum, the application of machine learning algorithms to the 2013 federal elections in the Greater Buenos Aires area was successful in detecting anomalies. Although this analysis should be extended – especially since anomalies might have been corrected in the definitive tally – the fact that the election examined was a very competitive one (the margin of difference being five points) and that anomalies seem to have favored the national challenger more than the incumbent candidate points to the importance of paying attention to the interplay between national and local races. In this particular case, incumbency at the local level was key to detecting anomalies in national election results. This was especially relevant since the electoral support of the two main electoral contenders varies strongly across municipalities. Qualitative knowledge about the electoral context proved valuable in identifying the relevant electoral variables.

4 SUMMARY

In this chapter we presented the application of machine learning approaches to the important problem of detecting electoral manipulation. The rapidly growing literature that uses various statistical techniques to detect potential electoral manipulation in election returns data has relied on relatively simple analytical tools, usually distribution tests, digit tests, or very simple linear models. Although those approaches have been productive – for example, the application of simple distribution tests in the first round of elections in 2003 in the Ukraine led to calls for new elections in that nation (Myagkov et al. 2009) – they are not likely to be useful in the near future. The problem with these simple analytical tools is that, because they are widely known, they are easily foiled by those who might wish to manipulate an election.

Thus, methodologists and statisticians will need to use increasingly sophisticated tools to keep up with those who might be trying to manipulate election outcomes. We believe that machine learning tools like we used here can be deployed to better detect and possibly even prevent future election fraud. These tools can be used to examine large election data sets, under flexible assumptions about model specification, and can help detect subtle forms of election fraud that may not be found so easily using simple distribution or digit tests. Clearly machine learning approaches merit further consideration as tools for detecting problems in the administration of elections – and most likely they have applications to other situations where analysts might be interested in finding potential fraud.

Notes

1. For an introduction to machine learning algorithms, see Hastie, Tibshirani, and Friedman (2009) and Lantz (2013).
2. Since the process involves a random component (i.e., the random selection of initial cluster centers), and since final results are often sensitive to initial conditions, the clustering procedure should be repeated. If cluster characteristics vary considerably between replicates, this might indicate that the total number of clusters is incorrect.
3. The independence assumption can also be problematic when certain levels of an electoral variable are never observed (in the training data) for one class of location, since this situation leads to degenerate posterior distributions (where fraud

is predicted to take place with probabilities 0 or 1 as a function of values taken by a single electoral indicator). For instance, suppose that in the previous example there was zero incidence of high turnout in clean electoral locations; then Bayes rule would predict that fraud takes place with probability 1 when turnout is high, regardless of values taken by other electoral variables predictive of the likelihood of electoral manipulation. A common way deal with this issue is to add an arbitrary count to cells in the contingency table.

4. In this chapter we implement tree-based classification using an algorithm known as C5.0 (Quinlin 2013). At each tree node, C5.0 determines the extent to which splitting the data based on a given electoral feature would produce an *information gain* by increasing homogeneity within partitions.

5. See Pomares et al. (2014); Alvarez et al. (2013); and Katz et al. (2011).

6. Our analysis only considered *mesas* with more than 100 voters where the total number of votes cast did not equal the number of registered voters and where each of the four largest electoral alliances (FPV, FR, FPCS, and ULT), as well as at least one of the remaining lists, received at least one vote. According to the law, there is a maximum of 350 registered voters per *mesa*. The data used for the analysis corresponds to the provisional tally under the responsibility of a unit within the Ministry of Interior (Dirección Nacional Electoral). Although this provisional tally does not count as the valid election result, it is the most technologically advanced. Some errors found in the provisional tally are corrected in the definitive tally.

7. The Greater Buenos Aires area surrounds the City of Buenos Aires and comprises 25% of the whole electoral register of Argentina. There is no unique way to define the boundaries of the suburbs of the City of Buenos Aires. We use the National Statistics Bureau's definition and include the 24 municipalities that surround the City of Buenos Aires.

8. To take into account the compositional nature of the data (the sum of abstention and vote shares measured as a proportion of the eligible electorate should add up to 1), we performed a log-ratio transformation of dependent variables. More specifically, dependent variables were set to the logarithm of the ratio between vote shares and the proportion of abstention. To ensure that estimates were not distorted by outliers, we first estimated regression models in the entire data set and then reestimated them excluding outliers before proceeding to using regression estimates to simulate clean data.

9. The first type of voter fraud is consistent with a situation where the perpetrator prevents votes from being cast for other parties by making opposition lists unavailable to voters (for instance, by removing them from the voting booth or *cuarto oscuro*).

10. In the case of the FPV, the lower mode in the distribution of vote shares in tainted data corresponds to situations where anomalies favor FR (and is smallest when vote stealing favors FR, when the share obtained by the FPV lies around 17%), and the higher mode corresponds to situations where anomalies favor FPV (and is largest when ballot box stuffing increases FPV vote shares, when the share obtained by the FPV lies around 37%). A similar pattern is assumed for vote shares obtained by the FR.

11. The simpler OneR rule learner leads to higher misclassification rates than the RIPPER rule learner. Specifically, with the OneR rule learner, the incidence of false positives equals 7%; the incidence of false negatives equals 7% (the main

reason being that 32% of units tainted with BS by FR are classified as clean); the proportion of units tainted with VS by one party classified as VS by the other party equals 21% and 22% for the FPV and FR, respectively; and the proportion of units tainted with BBS by one party classified as BBS by the other party equals 44% and 56% for the FPV and FR, respectively.

12. The composite index of unsatisfied basic needs (NBI) is calculated by Argentina's National Statistics and Census Institute based on three indicators: a household's living and economic conditions and access to schooling and health care services.

13. The measure of partisan support is a binary indicator of the incumbent party in the municipal government.

References

Alvarez, R. Michael, Lonna Rae Atkeson, and Thad E. Hall. 2012. *Evaluating Elections: A Handbook of Methods and Standards*. New York: Cambridge University Press.

Alvarez, R. Michael, Thad E. Hall, and Susan D. Hyde. 2008. *Election Fraud: Detecting and Deterring Electoral Manipulation*. Washington, DC: Brookings Institution Press.

Alvarez, R. Michael, Brian Kim, Ines Levin, and Julia Pomares. 2014. "Detecting Election Manipulation: Applications to Recent Elections in Venezuela." Unpublished Manuscript.

Alvarez, R. Michael, Ines Levin, Julia Pomares, and Marcelo Leiras. 2013. "Voting Made Safe and Easy: The Impact of e-voting on Citizen Perceptions." *Political Science Research and Methods* 1(1), 117–137.

Bjornlund, Eric C. 2004. *Beyond Free and Fair: Monitoring Elections and Building Democracy*. Baltimore, MD: Johns Hopkins University Press.

Ernesto Calvo and Marcelo Escolar. 2005. "La neuva politica de partidos en la Argentina." Crisis politica, realineamientos partidariso y reforma electoral. Buenos Aires: Prometeo.

Cantu, Francisco and Sebastian M. Saiegh. 2011. "Fraudulent Democracy? An Analysis of Argentina's Infamous Decade Using Supervised Machine Learning." *Political Analysis* 19(4): 409–433.

Cohen, William W. 1995. "Fast Effective Rule Reduction." *Proceedings of the Twelfth International Conference on Machine Learning*, Lake Tahoe, California

Hastie, Trevor, Robert Tibshirani, and Jerome Friedman. 2009. *The Elements of Statistical Learning: Data Mining, Inference, and Prediction*. Second Edition. New York: Springer.

Hornik, Kurt, Christian Buchta, Achim Zeileis. 2009. "Open-Source Machine Learning: R Meets Weka." *Computational Statistics* 24(2): 225–232.

Hyde, Susan D. 2007. "The Observer Effect in International Politics: Evidence from a Natural Experiment." *World Politics*, 60, 37–63.

Hyde, Susan D. 2011. *The Psuedo-Democrat's Dilemma: Why Election Monitoring Became an International Norm*. Ithaca, NY: Cornell University Press.

Katz, Gabriel, R. Michael Alvarez, Ernesto Calvo, Marcelo Escolar, and Julia Pomares. 2011. "Assessing the Impact of Alternative Voting Technologies on Multi-Party Elections: Design Features, Heuristic Processing and Voter Choice." *Political Behavior* 33, 247–270.

Kelley, Judith G. 2013. *Monitoring Democracy: When International Election Observation Works, and Why It Often Fails*. Princeton, NJ: Princeton University Press.

Lantz, Brett. 2013. *Machine Learning with R.* Birmingham: Packt Publishing.

Levin, Ines, Gabe A. Cohn, Peter C. Ordeshook, and R. Michael Alvarez. 2009. "Detecting Voter Fraud in an Electronic Voting Context: An Analysis of the Unlimited Reelection Vote in Venezuela." *Proceedings of the 2009 Electronic Voting Technology Workshop/Workshop on Trustworthy Elections* (EVT/WOTE '09), https://www.usenix.org/legacy/event/evtwote09/tech/full_papers/levin.pdf.

Levin, Ines and R. Michael Alvarez. 2012. "Introduction to the Virtual Issue: Election Fraud and Electoral Integrity." http://www.oxfordjournals.org/our_journals/polana/virtualissue3.html.

Liaw, Andy and Matthew Wiener. 2002. "Classification and Regression by random-Forest." *R News* 2(3): 18–22.

Meyer, David, Evgenia Dimitriadou, Kurt Hornik, Andreas Weingessel, and Friedrich Leisch. 2014. e1071: Misc Functions of the Department of Statistics (e1071), TU Wien. R package version 1.6-3. http://CRAN.R-project.org/package=e1071.

Myagkov, Mikhail, Peter C. Ordeshook, and Dimitri Shakin. 2009. *The Forensics of Election Fraud: Russia and Ukraine.* New York: Cambridge University Press.

Peters, Andrea and Torsten Hothorn. 2013. ipred: Improved Predictors. R package version 0.9-3. http://CRAN.R-project.org/package=ipred.

Pomares, Julia, Ines Levin, and R. Michael Alvarez. 2014. "Do Voters and Poll Workers Differ in their Attitudes toward E-voting? Evidence from the First E-election in Salta, Argentina." *USENIX Journal of Election Technology and Systems* 2(2), https://www.usenix.org/jets/issues/0202/pomares.

Pomares, Julia and Maria Page. 2014. "Elecciones 2013. Mitos, hechos e interrogantes sobre la fiscalización electoral en el conurbano bonaerense." Documentos de Políticas Públicas 124. Buenos Aires: CIPPEC.

Quinlan, J. Ross. 2013. Data Mining Tools See5 and C5.0. https://www.rulequest.com/see5-info.html.

Venables, William N. and Brian D. Ripley. 2002. *Modern Applied Statistics with S.* Fourth Edition. New York: Springer.

11

Centralized Analysis of Local Data, with Dollars and Lives on the Line

Lessons from the Home Radon Experience[*]

Phillip N. Price[†] and Andrew Gelman[‡]

In this chapter we elucidate four main themes. The first is that modern data analyses, including "big data" analyses, often rely on data from different sources, which can present challenges in constructing statistical models that can make effective use of all of the data. The second theme is that, although data analysis is usually centralized, frequently the final outcome is to provide information or allow decision making for individuals. Third, data analyses often have multiple uses by design: the outcomes of the analysis are intended to be used by more than one person or group, for more than one purpose. Finally, issues of privacy and confidentiality can cause problems in more subtle ways than are usually considered; we illustrate this point by discussing a case in which there is substantial and effective political opposition to simply acknowledging the geographic distribution of a health hazard.

A researcher analyzes some data and learns something important. What happens next? What does it take for the results to make a difference in people's lives? In this chapter we tell a story – a true story – about a statistical analysis that should have changed government policy, but did not. The project was a research success that did not make its way into policy, and we think it provides some useful insights into the interplay between locally collected data, statistical analysis, and individual decision making.

A DATA SET COMPILED FROM MANY LOCAL SOURCES

Before getting to our story we set the stage with a brief discussion of general issues regarding data availability. Some data analysis problems, even large or

---

[*] We thank Mike Alvarez for helpful comments and the National Science Foundation for partial support of this work.
[†] Environmental Energy Technologies Division, Lawrence Berkeley National Laboratory.
[‡] Department of Statistics, Columbia University, New York.

complicated ones, involve data from a single source or collected through a single mechanism. For example, the U.S. Census generates data on hundreds of millions of people using just a few different survey instruments. More typically, however, an analyses involves data from multiple sources. Moreover, although the input data might come from many sources and involve thousands or millions of people, at least some of the results of the analysis are often geared toward individuals. Some examples include the following:

- In evidence-based medicine (e.g., Lau, Ioannidis, and Schmid, 1997), information from many separate experiments and observational studies are combined in a meta-analysis, with the goal being to produce recommendations that can be adapted to individual patients by doctors or regulatory boards.
- Specialized online tools, such as those for traffic analysis, are used to gather and disseminate up-to-the-minute data so that people can get personalized estimates of travel time.
- Some websites gather and analyze information on housing sales, house characteristics, and neighborhood characteristics, so that they can provide estimated prices for individual houses on the market.

In addition to coming from multiple sources data have multiple uses, often by design. Most obviously, Google and Facebook appear to users as tools for answering queries or sharing information with friends, but at the same time they analyze the queries and social media posts to give advertisers a means of targeting potential customers. Scholastic testing is used to evaluate both individual students and schools or school systems. In this chapter, we use the term "big data" to refer to any analysis that combines data from several sources and generates results that are intended for multiple audiences, whether or not the data sets are actually "big" by modern standards.

From the perspective of the data analyst or of the user of the analysis, having more data is always better. One might choose to ignore data, even entire categories of data, if it is not clear how to use them in a statistical model or if the computational cost of analyzing them is too great, but on average there should be no *harm* in having more data. To the analyst, privacy and confidentiality protections are nuisances, rendering some data inaccessible and other data accessible only under inconvenient restrictions. For instance, access to data might be granted only if the researcher agrees that no raw data may be published. This may be acceptable inasmuch as it still allows publishing of summary statistics and derived quantities, but it might prevent publishing even exemplary plots or tables of raw data and might make it hard for others to evaluate the validity of the work. Imagine the problems of verifying global temperature changes if the raw data could not be shared.

Although the researcher or data analyst would always prefer access to all data that can be had, as well as the ability to publish all data and related analyses, owners or controllers of data often have good reasons not to share information or, if it is shared, to insist that the data be available only to a restricted group of researchers. Someone who is selling her house may not wish it known that the basement sometimes floods, and a political candidate might be reluctant to answer the question, "Have you ever had an affair?"

Data privacy issues can lead to a sort of prisoner's dilemma in which a group of people would benefit if they were *all* to share their data, but no single person's expected benefit is great enough to overcome their privacy concerns. Employees at a company might be able to bargain more effectively if everyone knew everyone else's salary, but each individual employee might see the negative impact of revealing his or her salary as being higher than the positive. An employee might reasonably think "I already know my salary, so adding my data to the pool does me no good at all, whereas it could cause me embarrassment or make co-workers unhappy with me; therefore I will not share," but if everyone follows this approach then the employees as a group are at an informational disadvantage compared to their employer. At times, the desire to prevent the free flow of information can have important consequences.

ASSESSING RISKS AND RECOMMENDING DECISIONS REGARDING
FOR INDOOR RADON EXPOSURE

Much of our thinking in this area has been influenced by an example we worked on in the mid-1990s on evaluating the risks of exposure to radon in the home (Lin et al., 1999). Radon is a naturally occurring radioactive gas that is drawn into houses from the surrounding soil due to wind- and temperature-driven pressure differences between the soil gas and the interior of the house. It has long been known to cause lung cancer if inhaled at high concentrations, an effect first recognized among miners. (To be technically correct, it is not radon that is dangerous; it is the decay products of radon, which are themselves radioactive. When we say "radon" in this article, we really mean "radon decay products.")

Radon concentrations are often far higher in mines than in homes, and it was not until the mid-1980s that it was recognized that even some homes have indoor radon concentrations that expose occupants to dangerous levels of radiation. (A book from that era that is still useful scientifically, but is now also an interesting historical document is Nazaroff and Nero, 1988). The most dramatic example is from 1984, when a Pennsylvanian who worked at a nuclear power plant kept triggering a radiation detector that was routinely used when workers left for the day. After some investigation, it was found that he was not being contaminated at work, but was carrying radon decay products to work with him on his clothes and that his annual exposure from living in his house was far higher than the occupational safety limit for uranium miners. Within a few years of this highly publicized discovery – which led to the discovery of many more high-radon houses across the country – radon monitoring and mitigation companies sprung up across the country, and state and federal agencies had developed advice and guidelines. Radon monitoring is quite inexpensive, just \$15–\$30 depending on test type; mitigation, which usually involves using a fan to depressurize the soil beneath the house, typically costs \$800–\$2,000 plus some energy cost to continuously run a fan.

Early on, the U.S. Environmental Protection Agency (EPA) established a recommendation that every house in the country should be tested for radon and that remediation actions should be performed if a home's long-term living-area-average radioactivity concentration exceeded 4 picoCuries per liter of air (4 pCi/L), a threshold known as the "action level." In many places in the country, radon is one of the items specifically called out as potential risks in mandatory paperwork when a house changes hands, along with termites, mold, and so on.

It was clear from the outset was that some areas of the country have much higher average radon concentrations than others, and a much higher chance of having homes with extremely high radon concentrations. This was no surprise, given known geographical variation in soil types and home construction. Within a few years of radon becoming a national issue, the U.S. Geological Survey had begun working on mapping "radon potential" (a somewhat ill-defined concept), and in the early 1990s it released maps for the coterminous United States (Schumann and Owen, 1988). However, these maps only attempted to identify areas of high, medium, and low "potential," and the official policy was (and still is) that "testing is the only way to know if you and your family are at risk from radon. EPA and the Surgeon General recommend testing all homes below the third floor for radon" (U.S. Environmental Protection Agency, 2012).

Contrary to federal policy, it would make sense to focus radon measurement and remediation efforts on homes with radon concentrations much higher than the recommended action level, first because the people in those houses are at greater individual risk and therefore stand to benefit most if their risks are identified and dealt with rapidly rather than slowly, but also because there is no question that residents of extremely high-radon houses are at *some* risk. The dose-response relationship for radon decay products is not well known at typical residential concentrations, and many people question whether the EPA's action level is too low: some people suggest there may be no additional risk of lung cancer at 4 pCi/L compared to, say, a typical outdoor level of 0.5 pCi/L. But there is no question that long-term exposure to the radon decay products generated by a concentration of 20 pCi/L causes a substantially increased risk of lung cancer. We believe (but many people disagree) that there is fairly convincing evidence that long-term residence in a house with a radon concentration of 4 pCi/L does in fact increase the risk of lung cancer (see Field et al., 2000, for example).

To determine the nationwide statistical distribution of indoor radon concentrations and to begin to map the geography of the problem, in the late 1980s and early 1990s the EPA measured long-term living-area-average radon concentrations in a stratified random sample of about 5,000 houses in the country and worked with state agencies to measure short-term (2- to 3-day) radon concentrations in winter on the lowest level of a sample of tens out thousands of houses from most of the 50 states. A short-term measurement in winter on the lowest floor of the house is called a "screening" measurement and tends to overestimate the long-term living-area-average concentration by a factor of 2 to 3.5, depending on details of climate and house construction, as well as being subject to considerable stochastic variability due to variation in the weather and physical constraints of the measuring device.

Although our analysis had many characteristics of a genuine big data problem, it differed from such problems in at least one important way: we did not in fact have a lot of data, with random-sample radon measurements from only about 60,000 homes throughout the country. Many individual counties had fewer than five samples. At least in some areas of the country there were much larger data sets that were potentially available from radon testing and mitigation contractors, but these data sets had a variety of problems and, after examining some of the data, we ultimately decided not to pursue obtaining and using them. The biggest problems were (1) inconsistent and often unrecorded measurement protocols and (2) the inclusion of multiple confirmatory measurements from houses with high initial test measurements, but with which measurements were duplicates. We found only low correlations between the random sample radon measurements and those from private databases in the same zip code or county. This example illustrates the important point that simply finding a way to get a larger data set does not guarantee a more accurate or more useful analysis.

LOCAL DATA, CENTRALIZED ANALYSIS, LOCAL DECISION MAKING

When we began to work on indoor radon mapping, we immediately ran into problems with combining data from different sources. For example, the nationwide radon survey performed long-term living-area measurements on each floor of the home, whereas the surveys conducted by the individual states almost all made one or two short-term measurements on the lowest level of each home, which was often an unoccupied basement. Also, radon measurements were made in individual homes, but the available data on soil uranium content (a useful predictive variable) were available only as spatial averages. Finding ways to jointly analyze all of the available data was a significant challenge (Price et al., 1996; Price and Nero, 1996).

We made several time-consuming false starts in our analyses when trying to figure out ways to exploit various types of data. For example, due to confidentiality constraints some of our data provided house locations only as zip codes, which are large enough in rural areas that we were unable to determine the local geology except in very crude terms. We spent considerable time and resources investigating whether more detailed location information would lead to better predictive models – this required both performing a new radon survey whose participants allowed us to make use of their exact house location, and digitizing old paper maps of local geology – only to find that this approach provided little benefit over the other variables we were already including in our models. Deciding what additional data are worth collecting is a part of many statistical modeling efforts.

In the end, having done the best we could to create a statistical model that used the radon measurement data, along with other information on the geographic distribution of radiation risks, we constructed a hierarchical model that yielded a (probabilistic) prediction of the radon level in any house, given its geographic location, information about the surface-soil radioactivity in its area, and house-specific information such as whether the house has a basement. This portion of our analysis yielded predictions of, and uncertainties in, the statistical distribution of indoor radon concentrations in every county in the conterminous United States. Counties that were heavily sampled in the radon surveys had small uncertainties, whereas sparsely sampled or unsampled counties had statistical distributions based purely on the explanatory variables and therefore had large uncertainties. The goal of this government-funded effort was to identify areas of the country with the highest radon concentrations, either in terms of average levels or the fraction of homes whose radon concentration greatly exceeded the recommended action level, so that special attention could be focused on those areas by way of increased public outreach and perhaps government programs to perform radon testing.

The good news was that, after some effort, we were able to construct a model that fit the data well, gave insight into the geographic distribution of radon risks, provided informative predictions, and performed well under cross-validation. The bad news was that, even though our mid-1990s efforts led to much more accurate maps of statistical distributions of radon concentrations than had previously been available, and in spite of the fact that much of our research had been federally funded, we found that our work had no effect on federal radon policy. Simply having radon maps that would have allowed specific counties around the country to be targeted for increased radon monitoring and mitigation did not lead to any such targeting, at least by federal agencies (some states do have targeted programs).

It was obvious to us that a targeted approach could be much cheaper than monitoring every home and could presumably save more lives as well: most people were ignoring the monitoring recommendations whether they lived in a high-radon area or not, whereas targeting high-radon areas would presumably improve compliance in those areas. Providing the ability to focus on high-radon areas did not promote change, but we thought, perhaps naively, that the government's radon policy would change if we illustrated the fact that a targeted policy could cost less money – and, depending on the policy and its reception by the public, could save more lives – than recommending testing in every house. Having fit the model, we were able to estimate the the potential cost in dollars and the potential savings in lives of various potential programs for the measurement and remediation of radon (Lin et al., 1999). This allowed us to compare the current policy of monitoring every house with a short-term test to various more targeted programs, such as focusing on certain counties or only certain types of houses in certain counties. Similar work was done by others at the same time (Ford et al., 1999).

Although certainly not a big data problem by today's standards or even the standards of the time, our analysis had some of the characteristics typical of such problems: we were putting together locally collected data in an aggregate context; our data came from disparate sources, and as with most real-world problems but not textbook problems, it was up to us to decide whether it was worth seeking out and trying to use other data sources (for example, maps of local geology). Our analysis also shared an unnoticed feature of many real-world data-based problems, which is that they are *dispersed*. In a classical decision problem there is a single decision tree, a single utility function, a single probability distribution, and a single decision to make. Here we were considering problems in which many different people each have to make decisions based in part on analysis of a large data set and in part on information that is specific to them. You can use a website to get summary statistics (or even raw data) about house prices or the reliability of different ages and models of used cars, but you then apply that information to deciding whether to buy a specific house or a specific car. This is related to the idea of Hand (2009) that statistics is the science of the individual as well as the aggregate.

Our radon analysis was centralized, and the government offers general recommendations, but the ultimate decisions, as well as the financial and health risks, are borne locally by individuals. Each homeowner needs to make his or her decision of what to do about home radon, and different people will make different decisions: the costs of measurement and remediation, as well as the risk of cancer, vary locally, and each person has her own risk tolerance and willingness to pay to reduce risk. We recommended that the government's simple decision rule, which was the same everywhere in the United States and that did not vary according to house-specific information, should be replaced by a more complicated rule that takes account of local knowledge of the statistical distribution of indoor radon concentrations, as well as information specific to each house (such as whether it has a basement). And if a homeowner measured her indoor radon concentration, our rule considered whether the measurement was short- or long-term and, if short term, in what season the measurement was made. Additionally, our rule allowed for variation in household size and makeup: smokers are at higher risk from radon than nonsmokers; the risk is different for men, women, and children; and all else equal a larger household has more chance of experiencing a radon-induced lung cancer than a smaller household.

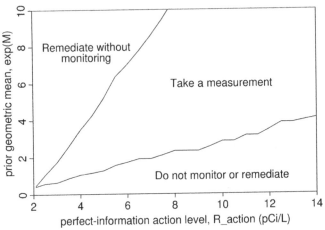

FIGURE 11.1. Recommended radon remediation/measurement decision as a function of two inputs at the individual level: (a) the perfect-information action level R_{action}, which represents an individual risk assessment, and (b) the prior geometric mean radon level e^M, which captures information about individual exposure. A homeowner can read off his or her recommended decision from this graph. (Wiggles in the lines are due to simulation variability in the calculations.) As can be seen from this figure, the output from our statistical and decision analysis is not a single decision, but rather is a decision function allowing different individual decisions under different conditions. From Gelman et al. (2013).

A homeowner's risk tolerance and household makeup, combined with the estimated dose-response relationship for men, women, and children exposed to radon decay products, determine a "perfect-information action level": if a homeowner knew for sure that her home's long-term living-area radon concentration exceeded this level, she should remediate her home to reduce the radon concentration. Given the perfect-information action level, the decision of whether or not to measure the radon concentration depends on the statistical distribution of radon concentrations for the home and some other parameters, such as the cost of testing and the uncertainty in the resulting measurement. For one set of assumptions about these matters, the results are shown in Figure 11.1.

What made this analysis work at a statistical level was hierarchical modeling, a statistical approach that estimates, and takes into account, variation that occurs at multiple levels of a hierarchy. There is variation in radon concentration between states, between counties within each state, between houses within each county, and between measurement locations within each house. A hierarchical model (as opposed to a simple linear regression) allowed us to get reasonable predictions of distributions of radon levels and of uncertainties in these distributions in every county, even those for which very few measurements were available (see Price, Nero, and Gelman, 1996). This allowed us to make decision recommendations that differ from county to county and from house type to house type.

Research on residential radon in support of government policy required communication among several groups: the people whose homes were measured, the EPA, us, and many other players, including commercial suppliers of radon test kits and home remediation, state-level regulatory officials, and public health officials. Some aspects of this communication went better than others. The EPA got excellent compliance in their radon survey, and it made the data available so that many different research groups could work on the radon prediction and remediation problem. But our own interactions with regulatory agencies and end users were not so effective. The people we spoke with at the EPA resisted our efforts to create a calibrated decision analysis with different recommendations for different counties and house types: instead, they wanted to stick with a uniform recommendation (measure all houses, then remediate all houses where the measured radon level exceeds some threshold), which we estimated would be a much less cost-effective way to reduce risk.

WHAT WENT WRONG: WHY IS THERE STILL A SINGLE NATIONWIDE RECOMMENDATION?

We thought at first that the resistance to a targeted radon monitoring approach was due to the belief that it would be too hard to implement. To try to demonstrate that such an approach was feasible, we created a high-tech (as of 2000!) website where anyone could click and find a map showing his or her county, along with estimated costs and benefits of radon measurement and remediation for a typical home in the county. Optionally, users could fill in additional information such as measurements in neighbors' houses that could inform the decision of whether to make a radon measurement, what type of measurement to make, and what they should use as their personal "action level" for remediation. We provided defaults for household size and makeup, as well as for risk tolerance, but users could change these as well if they wished. They could even change the assumed relationship between radon exposure and health risk.

We did not expect to reach a large number of individual homeowners through the website: as we stated in a companion article to our decision analysis paper (Lin et al., 1999b), by performing our analysis (and making the website), "we are hoping to influence government policy; we do not expect our recommendations to reach a substantial number of individual homeowners."

We had some small successes publicizing our maps, website, and research project (including, at one point, an article with maps in the *New York Times*; Fairfield, 2005), but it never became wildly popular: in total, fewer than forty thousand visitors used our site to get a recommendation. Over the years, different pieces of the webpage became nonfunctional – victims of software updates and the like – and we eventually abandoned it almost 10 years after it launched. The modest popularity of the site was neither disappointing nor surprising to us, because the public was not really the intended audience of the site: what we were trying to demonstrate was that the federal government could, if it chose, create and promote a targeted radon policy. The disappointment was that we never saw evidence that we had helped shift national policies toward targeted radon testing.

We believe one of the reasons targeted testing did not catch on is that there is pressure from homeowners and realtors not to identify specific areas as having elevated risk from radon. If you are a homeowner, you want to know if you are in a high-radon area so that you know to measure your home's radon concentration, but at the same time you may not want *other* people to know that you are in a high-radon area because this might decrease the value of your home. Concern about property values was evident even, or perhaps especially, in the first few years after high residential radon concentrations were discovered. As early as 1985 the state of Florida, which has very high radon concentrations on or near areas where phosphate mining has occurred, was considering requiring a formal warning to homeowners in those areas. A lobbyist said, "If they pass this notification thing, it's war with a capital W (Dunkelberger, 1985)." A few years later a *Chicago Tribune* article reported, "Lawyers and environmental specialists warned corporate relocation specialists gathering in Chicago last week that liability for environmental hazards in homes is likely to emerge soon as a major problem for sellers and real estate brokers," with radon specifically mentioned (Allen, 1989). Viewed in terms of a single home, the desire that a high radon test result should not be made public is just a routine data privacy and confidentiality issue. But because high-radon homes tend to occur in spatial clusters, many homeowners (or at least home sellers) in high-radon areas would strongly prefer that even the *statistical distribution* of radon should not be accurately mapped.

Interestingly, there is also a constituency – radon testing and mitigation companies – that does not want specific areas to be identified as having *low* risk from radon, because this will decrease the number of tests and mitigation installations. In fact, because of seasonal and short-term variability in indoor radon concentrations, and people's insistence on taking short-term rather than long-term tests, it is likely that in some relatively low-radon areas of the country a majority of radon mitigations are unnecessary, in the sense that the houses in question did not have long-term living-area radon concentrations in excess of the EPA's recommended action level (Lin et al., 1999).

The most enduring effect of our research is probably not in environmental policy but as an example of dispersed decision analysis that has appeared in two textbooks written by one of us (Gelman et al., 2013, Gelman and Hill, 2007). Having a good example is worth something: indeed, one of our original motivations in pushing through advanced statistical methods for this problem was to explore the application of hierarchical modeling for decision analysis.

We hope that the technical success of our work will motivate future uses of hierarchical modeling to enable effective localized decision recommendations.

And we hope people can learn from our social failures so as to better integrate future projects involving statistical analysis, policy makers, and local actors in real-world decision problems.

DENOUEMENT: INFORMATION WANTS TO BE FREE

We spent much of the past 15 years feeling disappointed that our work, of which we are proud, had no influence on radon policy. In addition to our personal disappointment, we have been unhappy about the inefficiency of having a single nationwide policy, and even angry about the loss of life and the waste of money compared to what a targeted radon policy could achieve.

But a funny thing has happened over the years: although the federal government still has a blanket recommendation, state policies and economic pressures have gradually led to a de facto targeting of high-radon areas. Some state governments, such as New York, have carried out radon mapping programs and information campaigns. Regions of the country with generally high radon concentrations tend to have more companies that perform testing and mitigation, and those companies advertise. Those regions have more news items about radon; a typical example is Minnick (2009), a short news article that reports, "Newlyweds Mark and Karen Hite learned about the high level of radon [in their area] months after they bought a north Raleigh home. A radon test revealed levels twice as high as the recommended EPA limit." Word of mouth in high-radon areas also leads to higher awareness.

Overall, the situation concerning radon measurement and mitigation decisions is far less efficient than it could be, but most radon measurements do seem to be made in high-radon areas, and although there are plenty of unnecessary mitigations and plenty of high-radon houses that escape remediation, many high-radon houses are found and fixed. The situation could be a lot better, but at least it is better than it used to be.

What are the implications for other researchers in data science who seek not just to perform good analyses but also to influence policy? First, we find hierarchical modeling to be a useful framework, both for statistical analysis and for mapping to policy recommendations: Modern-day consumers of big data analyses demand personalized (or, at least, localized) inferences to be constructed from the local data that they know are available. Second, as our radon example demonstrates, even if the results of an analysis are available, this does not mean they will make it into general use. Governments (and influential private organizations such as Google, Facebook, or Amazon, as well as intermediate-scale organizations such as businesses, school systems, or trade associations) play an essential role in turning research into policy.

Hence we find it valuable to consider the social and information exchanges involved at all stages of policy analysis – from the many local agents who gather or produce data, to the government agencies or private organizations that organize the collection or compilation of data, to researchers in academia and elsewhere who perform data analysis, to the government agencies or private organizations that transform these analyses into decision recommendations, to the dispersed individuals who make local decisions. In the radon example we saw the potential for doing policy-relevant analysis using data collected by thousands of homeowners across the country, along with the hurdles that have made it difficult for the knowledge thus gained to become widely available.

References

Allen, J. L. (1989). Radon new threat to home sales. *Chicago Tribune*, Apr. 8.

Dunkelberger, L. (1985). Realtors, builders fight radon warning bid. *Ocala Star-Banner*, Oct. 9.

Fairfield, H. (2005). In a new map, radon looks less risky for many. *New York Times*, Jan. 11.

Field, R. W., Steck, D. J., Smith, B. J., Brus, C. P., Neuberger, J. S., Fisher, E. F., Platz, C. E., Robinson, R. A., Woolson, R. F., and Lynch, C. F. (2000). Residential radon gas exposure and lung cancer: The Iowa radon lung cancer study. *American Journal of Epidemiology* **151**, 1091–1102.

Ford, E. S., Kelly, A. E., Teutsch, S. M., Thacker, S. B., and Garbe, P. L. (1999). Radon and lung cancer: A cost-effectiveness analysis. *American Journal of Public Health* **89**, 351–357.

Gelman, A., Carlin, J., Stern, H., Dunson, D., Vehtari, A., and Rubin, D. (2013). *Bayesian Data Analysis*, third edition. London: Chapman and Hall.

Gelman, A., and Hill, J. (2007). *Data Analysis Using Regression and Multilevel/Hierarchical Models*. New York: Cambridge University Press.

Hand, D. J. (2009). Modern statistics: The myth and the magic. *Journal of the Royal Statistical Society A* **172**, 287–306.

Lau, J., Ioannidis, J. P. A., and Schmid, C. H. (1997). Quantitative synthesis in systematic reviews. *Annals of Internal Medicine* **127**, 820–826.

Lin, C. Y., Gelman, A., Price, P. N., and Krantz, D. H. (1999). Analysis of local decisions using hierarchical modeling, applied to home radon measurement and remediation (with discussion). *Statistical Science* **14**, 305–337.

Minnick, B. (2009). High radon levels can be a problem in Triangle homes. WRAL.com, Raleigh-Durham-Fayetteville, June 22.

Nazaroff, W. W., and Nero, A. V., eds. (1988). *Radon and Its Decay Products in Indoor Air*. New York: Wiley.

Price, P. N., and Nero, A. V. (1996). Joint analysis of long- and short-term radon monitoring data from the northern US. *Environment International* 22 Suppl. 1, 699–714.

Price, P. N., Nero, A. V., and Gelman, A. (1996). Bayesian prediction of mean indoor radon concentrations for Minnesota counties. *Health Physics* **71**, 922–936.

Schumann, R. R., and Owen, D. E. (1988). *Relationships between Geology, Equivalent Uranium Concentration, and Radon in Soil Gas*. Fairfax County, VA: U.S. Geological Survey Open-File Report 88-18, 27 pp.

U.S. Environmental Protection Agency (2012). *A Citizen's Guide to Radon*. Washington, DC: EPA report 402/C-12/001.

CONCLUSION

Computational Social Science
Toward a Collaborative Future

Hanna Wallach
*Microsoft Research & University of Massachusetts Amherst**

Fifteen years ago, as an undergraduate computer science student in the United Kingdom, I read a popular science article (Matthews, 1999) profiling the research of my now colleague, Duncan Watts. This article, about the science of small-world networks, changed my life. To understand why, however, it is necessary to know that in the United Kingdom, there is (or at least was during the 1980s and 1990s) a profound "them-versus-us" split between the STEM (science, technology, engineering, and mathematics) fields and all other disciplines. This split is amplified or perhaps even caused by the fact that people specialize at a very young age, choosing at 15 or 16 whether they will ever take another math course or write another essay again. I, like everyone else in my degree program, had chosen STEM, but my decision had not been easy – I had also wanted to study the social sciences. The article about Duncan's research changed my life because it had never before occurred to me that math and computers could be used to study social phenomena. For the first time, I realized that, rather than studying *either* computer science *or* the social sciences, perhaps I could study both. This, then, became my motivating goal.

Ten years ago, as a PhD student studying machine learning, I was not really any closer to my goal. Sure, there was a growing number of researchers studying social networks, but for the most part these researchers were physicists, mathematicians, computer scientists, social scientists, with little interaction between the groups. In contrast, in 2015, we are on the cusp of a new era. Over the past five years, the nascent field of computational social science has taken off, with universities and corporations alike creating

* This work was supported in part by the Center for Intelligent Information Retrieval, in part by NSF grant #IIS-1320219, and in part by NSF grant #SBE-0965436. Any opinions, findings and conclusions, or recommedations expressed in this material are those of the author and do not necessarily reflect those of the sponsor.

307

interdisciplinary computational social science research institutes. This investment has, in part, been fueled an explosion of interest in "big data." Whereas this term used to refer to the massive data sets typically found in physics or biology, the data sets that fall under this new big data umbrella are, for the most part, granular, social data sets – that is, they document the attributes, actions, and interactions of individual people going about their everyday lives (Wallach, 2014). Consequently, research on aggregating and analyzing social data is more important (and better funded) than ever before. In turn, researchers have moved beyond the study of small-scale, static snapshots of networks onto nuanced, data-driven analyses of the structure, content, and dynamics of large-scale social processes. That said, we are still not quite there yet. Although this research is increasingly taking place in interdisciplinary environments, it is mostly being done by teams of socially minded computer scientists or teams of computationally minded social scientists. As a result, there is often a mismatch between the research being pursued by these teams, and, more importantly, there is a lack of agreement as to what even constitutes the big questions and scientific goals of computational social science as a field.

My aim for this chapter is therefore to characterize some of the differences between the computational social science research being done in computer science and that being done in the social sciences, as well as to outline some paths for moving forward as a truly interdisciplinary field. Although I am a computer scientist by training – specifically a machine learning researcher – most of my work over the past five years has been done in collaboration with social scientists, and this chapter constitutes a reflection of these experiences, rather than an infallible statement of hard-and-fast fact. That said, I hope my observations resonate with and motivate researchers in both fields.

To date, much of the computational social science research coming out of computer science – especially that appearing in machine learning, data mining, and data science conferences – has been driven by the fact that modern life is increasingly migrating online to new social platforms, often built by computer scientists, including Coursera, eBay, Facebook, Foursquare, LinkedIn, OKCupid, Stack Overflow, Twitter, and Wikipedia, to name just a few. This research therefore is primarily concerned with understanding social behavior as it relates to these platforms, often with an explicit end goal of improving user experience or generating additional revenue. Unsurprisingly, most of this research is driven by partnerships with industry and often involves a tight feedback loop of aggregating user data, analyzing these data to reveal new insights about social behavior, and using these insights to inform the next iteration of platform design. This type of research is appealing to computer scientists for several reasons. Not only do companies provide convenient and compelling data set, but also professors often have close ties to industry because most computer science students work at these companies after graduation. In other words, these companies are already an integral part of the broader computer science ecosystem. Moreover, this style of research is familiar: it dovetails with and draws on a long history of research on human–computer interaction and computer-supported cooperative work. And finally, for decades, computer science was internally focused – that is, focused on the computer itself – with researchers working on hardware, networks, operating systems, compilers, and so on. From a historical perspective, it is therefore unsurprising that socially minded computer scientists often choose to focus on analyzing platforms for social interaction built by other computer scientists.

This focus on improving social platforms is evidently conducive to fast-paced work with immediate real-world impact, but it also gives rise to certain biases. First, and most importantly, much of this research is concerned with modeling social behavior only insofar as it helps with predictive analyses; for example, modeling users' social networks in order to classify users into those who will make a purchase and those who will not, analyzing student discussion boards in order to predict who will drop an online course during the first two weeks, or quantifying users' preferences in order to select news stories for them. In other words, the emphasis is on "what" and "when" rather than "why." More generally, because studying social behavior is a means to an end, usually driven by short-term motivations rather than long-term, big-picture questions, the resultant findings do not necessarily transfer to other aspects – especially offline aspects – of society. Do we really want our understanding of social behavior to be tied to particular online platforms, with corresponding gaps in our knowledge relating to those aspects of life that take place elsewhere?

Second, it is often the case that this research is undertaken in the context of a single platform. This is understandable given the myriad of technical, legal, and ethical difficulties inherent in combining data sources – even for research purposes – that are the property of different companies, some of which may be in direct competition with one another. But, as a result, the constituent analyses and any methods or tools developed to perform them are intended for relatively homogeneous data sets, which can limit their applicability outside of this "single-source" setting. Finally, because of the scale of the data sets involved, computational efficiency is often prioritized over making accurate and accountable predictions. Although this is a justifiable tradeoff if the ultimate goal is to produce a platform that works well enough for the majority of a massive user base, this approach is not especially conducive to responsible, contextualized findings about social behavior.

In contrast, and as evidenced by the chapters in this book, the recent computational research arising from the social sciences has, for the most part, been fueled by longer term, bigger picture goals, usually with an explanatory bent. For example, Grimmer (Chapter 8) discusses the analysis of a large collection of House press releases in order to answer long-standing questions about the ways in which legislators use political communication to influence their relationships with constituents. Even researchers whose work involves data arising from online social platforms tend to use these data sets to answer questions extrinsic to the platforms themselves. For instance, Tucker et al.

(Chapter 7) draw on millions of geolocated tweets to examine the extent to which Twitter use during political protests reflects and even influences on-the-ground protest participation, as opposed to general international attention. Importantly, in both of these pieces of work – the research emphasis is firmly on "why" and "how," with "what" and "when" playing a secondary role. Moreover, Tucker et al.'s work explicitly focuses on the relationship between online and offline social behavior by studying whether and, more importantly, how behavior on online social platforms can affect behavior in offline contexts.

Although these two examples involve data arising from single data sources – House press releases and tweets, respectively – many other questions of substantive interest to social scientists cannot be answered in a single-source setting, usually because there is no single platform capable of producing the kind of aggregate data needed to answer these questions. As a result, there is a growing body of computational social science research, driven by social scientists, focused on combining and drawing conclusions from multiple, diverse data sources, often at radically different granularities or scales. Again taking chapters from this book as examples, Warshaw (Chapter 1) discusses the potential for using large, commercial public opinion data sets to augment small academic surveys, and the resultant need for new quantitative methods capable of analyzing the temporal dynamics of public opinion at a variety of scales. Meanwhile, Beieler et al. (Chapter 3) provide an extensive discussion of the opportunities and obstacles involved in automatically generating – in near-real time – massive political event data sets (for subsequent use by international relations scholars, among others) from news reports arising from a diverse range of international outlets. As evidenced by both of these pieces of work, there are nontrivial computational challenges involved in aggregating and analyzing signals from data sources with varying emphases, granularities, and formats – many of which do not arise when working with even massive quantities of relatively homogeneous data obtained from a single platform or source.

This focus on accurate and accountable explanations, often involving data from diverse sources, means that existing computer science methods – originally developed to facilitate efficient prediction or even data exploration, often at the expense of interpretability – are not always immediately applicable. Most notably, social scientists are usually interested in identifying not just whether and, if so, when certain social behaviors occur but also the conditions that explain those behaviors and any variation in them. As a result, analysis methods developed by social scientists typically provide the ability to incorporate observed covariates, so that the effects of those covariates on the behaviors of interest may be quantified. Because it is comparatively rare for computer scientists to prioritize interpretability and explanation in this way, it is often the case that methods arising from computer science have to be modified to capture the effects of observed covariates before they are adopted by social scientists. As a concrete example, the structural topic model of Roberts et al. (2014) (also the focus of Chapter 2) extends latent Dirichlet allocation

(Blei et al., 2003) – a statistical topic model developed by computer scientists for exploratory analysis of large document collections – to allow users to include a wide range of document-level covariates, thereby facilitating nuanced investigation of the ways in which thematic content varies with these covariates. The end result is not only a model better suited to the explanatory goals of social scientists but also a novel contribution, in and of itself, to the statistical topic modeling literature.

Finally, even those methods that are applicable in a supposedly "off-the-shelf" fashion often have "rough edges" that make using them to obtain accountable, even repeatable, findings a complex and time-consuming process. Continuing with the example of statistical topic modeling, Roberts et al. (Chapter 2) tackle the issue of nonconvexity and the resultant sensitivity of results to different initialization strategies. Although this issue has been long-acknowledged in the topic modeling literature, it is seldom addressed head-on, with researchers tending to gloss over its role in producing unrepeatable results. This situation is unsurprising: if one is primarily concerned with feasibility and computational efficiency, then nuanced issues affecting model stability may not be a priority. But if one is using these methods to explore substantive questions, whose answers have real-world social implications, then any issue that may affect repeatability and accountability matters a great deal. Roberts et al., like many others in the social sciences, have invested significant time in investigating not only when these kinds of rough edges occur and what causes their occurrence but also effective techniques for addressing or engaging with them. In some ways, this relationship between the computer and social sciences is reminiscent of the symbiosis between the Debian[1] and Ubuntu[2] Linux distributions.[3] Debian developers produce a comprehensive base distribution, primarily used by relatively technical users, such as other developers and system administrators; Ubuntu builds on this distribution, adding the interface and usability features needed to make it a reliable and easy-to-use operating system. Because many of Ubuntu's developments are contributed back "upstream" to Debian, this relationship has resulted not in only a more accessible distribution (which, in turn, has increased Linux adoption) but also in greater awareness of and attention to usability considerations within Debian – a net benefit to both groups.

To reiterate my earlier statement, we are on the cusp of a new era in computational social science. The past five years have seen some transformational changes to both the quantity and nature of research being undertaken by socially minded computer scientists and computationally minded social scientists. As someone whose long-term research goal is to develop computational methods for studying important social questions, I find these changes, and the foundation that they have laid, extremely exciting. Even more exciting to me, however, is the fact that computational social science is still evolving. As a result, I anticipate that the next few years will witness some even bigger changes, many of which will move the field toward a collaborative future characterized by truly interdisciplinary teams of computer scientists and social scientists and, increasingly, shared scientific goals. First, it is possible that engaging in platform-driven research will become increasingly difficult, at least for researchers in academic positions. Although privacy concerns have always made for a thorny path to navigate, especially for those researchers who do not have close ties to industry, 2014's controversial Facebook experiment highlighted the existence and importance of a range of ethical questions surrounding user experimentation (Grimmelmann, 2014). As long as these questions remain unanswered – and, realistically, they will not be answered for the foreseeable future while institutional review boards and other committees concerned with the oversight of human-subjects research rethink their policies, guidelines, and best practices – it is likely that many companies will be much more cautious about publicly engaging in experimentation for research purposes. In turn, this will make it much harder for researchers to study social behavior as it relates to understanding and improving online platforms. At the same time, I expect that many more socially minded computer scientists will start turning their attention to bigger picture social questions, most likely in collaboration with computationally minded social scientists. Here, the impetus is the outstanding methodological work coming out of the social sciences (some by contributors to this book) that concretely demonstrates how methods developed by computer scientists can be adapted and used to undertake accountable, substantively important, explanatory analyses. These pieces of work, many of which have been presented at computer science conferences and workshops in addition to social science venues, make it abundantly clear to socially minded computer scientists that there are some truly exciting and challenging opportunities for collaboration that go far beyond "run method X on data set Y."

So what can we do to ensure that this future of computational social science – characterized by interdisciplinary teams of researchers contributing equally to common, mutually beneficial research goals – actually materializes? Unfortunately, I do not think there are any "quick fix" answers to this question; if there were, we would likely have put them into practice already. That said, I do think there are a few things we can do that, when taken together, may increase our chances of achieving this future.

First, and most importantly, we need to understand each other's disciplinary norms, incentive structures, and research goals. Although this sounds simple enough, it is not – mostly because achieving this understanding is time consuming and we are all busy people who tend to prioritize sharing our own opinions (this chapter included!) over listening. But by taking the time to engage in conversations or to read papers outside of our own disciplines, we are also taking the first steps toward innovative and genuinely interdisciplinary research ideas that no discipline could have produced in isolation. One way to jump-start this process is to attend each other's conferences. Small, interdisciplinary workshops, co-located with larger, disciplinary meetings, are a particularly effective way to facilitate this attendance, not least because people can more easily justify the cost of attending. Personally, I have attended the American Political Science Association[4] meeting as a result of such a workshop,[5] and have also persuaded political scientists, sociologists, and economists to attend the Neural Information Processing Systems conference[6] (one of the leading machine learning conferences) by organizing two co-located workshops on computational social science, one in 2010[7] and one in 2011.[8] Of course, stand-alone interdisciplinary events, such as the now annual "New Directions in Text as Data" conference,[9] are another great way to bring together researchers with potentially overlapping interests. Again using my own experiences to highlight the benefits of attending such events, I met two of my political science collaborators by attending the "Text as Data" conference, in addition to many other political scientists, whose papers I now make sure to read. Naturally, because organizing a conference is potentially expensive (especially if participants are provided with travel funding), this is a great example of an area in which funding agencies and companies can help by covering either direct or indirect costs. Finally, even single-university seminar series can catalyze ongoing conversations and collaborations by bringing in external speakers whose research interests appeal broadly to both socially minded computer scientists and computationally minded social scientists. My own network of contacts in the social sciences exists, in large part, because of the seminar series run by the Computational Social Science Institute at the University of Massachusetts Amherst,[10] plus numerous invited talks I have given at other institutions.

Ironically, one of the biggest obstacles to producing truly interdisciplinary research is the need – shared by all researchers, regardless of discipline – to publish in high-quality venues in a timely fashion. Unlike within-discipline collaborations, interdisciplinary collaborations are seldom "force multipliers" from a perspective of publishing quickly – mostly because of the time that must be spent defining shared research goals and establishing a common language for communicating efficiently about them, before any actual research can even take place. As a result, bringing an interdisciplinary project to publication can involve a much bigger time investment than that required by a disciplinary project. Moreover, even when work is ready to be published, it is not always obvious where to publish it, because "standard" disciplinary venues may not be beneficial to all contributors, let alone appropriate for the work itself. A common strategy is therefore dual publication in a computer science conference and a social science journal, but this approach demands an even greater time investment. Unfortunately, these challenges are not always recognized by tenure and promotion committees, effectively disincentivizing researchers from pursuing this kind of work. Moving forward, it is therefore crucial that, at least in the short term, we – computational social science researchers – explicitly manage expectations by acknowledging and articulating to others the fact that publishing interdisciplinary research can be slower than publishing single-discipline research. In turn, any academic institution wishing to support and encourage interdisciplinary researchers must also acknowledge these issues when considering promotion and tenure cases. Longer term, we also need better publication strategies than dual publication in disciplinary venues. The most obvious, albeit nontrivial, way to address this need is to create new, high-quality publication venues, explicitly focused on interdisciplinary computational social science research.

I conclude by noting that the best way to ensure the long-term success of computational social science as an genuinely interdisciplinary field, characterized by a set of unifying social questions and scientific goals, is to think carefully about the next generation of computational social scientists and their educational trajectories. With some serious thought and resource investment, undertaken now, we can ensure that unlike the current generation – people like me who had to choose between computer science and the social sciences – this new generation will consist of people with training in both areas: people who therefore possess a deep understanding of the norms of multiple disciplinary communities and have been part of successful interdisciplinary collaborations long before they graduate. For this to be possible, however, academic departments, likely in different colleges or schools, will need to work together to create new educational opportunities. At the very least, students should be actively encouraged to enroll in dual-degree programs, in which they produce a single, interdisciplinary dissertation while satisfying the course requirements of two departments. Of course, much like the dual publication strategy mentioned earlier, dual degrees are time consuming, and not all departments are willing to bear this hit to their "time-to-graduation" records, let alone the cost of supporting a student for the additional duration. As a result, dual-degree enrollments are currently the exception rather than the rule, with faculty fighting for their students' rights to pursue such programs on a case-by-case basis. A better, and more sustainable, option is therefore the creation of new, interdisciplinary degree programs, devoted to training the next generation of computational social scientists. Although this option constitutes a much bigger change, requiring significant institutional investment both in terms of financial and strategic support, the long-term benefit to society – namely, the success of computational social science as an innovative, interdisciplinary field, dedicated to collaboratively answering some of society's biggest questions – seems well worth it.

Notes

1. http://debian.org/.
2. http://ubuntu.com/.
3. http://www.ubuntu.com/about/about-ubuntu/ubuntu-and-debian.
4. http://community.apsanet.org/annualmeeting/home.
5. http://poliinformatics.org/index.php/the-challenge/scheduled-research-challenges/apsa-political-science-challenge.
6. http://nips.cc/.

7. http://www.cs.umass.edu/~wallach/workshops/nips2010css.
8. http://www.cs.umass.edu/~wallach/workshops/nips2011css.
9. 2015 conference URL: http://textasdata.nyudatascience.org.
10. http://cssi.umass.edu/.

References

Blei, D. M., Ng, A. Y., and Jordan, M. I. (2003). Latent Dirichlet allocation. *Journal of Machine Learning Research*, 3:993–1022.

Grimmelmann, J. (2014). The Facebook emotional manipulation study: http://laboratorium.net/archive/2014/06/30/the_facebook_emotional_manipulation_study_source.

Matthews, R. E. (1999). Get connected. *New Scientist*, (2215).

Roberts, M. E., Stewart, B. M., Tingley, D., Lucas, C., Leder-Luis, J., Gadarian, S. K., Albertson, B., and Rand, D. G. (2014). Structural topic models for open-ended survey responses. *American Journal of Political Science*, 58:1064–1082.

Wallach, H. (2014). Big data, machine learning, and the social sciences: Fairness, accountability, and transparency. https://medium.com/@hannawallach/big-data-machine-learning-and-the-social-sciences-927a8e20460d.

Index

ACLED (recent event data set), 110
"action level," and radon remediation, 298, 303
Affordable Care Act, 239–40
Africa, estimated population of U.S. citizens in, 258, 259, 260
Agence France-Presse (AFP), 99, 102
aggregations, of topic models, 67–9, 70
Agricultural Quarantine Inspection Monitoring (AQIM), 248–50
agriculture: and expressed priorities of legislators, 236; social marketing and government policies on invasive species, 247–53, 261–3
Airoldi, Edoardo M., 227
Akin, Todd, 240
Alexander, Rodney, 234
alignment, of topic models, 65
Allan, J., 110
alternative distance measures, of topic models, 76, 78
Alvarez, R. Michael, 11, 21n5
American National Election Study (ANES), 2, 28, 29, 44n3
American Political Science Association (APSA), 19, 137n1, 313
American Political Science Review (journal), 1–2
Analytical Methods for Social Research (journal), 1
Anandkumar, Anima, 90n33
anchor selection methods, and topic models, 90n30

Animal and Plant Health Inspection Service (APHIS), 247–53, 261–3
Annenberg School of Communications (University of Pennsylvania), 29
anonymity, as critical issue in computational social science, 13–14. *See also* privacy
Ansolabehere, Stephen, 31
Appropriations Committee (House of Representatives), 236–7
Arab Spring Revolutions (2011), 201, 212
archival depth, of political event data, 100
area-probability sampling, 30
Argentina, machine learning algorithms for detection of election fraud in, 275–91
Arora, Sanjeev, 83, 84, 85, 86, 90n30
audio, progress in data analysis of, 16
automated approaches, for review of topic models, 61–2
automated dictionary updates, and political event data, 102–105
Axelrod, Robert, 13

Bafumi, Joseph, 32, 42
bagging: and ensemble methods for machine learning algorithms, 274; and random forests, 173
Bagozzi, B. E., 106, 109
Ball, P., 108
ballot box stuffing (BBS), and detection of election fraud, 271, 277, 281, 285, 286, 292n10–11
Barbera, Pablo, 9

Made in the USA
Coppell, TX
20 February 2021